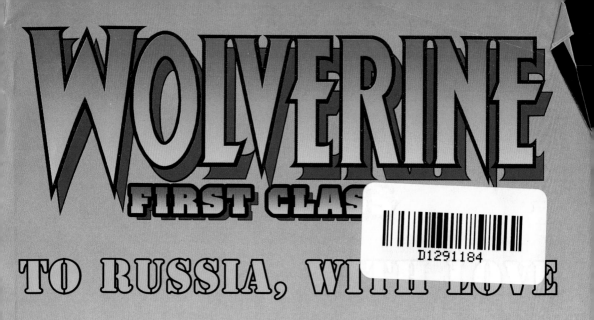

WOLVERINE
FIRST CLASS
TO RUSSIA, WITH LOVE

WRITER: *Fred Van Lente*
PENCILS: *Clayton Henry, Salva Espin & Steven Cummings*
INKS: ifuentes
COLORISTS: Deron Bennett
LETTERERS: Rus Wooton
COVER ART chael Golden

UNCANNY X-MEN #139-140
WRITER: *Chris Claremont*
PLOT/PENCILS: *John Byrne*
INKS: *Terry Austin*
LETTERER: *Tom Orzechowski*
COLORIST: *Glynis Wein*

WOLVERINE AND POWER PACK #1
WRITER: *Marc Sumerak*
ART: *GuriHiru*
LETTERER: *Dave Sharpe*
EDITOR: *Nate Cosby*

COLLECTION EDITOR: *Alex Starbuck* • **ASSISTANT EDITORS:** *Cory Levine & John Denning*
EDITORS, SPECIAL PROJECTS: *Jennifer Grünwald & Mark D. Beazley*
SENIOR EDITOR, SPECIAL PROJECTS: *Jeff Youngquist*
PRODUCTION: *Jerron Quality Color* • **SENIOR VICE PRESIDENT OF SALES:** *David Gabriel*

EDITOR IN CHIEF: *Joe Quesada*

PUBLISHER: *Dan Buckley*

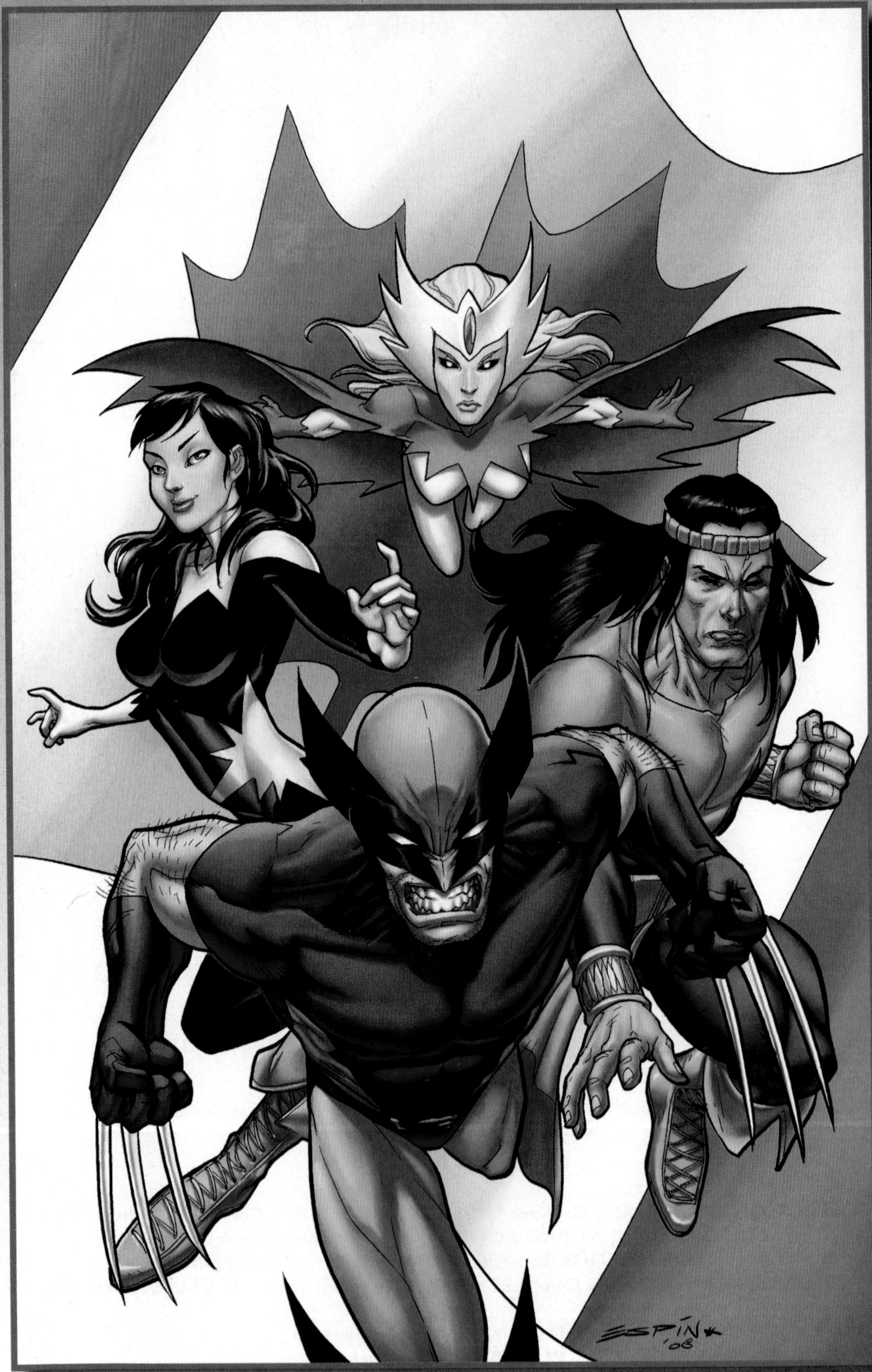
ESPÍN '08

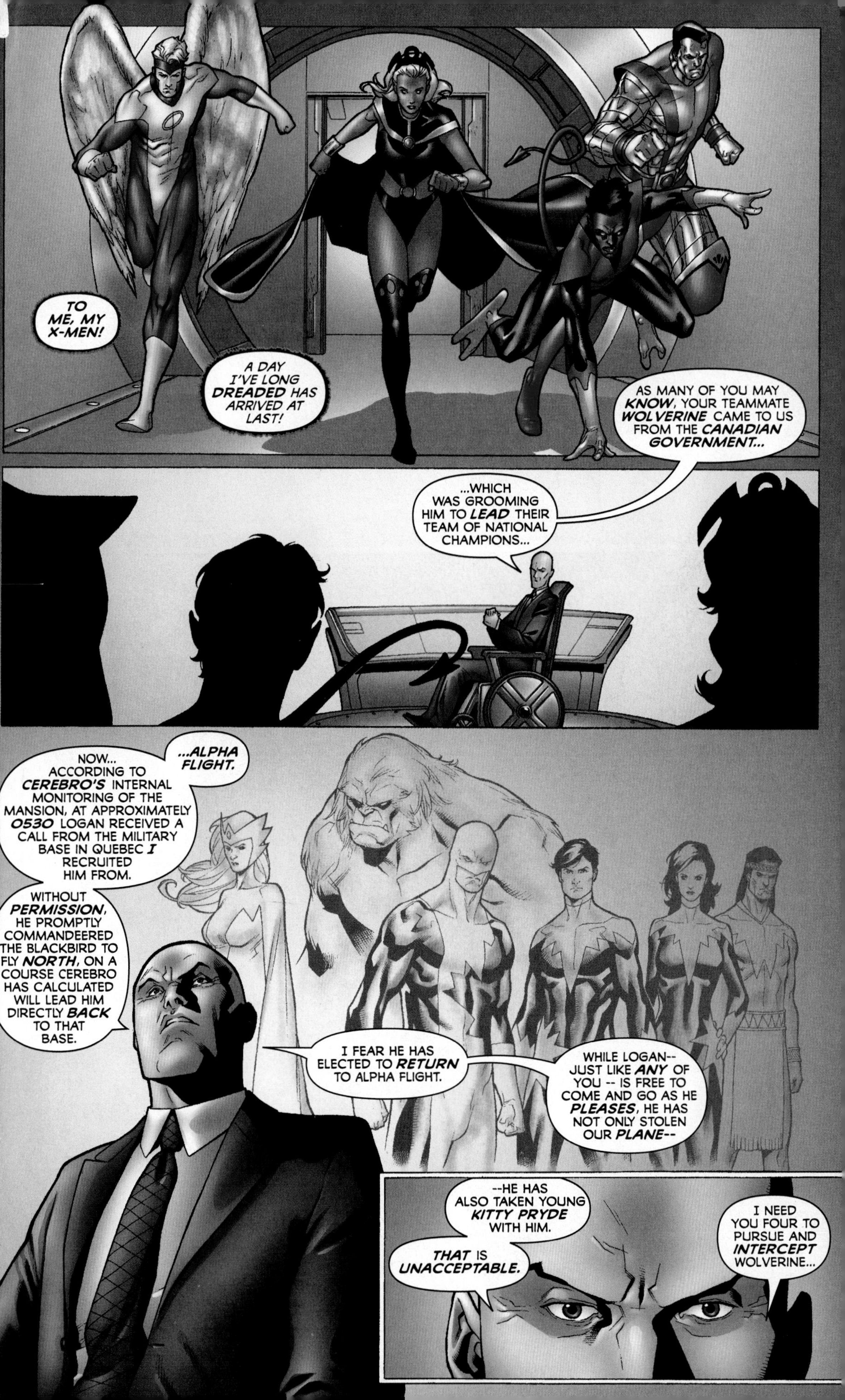
TO ME, MY X-MEN!
A DAY I'VE LONG DREADED HAS ARRIVED AT LAST!
AS MANY OF YOU MAY KNOW, YOUR TEAMMATE WOLVERINE CAME TO US FROM THE CANADIAN GOVERNMENT...
...WHICH WAS GROOMING HIM TO LEAD THEIR TEAM OF NATIONAL CHAMPIONS...
...ALPHA FLIGHT.
NOW... ACCORDING TO CEREBRO'S INTERNAL MONITORING OF THE MANSION, AT APPROXIMATELY 0530 LOGAN RECEIVED A CALL FROM THE MILITARY BASE IN QUEBEC I RECRUITED HIM FROM.
WITHOUT PERMISSION, HE PROMPTLY COMMANDEERED THE BLACKBIRD TO FLY NORTH, ON A COURSE CEREBRO HAS CALCULATED WILL LEAD HIM DIRECTLY BACK TO THAT BASE.
I FEAR HE HAS ELECTED TO RETURN TO ALPHA FLIGHT.
WHILE LOGAN-- JUST LIKE ANY OF YOU -- IS FREE TO COME AND GO AS HE PLEASES, HE HAS NOT ONLY STOLEN OUR PLANE--
--HE HAS ALSO TAKEN YOUNG KITTY PRYDE WITH HIM.
THAT IS UNACCEPTABLE.
I NEED YOU FOUR TO PURSUE AND INTERCEPT WOLVERINE...

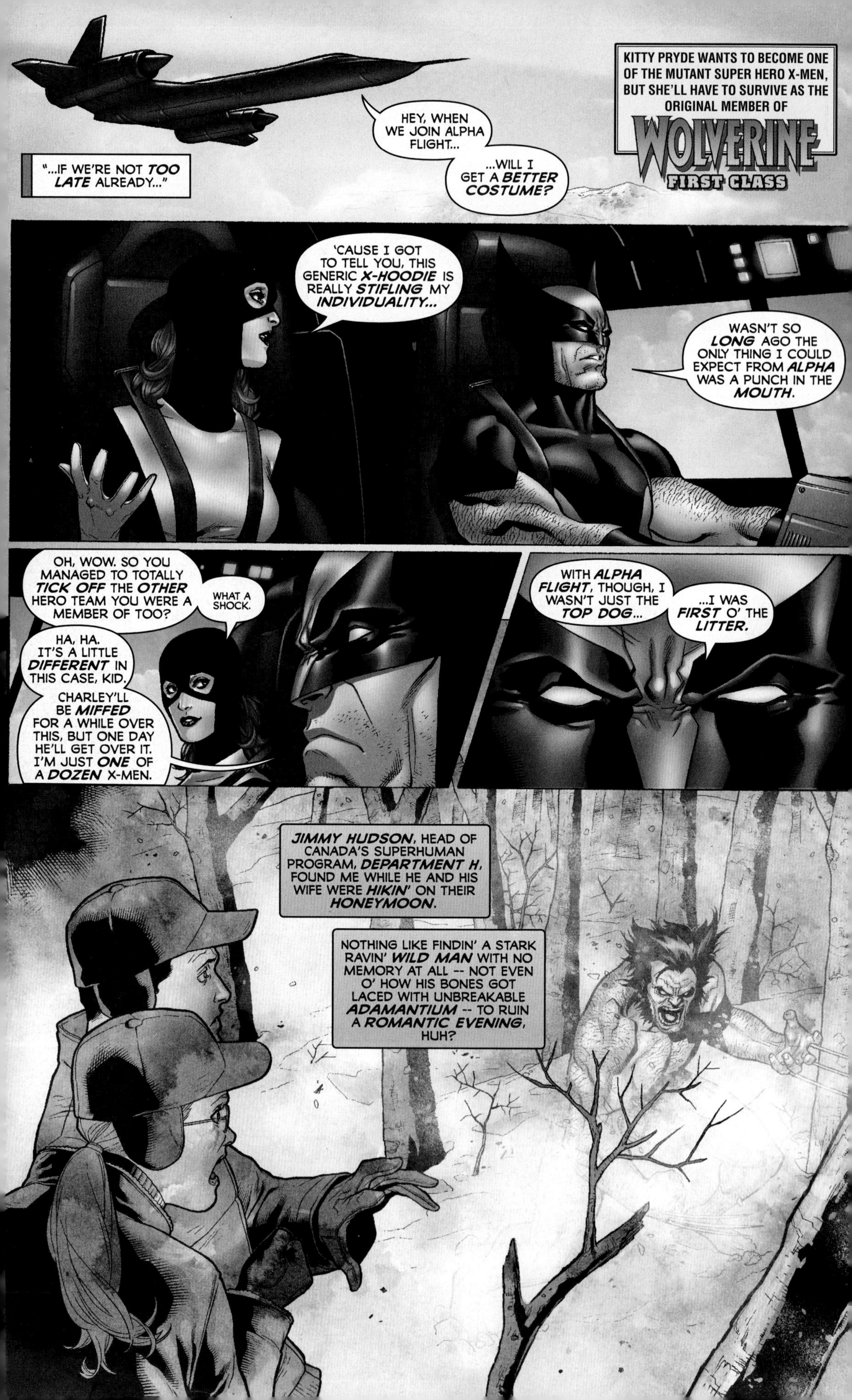
KITTY PRYDE WANTS TO BECOME ONE OF THE MUTANT SUPER HERO X-MEN, BUT SHE'LL HAVE TO SURVIVE AS THE ORIGINAL MEMBER OF
WOLVERINE
FIRST CLASS
"...IF WE'RE NOT TOO LATE ALREADY..."
HEY, WHEN WE JOIN ALPHA FLIGHT...
...WILL I GET A BETTER COSTUME?
'CAUSE I GOT TO TELL YOU, THIS GENERIC X-HOODIE IS REALLY STIFLING MY INDIVIDUALITY...
WASN'T SO LONG AGO THE ONLY THING I COULD EXPECT FROM ALPHA WAS A PUNCH IN THE MOUTH.
OH, WOW. SO YOU MANAGED TO TOTALLY TICK OFF THE OTHER HERO TEAM YOU WERE A MEMBER OF TOO?
WHAT A SHOCK.
HA, HA. IT'S A LITTLE DIFFERENT IN THIS CASE, KID.
CHARLEY'LL BE MIFFED FOR A WHILE OVER THIS, BUT ONE DAY HE'LL GET OVER IT. I'M JUST ONE OF A DOZEN X-MEN.
WITH ALPHA FLIGHT, THOUGH, I WASN'T JUST THE TOP DOG...
...I WAS FIRST O' THE LITTER.
JIMMY HUDSON, HEAD OF CANADA'S SUPERHUMAN PROGRAM, DEPARTMENT H, FOUND ME WHILE HE AND HIS WIFE WERE HIKIN' ON THEIR HONEYMOON.
NOTHING LIKE FINDIN' A STARK RAVIN' WILD MAN WITH NO MEMORY AT ALL -- NOT EVEN O' HOW HIS BONES GOT LACED WITH UNBREAKABLE ADAMANTIUM -- TO RUIN A ROMANTIC EVENING, HUH?

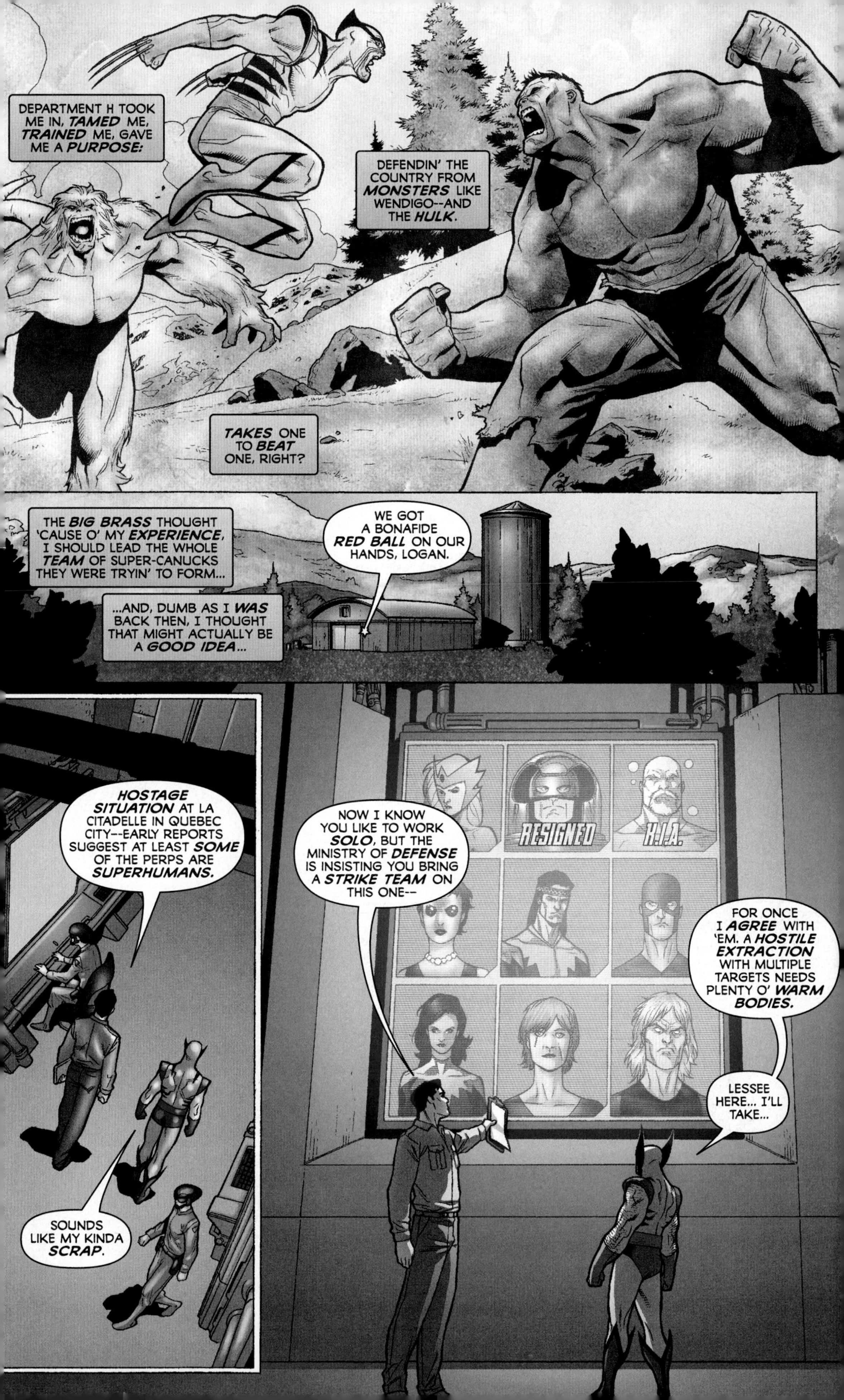
DEPARTMENT H TOOK ME IN, TAMED ME, TRAINED ME, GAVE ME A PURPOSE:
DEFENDIN' THE COUNTRY FROM MONSTERS LIKE WENDIGO--AND THE HULK.
TAKES ONE TO BEAT ONE, RIGHT?
THE BIG BRASS THOUGHT 'CAUSE O' MY EXPERIENCE, I SHOULD LEAD THE WHOLE TEAM OF SUPER-CANUCKS THEY WERE TRYIN' TO FORM...
...AND, DUMB AS I WAS BACK THEN, I THOUGHT THAT MIGHT ACTUALLY BE A GOOD IDEA...
WE GOT A BONAFIDE RED BALL ON OUR HANDS, LOGAN.
HOSTAGE SITUATION AT LA CITADELLE IN QUEBEC CITY--EARLY REPORTS SUGGEST AT LEAST SOME OF THE PERPS ARE SUPERHUMANS.
SOUNDS LIKE MY KINDA SCRAP.
NOW I KNOW YOU LIKE TO WORK SOLO, BUT THE MINISTRY OF DEFENSE IS INSISTING YOU BRING A STRIKE TEAM ON THIS ONE--
RESIGNED
K.I.A.
FOR ONCE I AGREE WITH 'EM. A HOSTILE EXTRACTION WITH MULTIPLE TARGETS NEEDS PLENTY O' WARM BODIES.
LESSEE HERE... I'LL TAKE...

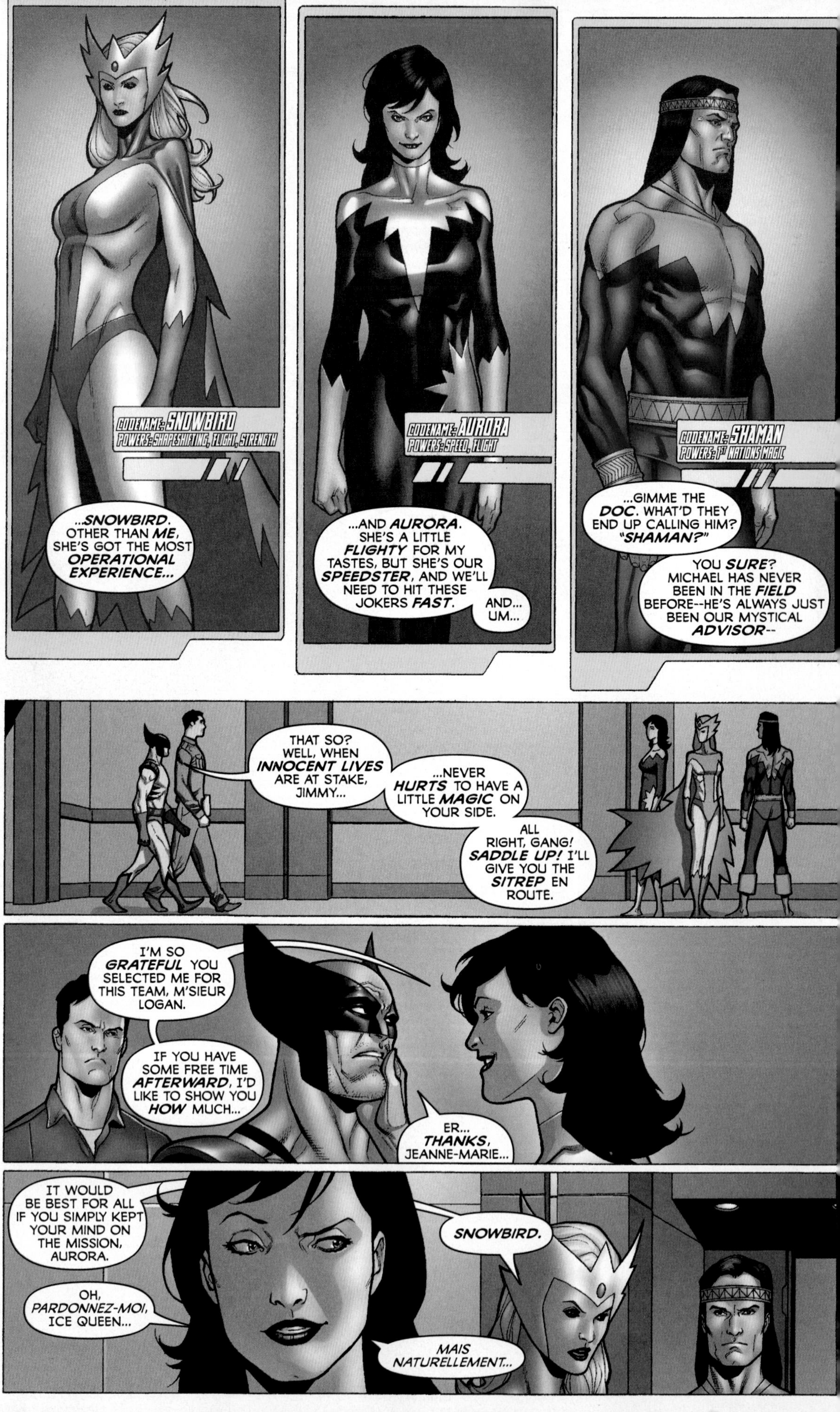
CODENAME: SNOWBIRD
POWERS: SHAPESHIFTING, FLIGHT, STRENGTH
...SNOWBIRD. OTHER THAN ME, SHE'S GOT THE MOST OPERATIONAL EXPERIENCE...
CODENAME: AURORA
POWERS: SPEED, FLIGHT
...AND AURORA. SHE'S A LITTLE FLIGHTY FOR MY TASTES, BUT SHE'S OUR SPEEDSTER, AND WE'LL NEED TO HIT THESE JOKERS FAST.
AND... UM...
CODENAME: SHAMAN
POWERS: 1ST NATIONS MAGIC
...GIMME THE DOC. WHAT'D THEY END UP CALLING HIM? "SHAMAN?"
YOU SURE? MICHAEL HAS NEVER BEEN IN THE FIELD BEFORE--HE'S ALWAYS JUST BEEN OUR MYSTICAL ADVISOR--
THAT SO? WELL, WHEN INNOCENT LIVES ARE AT STAKE, JIMMY...
...NEVER HURTS TO HAVE A LITTLE MAGIC ON YOUR SIDE.
ALL RIGHT, GANG! SADDLE UP! I'LL GIVE YOU THE SITREP EN ROUTE.
I'M SO GRATEFUL YOU SELECTED ME FOR THIS TEAM, M'SIEUR LOGAN.
IF YOU HAVE SOME FREE TIME AFTERWARD, I'D LIKE TO SHOW YOU HOW MUCH...
ER... THANKS, JEANNE-MARIE...
IT WOULD BE BEST FOR ALL IF YOU SIMPLY KEPT YOUR MIND ON THE MISSION, AURORA.
SNOWBIRD.
OH, PARDONNEZ-MOI, ICE QUEEN...
MAIS NATURELLEMENT...

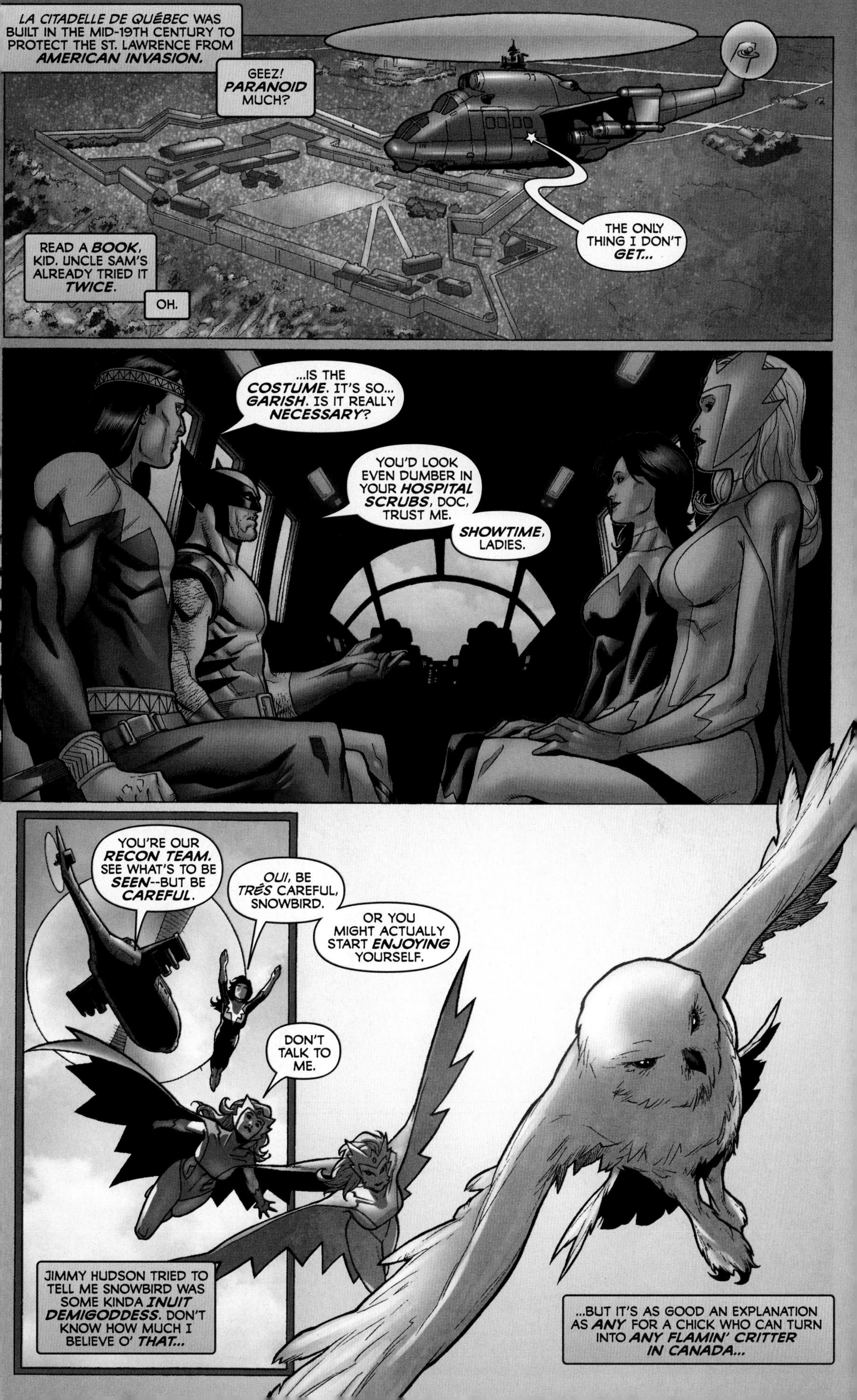
LA CITADELLE DE QUÉBEC WAS BUILT IN THE MID-19TH CENTURY TO PROTECT THE ST. LAWRENCE FROM AMERICAN INVASION.
GEEZ! PARANOID MUCH?
READ A BOOK, KID. UNCLE SAM'S ALREADY TRIED IT TWICE.
OH.
THE ONLY THING I DON'T GET...
...IS THE COSTUME. IT'S SO... GARISH. IS IT REALLY NECESSARY?
YOU'D LOOK EVEN DUMBER IN YOUR HOSPITAL SCRUBS, DOC, TRUST ME.
SHOWTIME, LADIES.
YOU'RE OUR RECON TEAM. SEE WHAT'S TO BE SEEN--BUT BE CAREFUL.
OUI, BE TRÉS CAREFUL, SNOWBIRD.
OR YOU MIGHT ACTUALLY START ENJOYING YOURSELF.
DON'T TALK TO ME.
JIMMY HUDSON TRIED TO TELL ME SNOWBIRD WAS SOME KINDA INUIT DEMIGODDESS. DON'T KNOW HOW MUCH I BELIEVE O' THAT...
...BUT IT'S AS GOOD AN EXPLANATION AS ANY FOR A CHICK WHO CAN TURN INTO ANY FLAMIN' CRITTER IN CANADA...

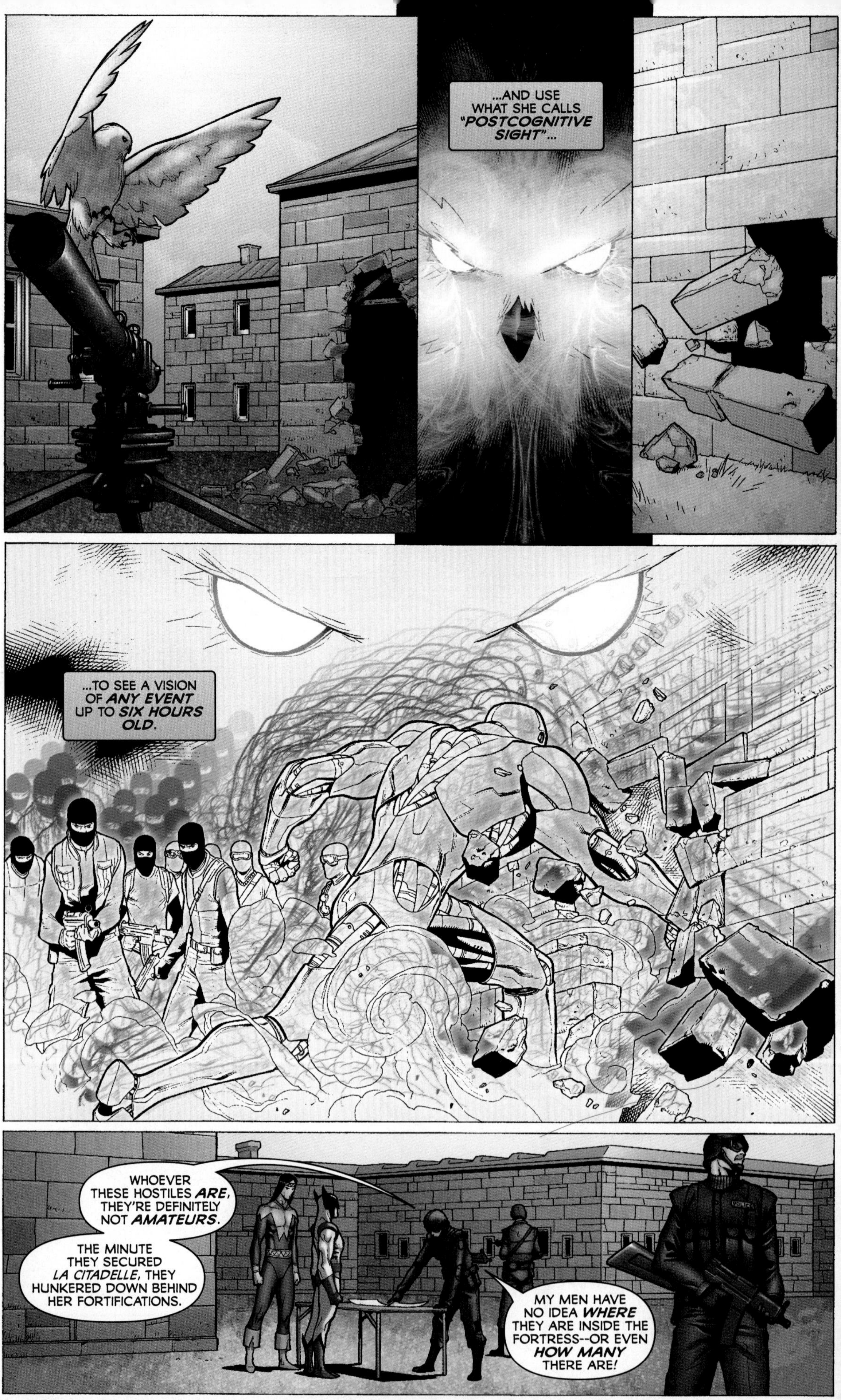
...AND USE WHAT SHE CALLS "POSTCOGNITIVE SIGHT"...
...TO SEE A VISION OF ANY EVENT UP TO SIX HOURS OLD.
WHOEVER THESE HOSTILES ARE, THEY'RE DEFINITELY NOT AMATEURS.
THE MINUTE THEY SECURED LA CITADELLE, THEY HUNKERED DOWN BEHIND HER FORTIFICATIONS.
MY MEN HAVE NO IDEA WHERE THEY ARE INSIDE THE FORTRESS--OR EVEN HOW MANY THERE ARE!

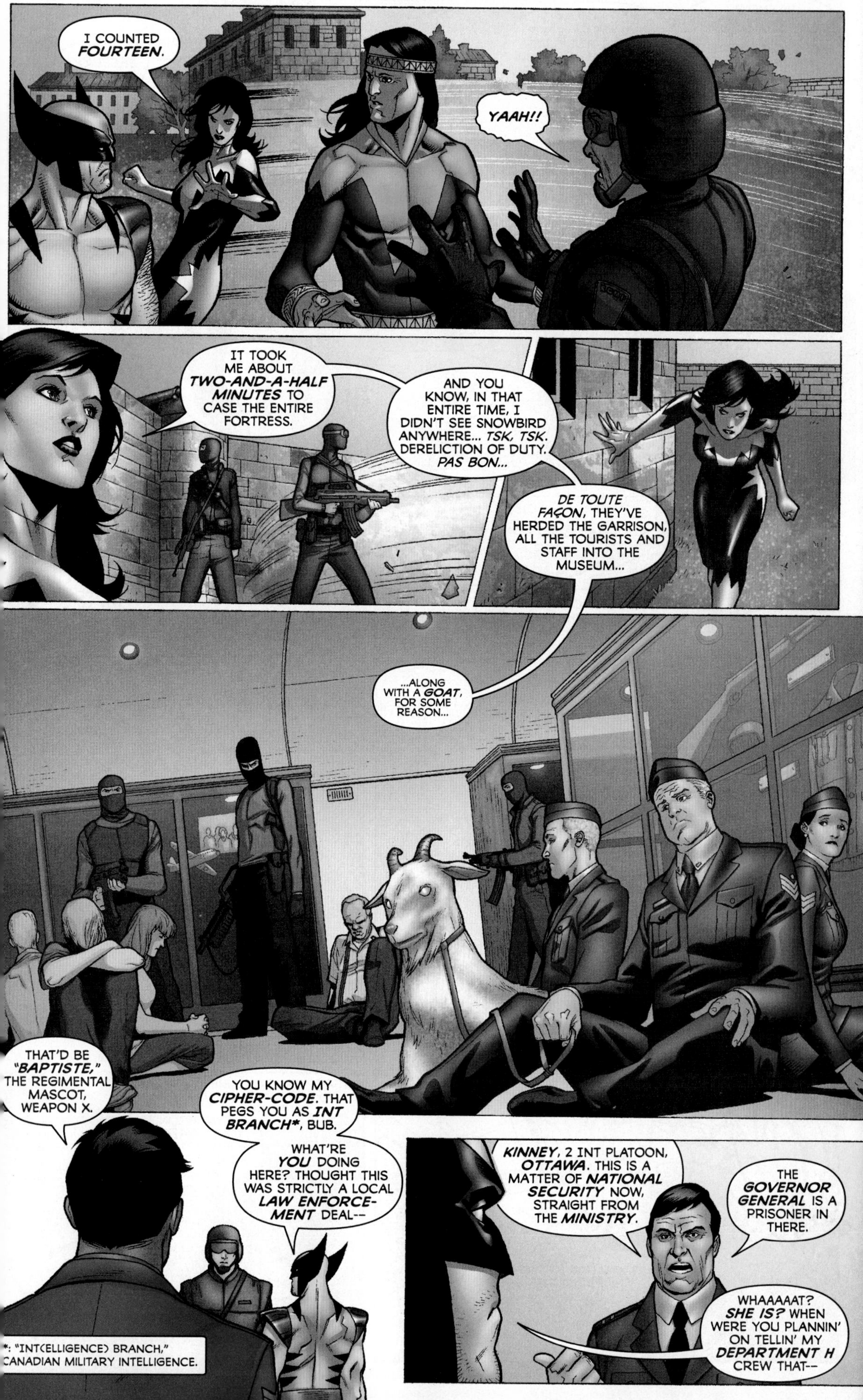
I COUNTED FOURTEEN.
YAAH!!
IT TOOK ME ABOUT TWO-AND-A-HALF MINUTES TO CASE THE ENTIRE FORTRESS.
AND YOU KNOW, IN THAT ENTIRE TIME, I DIDN'T SEE SNOWBIRD ANYWHERE... TSK, TSK. DERELICTION OF DUTY. PAS BON...
DE TOUTE FAÇON, THEY'VE HERDED THE GARRISON, ALL THE TOURISTS AND STAFF INTO THE MUSEUM...
...ALONG WITH A GOAT, FOR SOME REASON...
THAT'D BE "BAPTISTE," THE REGIMENTAL MASCOT, WEAPON X.
YOU KNOW MY CIPHER-CODE. THAT PEGS YOU AS INT BRANCH*, BUB.
WHAT'RE YOU DOING HERE? THOUGHT THIS WAS STRICTLY A LOCAL LAW ENFORCE-MENT DEAL--
*: "INT(ELLIGENCE) BRANCH," CANADIAN MILITARY INTELLIGENCE.
KINNEY, 2 INT PLATOON, OTTAWA. THIS IS A MATTER OF NATIONAL SECURITY NOW, STRAIGHT FROM THE MINISTRY.
THE GOVERNOR GENERAL IS A PRISONER IN THERE.
WHAAAAAT? SHE IS? WHEN WERE YOU PLANNIN' ON TELLIN' MY DEPARTMENT H CREW THAT--

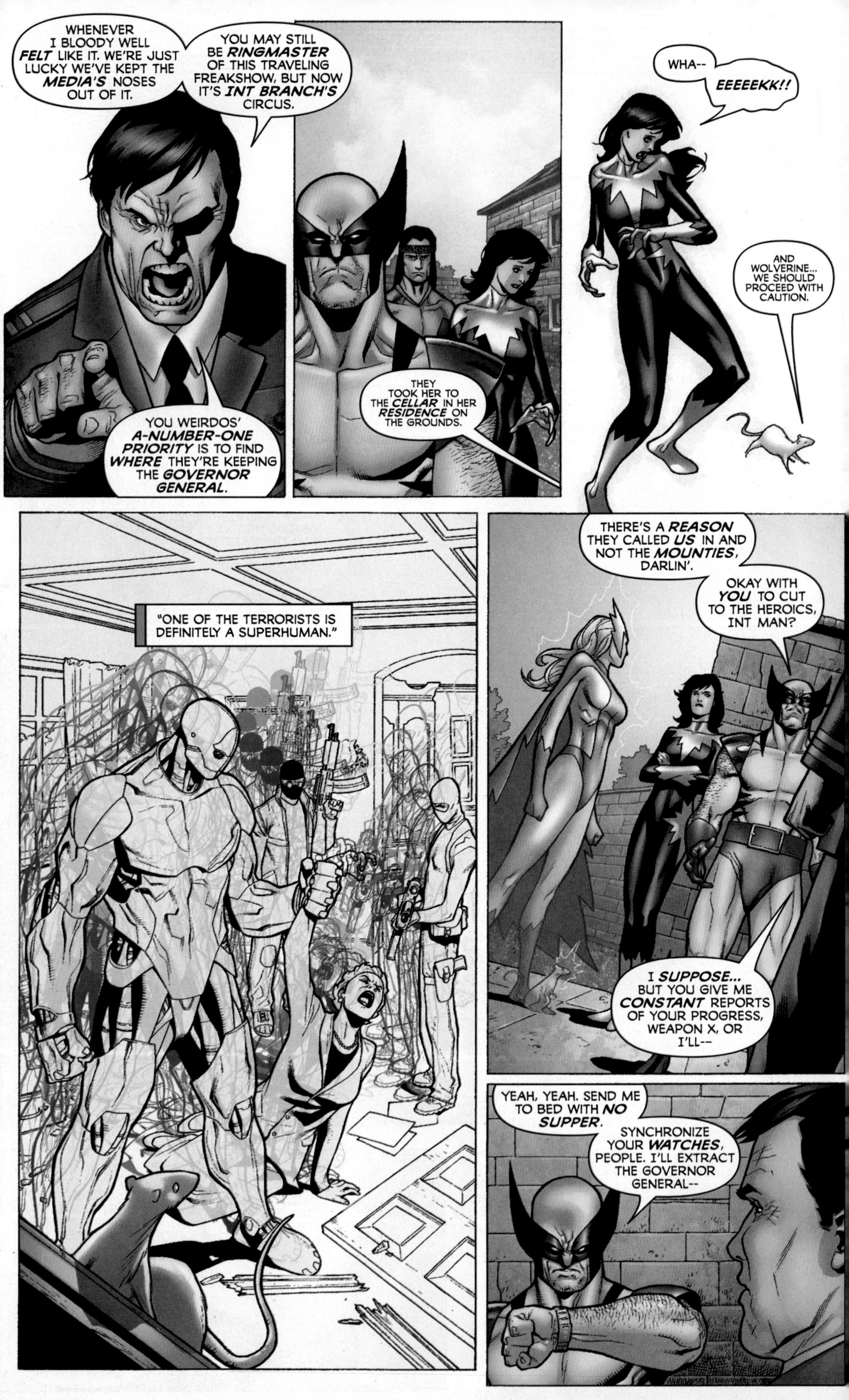
WHENEVER I BLOODY WELL FELT LIKE IT. WE'RE JUST LUCKY WE'VE KEPT THE MEDIA'S NOSES OUT OF IT.
YOU MAY STILL BE RINGMASTER OF THIS TRAVELING FREAKSHOW, BUT NOW IT'S INT BRANCH'S CIRCUS.
YOU WEIRDOS' A-NUMBER-ONE PRIORITY IS TO FIND WHERE THEY'RE KEEPING THE GOVERNOR GENERAL.
THEY TOOK HER TO THE CELLAR IN HER RESIDENCE ON THE GROUNDS.
WHA--
EEEEEKK!!
AND WOLVERINE... WE SHOULD PROCEED WITH CAUTION.
"ONE OF THE TERRORISTS IS DEFINITELY A SUPERHUMAN."
THERE'S A REASON THEY CALLED US IN AND NOT THE MOUNTIES, DARLIN'.
OKAY WITH YOU TO CUT TO THE HEROICS, INT MAN?
I SUPPOSE... BUT YOU GIVE ME CONSTANT REPORTS OF YOUR PROGRESS, WEAPON X, OR I'LL--
YEAH, YEAH. SEND ME TO BED WITH NO SUPPER.
SYNCHRONIZE YOUR WATCHES, PEOPLE. I'LL EXTRACT THE GOVERNOR GENERAL--

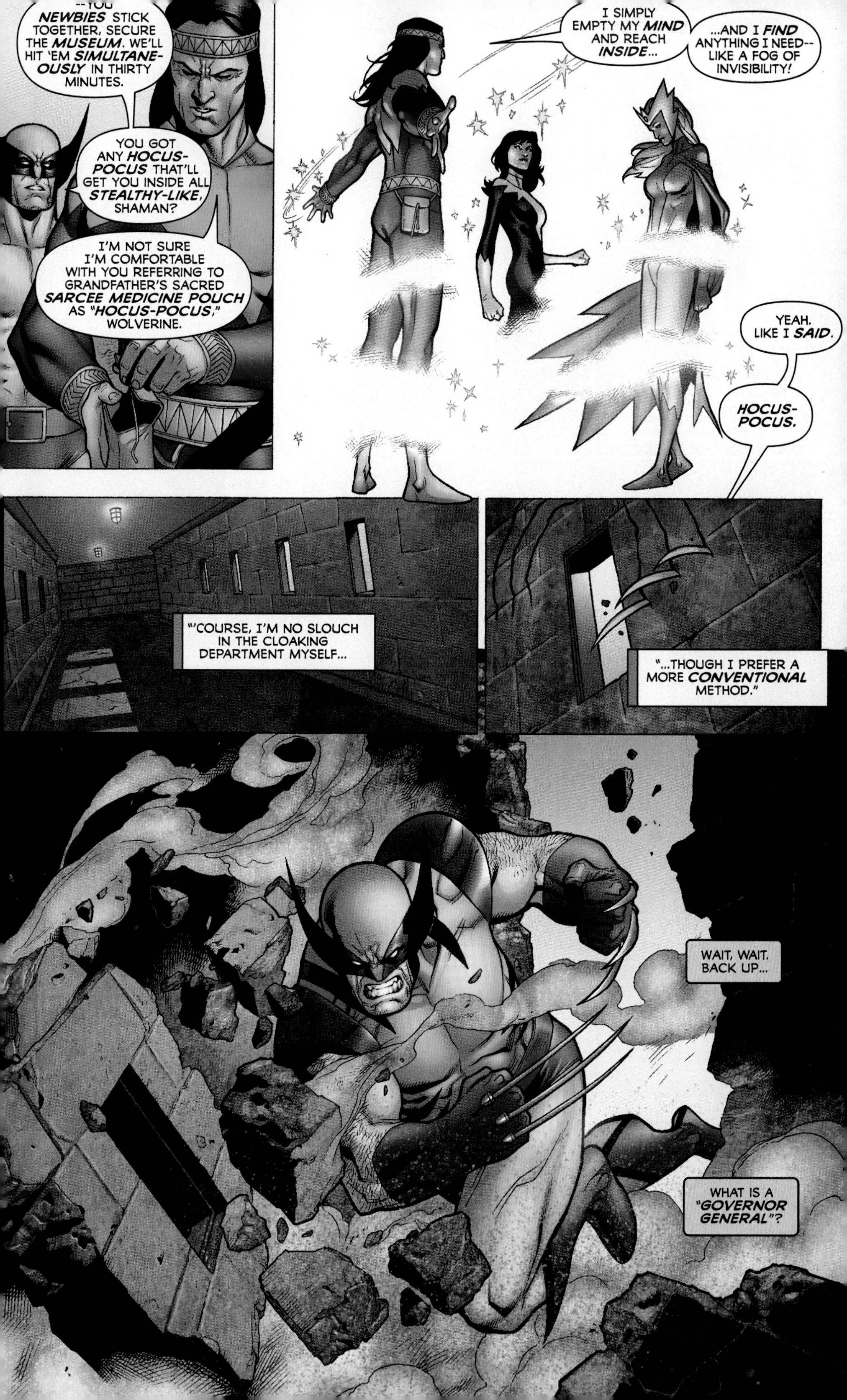
--YOU NEWBIES STICK TOGETHER, SECURE THE MUSEUM. WE'LL HIT 'EM SIMULTANEOUSLY IN THIRTY MINUTES.
YOU GOT ANY HOCUS-POCUS THAT'LL GET YOU INSIDE ALL STEALTHY-LIKE, SHAMAN?
I'M NOT SURE I'M COMFORTABLE WITH YOU REFERRING TO GRANDFATHER'S SACRED SARCEE MEDICINE POUCH AS "HOCUS-POCUS," WOLVERINE.
I SIMPLY EMPTY MY MIND AND REACH INSIDE...
...AND I FIND ANYTHING I NEED--LIKE A FOG OF INVISIBILITY!
YEAH. LIKE I SAID.
HOCUS-POCUS.
"'COURSE, I'M NO SLOUCH IN THE CLOAKING DEPARTMENT MYSELF...
"...THOUGH I PREFER A MORE CONVENTIONAL METHOD."
WAIT, WAIT. BACK UP...
WHAT IS A "GOVERNOR GENERAL"?

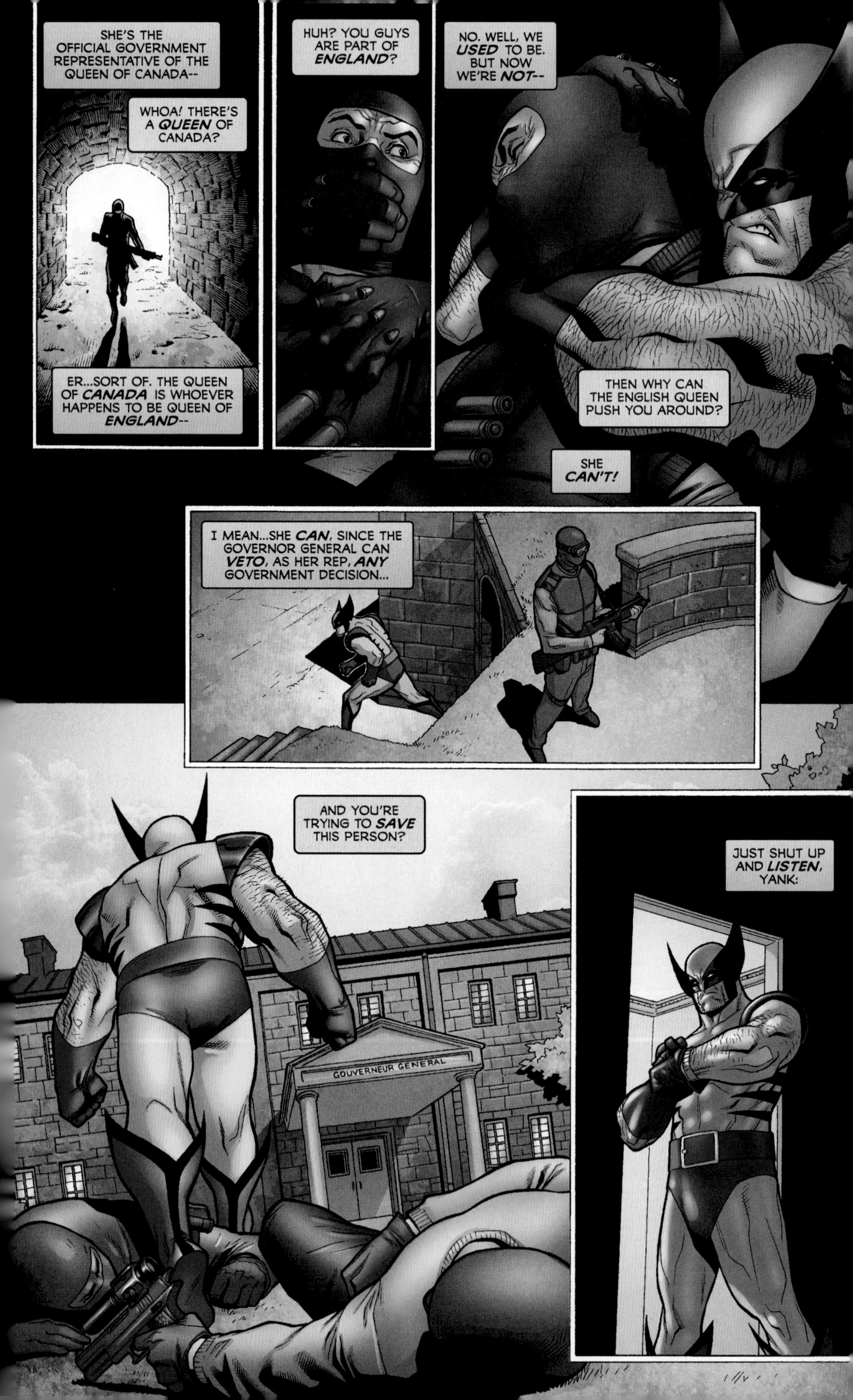
SHE'S THE OFFICIAL GOVERNMENT REPRESENTATIVE OF THE QUEEN OF CANADA--
WHOA! THERE'S A QUEEN OF CANADA?
ER...SORT OF. THE QUEEN OF CANADA IS WHOEVER HAPPENS TO BE QUEEN OF ENGLAND--
HUH? YOU GUYS ARE PART OF ENGLAND?
NO. WELL, WE USED TO BE. BUT NOW WE'RE NOT--
THEN WHY CAN THE ENGLISH QUEEN PUSH YOU AROUND?
SHE CAN'T!
I MEAN...SHE CAN, SINCE THE GOVERNOR GENERAL CAN VETO, AS HER REP, ANY GOVERNMENT DECISION...
AND YOU'RE TRYING TO SAVE THIS PERSON?
GOUVERNEUR GENERAL
JUST SHUT UP AND LISTEN, YANK:

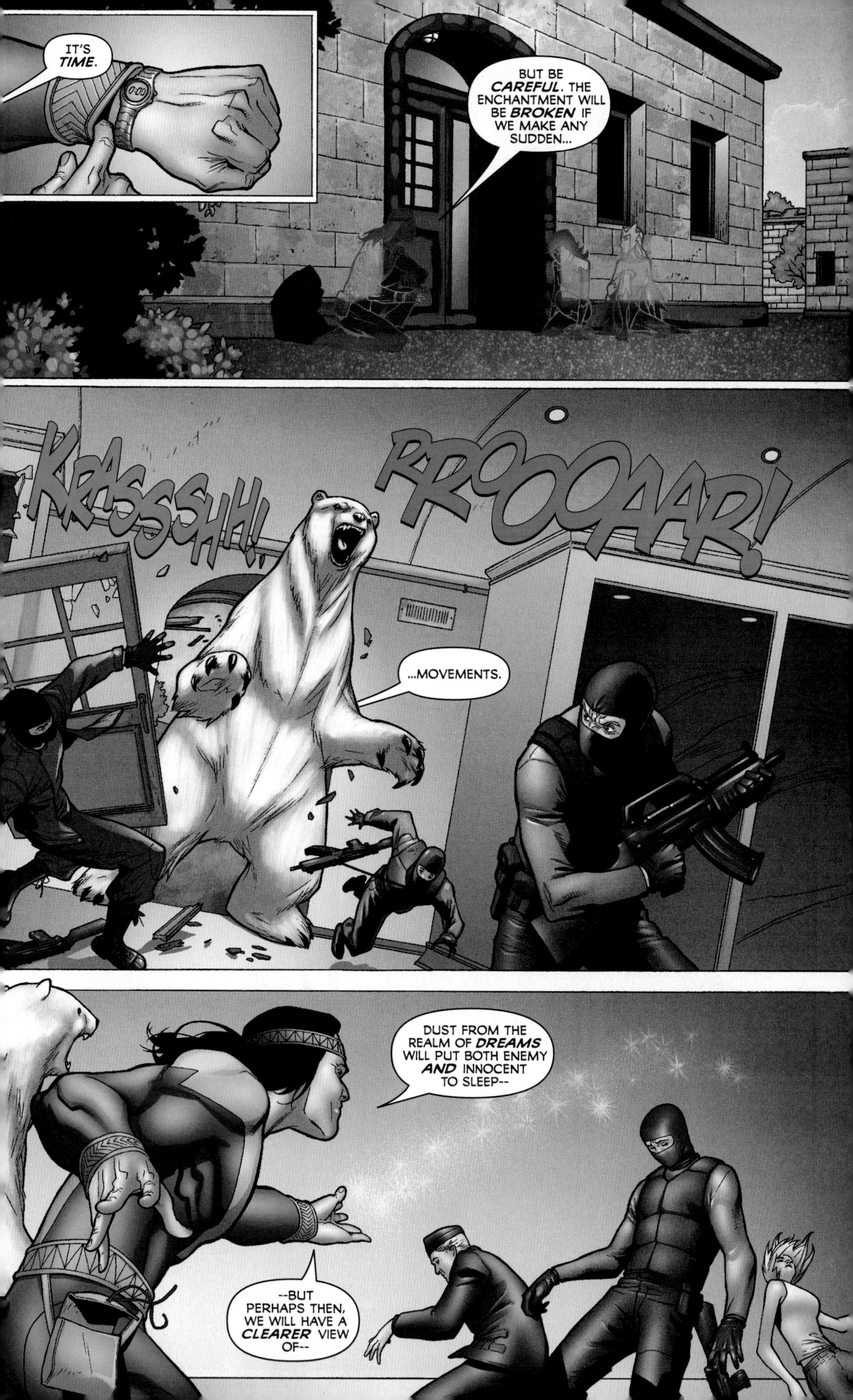

IT'S *TIME*.
BUT BE *CAREFUL*. THE ENCHANTMENT WILL BE *BROKEN* IF WE MAKE ANY SUDDEN...
KRASSSHH!
RROOOAAR!
...MOVEMENTS.
DUST FROM THE REALM OF *DREAMS* WILL PUT BOTH ENEMY *AND* INNOCENT TO SLEEP--
--BUT PERHAPS THEN, WE WILL HAVE A *CLEARER* VIEW OF--

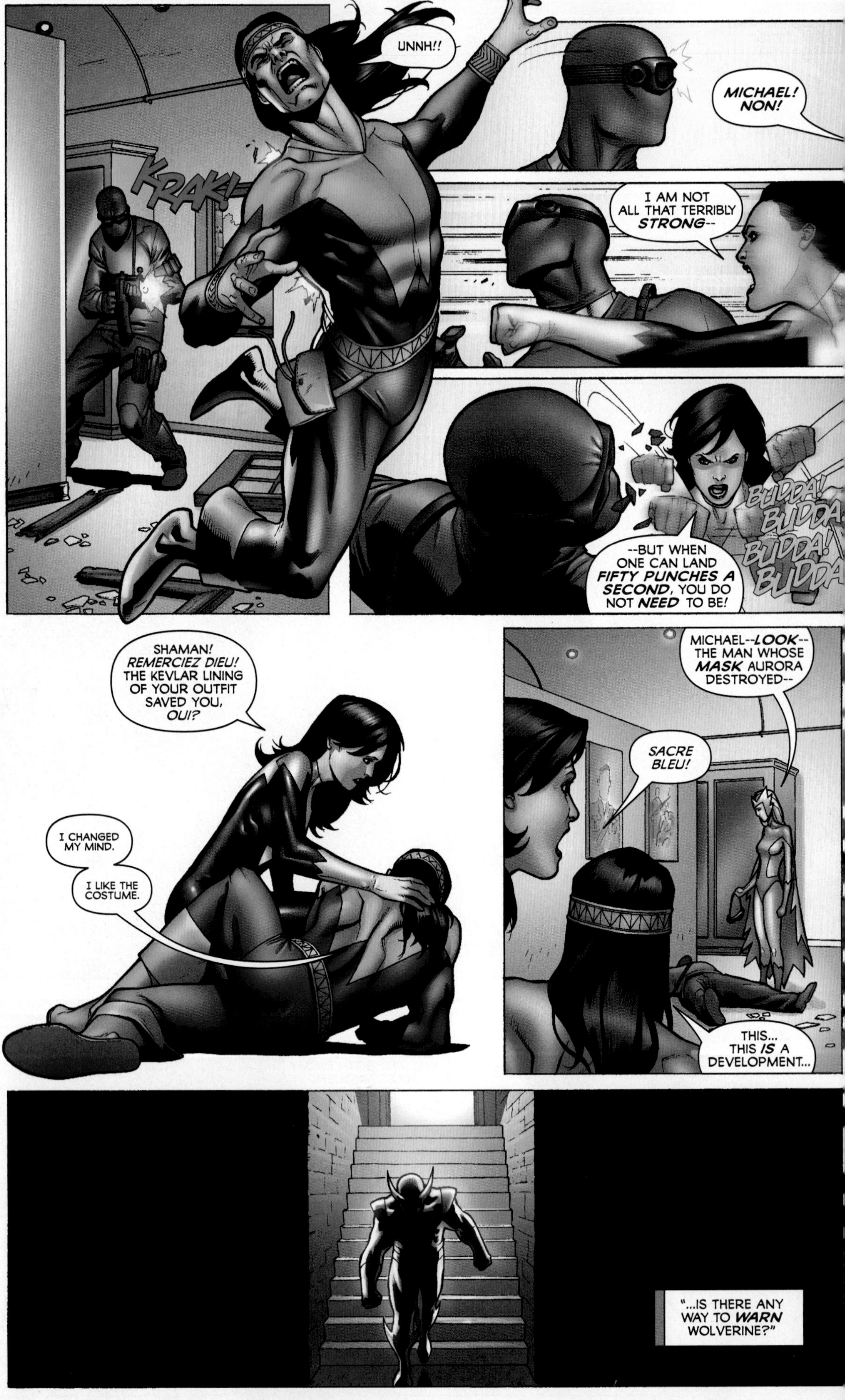
UNNH!!
KRAK!
MICHAEL! NON!
I AM NOT ALL THAT TERRIBLY STRONG--
--BUT WHEN ONE CAN LAND FIFTY PUNCHES A SECOND, YOU DO NOT NEED TO BE!
BUDDA! BUDDA! BUDDA! BUDDA!
SHAMAN! REMERCIEZ DIEU! THE KEVLAR LINING OF YOUR OUTFIT SAVED YOU, OUI?
I CHANGED MY MIND.
I LIKE THE COSTUME.
MICHAEL--LOOK-- THE MAN WHOSE MASK AURORA DESTROYED--
SACRE BLEU!
THIS... THIS IS A DEVELOPMENT...
"...IS THERE ANY WAY TO WARN WOLVERINE?"

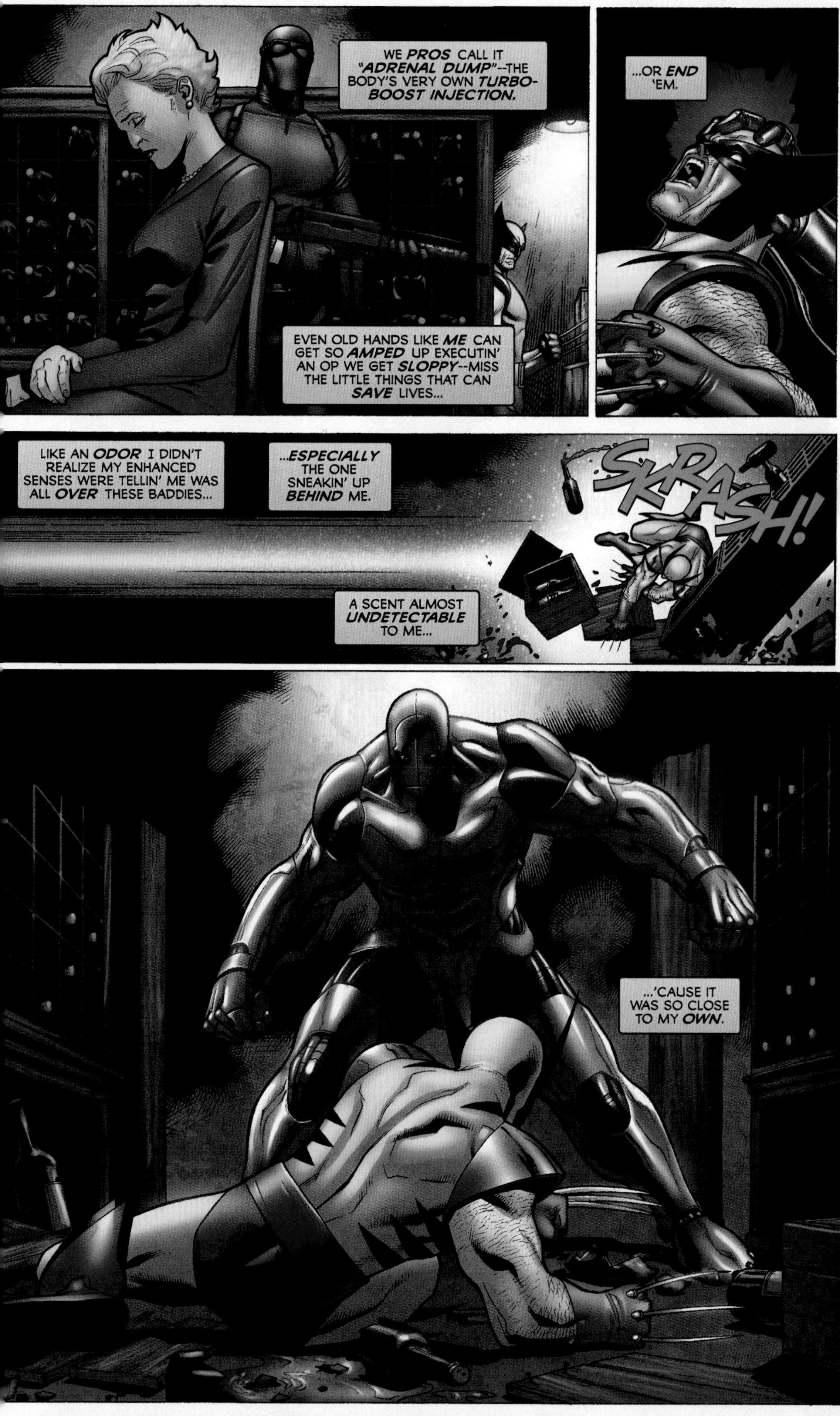
WE PROS CALL IT "ADRENAL DUMP"--THE BODY'S VERY OWN TURBO-BOOST INJECTION.
EVEN OLD HANDS LIKE ME CAN GET SO AMPED UP EXECUTIN' AN OP WE GET SLOPPY--MISS THE LITTLE THINGS THAT CAN SAVE LIVES...
...OR END 'EM.
LIKE AN ODOR I DIDN'T REALIZE MY ENHANCED SENSES WERE TELLIN' ME WAS ALL OVER THESE BADDIES...
...ESPECIALLY THE ONE SNEAKIN' UP BEHIND ME.
SKRASH!
A SCENT ALMOST UNDETECTABLE TO ME...
...'CAUSE IT WAS SO CLOSE TO MY OWN.

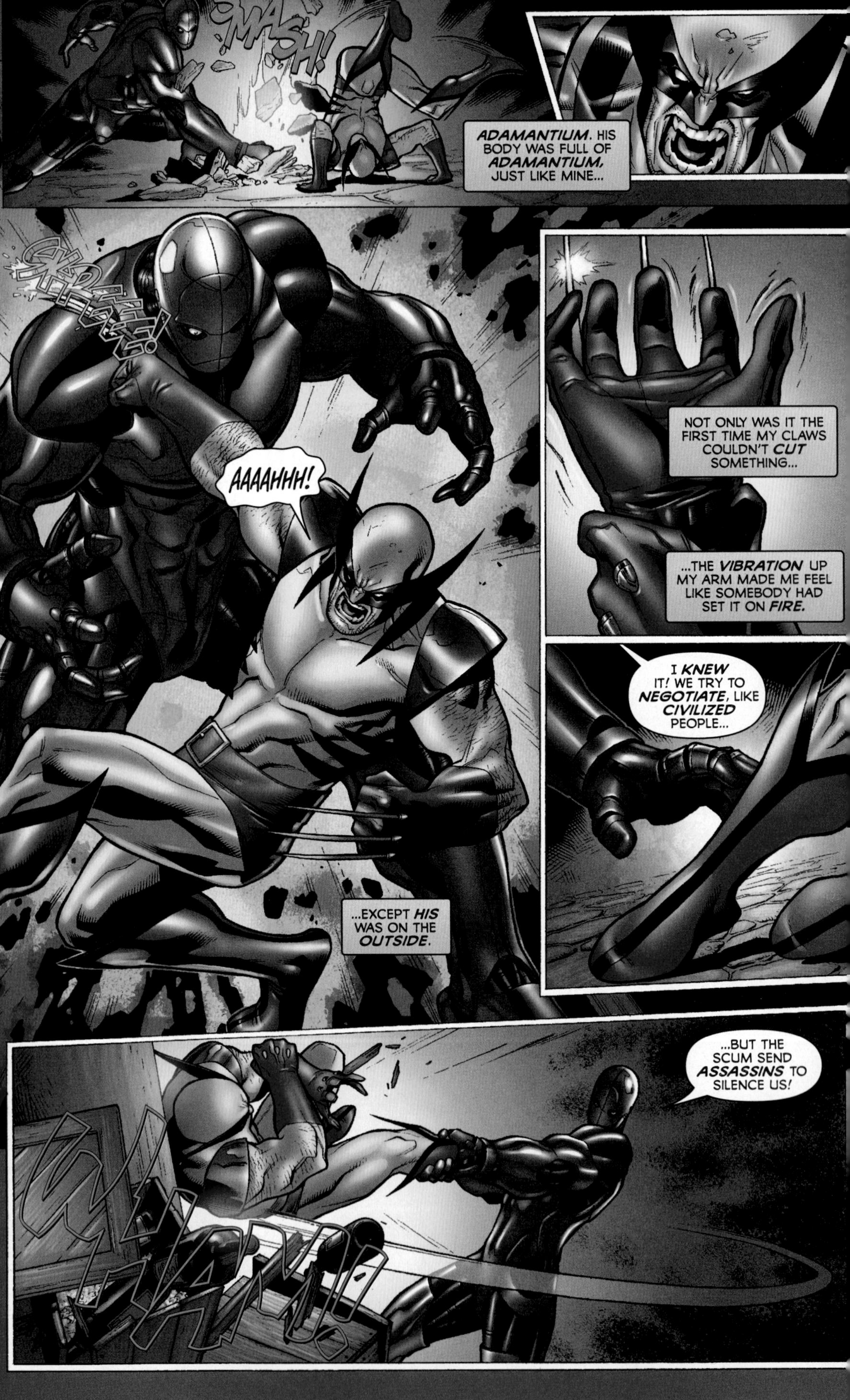
SMASH!
ADAMANTIUM. HIS BODY WAS FULL OF ADAMANTIUM, JUST LIKE MINE...
AAAAHHH!
...EXCEPT HIS WAS ON THE OUTSIDE.
NOT ONLY WAS IT THE FIRST TIME MY CLAWS COULDN'T CUT SOMETHING...
...THE VIBRATION UP MY ARM MADE ME FEEL LIKE SOMEBODY HAD SET IT ON FIRE.
I KNEW IT! WE TRY TO NEGOTIATE, LIKE CIVILIZED PEOPLE...
...BUT THE SCUM SEND ASSASSINS TO SILENCE US!

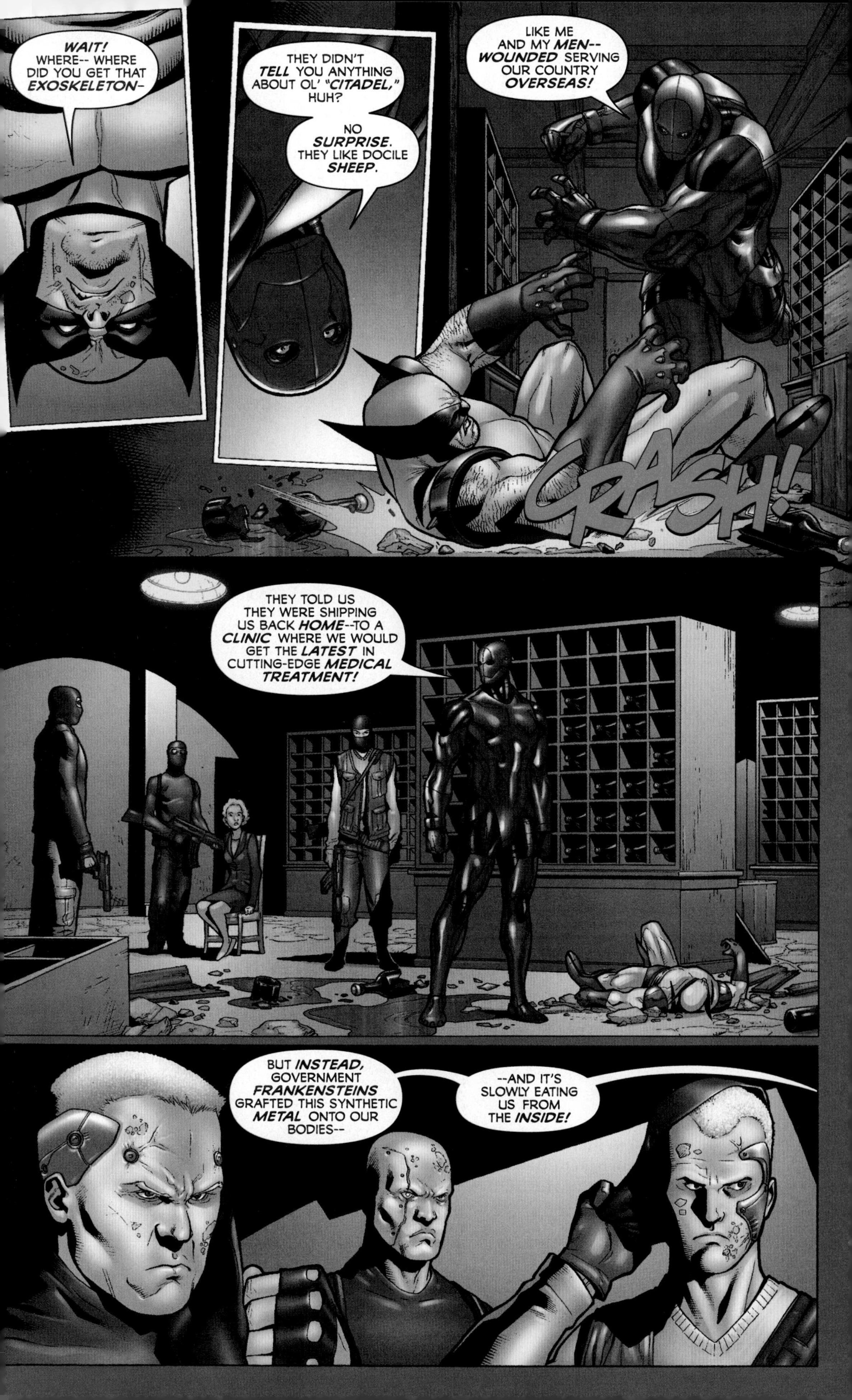
WAIT! WHERE-- WHERE DID YOU GET THAT EXOSKELETON-
THEY DIDN'T TELL YOU ANYTHING ABOUT OL' "CITADEL," HUH?
NO SURPRISE. THEY LIKE DOCILE SHEEP.
LIKE ME AND MY MEN-- WOUNDED SERVING OUR COUNTRY OVERSEAS!
CRASH!
THEY TOLD US THEY WERE SHIPPING US BACK HOME--TO A CLINIC WHERE WE WOULD GET THE LATEST IN CUTTING-EDGE MEDICAL TREATMENT!
BUT INSTEAD, GOVERNMENT FRANKENSTEINS GRAFTED THIS SYNTHETIC METAL ONTO OUR BODIES--
--AND IT'S SLOWLY EATING US FROM THE INSIDE!

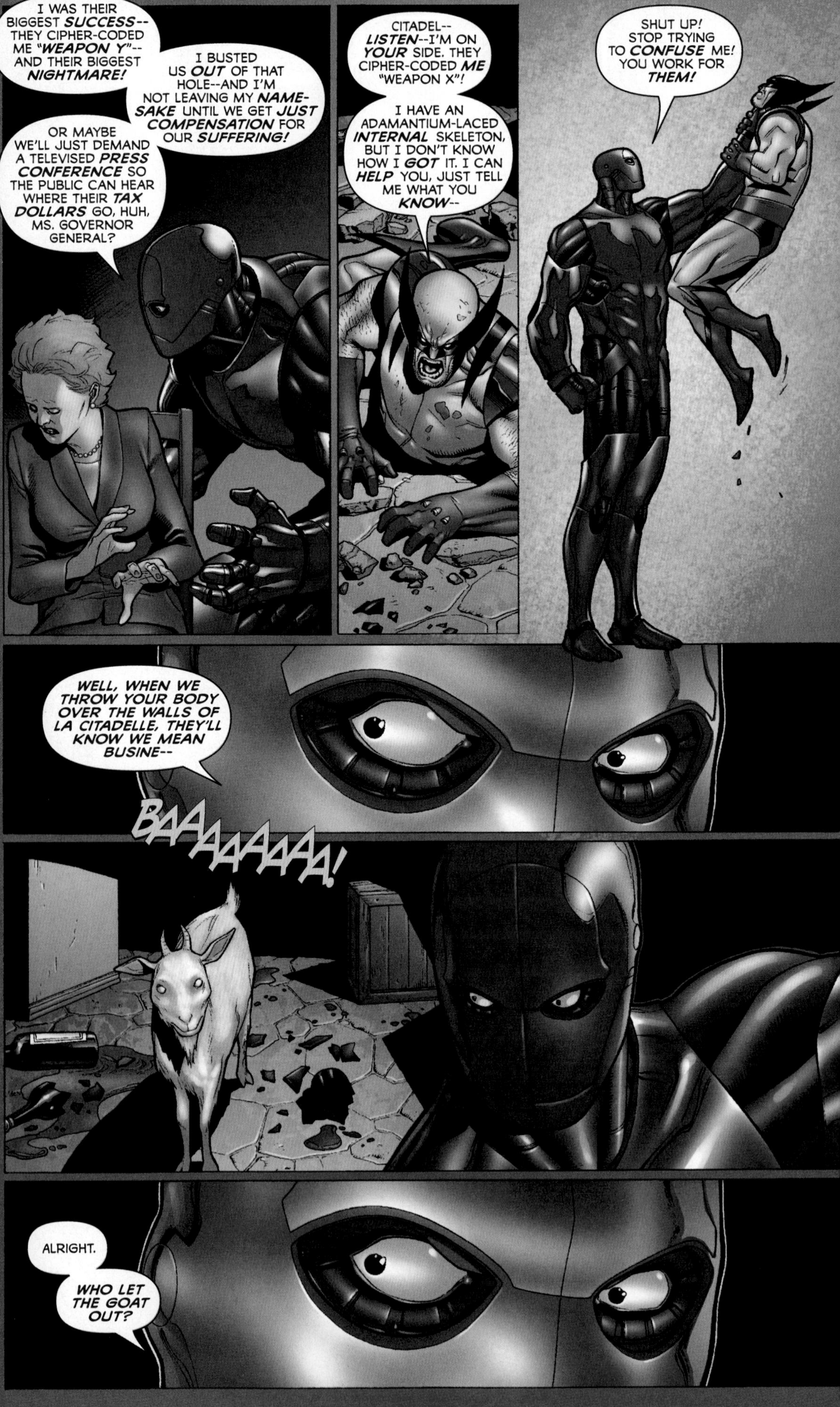

I WAS THEIR BIGGEST SUCCESS--THEY CIPHER-CODED ME "WEAPON Y"--AND THEIR BIGGEST NIGHTMARE!
I BUSTED US OUT OF THAT HOLE--AND I'M NOT LEAVING MY NAME-SAKE UNTIL WE GET JUST COMPENSATION FOR OUR SUFFERING!
OR MAYBE WE'LL JUST DEMAND A TELEVISED PRESS CONFERENCE SO THE PUBLIC CAN HEAR WHERE THEIR TAX DOLLARS GO, HUH, MS. GOVERNOR GENERAL?
CITADEL--LISTEN--I'M ON YOUR SIDE. THEY CIPHER-CODED ME "WEAPON X"!
I HAVE AN ADAMANTIUM-LACED INTERNAL SKELETON, BUT I DON'T KNOW HOW I GOT IT. I CAN HELP YOU, JUST TELL ME WHAT YOU KNOW--
SHUT UP! STOP TRYING TO CONFUSE ME! YOU WORK FOR THEM!
WELL, WHEN WE THROW YOUR BODY OVER THE WALLS OF LA CITADELLE, THEY'LL KNOW WE MEAN BUSINE--
BAAAAAAAA!
ALRIGHT.
WHO LET THE GOAT OUT?

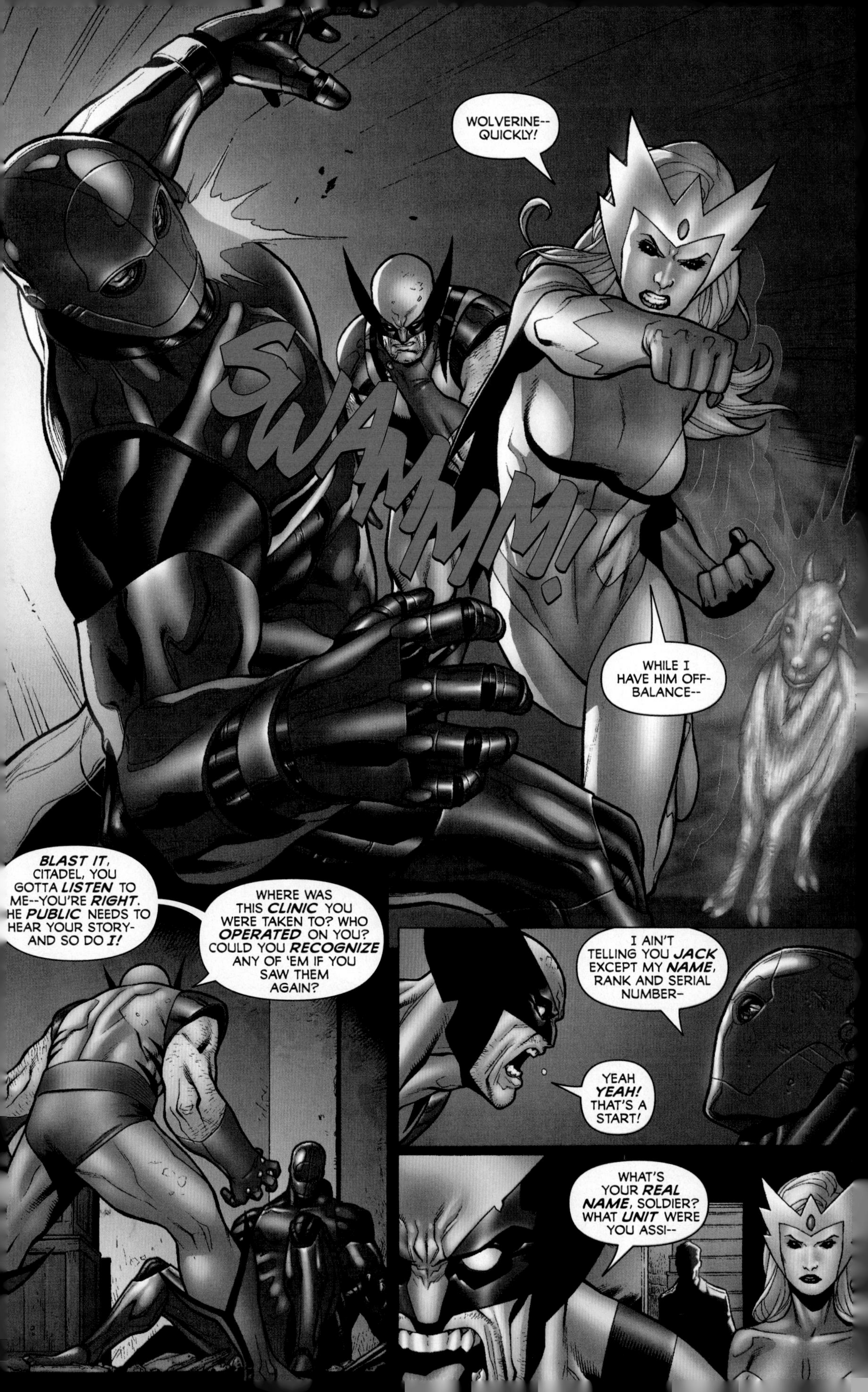
WOLVERINE--
QUICKLY!
SWAMMM!
WHILE I HAVE HIM OFF-BALANCE--
BLAST IT, CITADEL, YOU GOTTA LISTEN TO ME--YOU'RE RIGHT. HE PUBLIC NEEDS TO HEAR YOUR STORY-AND SO DO I!
WHERE WAS THIS CLINIC YOU WERE TAKEN TO? WHO OPERATED ON YOU? COULD YOU RECOGNIZE ANY OF 'EM IF YOU SAW THEM AGAIN?
I AIN'T TELLING YOU JACK EXCEPT MY NAME, RANK AND SERIAL NUMBER–
YEAH YEAH! THAT'S A START!
WHAT'S YOUR REAL NAME, SOLDIER? WHAT UNIT WERE YOU ASSI--

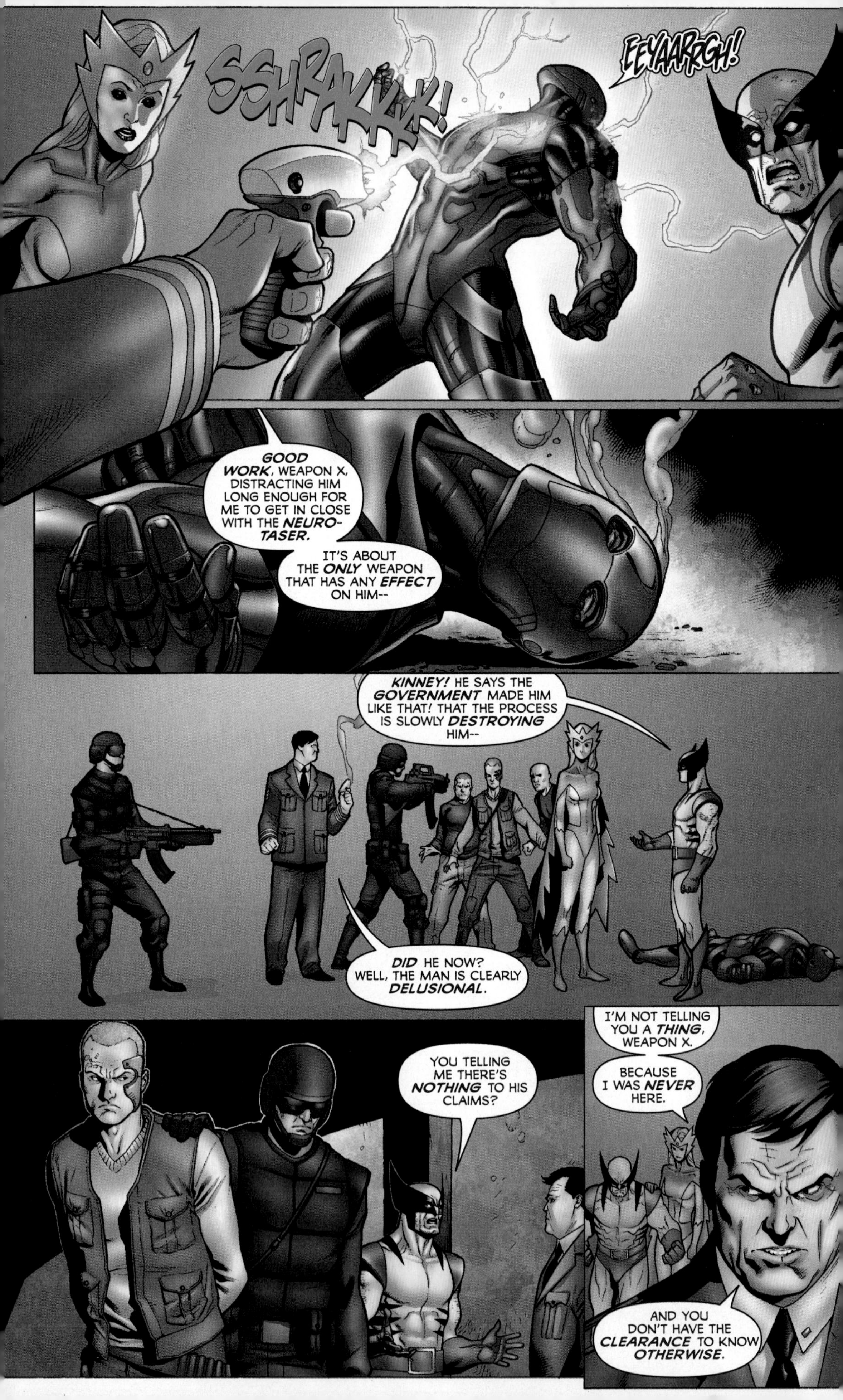
SSHRAKKKK!
EEYAARRGH!
GOOD WORK, WEAPON X, DISTRACTING HIM LONG ENOUGH FOR ME TO GET IN CLOSE WITH THE NEURO-TASER.
IT'S ABOUT THE ONLY WEAPON THAT HAS ANY EFFECT ON HIM--
KINNEY! HE SAYS THE GOVERNMENT MADE HIM LIKE THAT! THAT THE PROCESS IS SLOWLY DESTROYING HIM--
DID HE NOW? WELL, THE MAN IS CLEARLY DELUSIONAL.
YOU TELLING ME THERE'S NOTHING TO HIS CLAIMS?
I'M NOT TELLING YOU A THING, WEAPON X.
BECAUSE I WAS NEVER HERE.
AND YOU DON'T HAVE THE CLEARANCE TO KNOW OTHERWISE.

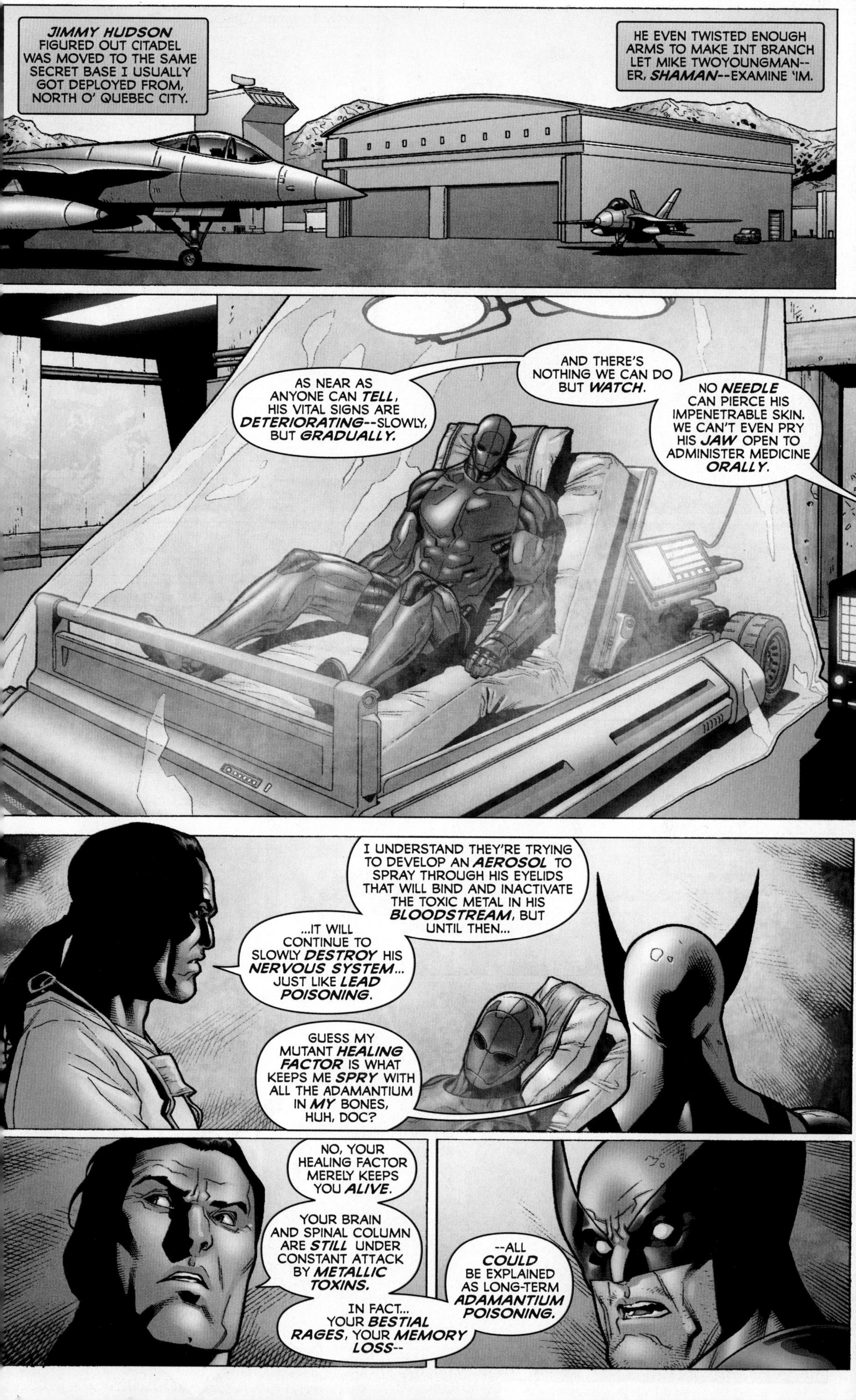
JIMMY HUDSON FIGURED OUT CITADEL WAS MOVED TO THE SAME SECRET BASE I USUALLY GOT DEPLOYED FROM, NORTH O' QUEBEC CITY.
HE EVEN TWISTED ENOUGH ARMS TO MAKE INT BRANCH LET MIKE TWOYOUNGMAN-- ER, SHAMAN--EXAMINE 'IM.
AS NEAR AS ANYONE CAN TELL, HIS VITAL SIGNS ARE DETERIORATING--SLOWLY, BUT GRADUALLY.
AND THERE'S NOTHING WE CAN DO BUT WATCH.
NO NEEDLE CAN PIERCE HIS IMPENETRABLE SKIN. WE CAN'T EVEN PRY HIS JAW OPEN TO ADMINISTER MEDICINE ORALLY.
I UNDERSTAND THEY'RE TRYING TO DEVELOP AN AEROSOL TO SPRAY THROUGH HIS EYELIDS THAT WILL BIND AND INACTIVATE THE TOXIC METAL IN HIS BLOODSTREAM, BUT UNTIL THEN...
...IT WILL CONTINUE TO SLOWLY DESTROY HIS NERVOUS SYSTEM... JUST LIKE LEAD POISONING.
GUESS MY MUTANT HEALING FACTOR IS WHAT KEEPS ME SPRY WITH ALL THE ADAMANTIUM IN MY BONES, HUH, DOC?
NO, YOUR HEALING FACTOR MERELY KEEPS YOU ALIVE.
YOUR BRAIN AND SPINAL COLUMN ARE STILL UNDER CONSTANT ATTACK BY METALLIC TOXINS.
IN FACT... YOUR BESTIAL RAGES, YOUR MEMORY LOSS--
--ALL COULD BE EXPLAINED AS LONG-TERM ADAMANTIUM POISONING.

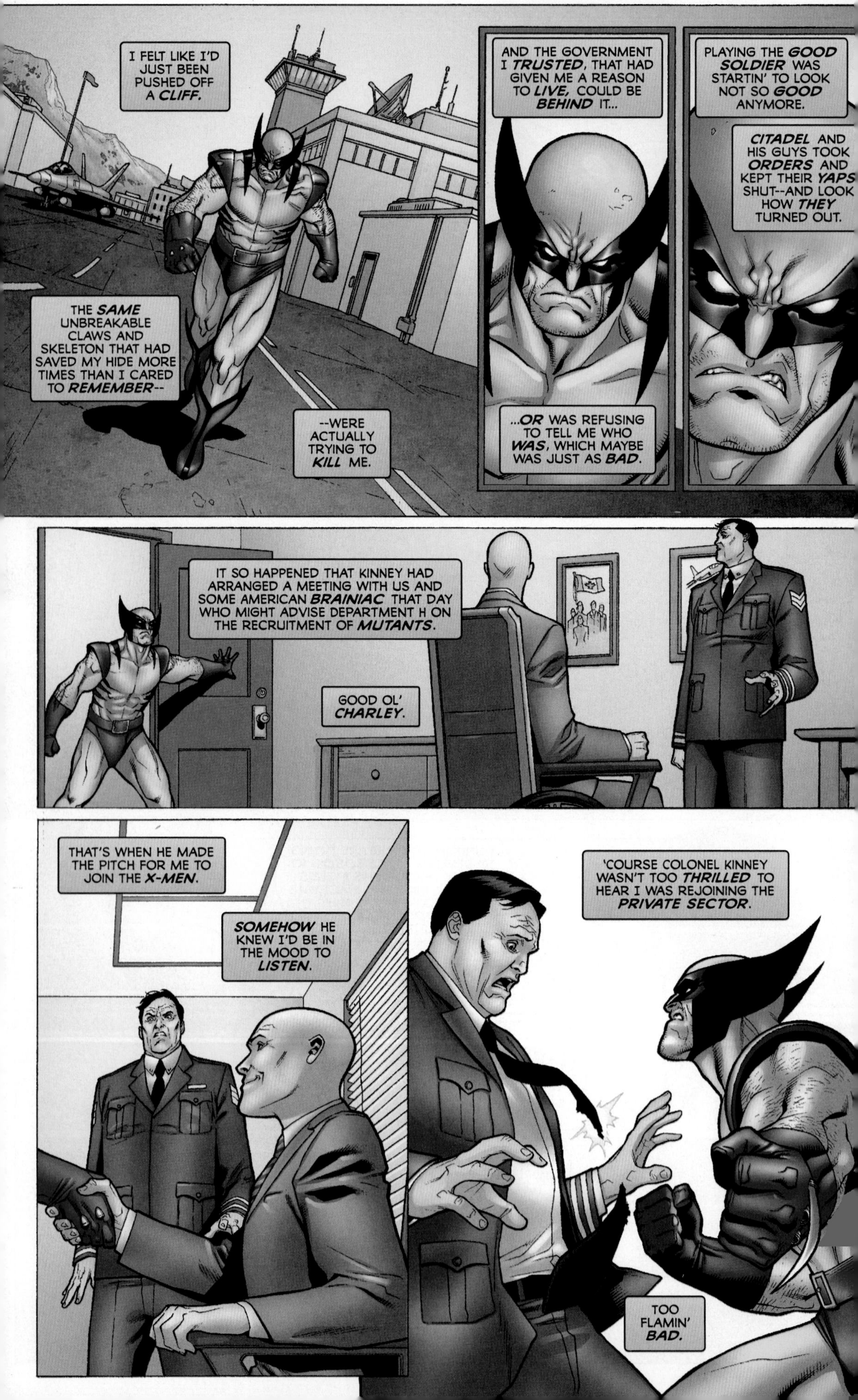
I FELT LIKE I'D JUST BEEN PUSHED OFF A CLIFF.
THE SAME UNBREAKABLE CLAWS AND SKELETON THAT HAD SAVED MY HIDE MORE TIMES THAN I CARED TO REMEMBER--
--WERE ACTUALLY TRYING TO KILL ME.
AND THE GOVERNMENT I TRUSTED, THAT HAD GIVEN ME A REASON TO LIVE, COULD BE BEHIND IT...
...OR WAS REFUSING TO TELL ME WHO WAS, WHICH MAYBE WAS JUST AS BAD.
PLAYING THE GOOD SOLDIER WAS STARTIN' TO LOOK NOT SO GOOD ANYMORE.
CITADEL AND HIS GUYS TOOK ORDERS AND KEPT THEIR YAPS SHUT--AND LOOK HOW THEY TURNED OUT.
IT SO HAPPENED THAT KINNEY HAD ARRANGED A MEETING WITH US AND SOME AMERICAN BRAINIAC THAT DAY WHO MIGHT ADVISE DEPARTMENT H ON THE RECRUITMENT OF MUTANTS.
GOOD OL' CHARLEY.
THAT'S WHEN HE MADE THE PITCH FOR ME TO JOIN THE X-MEN.
SOMEHOW HE KNEW I'D BE IN THE MOOD TO LISTEN.
'COURSE COLONEL KINNEY WASN'T TOO THRILLED TO HEAR I WAS REJOINING THE PRIVATE SECTOR.
TOO FLAMIN' BAD.

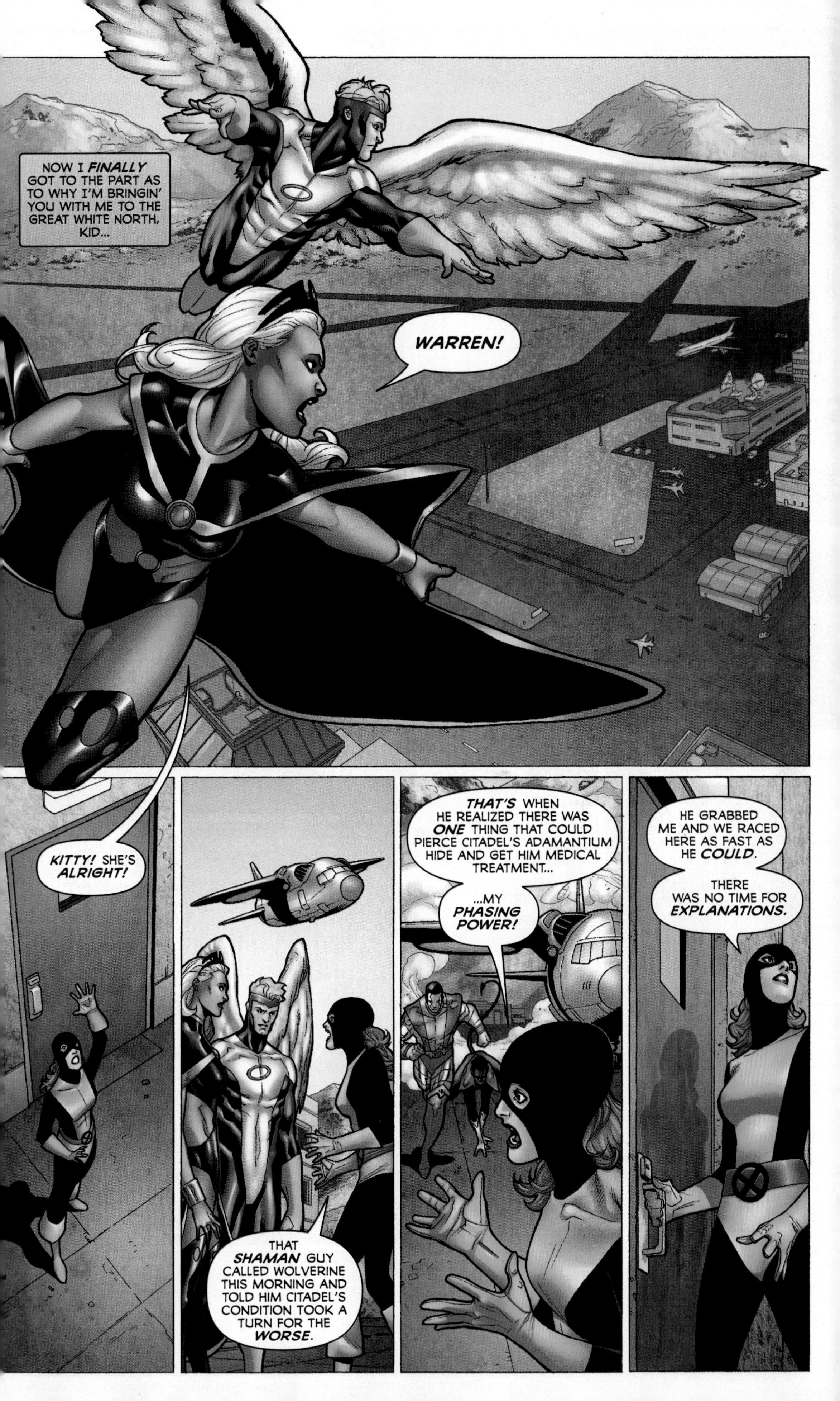
NOW I *FINALLY* GOT TO THE PART AS TO WHY I'M BRINGIN' YOU WITH ME TO THE GREAT WHITE NORTH, KID...
WARREN!
KITTY! SHE'S *ALRIGHT!*
THAT *SHAMAN* GUY CALLED WOLVERINE THIS MORNING AND TOLD HIM CITADEL'S CONDITION TOOK A TURN FOR THE *WORSE*.
THAT'S WHEN HE REALIZED THERE WAS *ONE* THING THAT COULD PIERCE CITADEL'S ADAMANTIUM HIDE AND GET HIM MEDICAL TREATMENT...
...MY *PHASING POWER!*
HE GRABBED ME AND WE RACED HERE AS FAST AS HE *COULD*.
THERE WAS NO TIME FOR *EXPLANATIONS.*

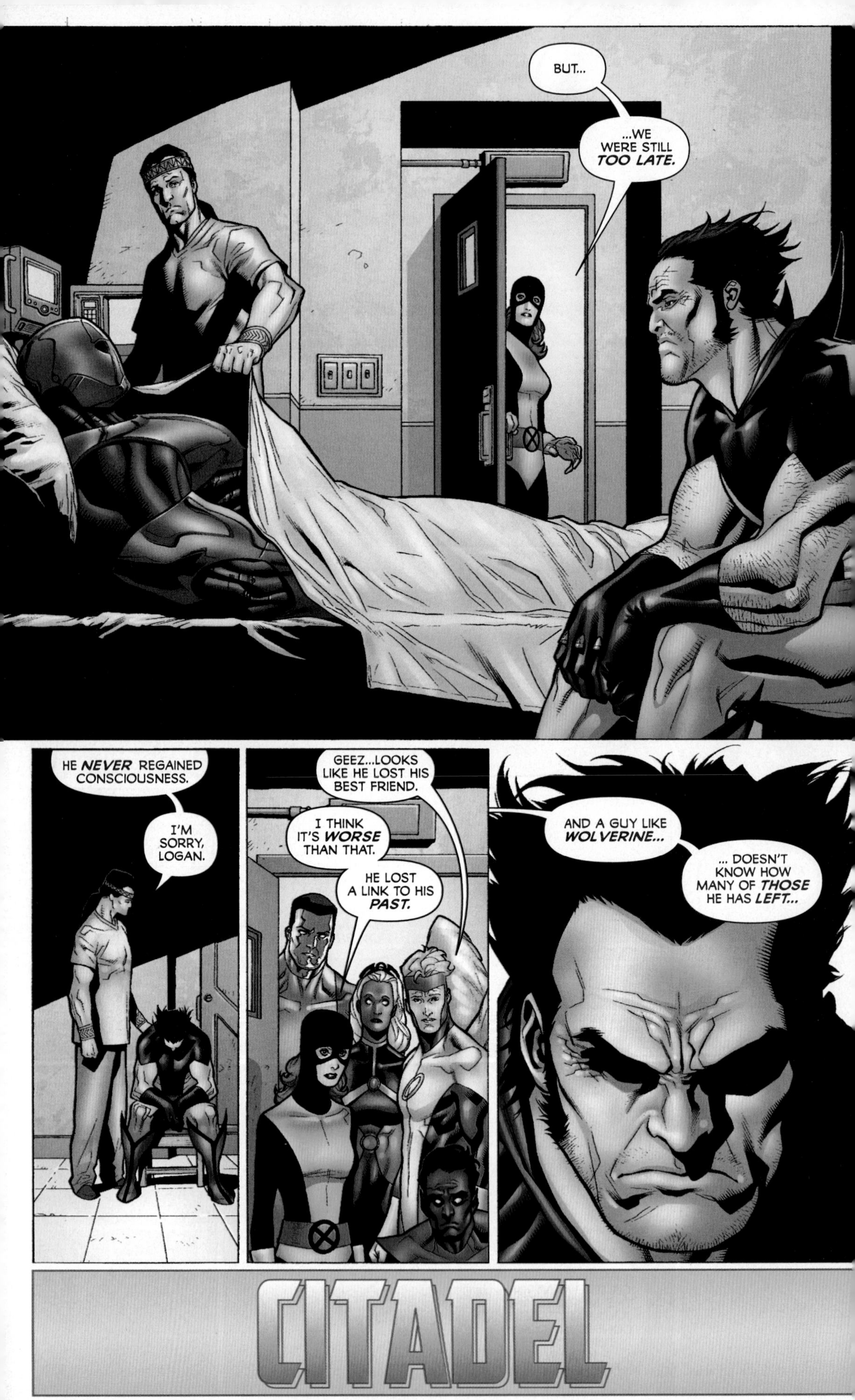

BUT...
...WE WERE STILL TOO LATE.
HE NEVER REGAINED CONSCIOUSNESS.
I'M SORRY, LOGAN.
GEEZ...LOOKS LIKE HE LOST HIS BEST FRIEND.
I THINK IT'S WORSE THAN THAT.
HE LOST A LINK TO HIS PAST.
AND A GUY LIKE WOLVERINE...
... DOESN'T KNOW HOW MANY OF THOSE HE HAS LEFT...
CITADEL

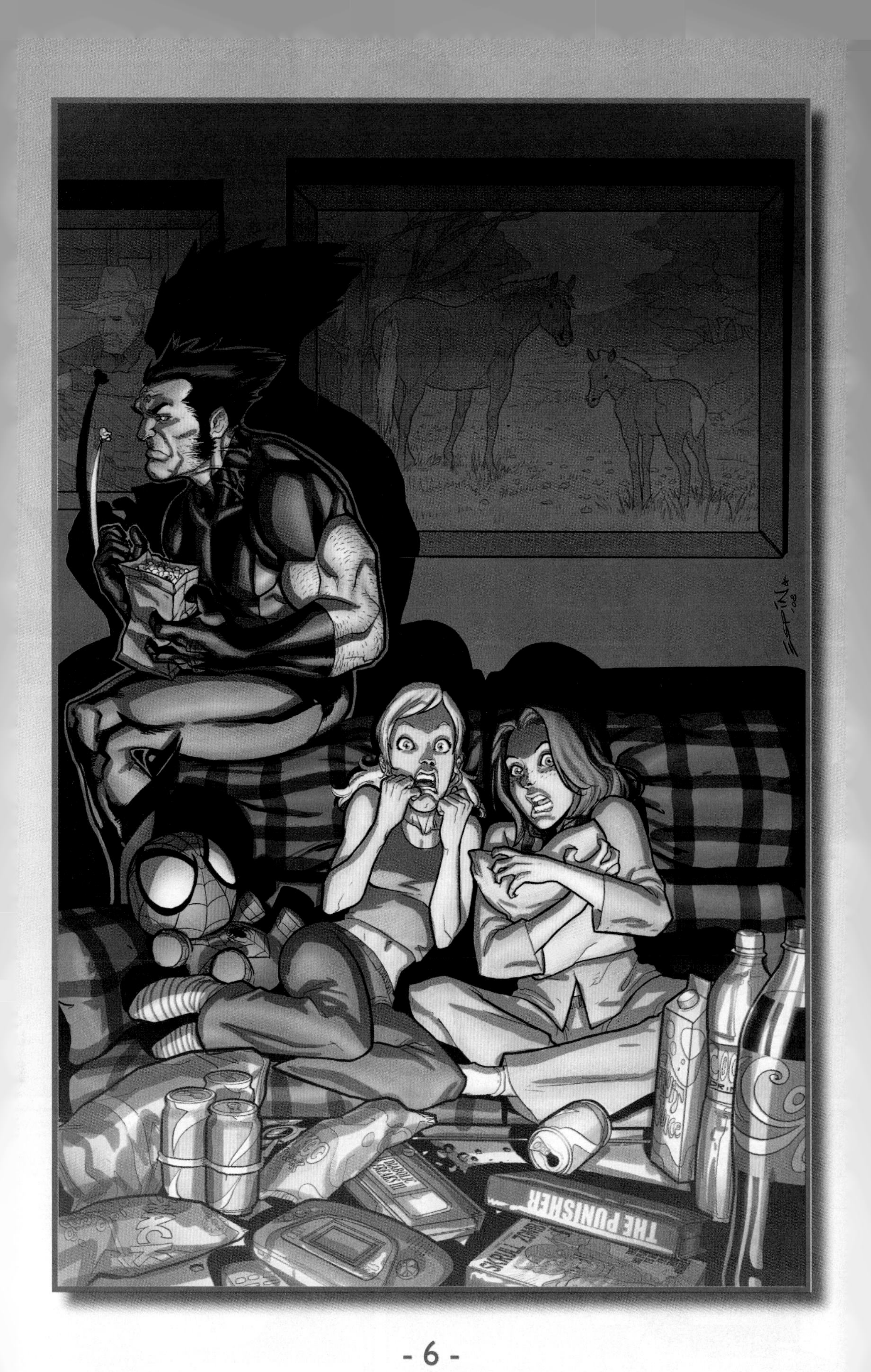
THE PUNISHER

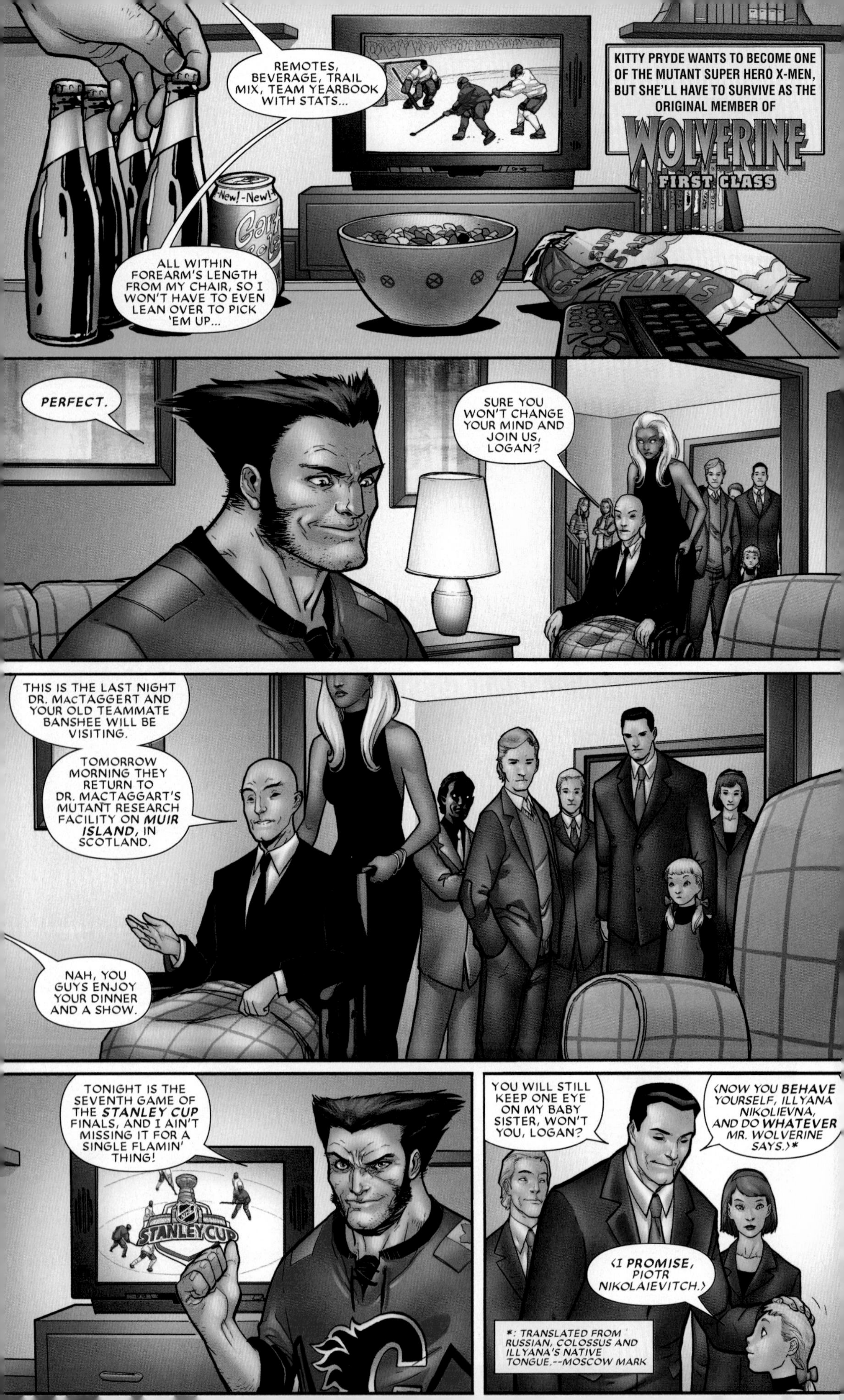
REMOTES, BEVERAGE, TRAIL MIX, TEAM YEARBOOK WITH STATS...
KITTY PRYDE WANTS TO BECOME ONE OF THE MUTANT SUPER HERO X-MEN, BUT SHE'LL HAVE TO SURVIVE AS THE ORIGINAL MEMBER OF
WOLVERINE FIRST CLASS
-New! -New!
ALL WITHIN FOREARM'S LENGTH FROM MY CHAIR, SO I WON'T HAVE TO EVEN LEAN OVER TO PICK 'EM UP...
PERFECT.
SURE YOU WON'T CHANGE YOUR MIND AND JOIN US, LOGAN?
THIS IS THE LAST NIGHT DR. MacTAGGERT AND YOUR OLD TEAMMATE BANSHEE WILL BE VISITING.
TOMORROW MORNING THEY RETURN TO DR. MACTAGGART'S MUTANT RESEARCH FACILITY ON MUIR ISLAND, IN SCOTLAND.
NAH, YOU GUYS ENJOY YOUR DINNER AND A SHOW.
TONIGHT IS THE SEVENTH GAME OF THE STANLEY CUP FINALS, AND I AIN'T MISSING IT FOR A SINGLE FLAMIN' THING!
STANLEY CUP
YOU WILL STILL KEEP ONE EYE ON MY BABY SISTER, WON'T YOU, LOGAN?
‹NOW YOU BEHAVE YOURSELF, ILLYANA NIKOLIEVNA, AND DO WHATEVER MR. WOLVERINE SAYS.›*
‹I PROMISE, PIOTR NIKOLAIEVITCH.›
*: TRANSLATED FROM RUSSIAN, COLOSSUS AND ILLYANA'S NATIVE TONGUE.--MOSCOW MARK

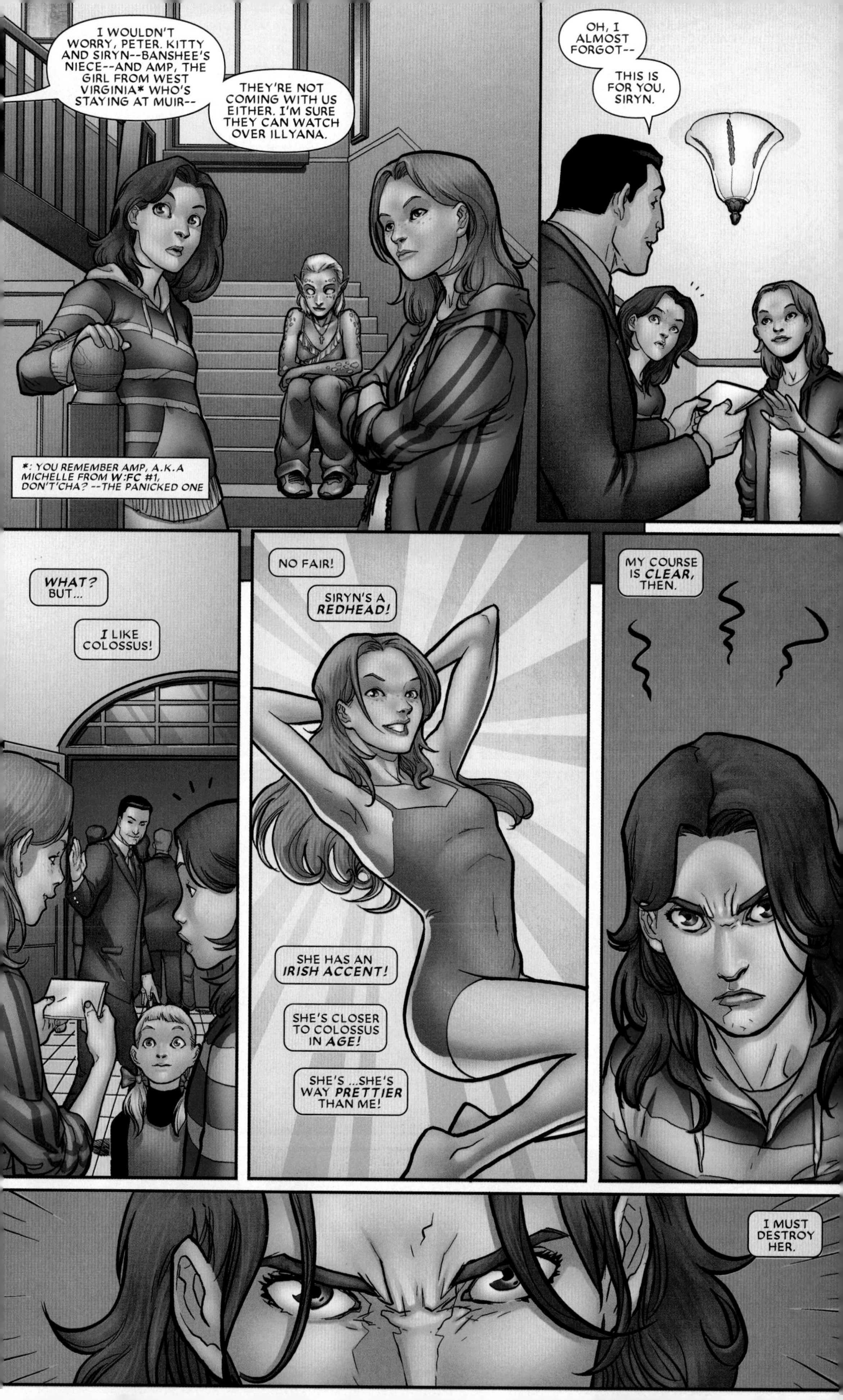
I WOULDN'T WORRY, PETER. KITTY AND SIRYN--BANSHEE'S NIECE--AND AMP, THE GIRL FROM WEST VIRGINIA* WHO'S STAYING AT MUIR--
THEY'RE NOT COMING WITH US EITHER. I'M SURE THEY CAN WATCH OVER ILLYANA.
*: YOU REMEMBER AMP, A.K.A MICHELLE FROM W:FC #1, DON'T'CHA? --THE PANICKED ONE
OH, I ALMOST FORGOT--
THIS IS FOR YOU, SIRYN.
WHAT? BUT...
I LIKE COLOSSUS!
NO FAIR!
SIRYN'S A REDHEAD!
SHE HAS AN IRISH ACCENT!
SHE'S CLOSER TO COLOSSUS IN AGE!
SHE'S ...SHE'S WAY PRETTIER THAN ME!
MY COURSE IS CLEAR, THEN.
I MUST DESTROY HER.

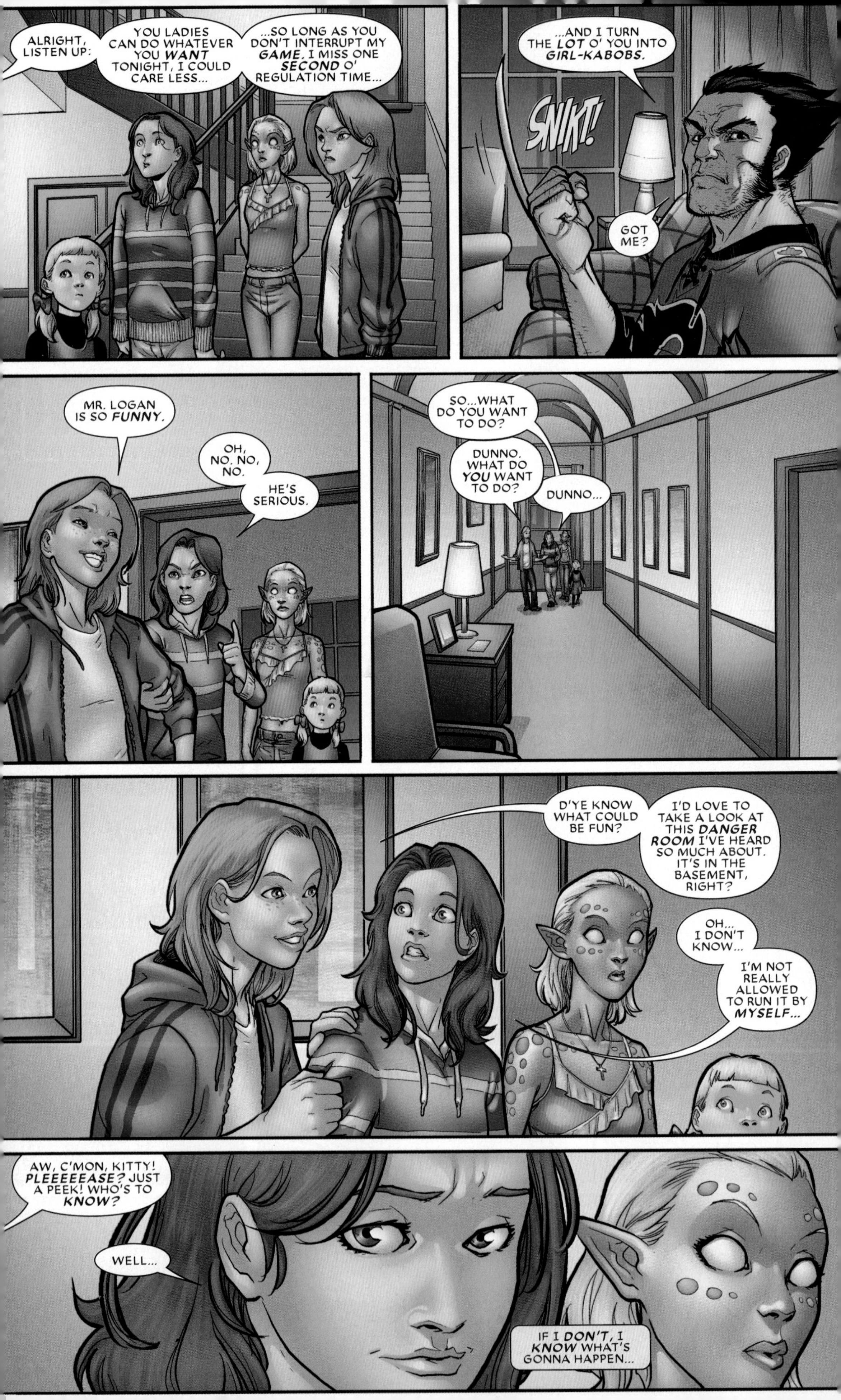
ALRIGHT, LISTEN UP:
YOU LADIES CAN DO WHATEVER YOU *WANT* TONIGHT, I COULD CARE LESS...
...SO LONG AS YOU DON'T INTERRUPT MY *GAME*. I MISS ONE *SECOND* O' REGULATION TIME...
...AND I TURN THE *LOT* O' YOU INTO *GIRL-KABOBS*.
SNIKT!
GOT ME?
MR. LOGAN IS SO *FUNNY*.
OH, NO. NO, NO.
HE'S SERIOUS.
SO...WHAT DO YOU WANT TO DO?
DUNNO. WHAT DO *YOU* WANT TO DO?
DUNNO...
D'YE KNOW WHAT COULD BE FUN?
I'D LOVE TO TAKE A LOOK AT THIS *DANGER ROOM* I'VE HEARD SO MUCH ABOUT. IT'S IN THE BASEMENT, RIGHT?
OH... I DON'T KNOW...
I'M NOT REALLY ALLOWED TO RUN IT BY *MYSELF*...
AW, C'MON, KITTY! *PLEEEEEASE?* JUST A PEEK! WHO'S TO *KNOW?*
WELL...
IF I *DON'T*, I *KNOW* WHAT'S GONNA HAPPEN...

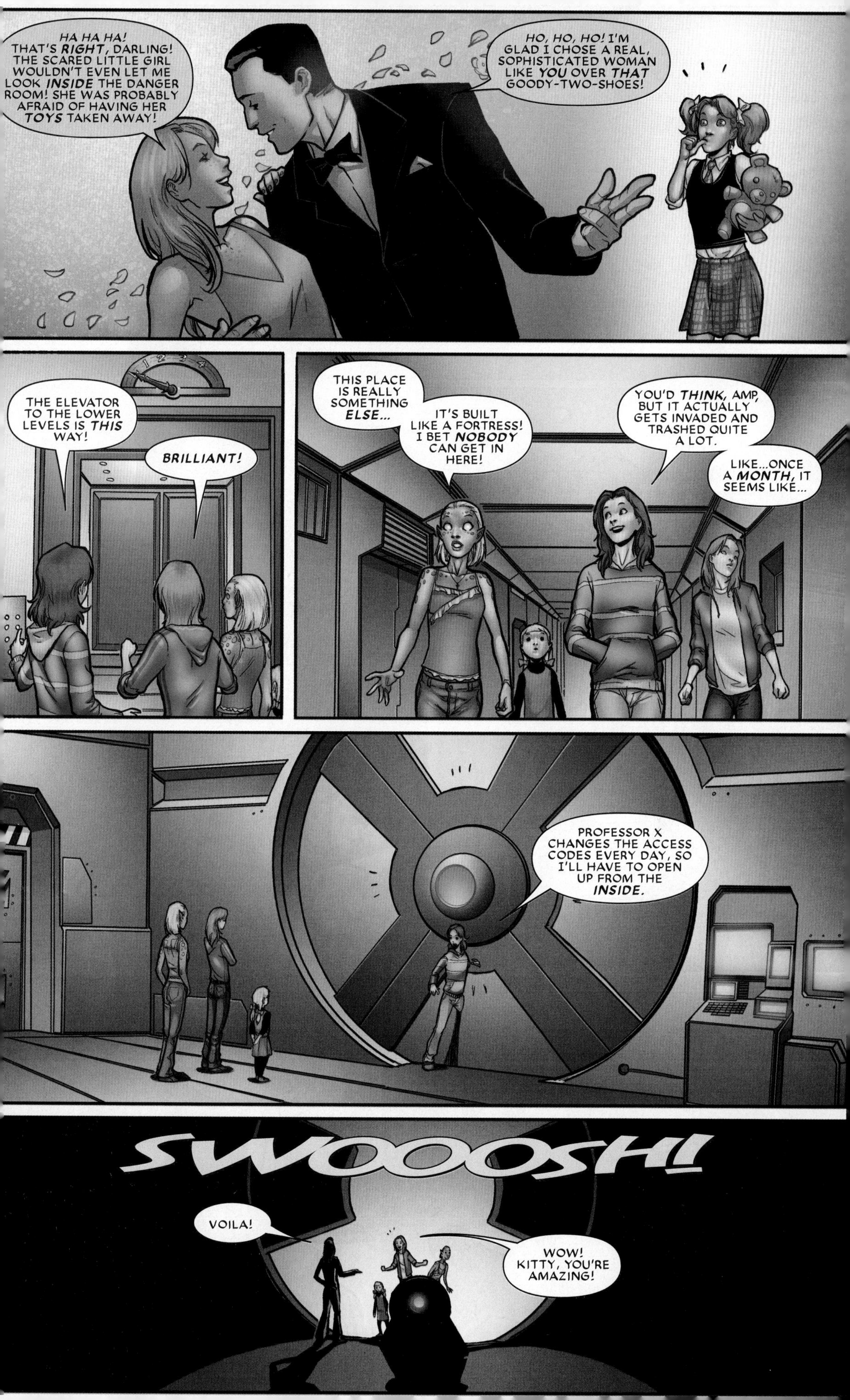
HA HA HA! THAT'S RIGHT, DARLING! THE SCARED LITTLE GIRL WOULDN'T EVEN LET ME LOOK INSIDE THE DANGER ROOM! SHE WAS PROBABLY AFRAID OF HAVING HER TOYS TAKEN AWAY!
HO, HO, HO! I'M GLAD I CHOSE A REAL, SOPHISTICATED WOMAN LIKE YOU OVER THAT GOODY-TWO-SHOES!
1 2 3 4
THE ELEVATOR TO THE LOWER LEVELS IS THIS WAY!
BRILLIANT!
THIS PLACE IS REALLY SOMETHING ELSE...
IT'S BUILT LIKE A FORTRESS! I BET NOBODY CAN GET IN HERE!
YOU'D THINK, AMP, BUT IT ACTUALLY GETS INVADED AND TRASHED QUITE A LOT.
LIKE...ONCE A MONTH, IT SEEMS LIKE...
PROFESSOR X CHANGES THE ACCESS CODES EVERY DAY, SO I'LL HAVE TO OPEN UP FROM THE INSIDE.
SWOOOSH!
VOILA!
WOW! KITTY, YOU'RE AMAZING!

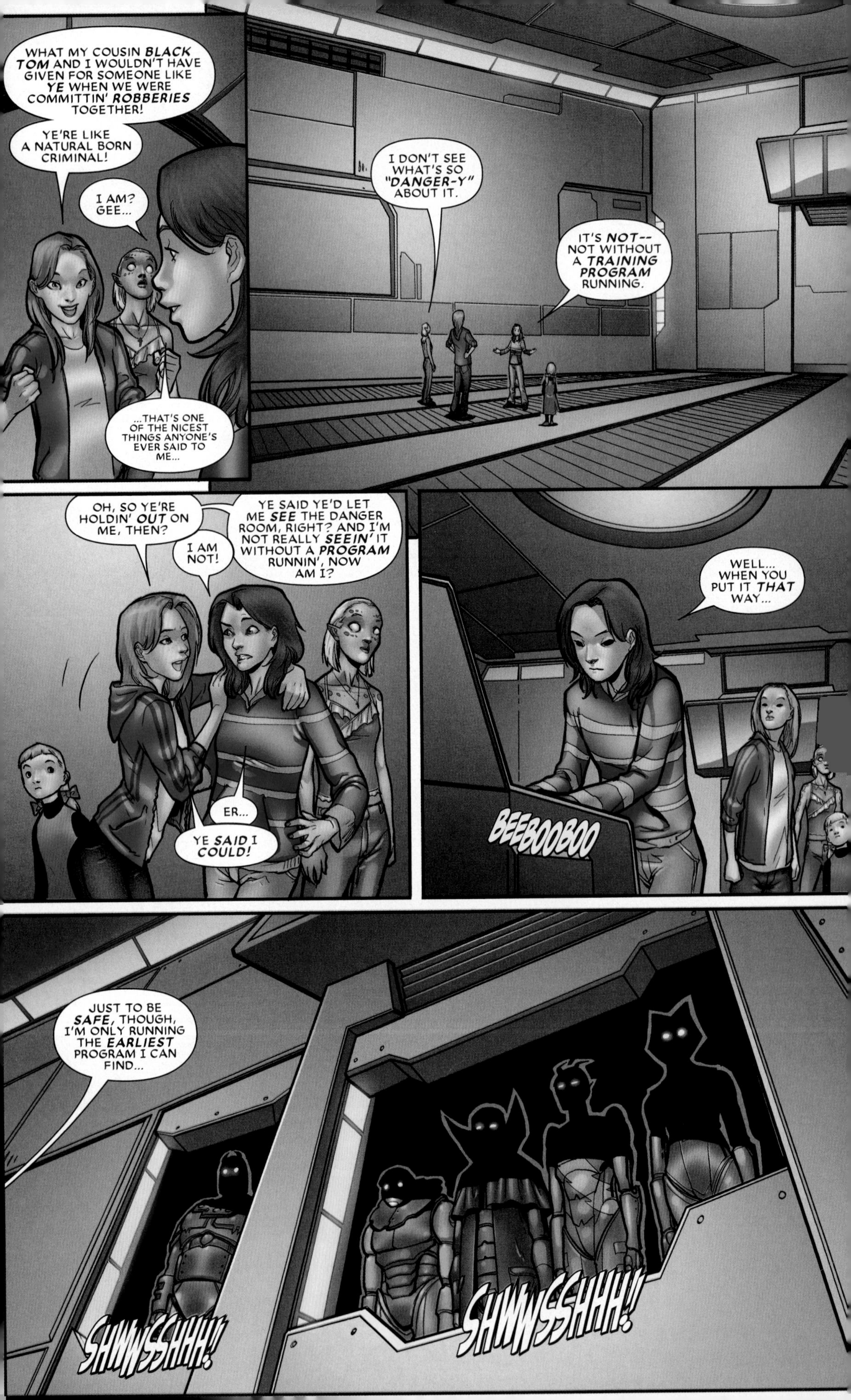

WHAT MY COUSIN BLACK TOM AND I WOULDN'T HAVE GIVEN FOR SOMEONE LIKE YE WHEN WE WERE COMMITTIN' ROBBERIES TOGETHER!
YE'RE LIKE A NATURAL BORN CRIMINAL!
I AM? GEE...
...THAT'S ONE OF THE NICEST THINGS ANYONE'S EVER SAID TO ME...
I DON'T SEE WHAT'S SO "DANGER-Y" ABOUT IT.
IT'S NOT-- NOT WITHOUT A TRAINING PROGRAM RUNNING.
OH, SO YE'RE HOLDIN' OUT ON ME, THEN?
I AM NOT!
YE SAID YE'D LET ME SEE THE DANGER ROOM, RIGHT? AND I'M NOT REALLY SEEIN' IT WITHOUT A PROGRAM RUNNIN', NOW AM I?
ER...
YE SAID I COULD!
WELL... WHEN YOU PUT IT THAT WAY...
BEEBOOBOO
JUST TO BE SAFE, THOUGH, I'M ONLY RUNNING THE EARLIEST PROGRAM I CAN FIND...
SHWWSSHHH!!
SHWWSSHHH!!

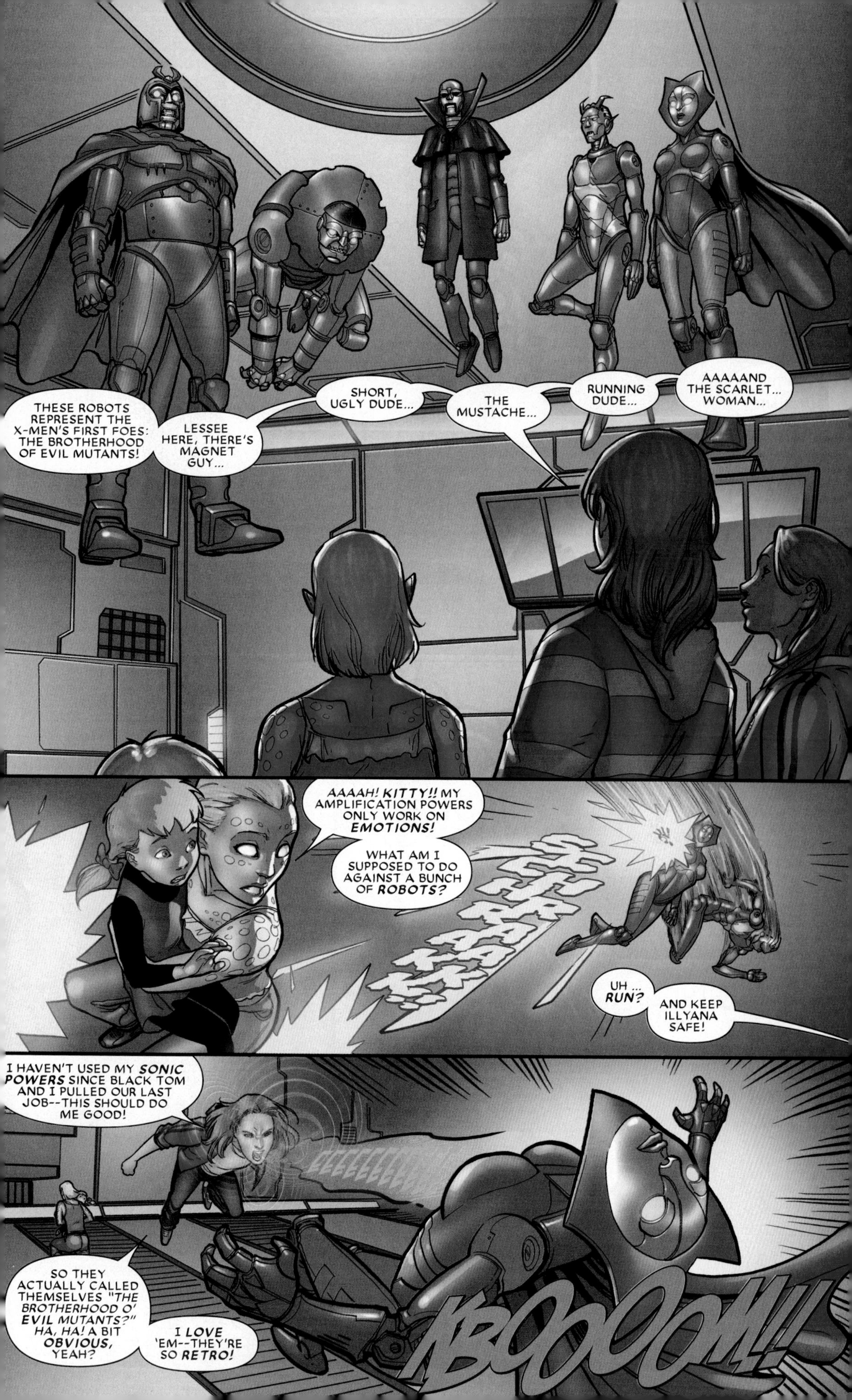

THESE ROBOTS REPRESENT THE X-MEN'S FIRST FOES: THE BROTHERHOOD OF EVIL MUTANTS!
LESSEE HERE, THERE'S MAGNET GUY...
SHORT, UGLY DUDE...
THE MUSTACHE...
RUNNING DUDE...
AAAAAND THE SCARLET... WOMAN...
AAAAH! KITTY!! MY AMPLIFICATION POWERS ONLY WORK ON EMOTIONS!
WHAT AM I SUPPOSED TO DO AGAINST A BUNCH OF ROBOTS?
UH ... RUN?
AND KEEP ILLYANA SAFE!
I HAVEN'T USED MY SONIC POWERS SINCE BLACK TOM AND I PULLED OUR LAST JOB--THIS SHOULD DO ME GOOD!
EEEEEEEE
SO THEY ACTUALLY CALLED THEMSELVES "THE BROTHERHOOD O' EVIL MUTANTS?" HA, HA! A BIT OBVIOUS, YEAH?
I LOVE 'EM--THEY'RE SO RETRO!
KBOOOOM!!

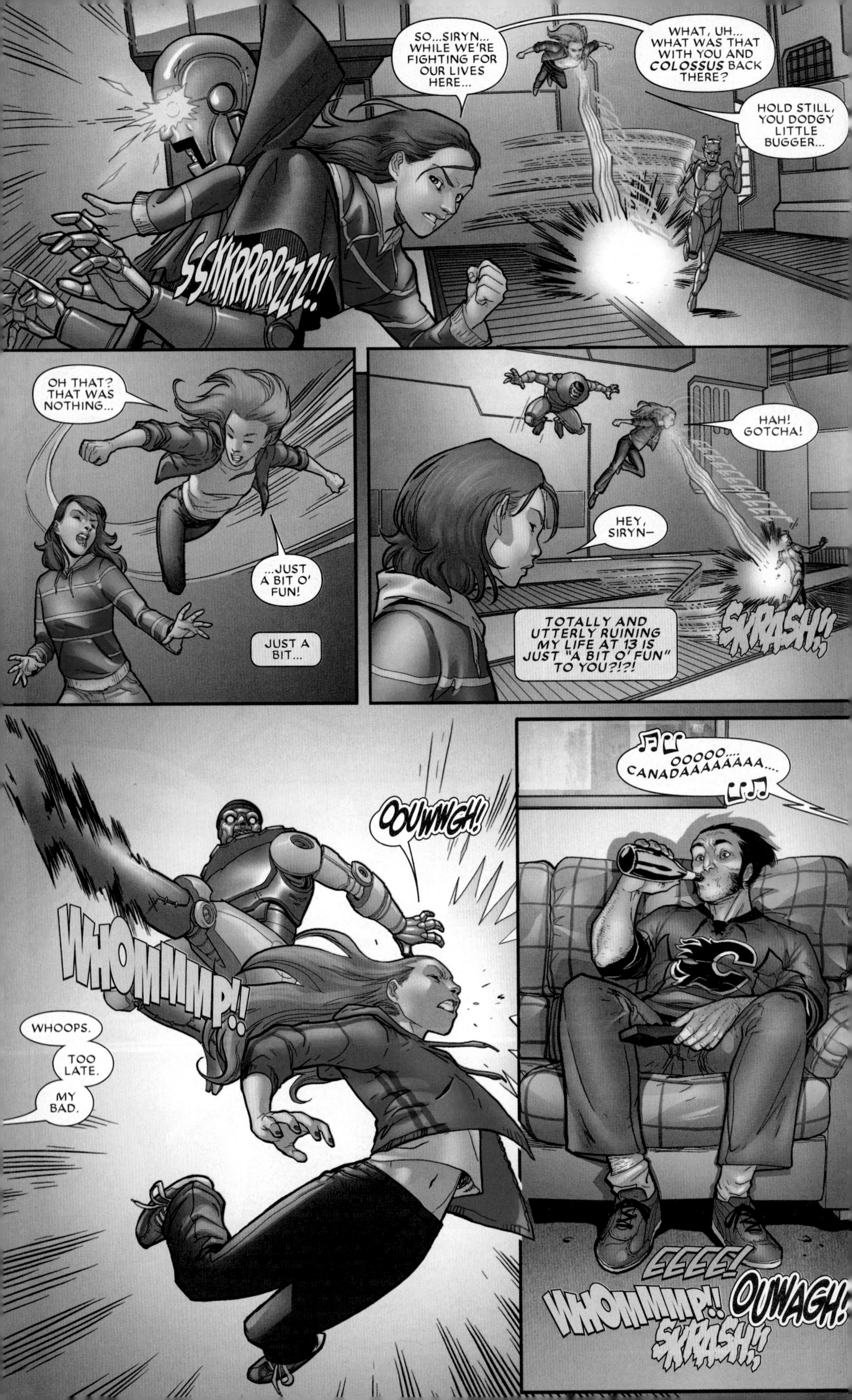
SO...SIRYN... WHILE WE'RE FIGHTING FOR OUR LIVES HERE...
WHAT, UH... WHAT WAS THAT WITH YOU AND COLOSSUS BACK THERE?
HOLD STILL, YOU DODGY LITTLE BUGGER...
SSKKRRRRZZZ!!
OH THAT? THAT WAS NOTHING...
...JUST A BIT O' FUN!
JUST A BIT...
HAH! GOTCHA!
HEY, SIRYN—
TOTALLY AND UTTERLY RUINING MY LIFE AT 13 IS JUST "A BIT O' FUN" TO YOU?!?!
SKRASH!!
OOUWWGH!
WHOMMMP!!
WHOOPS.
TOO LATE.
MY BAD.
OOOOO.... CANADAAAAAAAA....
EEEE!
WHOMMMP!!
OUWAGH!
SKRASH!!

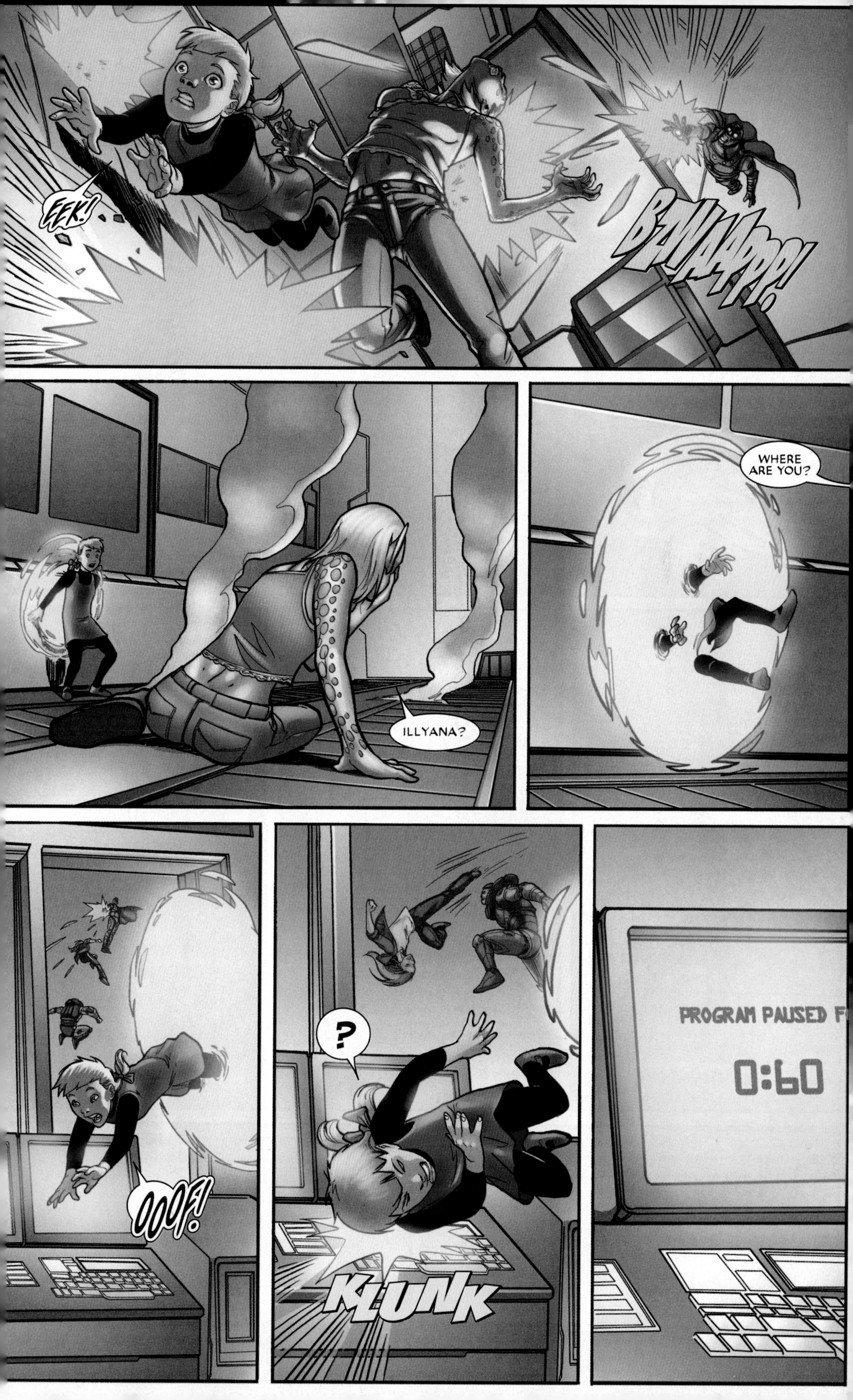
EEK!
BZWAAPP!
ILLYANA?
WHERE ARE YOU?
OOOF!
?
KLUNK
PROGRAM PAUSED F
0:60

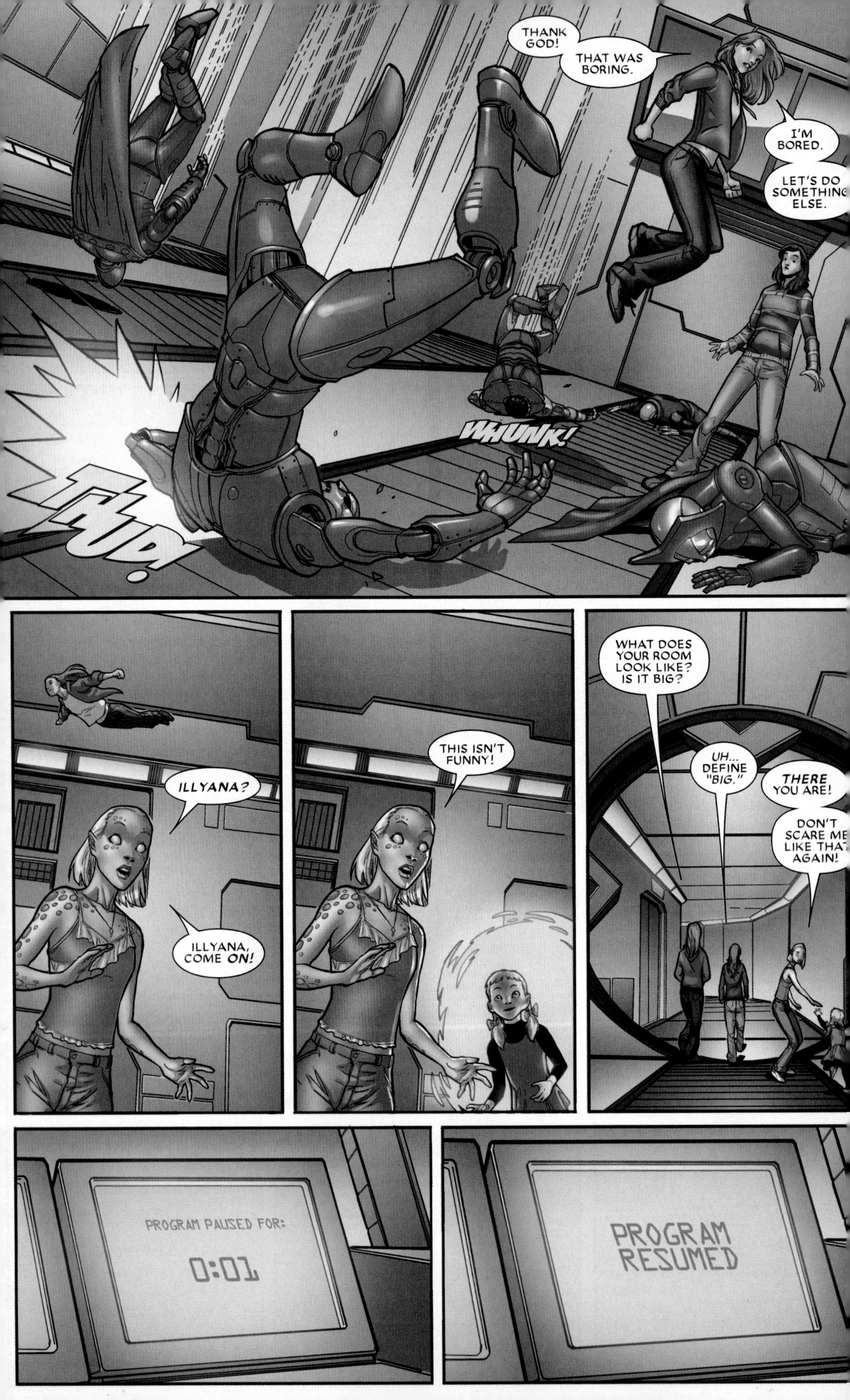
THANK GOD!
THAT WAS BORING.
I'M BORED.
LET'S DO SOMETHING ELSE.
WHUNK!
THUD!
ILLYANA?
ILLYANA, COME ON!
THIS ISN'T FUNNY!
WHAT DOES YOUR ROOM LOOK LIKE? IS IT BIG?
UH... DEFINE "BIG."
THERE YOU ARE!
DON'T SCARE ME LIKE THAT AGAIN!
PROGRAM PAUSED FOR:
0:01
PROGRAM RESUMED

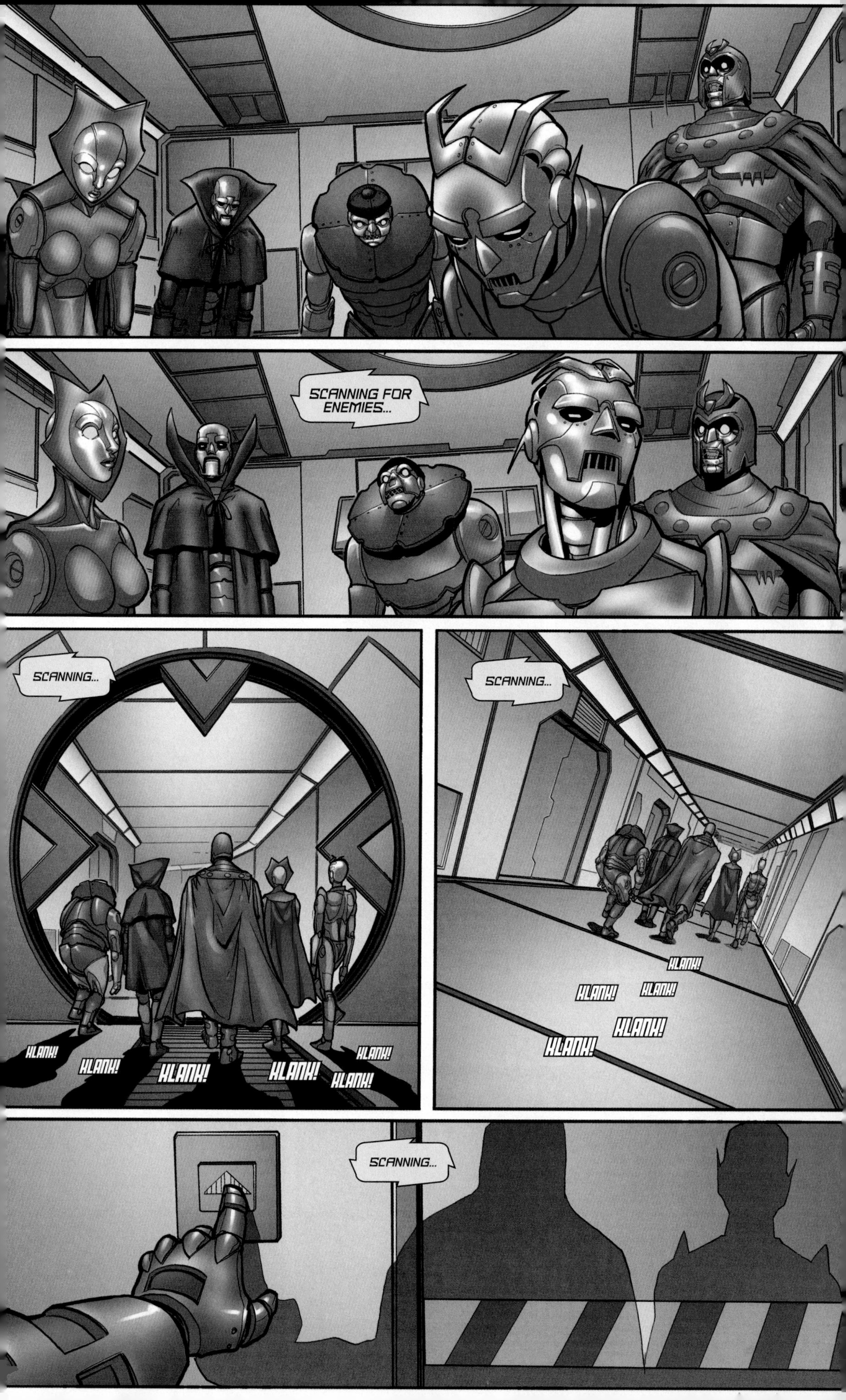
SCANNING FOR ENEMIES...
SCANNING...
KLANK!
KLANK!
KLANK!
KLANK!
KLANK!
KLANK!
SCANNING...
KLANK!
KLANK!
KLANK!
KLANK!
KLANK!
SCANNING...

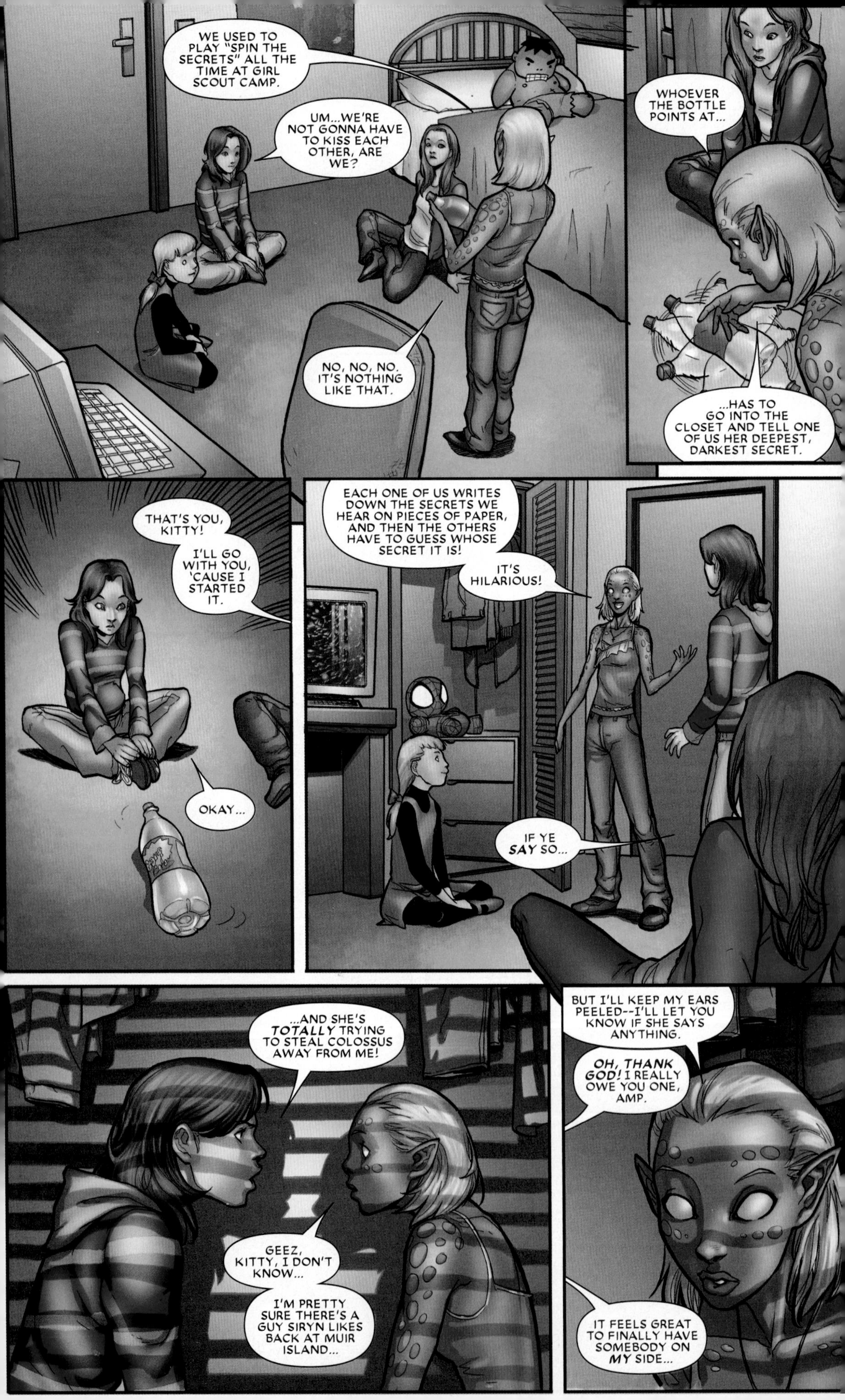
WE USED TO PLAY "SPIN THE SECRETS" ALL THE TIME AT GIRL SCOUT CAMP.
UM...WE'RE NOT GONNA HAVE TO KISS EACH OTHER, ARE WE?
NO, NO, NO. IT'S NOTHING LIKE THAT.
WHOEVER THE BOTTLE POINTS AT...
...HAS TO GO INTO THE CLOSET AND TELL ONE OF US HER DEEPEST, DARKEST SECRET.
THAT'S YOU, KITTY!
I'LL GO WITH YOU, 'CAUSE I STARTED IT.
OKAY...
EACH ONE OF US WRITES DOWN THE SECRETS WE HEAR ON PIECES OF PAPER, AND THEN THE OTHERS HAVE TO GUESS WHOSE SECRET IT IS!
IT'S HILARIOUS!
IF YE *SAY* SO...
...AND SHE'S *TOTALLY* TRYING TO STEAL COLOSSUS AWAY FROM ME!
GEEZ, KITTY, I DON'T KNOW...
I'M PRETTY SURE THERE'S A GUY SIRYN LIKES BACK AT MUIR ISLAND...
BUT I'LL KEEP MY EARS PEELED--I'LL LET YOU KNOW IF SHE SAYS ANYTHING.
OH, THANK GOD! I REALLY OWE YOU ONE, AMP.
IT FEELS GREAT TO FINALLY HAVE SOMEBODY ON *MY* SIDE...

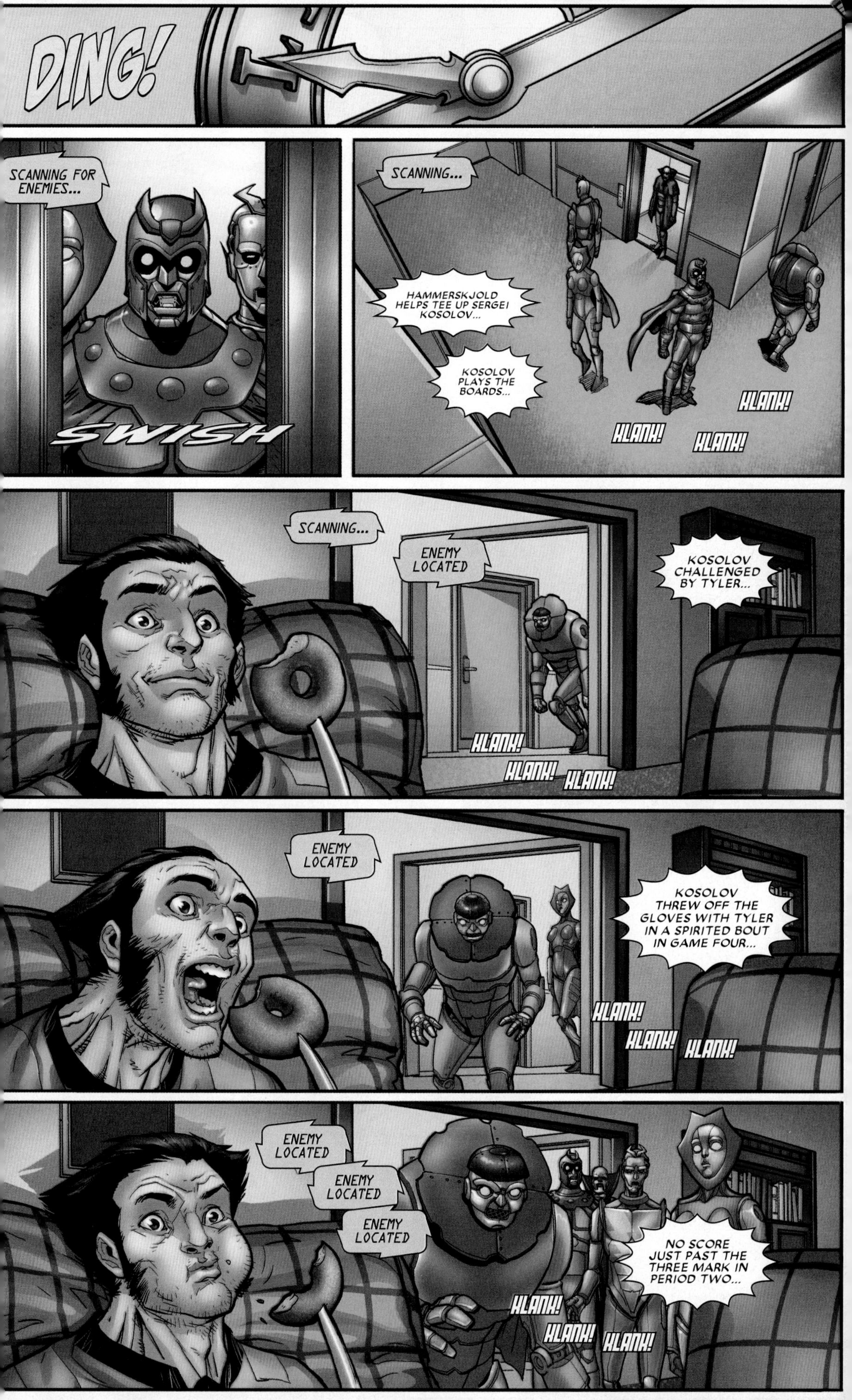
DING!
SCANNING FOR ENEMIES...
SWISH
SCANNING...
HAMMERSKJOLD HELPS TEE UP SERGEI KOSOLOV...
KOSOLOV PLAYS THE BOARDS...
KLANK!
KLANK!
KLANK!
SCANNING...
ENEMY LOCATED
KOSOLOV CHALLENGED BY TYLER...
KLANK!
KLANK!
KLANK!
ENEMY LOCATED
KOSOLOV THREW OFF THE GLOVES WITH TYLER IN A SPIRITED BOUT IN GAME FOUR...
KLANK!
KLANK!
KLANK!
ENEMY LOCATED
ENEMY LOCATED
ENEMY LOCATED
NO SCORE JUST PAST THE THREE MARK IN PERIOD TWO...
KLANK!
KLANK!
KLANK!

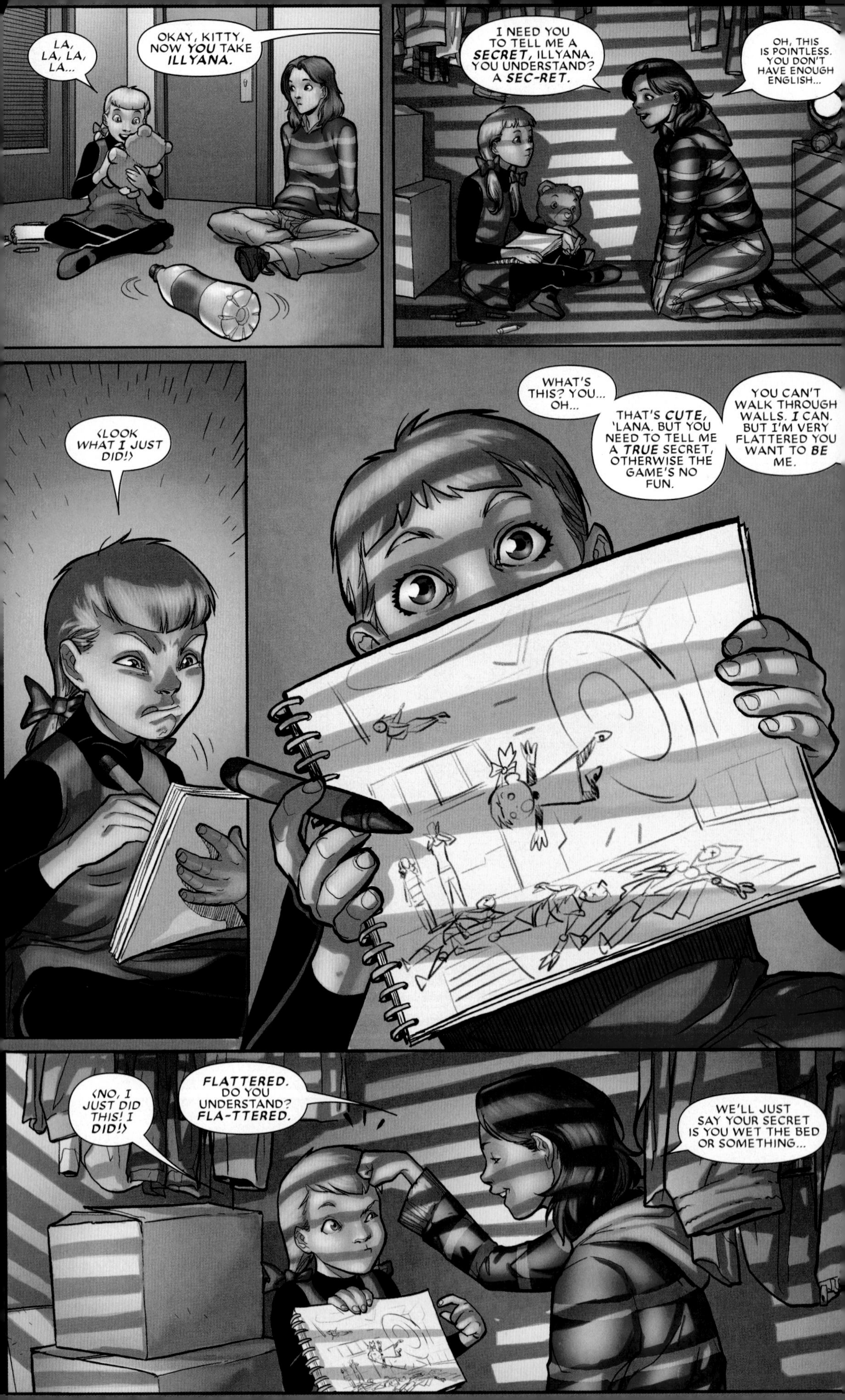
LA, LA, LA, LA...
OKAY, KITTY, NOW YOU TAKE ILLYANA.
I NEED YOU TO TELL ME A SECRET, ILLYANA. YOU UNDERSTAND? A SEC-RET.
OH, THIS IS POINTLESS. YOU DON'T HAVE ENOUGH ENGLISH...
<LOOK WHAT I JUST DID!>
WHAT'S THIS? YOU... OH...
THAT'S CUTE, 'LANA. BUT YOU NEED TO TELL ME A TRUE SECRET, OTHERWISE THE GAME'S NO FUN.
YOU CAN'T WALK THROUGH WALLS. I CAN. BUT I'M VERY FLATTERED YOU WANT TO BE ME.
<NO, I JUST DID THIS! I DID!>
FLATTERED. DO YOU UNDERSTAND? FLA-TTERED.
WE'LL JUST SAY YOUR SECRET IS YOU WET THE BED OR SOMETHING...

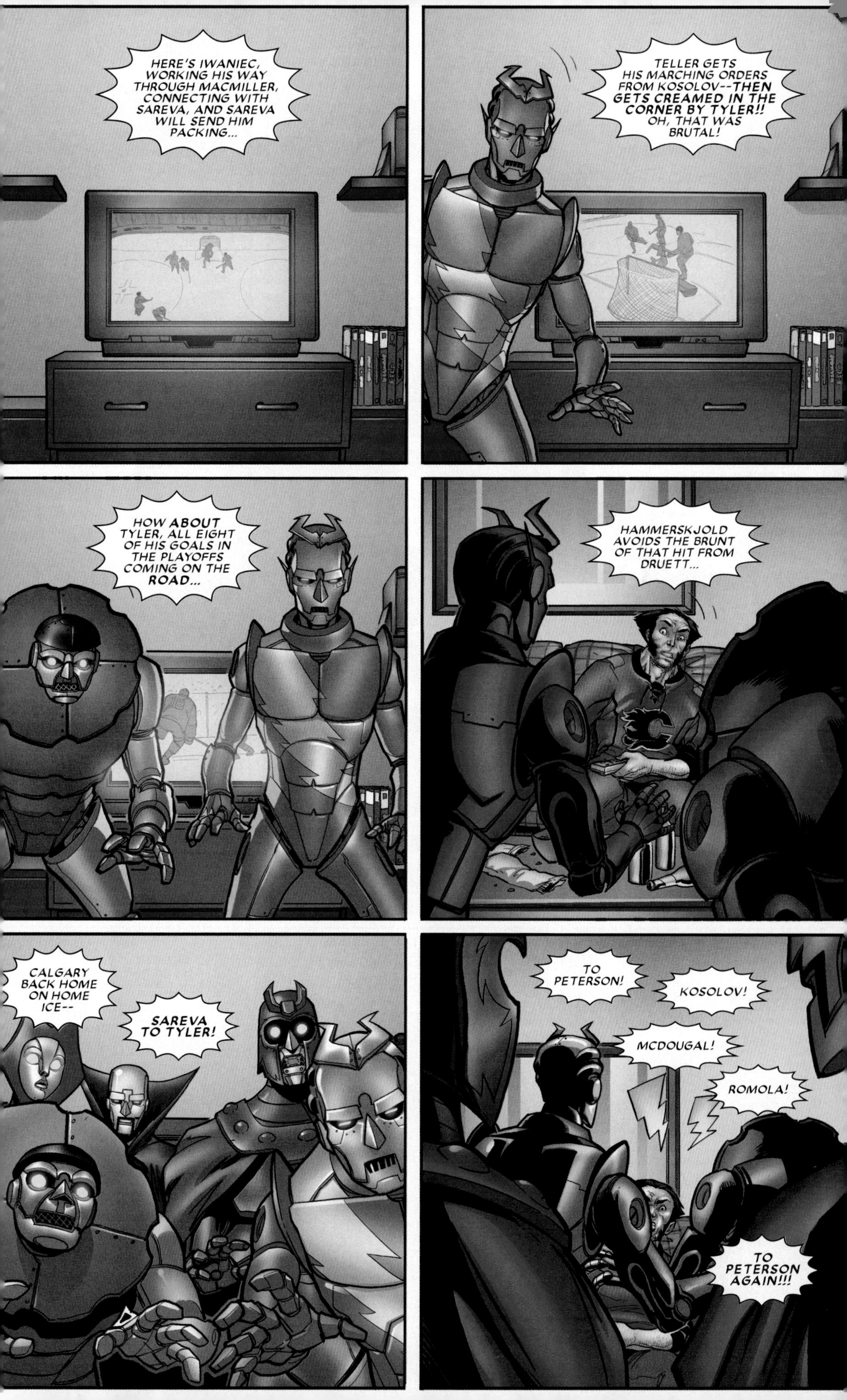
HERE'S IWANIEC, WORKING HIS WAY THROUGH MACMILLER, CONNECTING WITH SAREVA, AND SAREVA WILL SEND HIM PACKING...
TELLER GETS HIS MARCHING ORDERS FROM KOSOLOV--THEN GETS CREAMED IN THE CORNER BY TYLER!! OH, THAT WAS BRUTAL!
HOW ABOUT TYLER, ALL EIGHT OF HIS GOALS IN THE PLAYOFFS COMING ON THE ROAD...
HAMMERSKJOLD AVOIDS THE BRUNT OF THAT HIT FROM DRUETT...
CALGARY BACK HOME ON HOME ICE--
SAREVA TO TYLER!
TO PETERSON!
KOSOLOV!
MCDOUGAL!
ROMOLA!
TO PETERSON AGAIN!!!

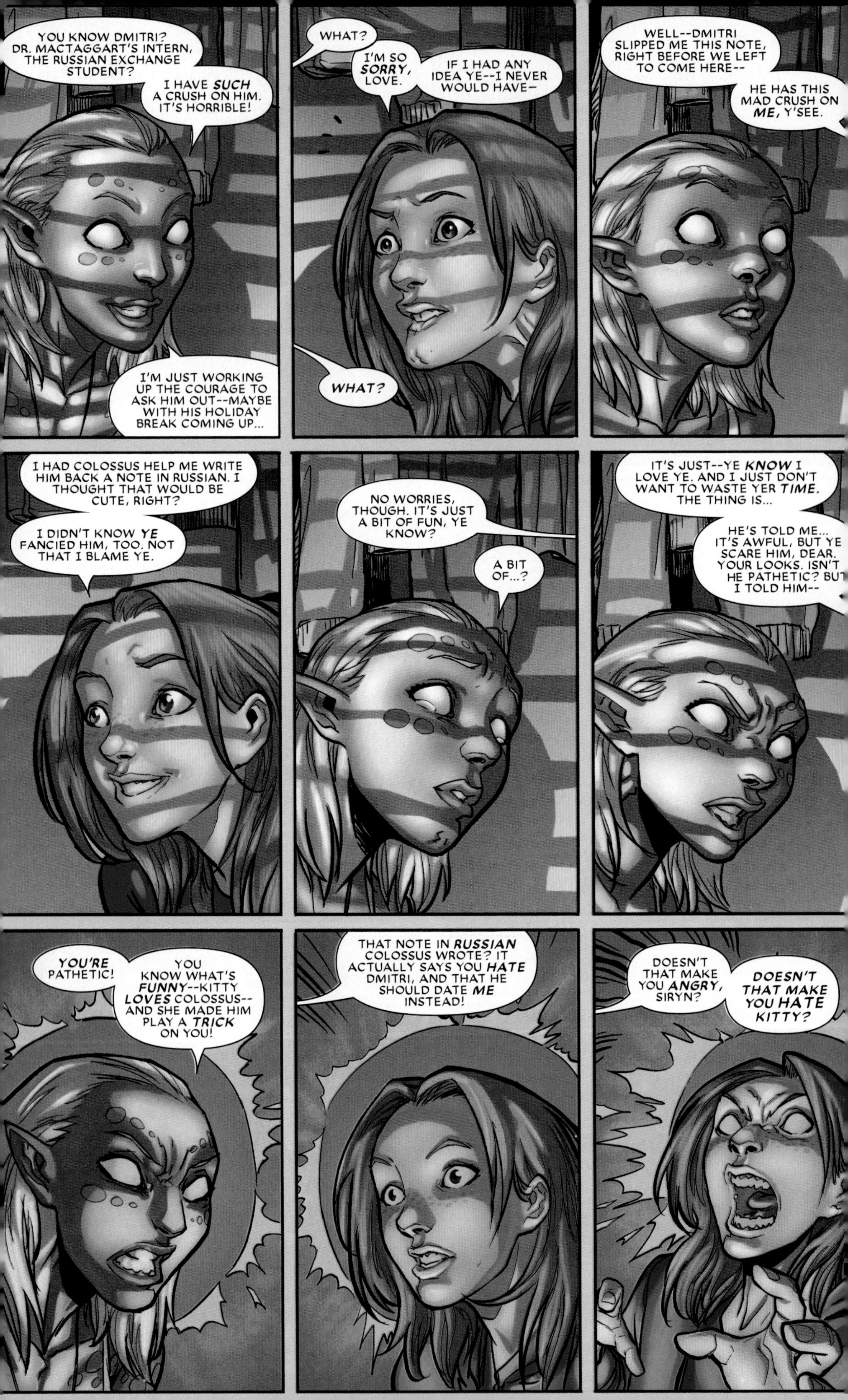
YOU KNOW DMITRI? DR. MACTAGGART'S INTERN, THE RUSSIAN EXCHANGE STUDENT?
I HAVE SUCH A CRUSH ON HIM. IT'S HORRIBLE!
I'M JUST WORKING UP THE COURAGE TO ASK HIM OUT--MAYBE WITH HIS HOLIDAY BREAK COMING UP...
WHAT?
I'M SO SORRY, LOVE.
IF I HAD ANY IDEA YE--I NEVER WOULD HAVE--
WHAT?
WELL--DMITRI SLIPPED ME THIS NOTE, RIGHT BEFORE WE LEFT TO COME HERE--
HE HAS THIS MAD CRUSH ON ME, Y'SEE.
I HAD COLOSSUS HELP ME WRITE HIM BACK A NOTE IN RUSSIAN. I THOUGHT THAT WOULD BE CUTE, RIGHT?
I DIDN'T KNOW YE FANCIED HIM, TOO. NOT THAT I BLAME YE.
NO WORRIES, THOUGH. IT'S JUST A BIT OF FUN, YE KNOW?
A BIT OF...?
IT'S JUST--YE KNOW I LOVE YE. AND I JUST DON'T WANT TO WASTE YER TIME. THE THING IS...
HE'S TOLD ME... IT'S AWFUL, BUT YE SCARE HIM, DEAR. YOUR LOOKS. ISN'T HE PATHETIC? BUT I TOLD HIM--
YOU'RE PATHETIC!
YOU KNOW WHAT'S FUNNY--KITTY LOVES COLOSSUS--AND SHE MADE HIM PLAY A TRICK ON YOU!
THAT NOTE IN RUSSIAN COLOSSUS WROTE? IT ACTUALLY SAYS YOU HATE DMITRI, AND THAT HE SHOULD DATE ME INSTEAD!
DOESN'T THAT MAKE YOU ANGRY, SIRYN?
DOESN'T THAT MAKE YOU HATE KITTY?

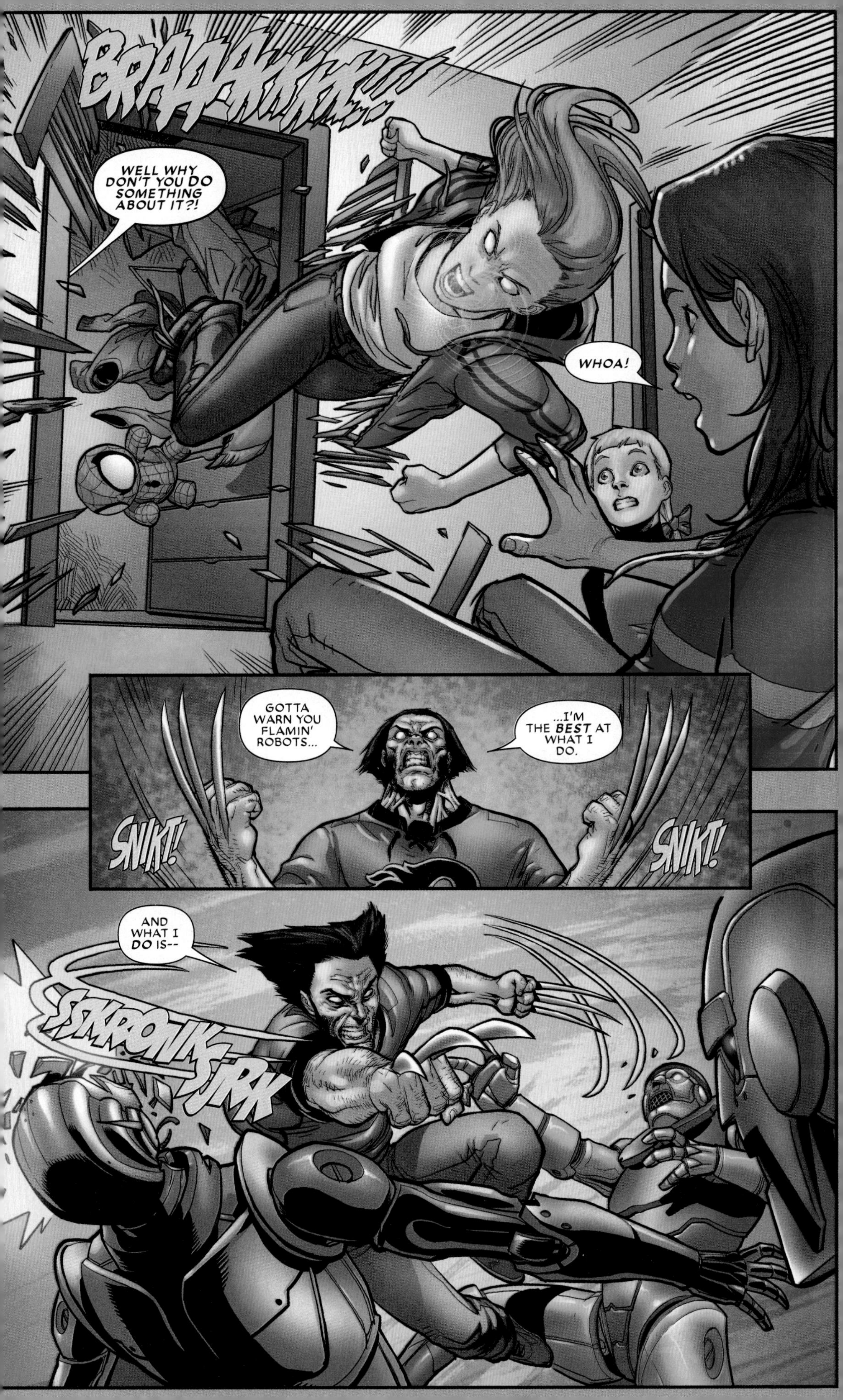
BRAAAKKKK!!
WELL WHY DON'T YOU DO SOMETHING ABOUT IT?!
WHOA!
GOTTA WARN YOU FLAMIN' ROBOTS...
...I'M THE BEST AT WHAT I DO.
SNIKT!
SNIKT!
AND WHAT I DO IS--
SSKRONK
SHRK

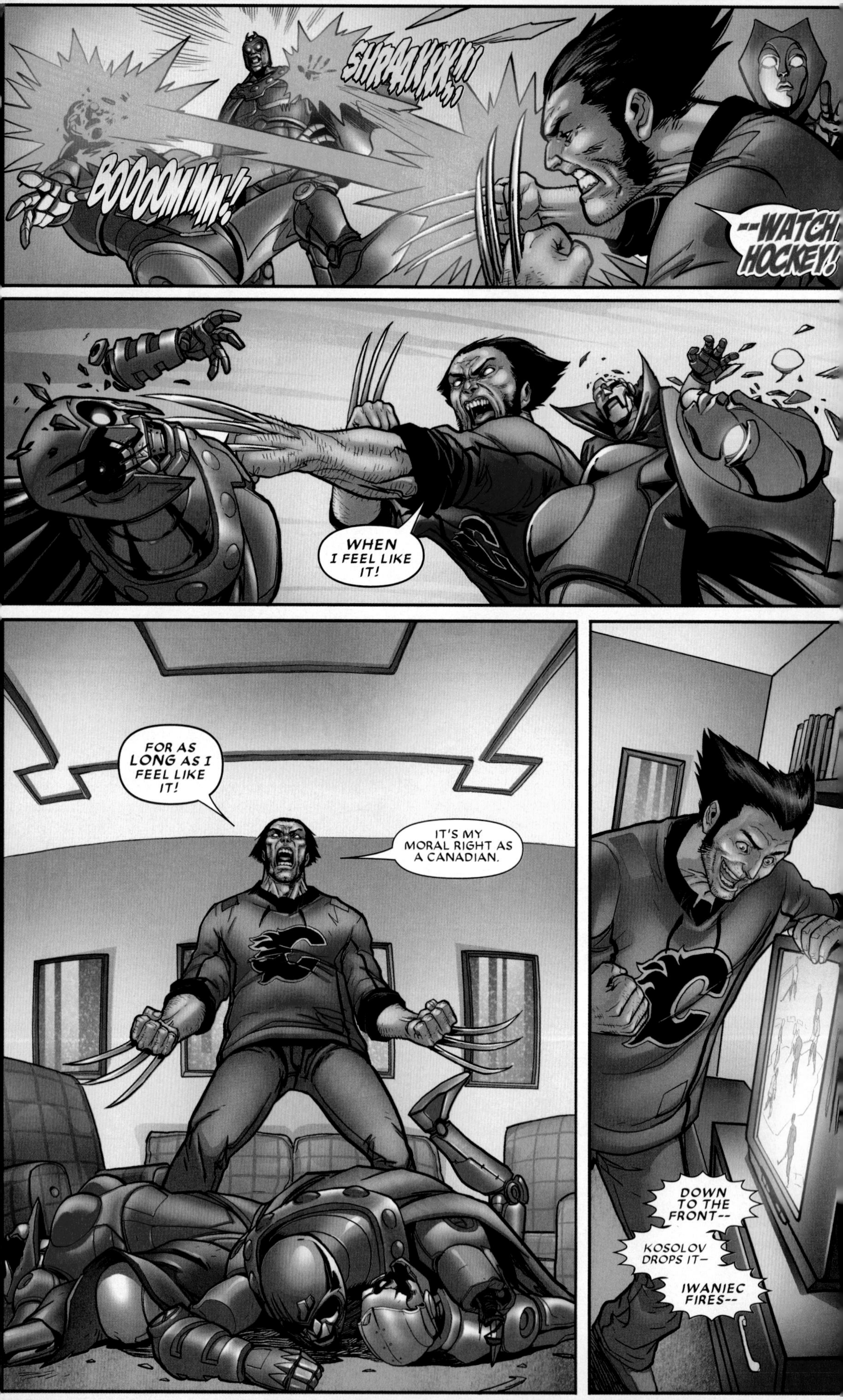
SHRAAKKK!!
BOOOOMMM!!
--WATCH HOCKEY!
WHEN I FEEL LIKE IT!
FOR AS LONG AS I FEEL LIKE IT!
IT'S MY MORAL RIGHT AS A CANADIAN.
DOWN TO THE FRONT--
KOSOLOV DROPS IT--
IWANIEC FIRES--

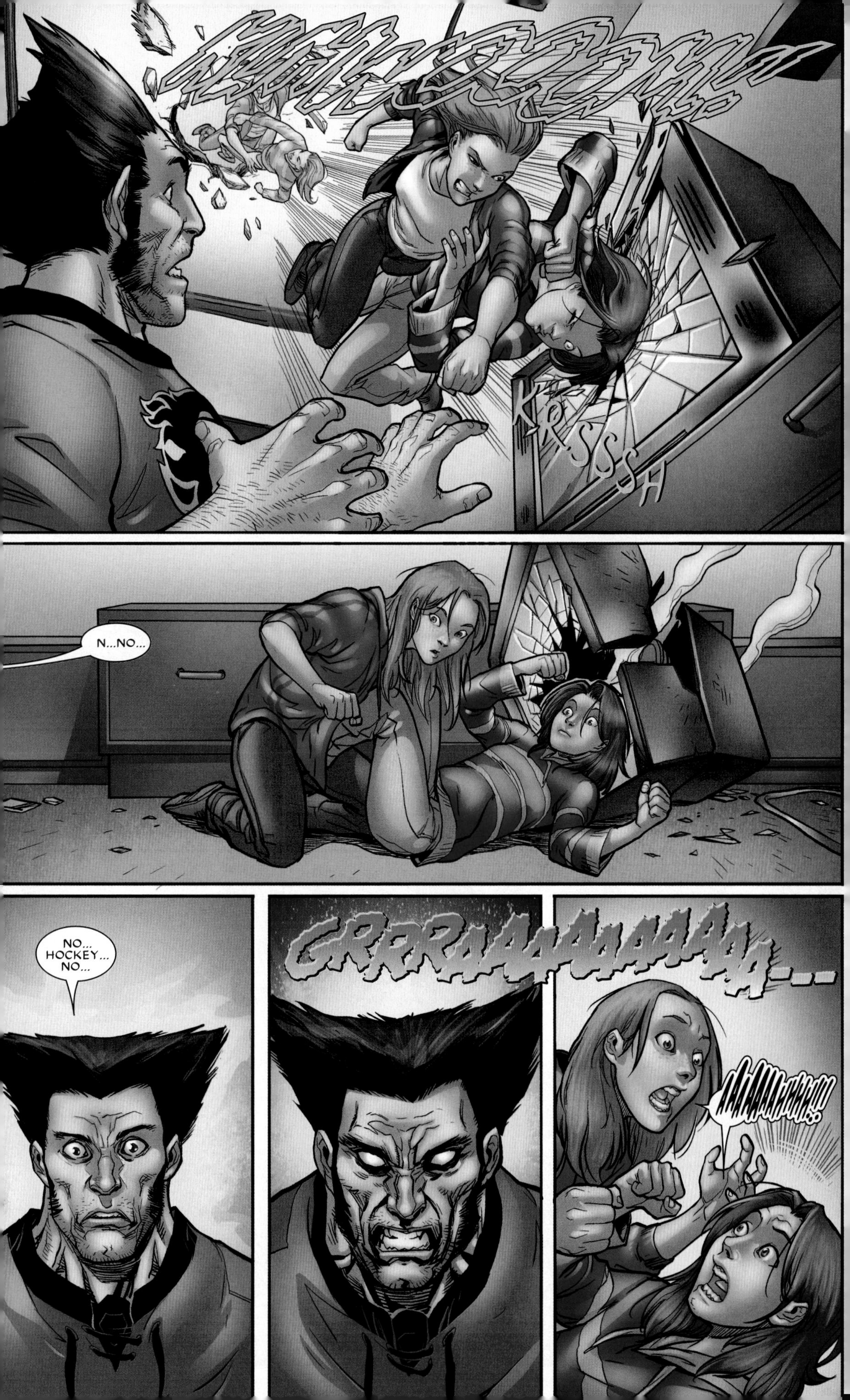
KRSSSH
N...NO...
NO... HOCKEY... NO...
GRRRAAAAAAAAA--...
AAAAAAAHHH!!!

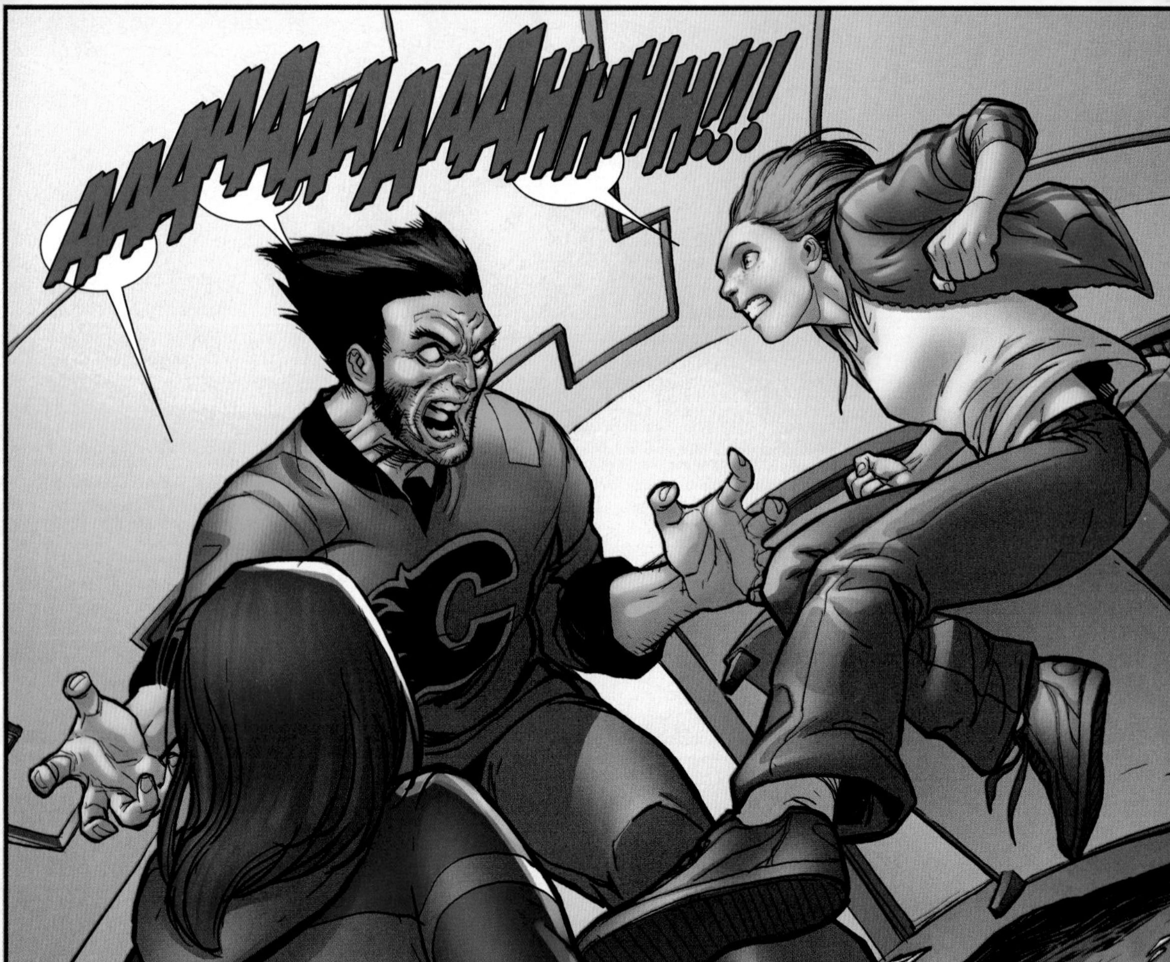
AAAAAAAAAAAHHHH!!!

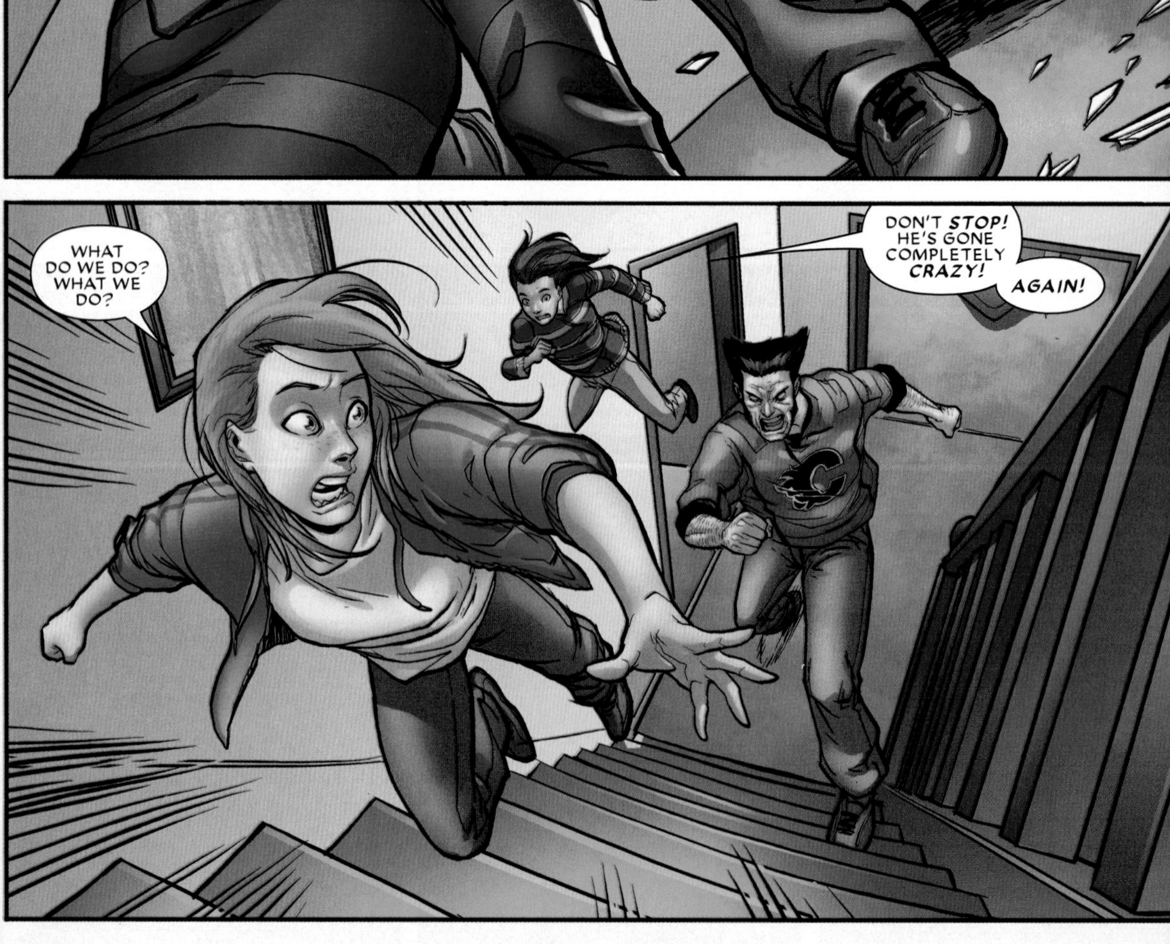
WHAT DO WE DO? WHAT WE DO?
DON'T STOP! HE'S GONE COMPLETELY CRAZY!
AGAIN!

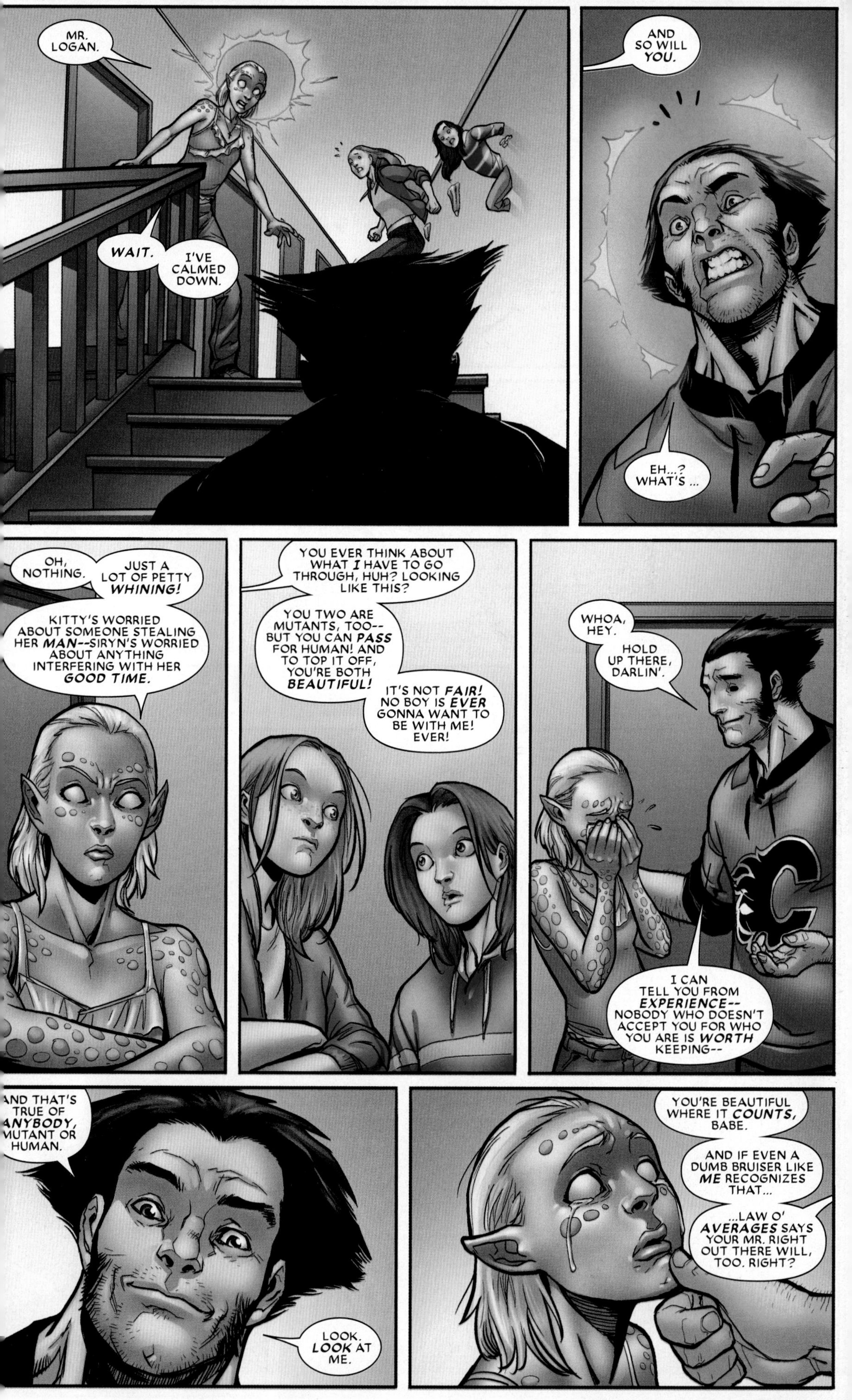
MR. LOGAN.
WAIT.
I'VE CALMED DOWN.
AND SO WILL YOU.
EH...? WHAT'S ...
OH, NOTHING.
JUST A LOT OF PETTY WHINING!
KITTY'S WORRIED ABOUT SOMEONE STEALING HER MAN--SIRYN'S WORRIED ABOUT ANYTHING INTERFERING WITH HER GOOD TIME.
YOU EVER THINK ABOUT WHAT I HAVE TO GO THROUGH, HUH? LOOKING LIKE THIS?
YOU TWO ARE MUTANTS, TOO-- BUT YOU CAN PASS FOR HUMAN! AND TO TOP IT OFF, YOU'RE BOTH BEAUTIFUL!
IT'S NOT FAIR! NO BOY IS EVER GONNA WANT TO BE WITH ME! EVER!
WHOA, HEY.
HOLD UP THERE, DARLIN'.
I CAN TELL YOU FROM EXPERIENCE-- NOBODY WHO DOESN'T ACCEPT YOU FOR WHO YOU ARE IS WORTH KEEPING--
AND THAT'S TRUE OF ANYBODY, MUTANT OR HUMAN.
LOOK. LOOK AT ME.
YOU'RE BEAUTIFUL WHERE IT COUNTS, BABE.
AND IF EVEN A DUMB BRUISER LIKE ME RECOGNIZES THAT...
...LAW O' AVERAGES SAYS YOUR MR. RIGHT OUT THERE WILL, TOO. RIGHT?

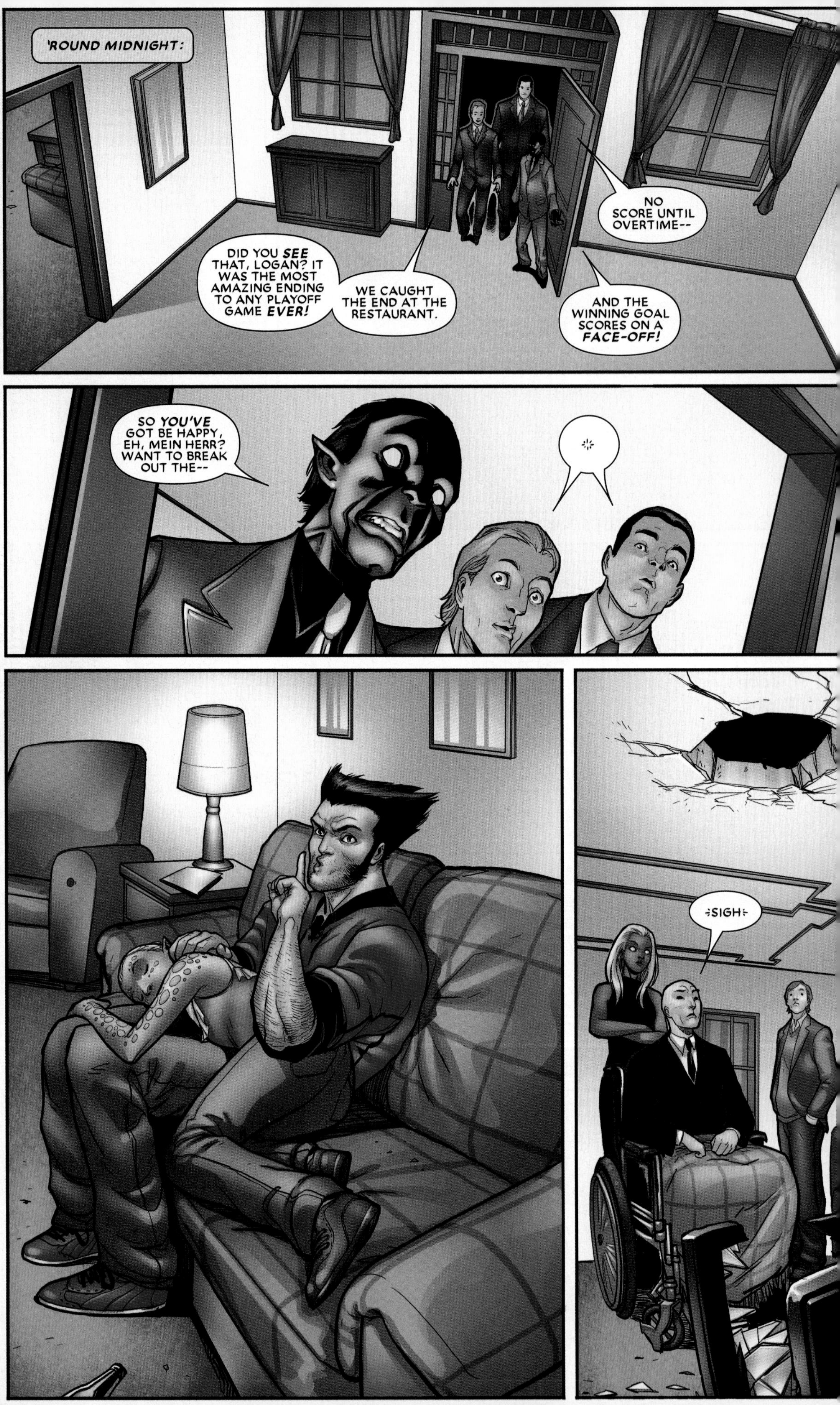

'ROUND MIDNIGHT:
DID YOU SEE THAT, LOGAN? IT WAS THE MOST AMAZING ENDING TO ANY PLAYOFF GAME EVER!
WE CAUGHT THE END AT THE RESTAURANT.
NO SCORE UNTIL OVERTIME--
AND THE WINNING GOAL SCORES ON A FACE-OFF!
SO YOU'VE GOT BE HAPPY, EH, MEIN HERR? WANT TO BREAK OUT THE--
SIGH

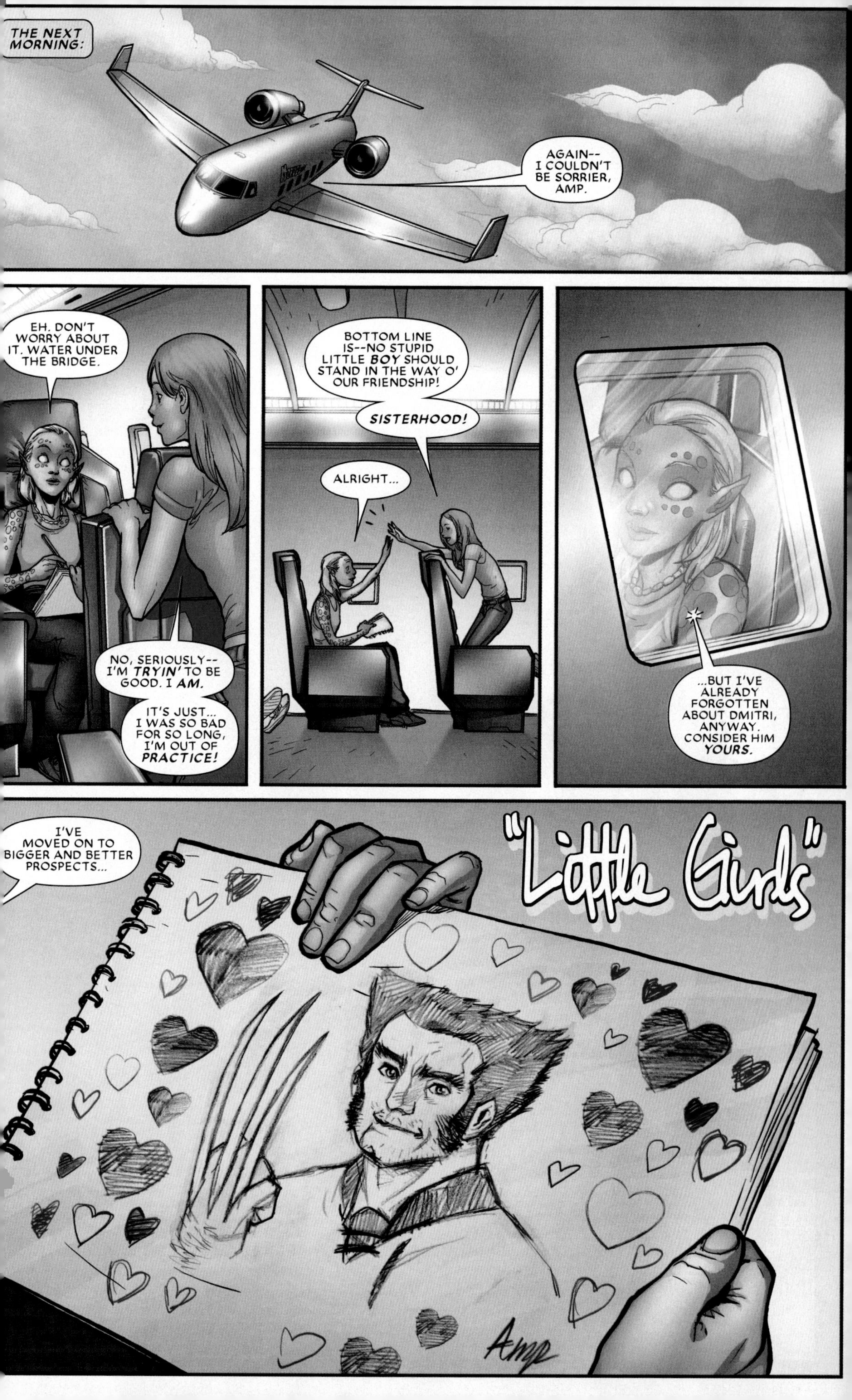
THE NEXT MORNING:
AGAIN-- I COULDN'T BE SORRIER, AMP.
EH. DON'T WORRY ABOUT IT. WATER UNDER THE BRIDGE.
NO, SERIOUSLY-- I'M TRYIN' TO BE GOOD. I AM.
IT'S JUST... I WAS SO BAD FOR SO LONG, I'M OUT OF PRACTICE!
BOTTOM LINE IS--NO STUPID LITTLE BOY SHOULD STAND IN THE WAY O' OUR FRIENDSHIP!
SISTERHOOD!
ALRIGHT...
...BUT I'VE ALREADY FORGOTTEN ABOUT DMITRI, ANYWAY. CONSIDER HIM YOURS.
I'VE MOVED ON TO BIGGER AND BETTER PROSPECTS...
"Little Girls"
Amp

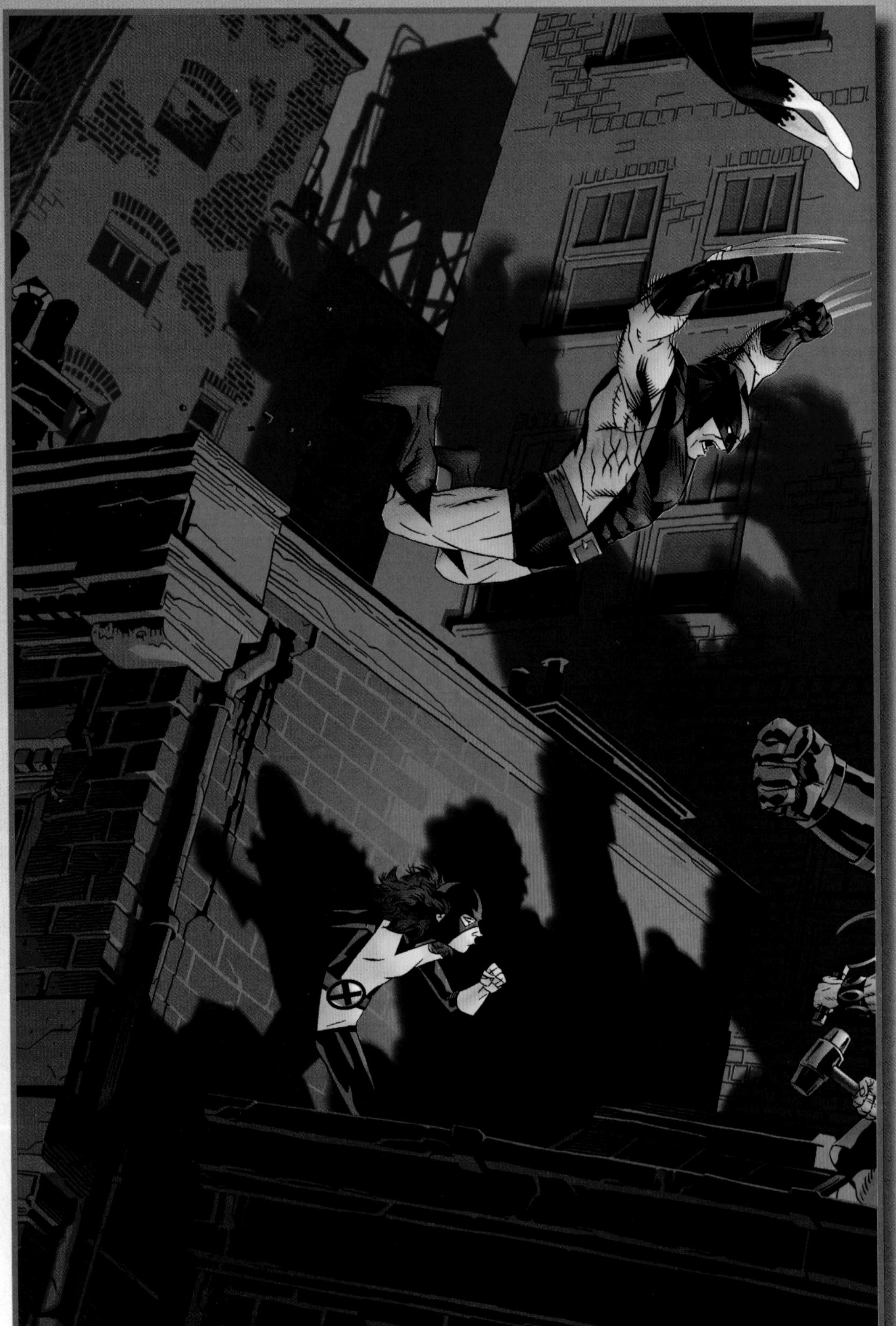

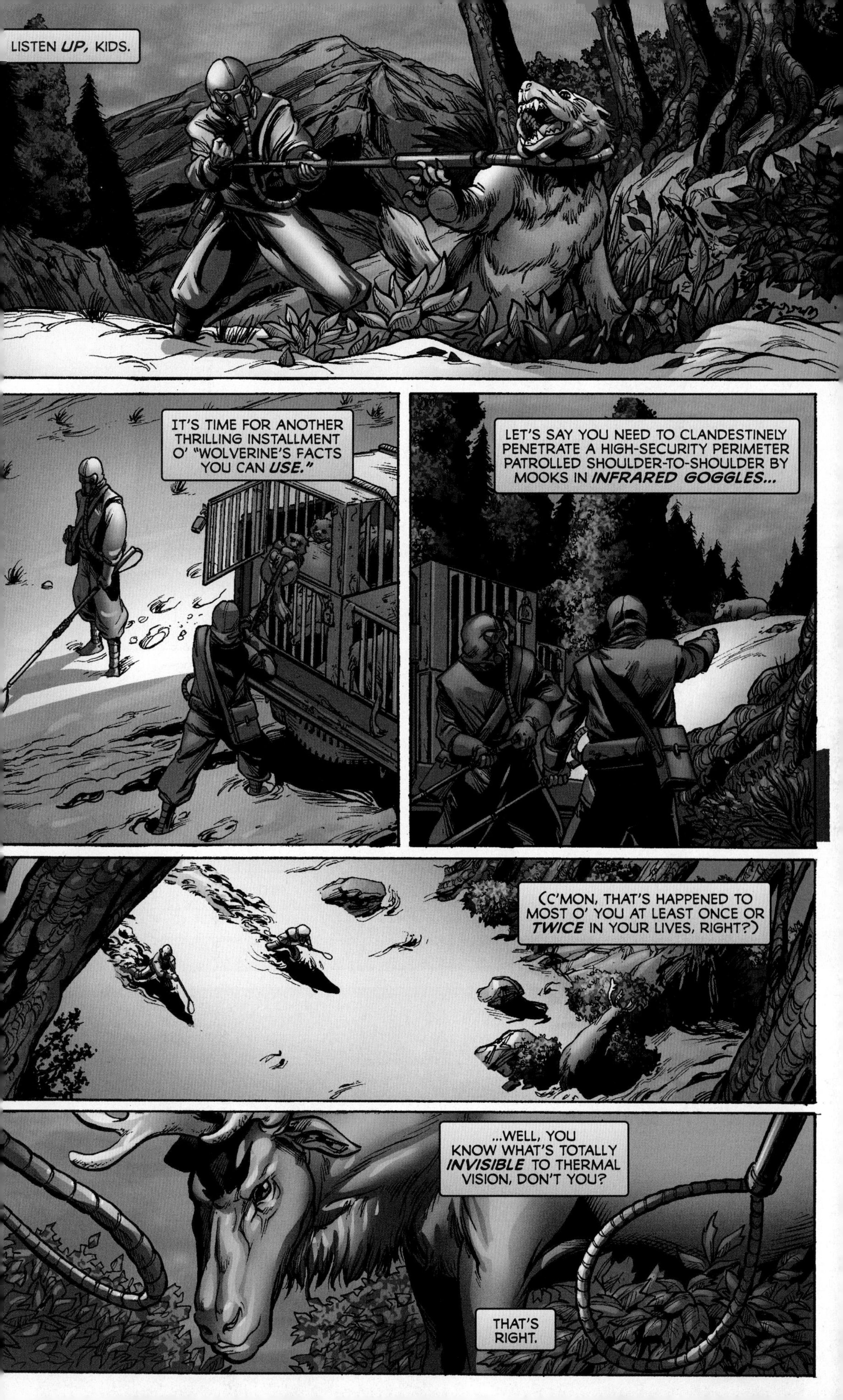
LISTEN *UP,* KIDS.
IT'S TIME FOR ANOTHER THRILLING INSTALLMENT O' "WOLVERINE'S FACTS YOU CAN *USE.*"
LET'S SAY YOU NEED TO CLANDESTINELY PENETRATE A HIGH-SECURITY PERIMETER PATROLLED SHOULDER-TO-SHOULDER BY MOOKS IN *INFRARED GOGGLES...*
(C'MON, THAT'S HAPPENED TO MOST O' YOU AT LEAST ONCE OR *TWICE* IN YOUR LIVES, RIGHT?)
...WELL, YOU KNOW WHAT'S TOTALLY *INVISIBLE* TO THERMAL VISION, DON'T YOU?
THAT'S RIGHT.

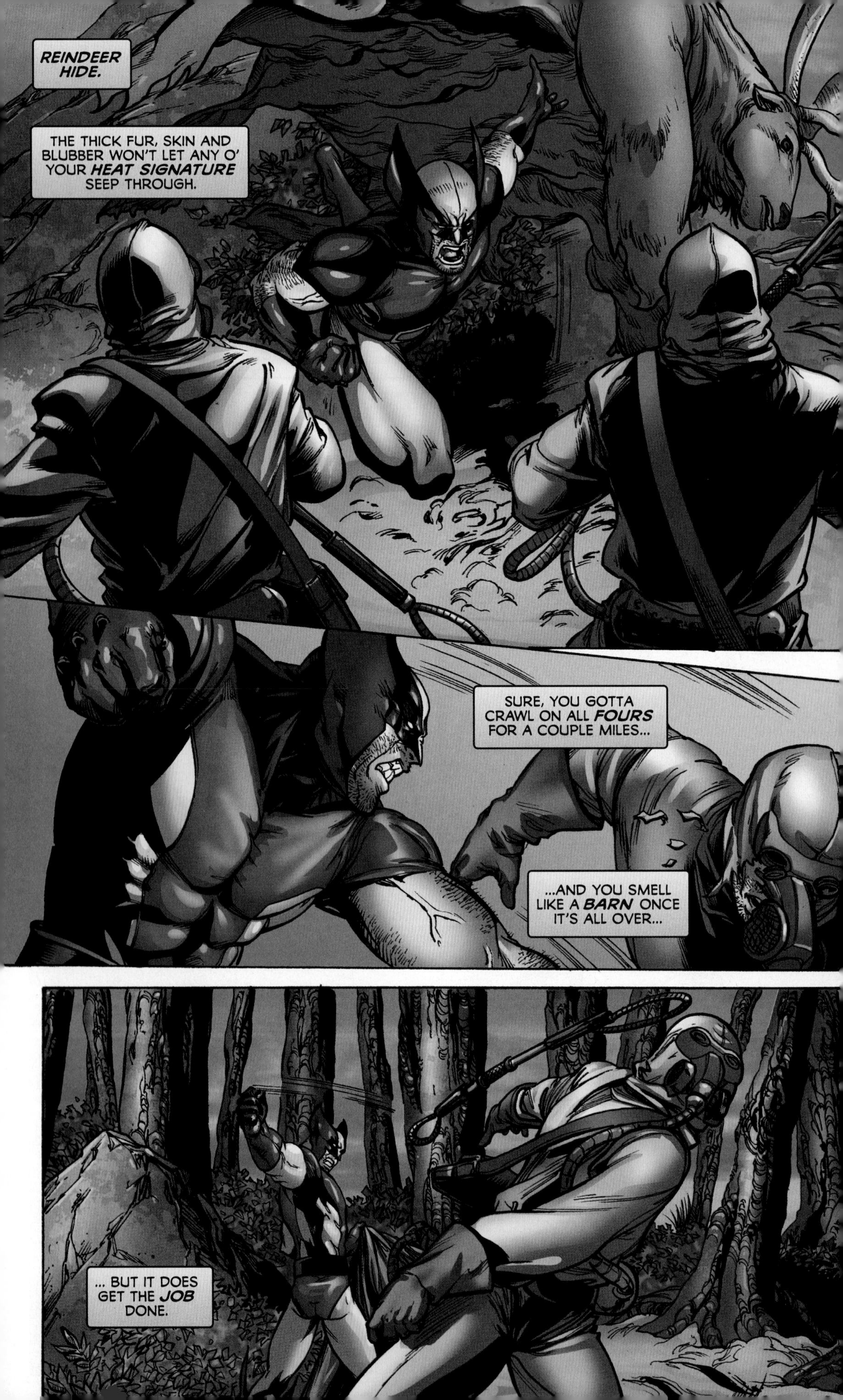
REINDEER HIDE.
THE THICK FUR, SKIN AND BLUBBER WON'T LET ANY O' YOUR HEAT SIGNATURE SEEP THROUGH.
SURE, YOU GOTTA CRAWL ON ALL FOURS FOR A COUPLE MILES...
...AND YOU SMELL LIKE A BARN ONCE IT'S ALL OVER...
... BUT IT DOES GET THE JOB DONE.

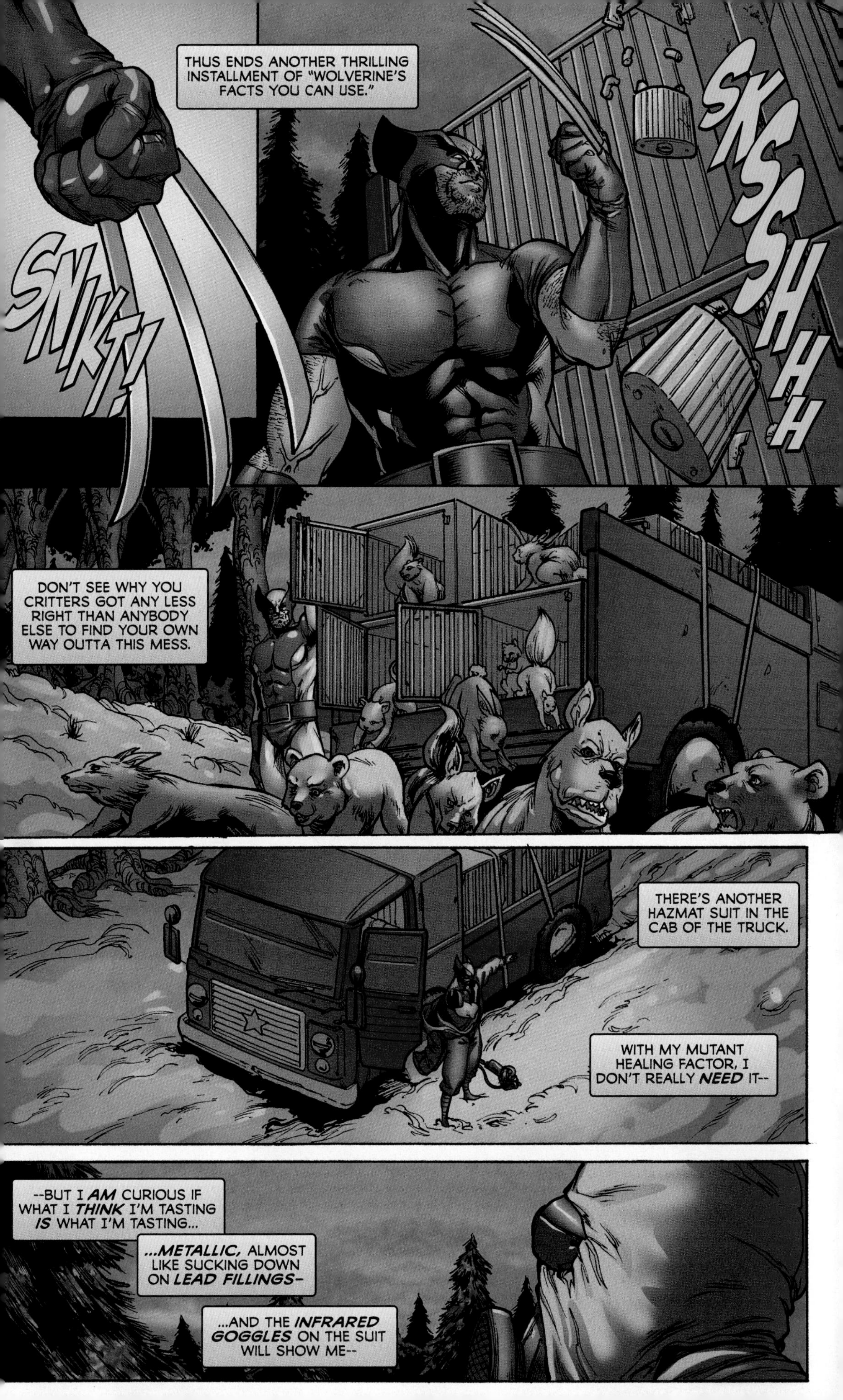
THUS ENDS ANOTHER THRILLING INSTALLMENT OF "WOLVERINE'S FACTS YOU CAN USE."
SNIKT!
SKSSHHHH
DON'T SEE WHY YOU CRITTERS GOT ANY LESS RIGHT THAN ANYBODY ELSE TO FIND YOUR OWN WAY OUTTA THIS MESS.
THERE'S ANOTHER HAZMAT SUIT IN THE CAB OF THE TRUCK.
WITH MY MUTANT HEALING FACTOR, I DON'T REALLY NEED IT--
--BUT I AM CURIOUS IF WHAT I THINK I'M TASTING IS WHAT I'M TASTING...
...METALLIC, ALMOST LIKE SUCKING DOWN ON LEAD FILLINGS--
...AND THE INFRARED GOGGLES ON THE SUIT WILL SHOW ME--

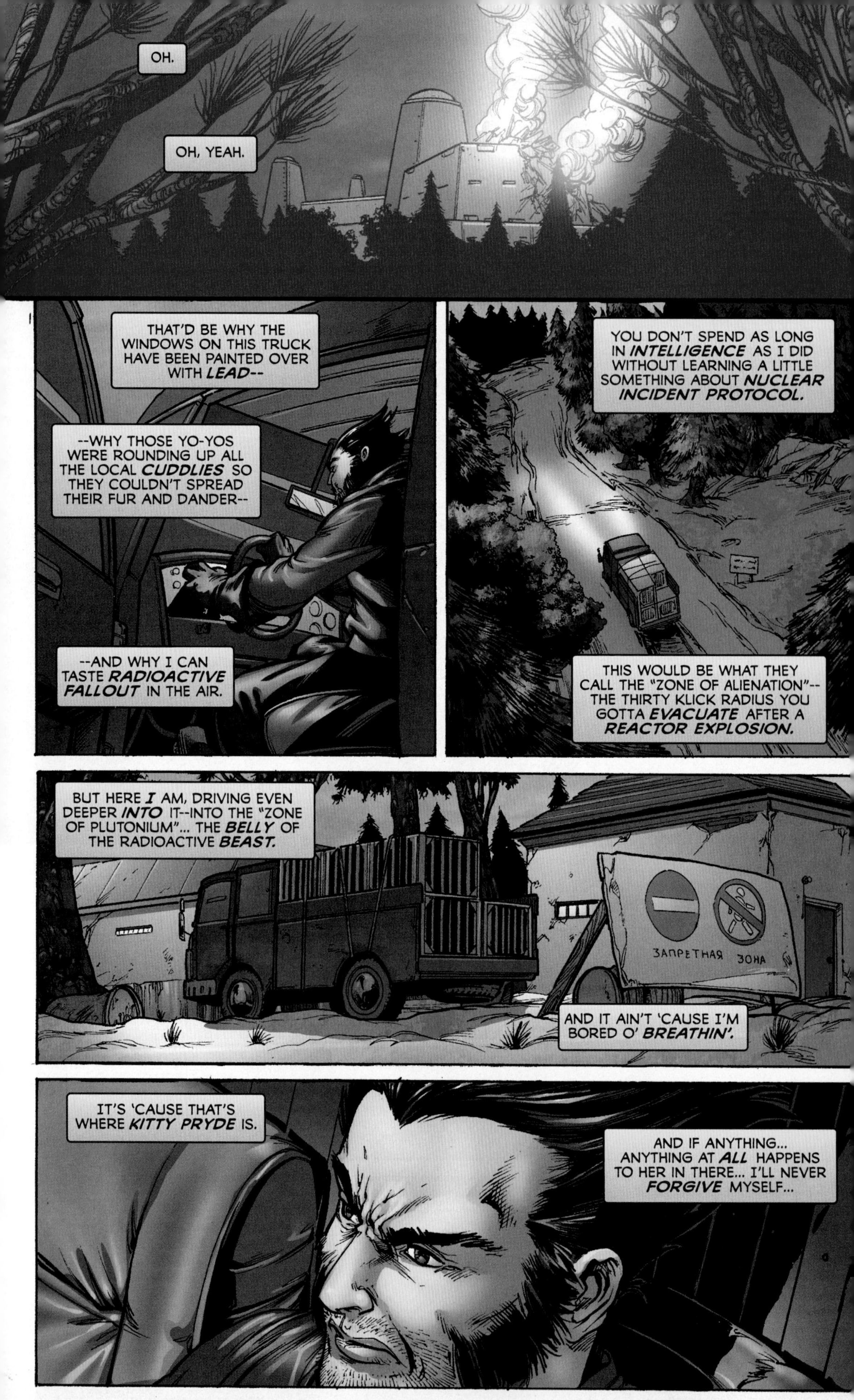
OH.
OH, YEAH.
THAT'D BE WHY THE WINDOWS ON THIS TRUCK HAVE BEEN PAINTED OVER WITH *LEAD--*
--WHY THOSE YO-YOS WERE ROUNDING UP ALL THE LOCAL *CUDDLIES* SO THEY COULDN'T SPREAD THEIR FUR AND DANDER--
--AND WHY I CAN TASTE *RADIOACTIVE FALLOUT* IN THE AIR.
YOU DON'T SPEND AS LONG IN *INTELLIGENCE* AS I DID WITHOUT LEARNING A LITTLE SOMETHING ABOUT *NUCLEAR INCIDENT PROTOCOL.*
THIS WOULD BE WHAT THEY CALL THE "ZONE OF ALIENATION"-- THE THIRTY KLICK RADIUS YOU GOTTA *EVACUATE* AFTER A *REACTOR EXPLOSION.*
BUT HERE *I* AM, DRIVING EVEN DEEPER *INTO* IT--INTO THE "ZONE OF PLUTONIUM"... THE *BELLY* OF THE RADIOACTIVE *BEAST.*
ЗАПРЕТНАЯ ЗОНА
AND IT AIN'T 'CAUSE I'M BORED O' *BREATHIN'.*
IT'S 'CAUSE THAT'S WHERE *KITTY PRYDE* IS.
AND IF ANYTHING... ANYTHING AT *ALL* HAPPENS TO HER IN THERE... I'LL NEVER *FORGIVE* MYSELF...

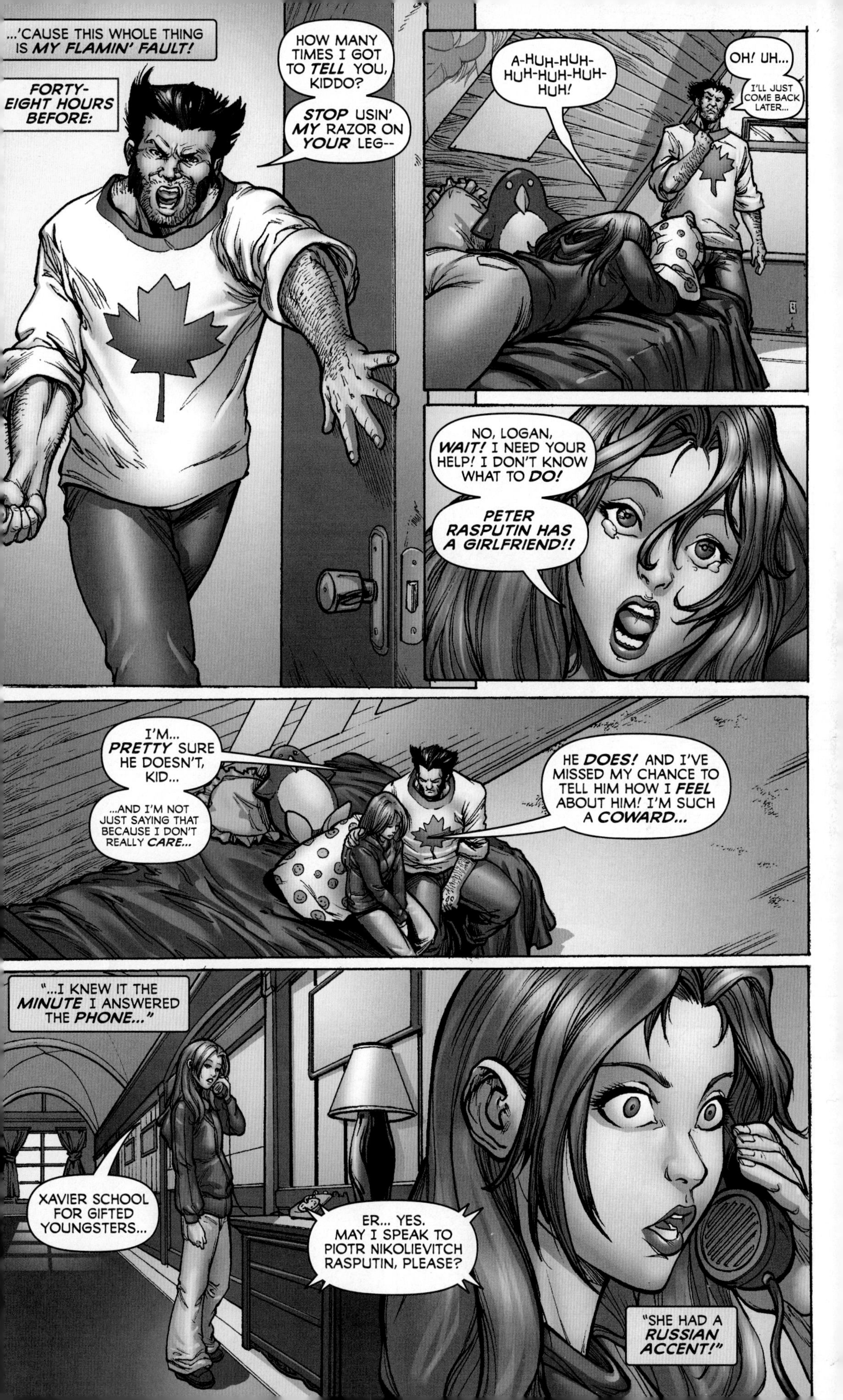
...'CAUSE THIS WHOLE THING IS MY FLAMIN' FAULT!
FORTY-EIGHT HOURS BEFORE:
HOW MANY TIMES I GOT TO TELL YOU, KIDDO?
STOP USIN' MY RAZOR ON YOUR LEG--
A-HUH-HUH-HUH-HUH-HUH-HUH!
OH! UH...
I'LL JUST COME BACK LATER...
NO, LOGAN, WAIT! I NEED YOUR HELP! I DON'T KNOW WHAT TO DO!
PETER RASPUTIN HAS A GIRLFRIEND!!
I'M... PRETTY SURE HE DOESN'T, KID...
...AND I'M NOT JUST SAYING THAT BECAUSE I DON'T REALLY CARE...
HE DOES! AND I'VE MISSED MY CHANCE TO TELL HIM HOW I FEEL ABOUT HIM! I'M SUCH A COWARD...
"...I KNEW IT THE MINUTE I ANSWERED THE PHONE..."
XAVIER SCHOOL FOR GIFTED YOUNGSTERS...
ER... YES. MAY I SPEAK TO PIOTR NIKOLIEVITCH RASPUTIN, PLEASE?
"SHE HAD A RUSSIAN ACCENT!"

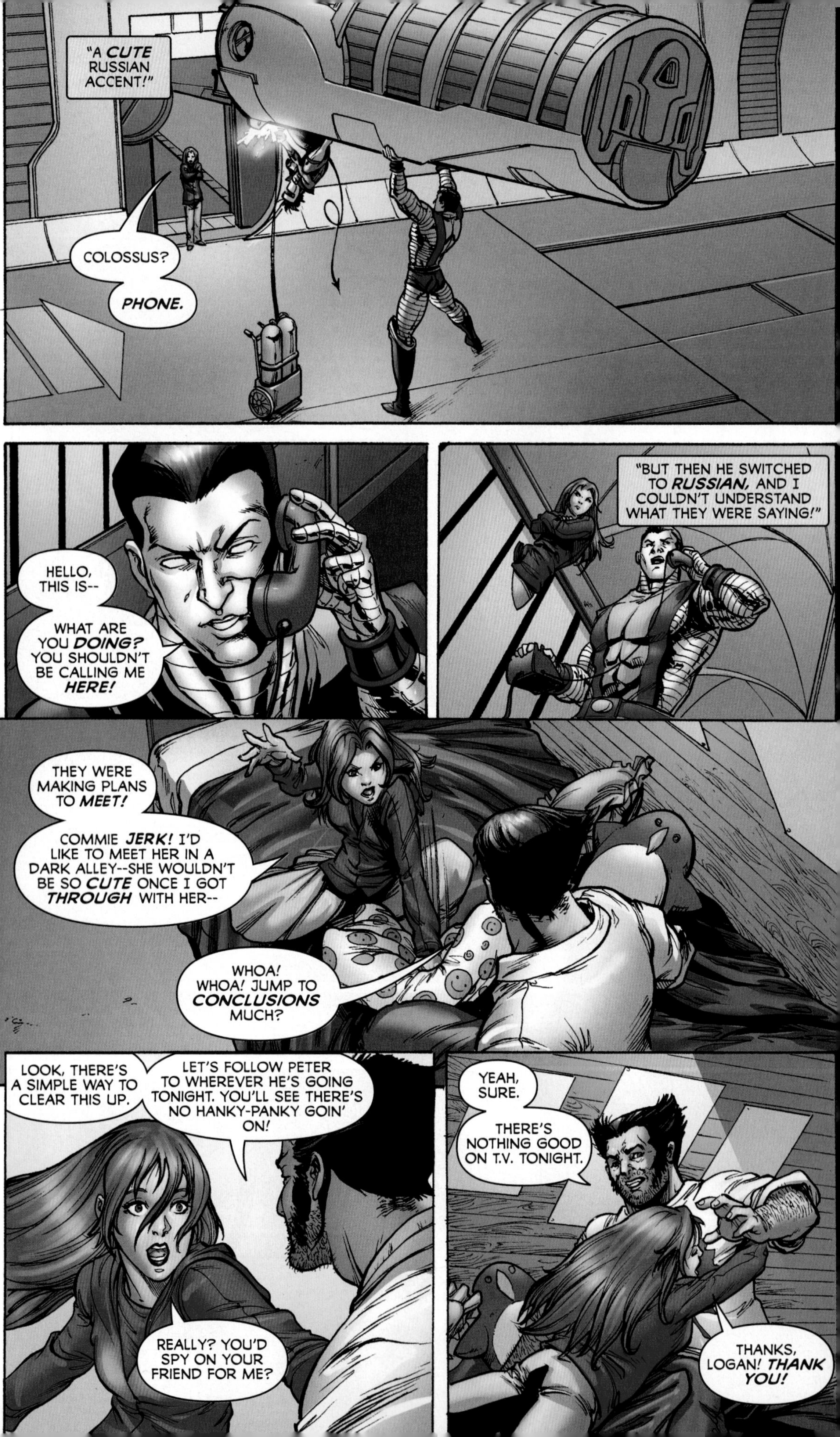
"A CUTE RUSSIAN ACCENT!"
COLOSSUS?
PHONE.
HELLO, THIS IS--
WHAT ARE YOU DOING? YOU SHOULDN'T BE CALLING ME HERE!
"BUT THEN HE SWITCHED TO RUSSIAN, AND I COULDN'T UNDERSTAND WHAT THEY WERE SAYING!"
THEY WERE MAKING PLANS TO MEET!
COMMIE JERK! I'D LIKE TO MEET HER IN A DARK ALLEY--SHE WOULDN'T BE SO CUTE ONCE I GOT THROUGH WITH HER--
WHOA! WHOA! JUMP TO CONCLUSIONS MUCH?
LOOK, THERE'S A SIMPLE WAY TO CLEAR THIS UP.
LET'S FOLLOW PETER TO WHEREVER HE'S GOING TONIGHT. YOU'LL SEE THERE'S NO HANKY-PANKY GOIN' ON!
REALLY? YOU'D SPY ON YOUR FRIEND FOR ME?
YEAH, SURE.
THERE'S NOTHING GOOD ON T.V. TONIGHT.
THANKS, LOGAN! THANK YOU!

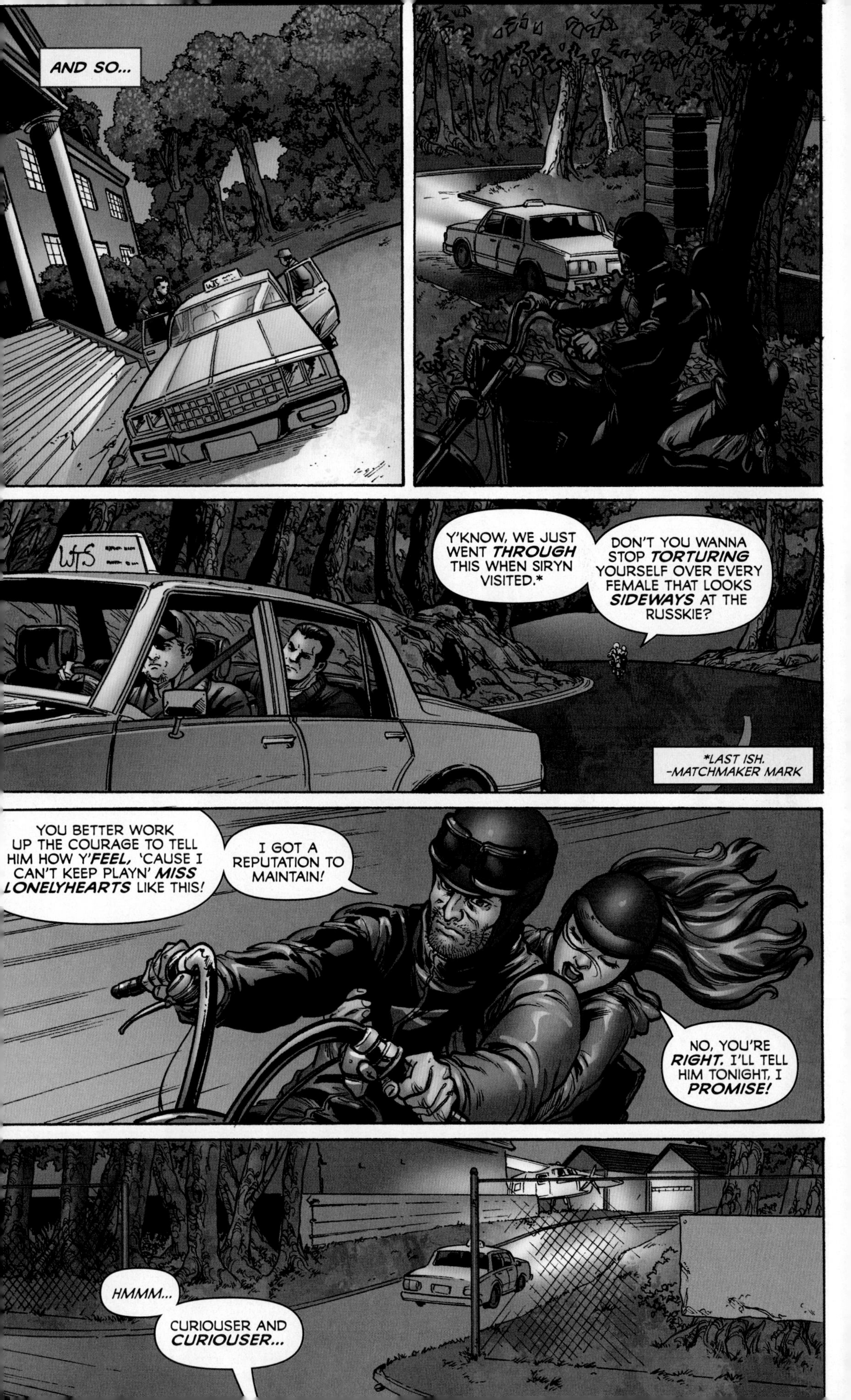
AND SO...
Y'KNOW, WE JUST WENT THROUGH THIS WHEN SIRYN VISITED.*
DON'T YOU WANNA STOP TORTURING YOURSELF OVER EVERY FEMALE THAT LOOKS SIDEWAYS AT THE RUSSKIE?
*LAST ISH. -MATCHMAKER MARK
YOU BETTER WORK UP THE COURAGE TO TELL HIM HOW Y'FEEL, 'CAUSE I CAN'T KEEP PLAYN' MISS LONELYHEARTS LIKE THIS!
I GOT A REPUTATION TO MAINTAIN!
NO, YOU'RE RIGHT. I'LL TELL HIM TONIGHT, I PROMISE!
HMMM...
CURIOUSER AND CURIOUSER...

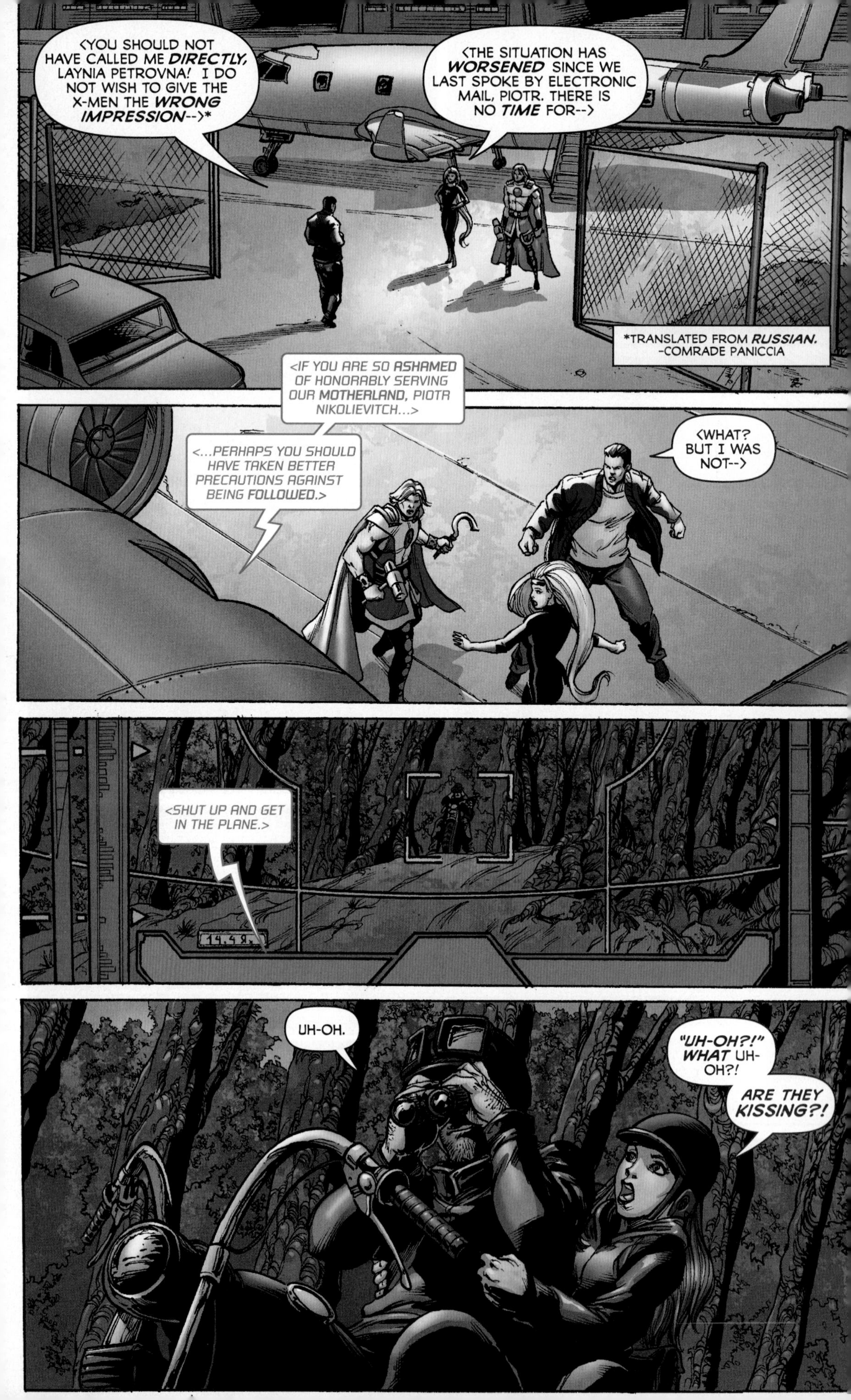
<YOU SHOULD NOT HAVE CALLED ME DIRECTLY, LAYNIA PETROVNA! I DO NOT WISH TO GIVE THE X-MEN THE WRONG IMPRESSION-->*
<THE SITUATION HAS WORSENED SINCE WE LAST SPOKE BY ELECTRONIC MAIL, PIOTR. THERE IS NO TIME FOR-->
*TRANSLATED FROM RUSSIAN. -COMRADE PANICCIA
<IF YOU ARE SO ASHAMED OF HONORABLY SERVING OUR MOTHERLAND, PIOTR NIKOLIEVITCH...>
<...PERHAPS YOU SHOULD HAVE TAKEN BETTER PRECAUTIONS AGAINST BEING FOLLOWED.>
<WHAT? BUT I WAS NOT-->
<SHUT UP AND GET IN THE PLANE.>
UH-OH.
"UH-OH?!" WHAT UH-OH?!
ARE THEY KISSING?!

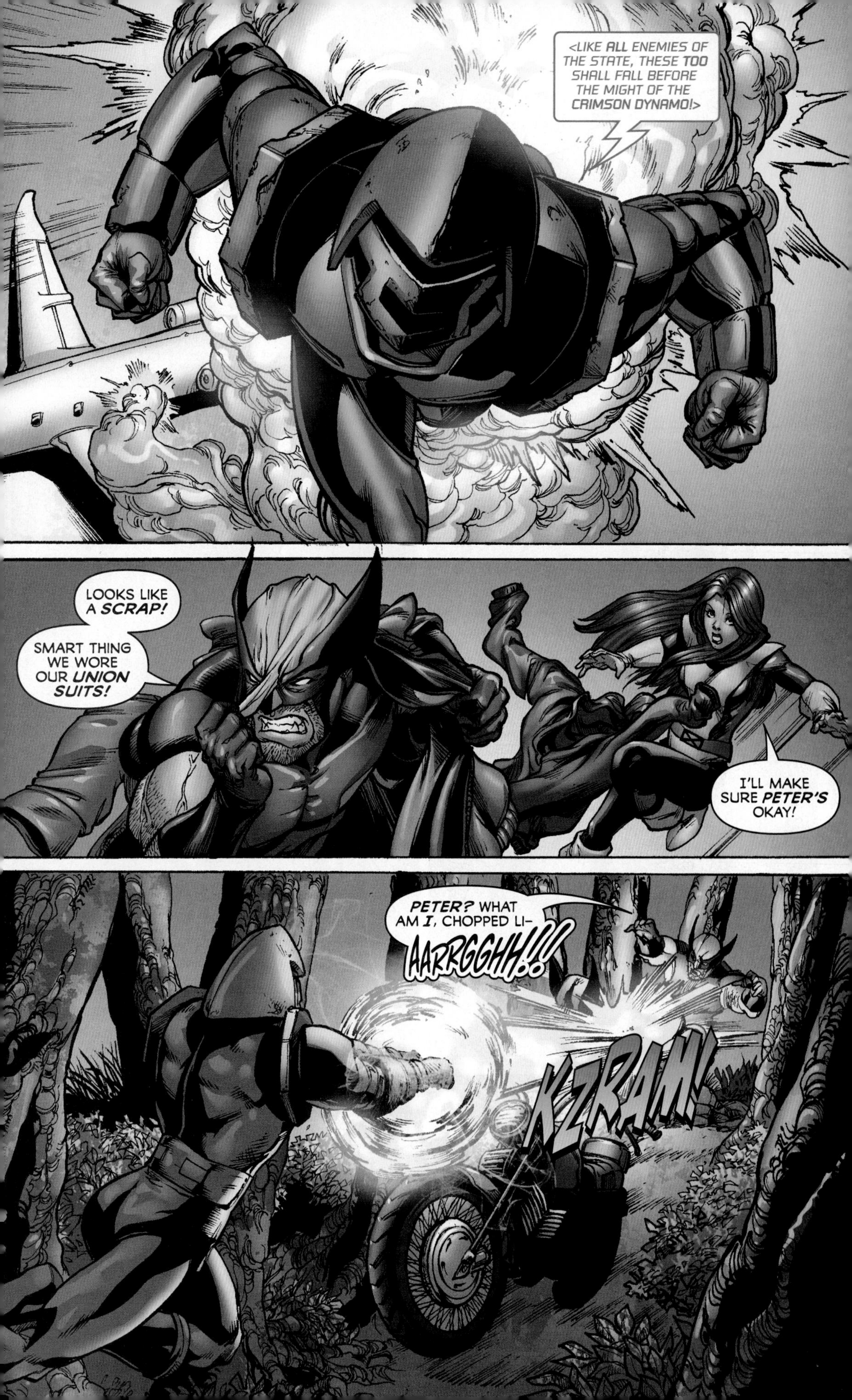
<LIKE ALL ENEMIES OF THE STATE, THESE TOO SHALL FALL BEFORE THE MIGHT OF THE CRIMSON DYNAMO!>
LOOKS LIKE A SCRAP!
SMART THING WE WORE OUR UNION SUITS!
I'LL MAKE SURE PETER'S OKAY!
PETER? WHAT AM I, CHOPPED LI-
AARRGGHH!!!
KZRAM!

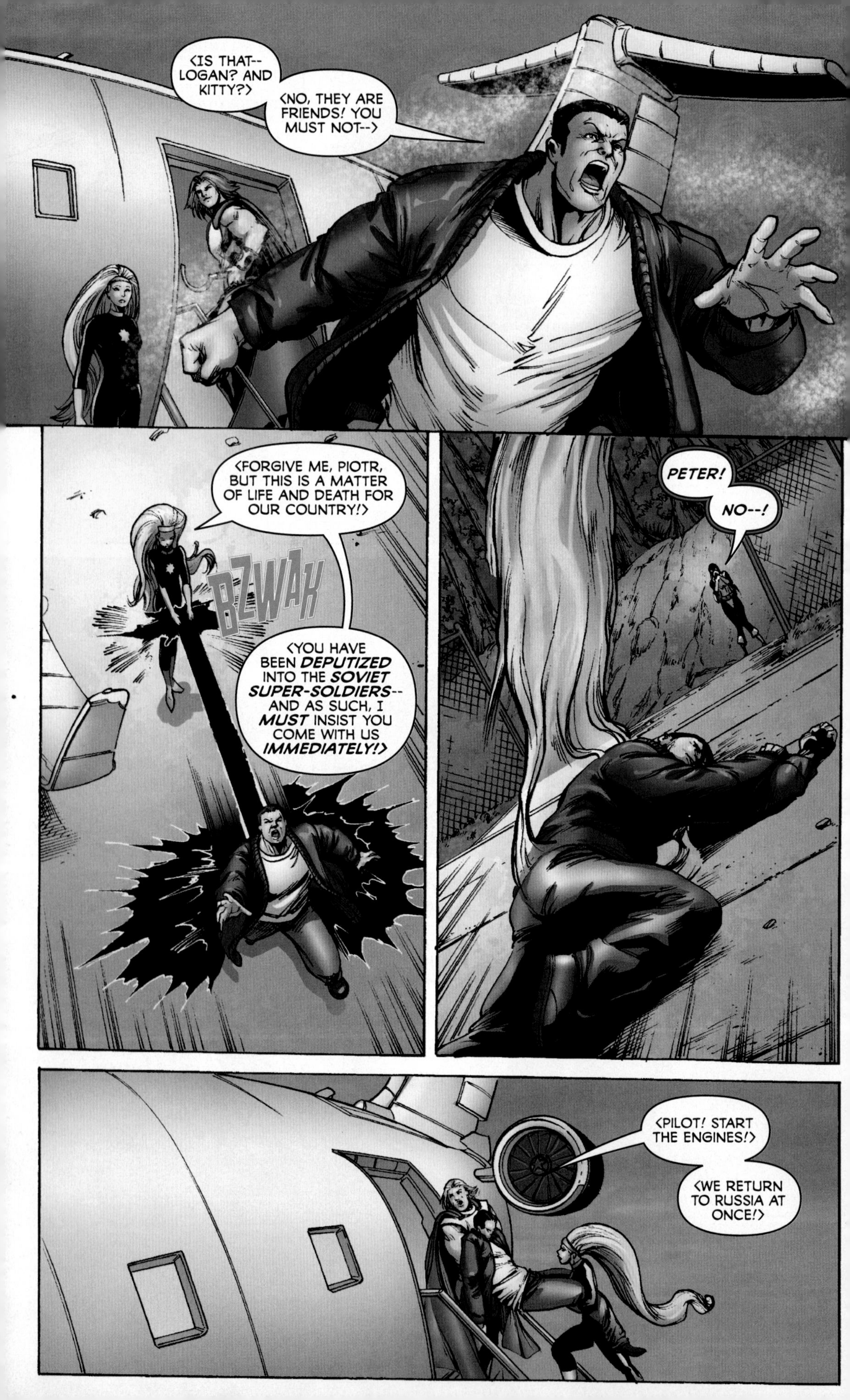

<IS THAT-- LOGAN? AND KITTY?>
<NO, THEY ARE FRIENDS! YOU MUST NOT-->
<FORGIVE ME, PIOTR, BUT THIS IS A MATTER OF LIFE AND DEATH FOR OUR COUNTRY!>
BZWAK
<YOU HAVE BEEN *DEPUTIZED* INTO THE *SOVIET SUPER-SOLDIERS*-- AND AS SUCH, I *MUST* INSIST YOU COME WITH US *IMMEDIATELY!*>
PETER!
NO--!
<PILOT! START THE ENGINES!>
<WE RETURN TO RUSSIA AT ONCE!>

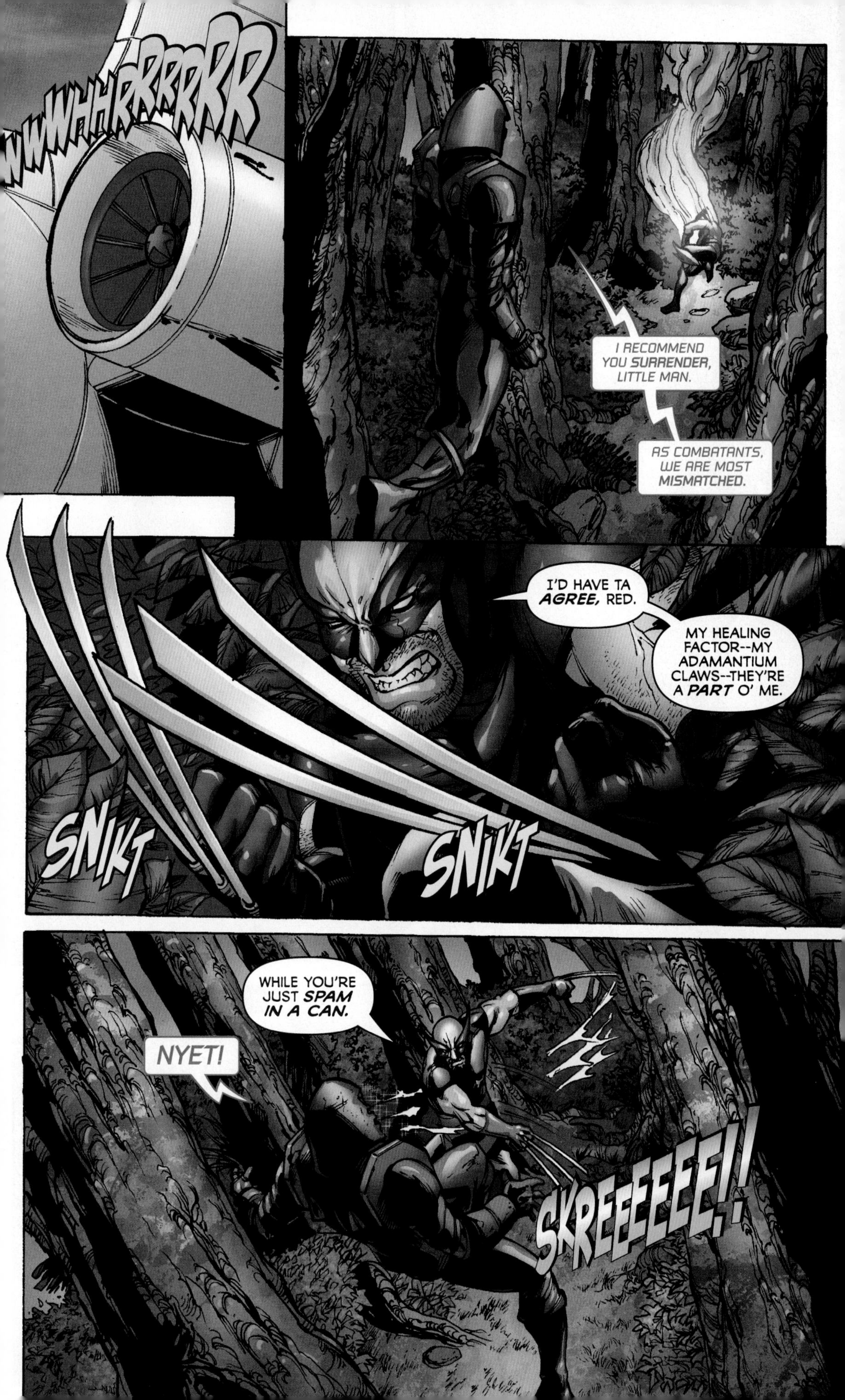
WWWHHRRRRRR
I RECOMMEND YOU SURRENDER, LITTLE MAN.
AS COMBATANTS, WE ARE MOST MISMATCHED.
I'D HAVE TA AGREE, RED.
MY HEALING FACTOR--MY ADAMANTIUM CLAWS--THEY'RE A PART O' ME.
SNIKT
SNIKT
WHILE YOU'RE JUST SPAM IN A CAN.
NYET!
SKREEEEEE!!

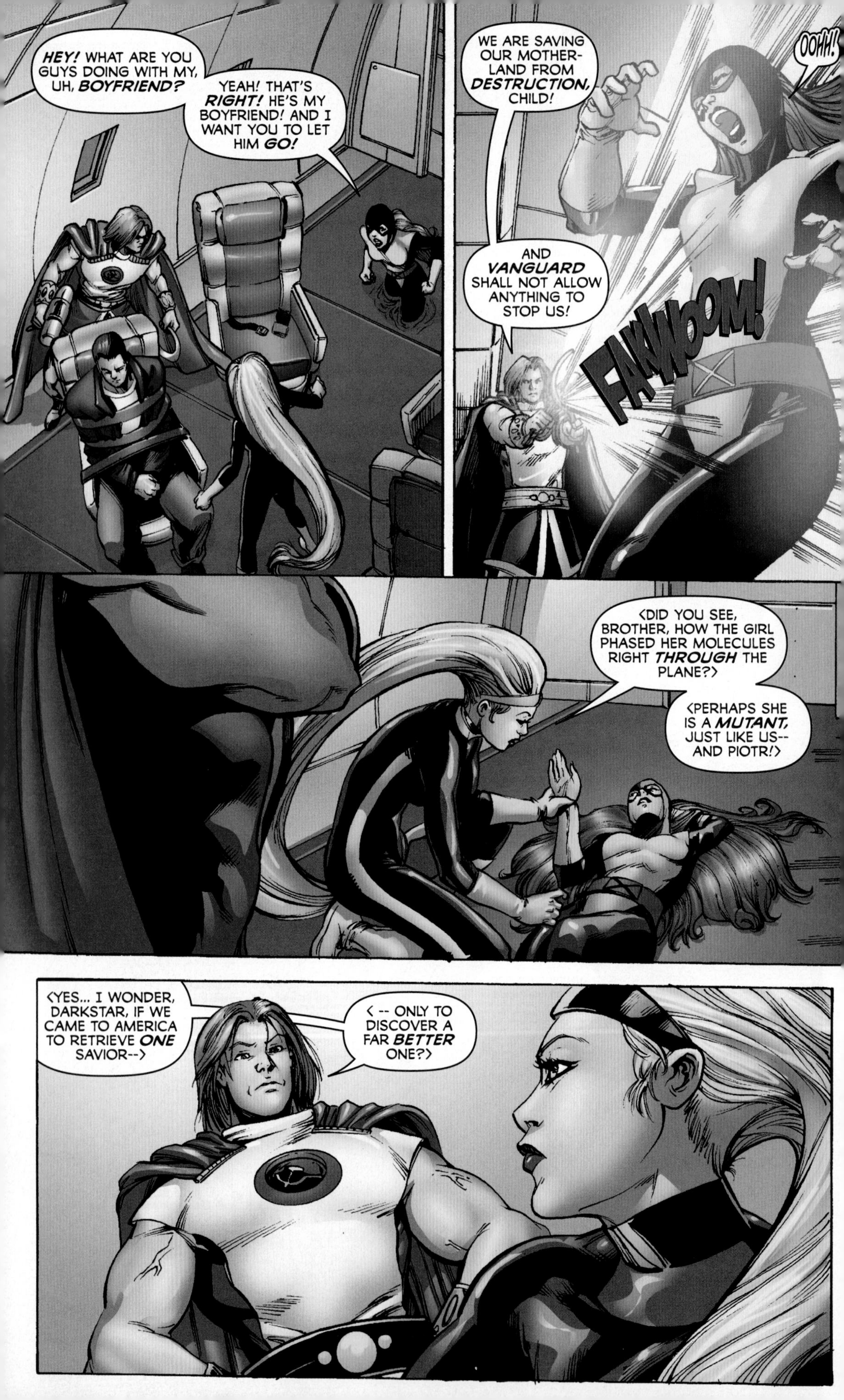
HEY! WHAT ARE YOU GUYS DOING WITH MY, UH, BOYFRIEND?
YEAH! THAT'S RIGHT! HE'S MY BOYFRIEND! AND I WANT YOU TO LET HIM GO!
WE ARE SAVING OUR MOTHER-LAND FROM DESTRUCTION, CHILD!
OOHH!
AND VANGUARD SHALL NOT ALLOW ANYTHING TO STOP US!
FAKWOOM!
<DID YOU SEE, BROTHER, HOW THE GIRL PHASED HER MOLECULES RIGHT THROUGH THE PLANE?>
<PERHAPS SHE IS A MUTANT, JUST LIKE US-- AND PIOTR!>
<YES... I WONDER, DARKSTAR, IF WE CAME TO AMERICA TO RETRIEVE ONE SAVIOR-->
< -- ONLY TO DISCOVER A FAR BETTER ONE?>

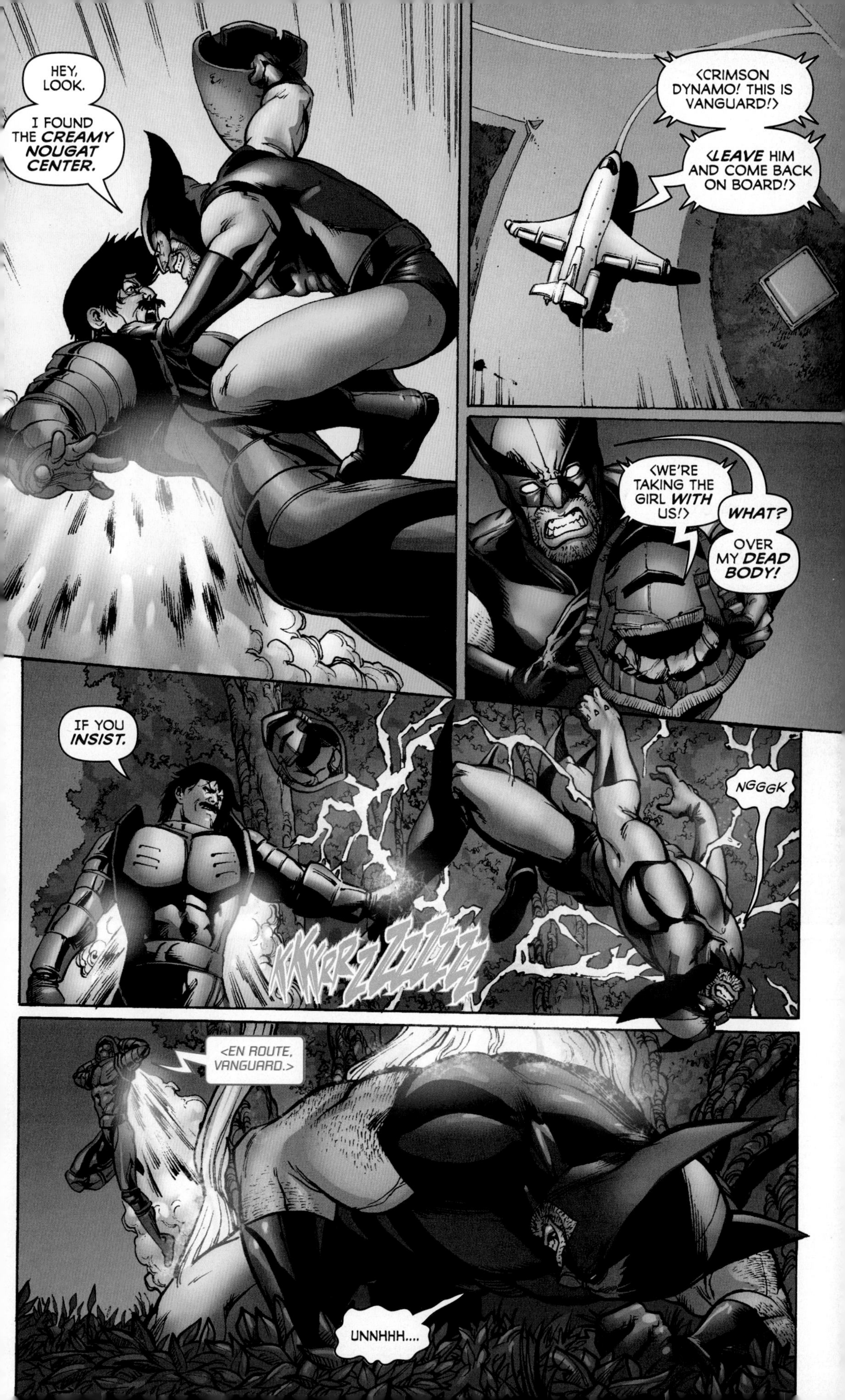
HEY, LOOK.
I FOUND THE *CREAMY NOUGAT CENTER.*
<CRIMSON DYNAMO! THIS IS VANGUARD!>
<*LEAVE* HIM AND COME BACK ON BOARD!>
<WE'RE TAKING THE GIRL *WITH* US!>
WHAT?
OVER MY *DEAD BODY!*
IF YOU *INSIST.*
NGGGK
KKKRRZZZZZZZ
<EN ROUTE, VANGUARD.>
UNNHHH....

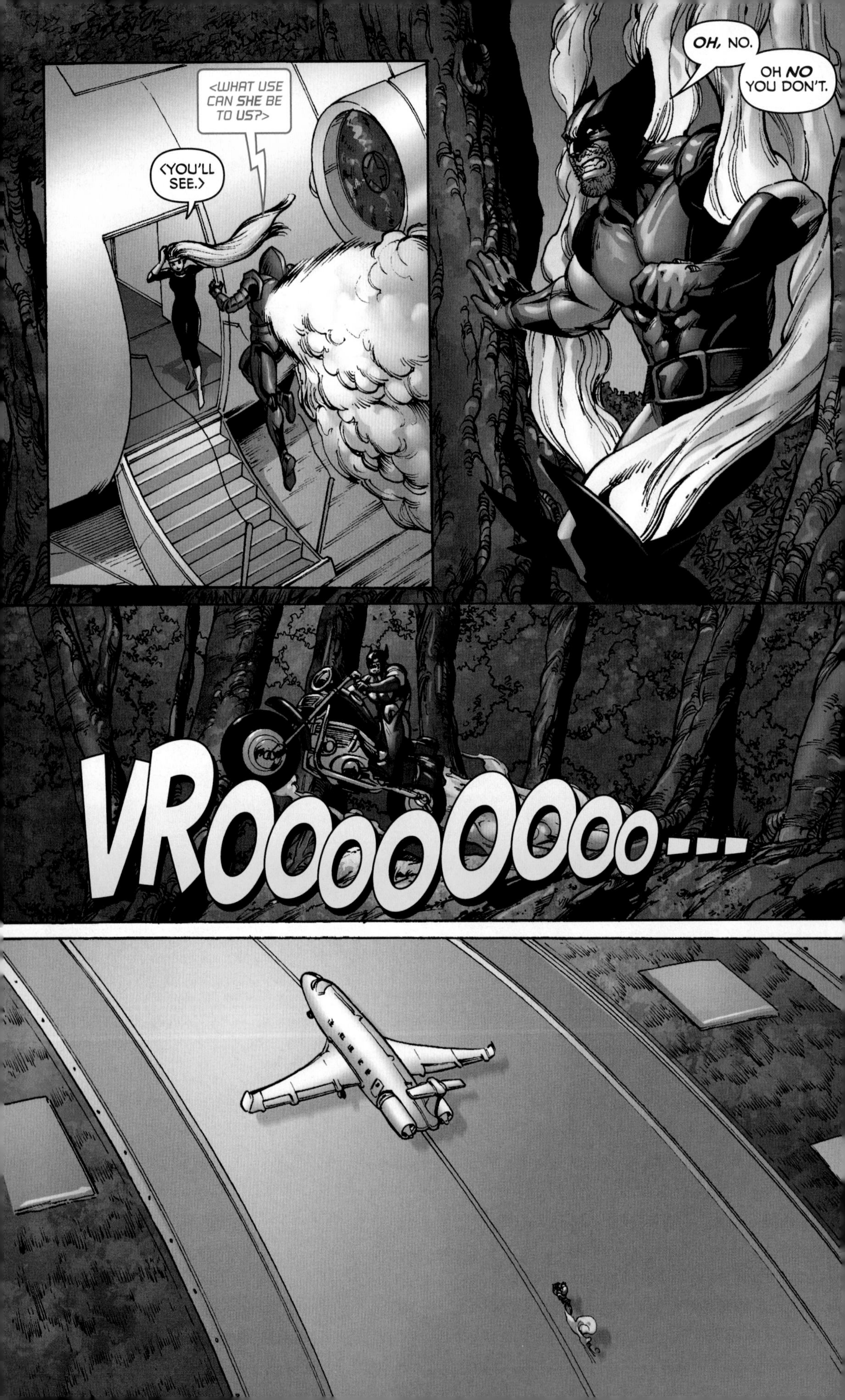
<WHAT USE CAN SHE BE TO US?>
<YOU'LL SEE.>
OH, NO.
OH NO YOU DON'T.
VROOOOOOOOO...

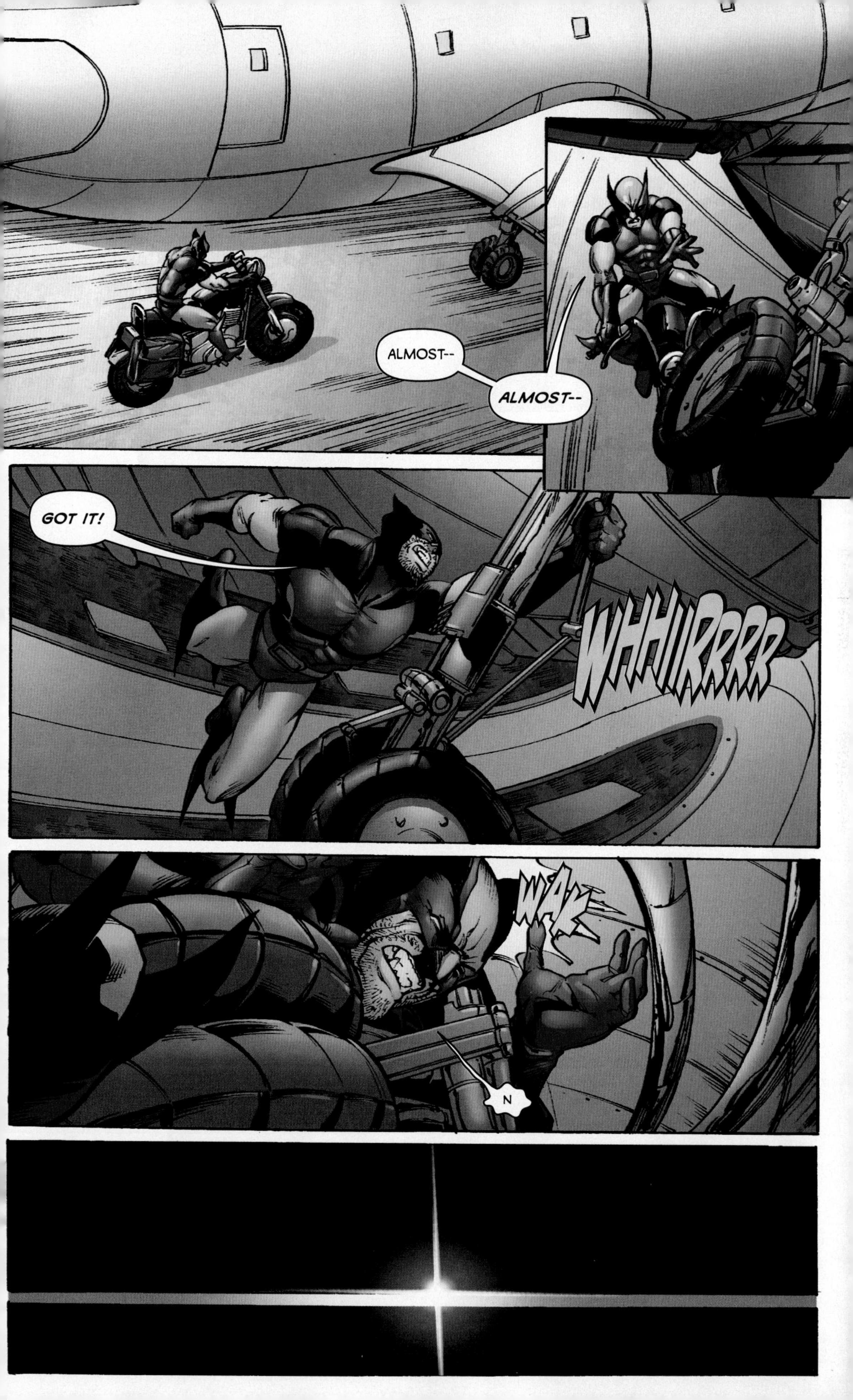
ALMOST--
ALMOST--
GOT IT!
WHHIRRRR
WAK
N

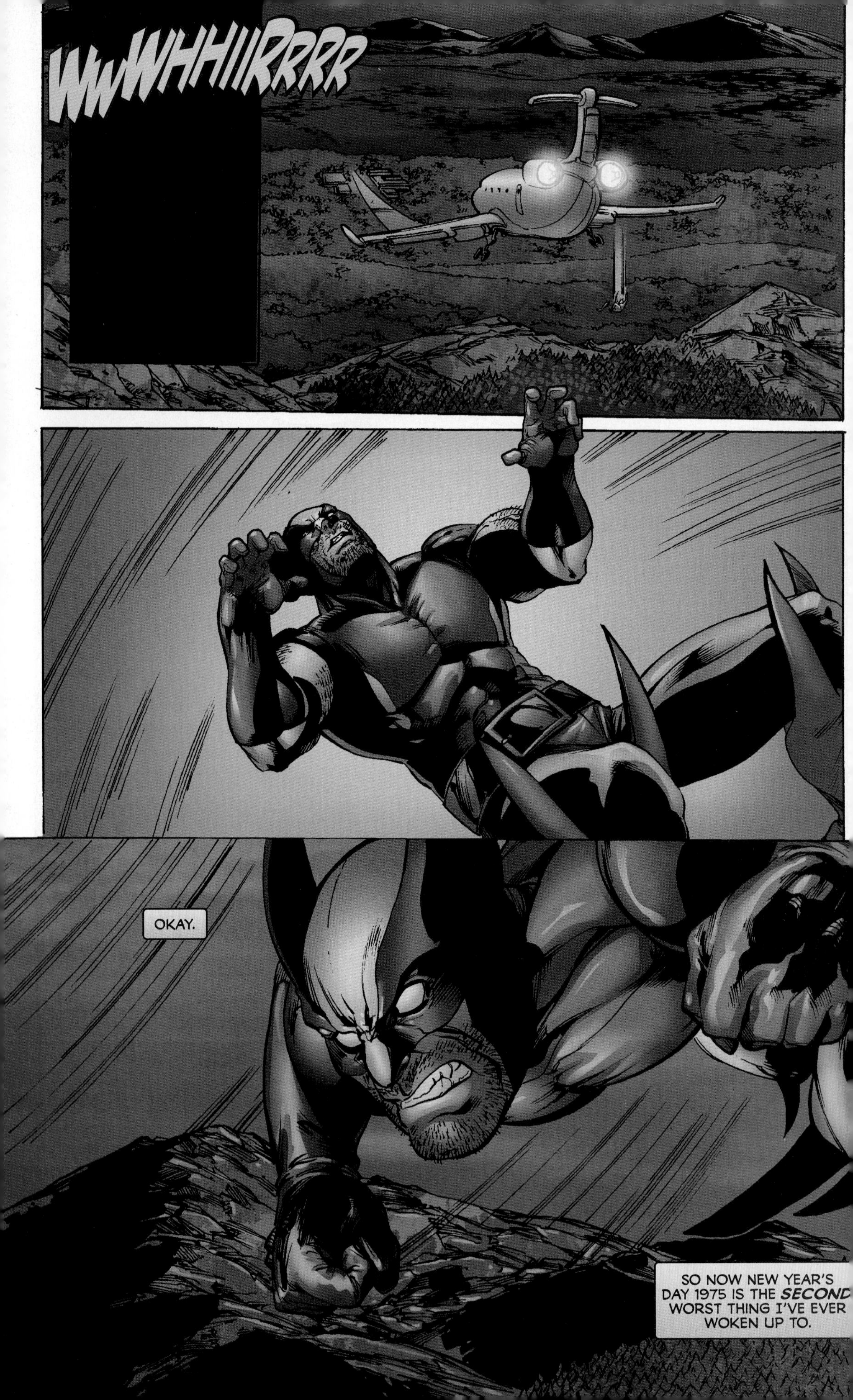
WwWHHIIRRRR
[redacted]
OKAY.
SO NOW NEW YEAR'S DAY 1975 IS THE *SECOND* WORST THING I'VE EVER WOKEN UP TO.

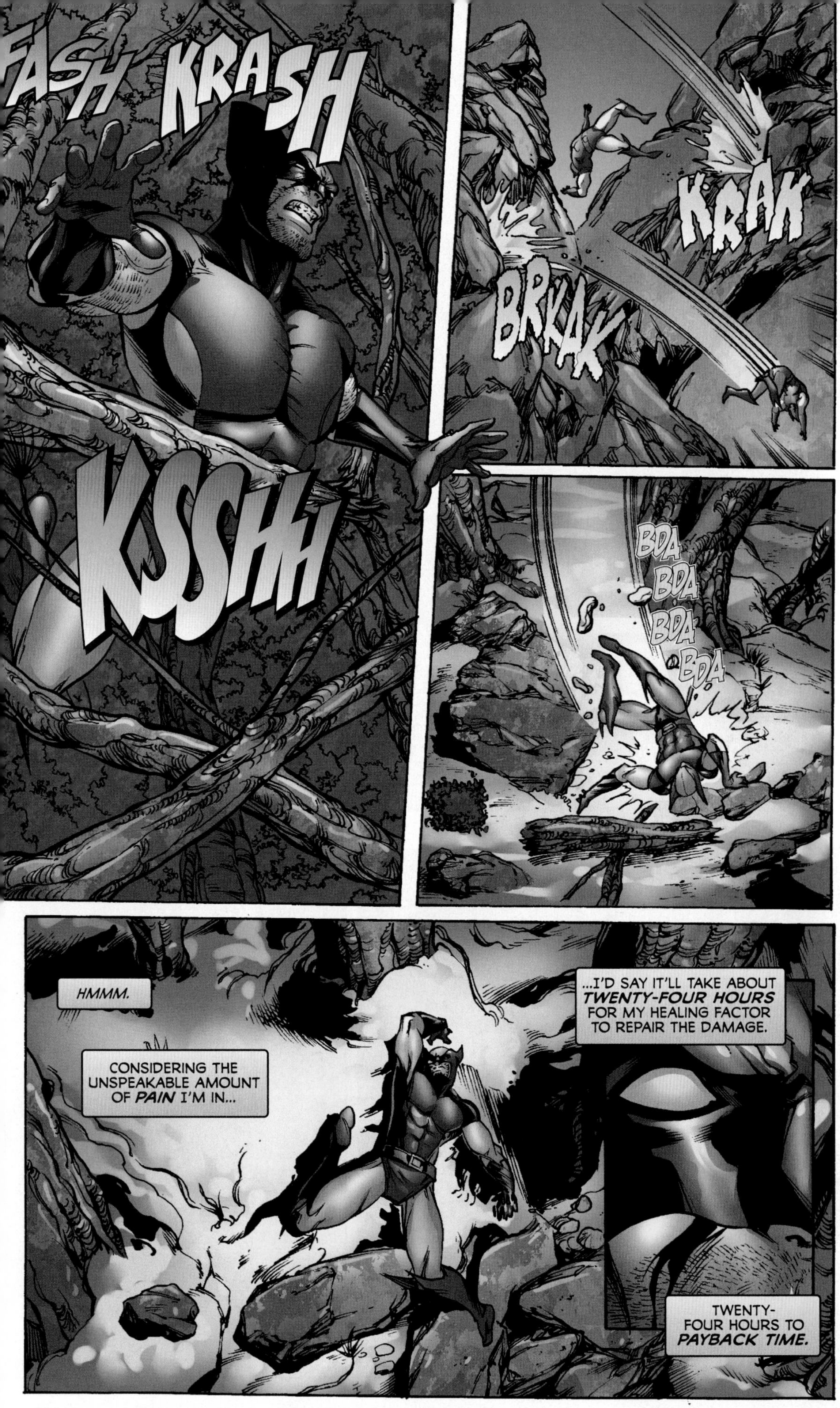
FASH KRASH
KSSHH
BRAK
KRAK
BDA BDA BDA BDA
HMMM.
CONSIDERING THE UNSPEAKABLE AMOUNT OF *PAIN* I'M IN...
...I'D SAY IT'LL TAKE ABOUT ***TWENTY-FOUR HOURS*** FOR MY HEALING FACTOR TO REPAIR THE DAMAGE.
TWENTY-FOUR HOURS TO ***PAYBACK TIME.***

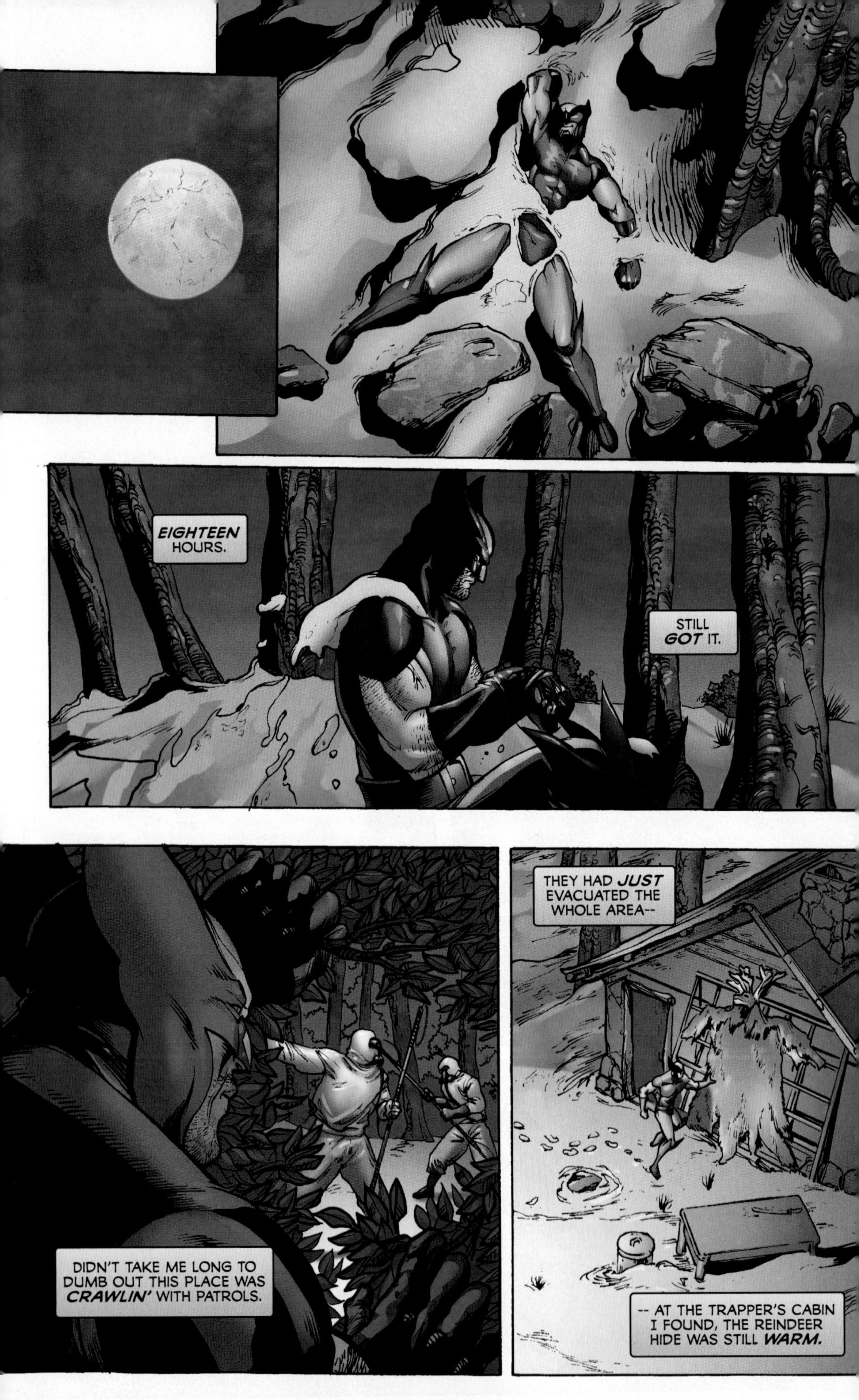
EIGHTEEN HOURS.
STILL GOT IT.
DIDN'T TAKE ME LONG TO DUMB OUT THIS PLACE WAS CRAWLIN' WITH PATROLS.
THEY HAD JUST EVACUATED THE WHOLE AREA--
-- AT THE TRAPPER'S CABIN I FOUND, THE REINDEER HIDE WAS STILL WARM.

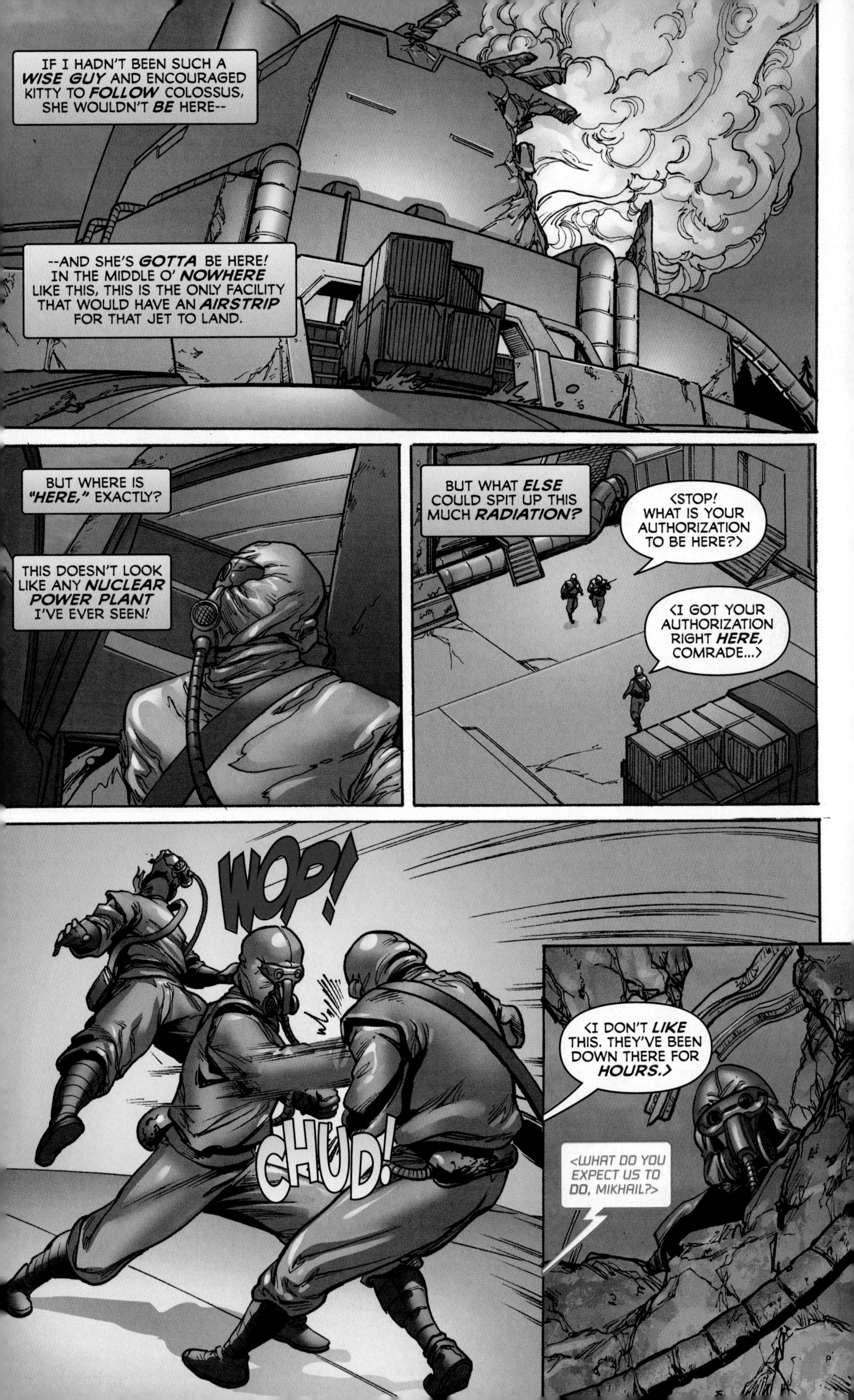

IF I HADN'T BEEN SUCH A WISE GUY AND ENCOURAGED KITTY TO FOLLOW COLOSSUS, SHE WOULDN'T BE HERE--
--AND SHE'S GOTTA BE HERE! IN THE MIDDLE O' NOWHERE LIKE THIS, THIS IS THE ONLY FACILITY THAT WOULD HAVE AN AIRSTRIP FOR THAT JET TO LAND.
BUT WHERE IS "HERE," EXACTLY?
THIS DOESN'T LOOK LIKE ANY NUCLEAR POWER PLANT I'VE EVER SEEN!
BUT WHAT ELSE COULD SPIT UP THIS MUCH RADIATION?
<STOP! WHAT IS YOUR AUTHORIZATION TO BE HERE?>
<I GOT YOUR AUTHORIZATION RIGHT HERE, COMRADE...>
WOP!
CHUD!
<I DON'T LIKE THIS. THEY'VE BEEN DOWN THERE FOR HOURS.>
<WHAT DO YOU EXPECT US TO DO, MIKHAIL?>

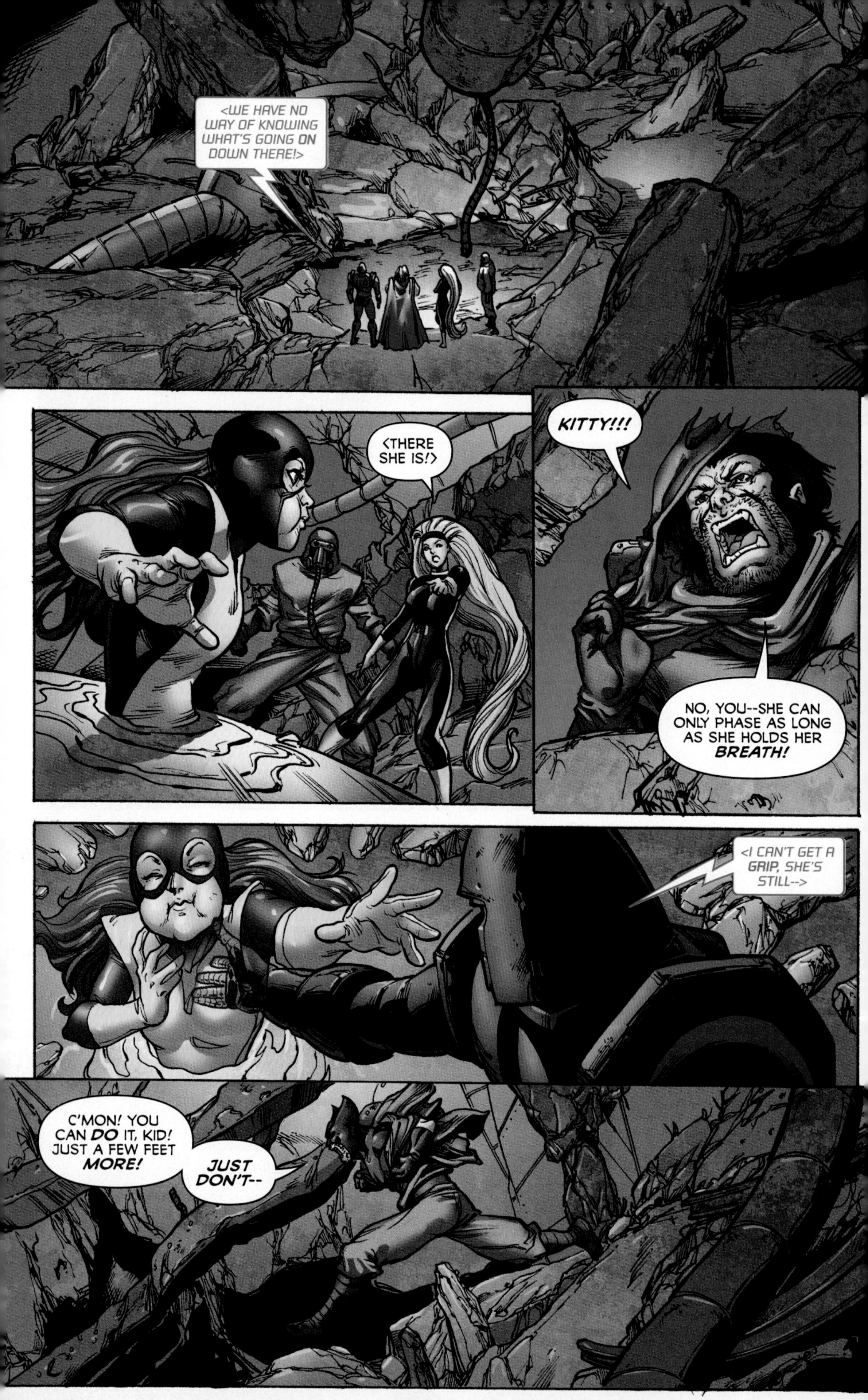

<WE HAVE NO WAY OF KNOWING WHAT'S GOING ON DOWN THERE!>
<THERE SHE IS!>
KITTY!!!
NO, YOU--SHE CAN ONLY PHASE AS LONG AS SHE HOLDS HER BREATH!
<I CAN'T GET A GRIP, SHE'S STILL-->
C'MON! YOU CAN DO IT, KID! JUST A FEW FEET MORE!
JUST DON'T--

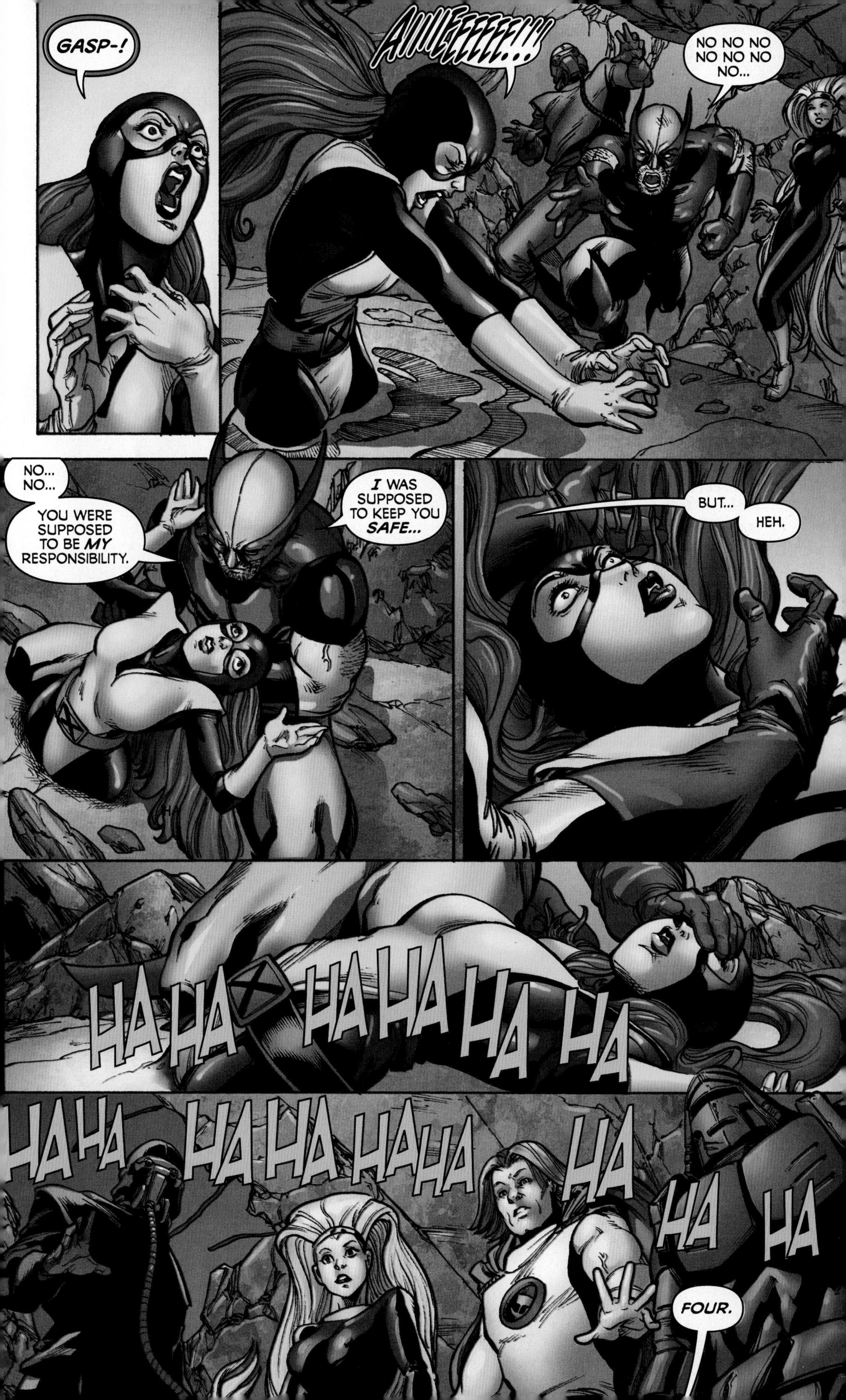
GASP-!
AIIIIEEEEEE!!!
NO NO NO
NO NO NO
NO...
NO...
NO...
YOU WERE SUPPOSED TO BE MY RESPONSIBILITY.
I WAS SUPPOSED TO KEEP YOU SAFE...
BUT...
HEH.
HAHA HAHA HA HA
HAHA HAHAHAHAHA HA HA HA
FOUR.

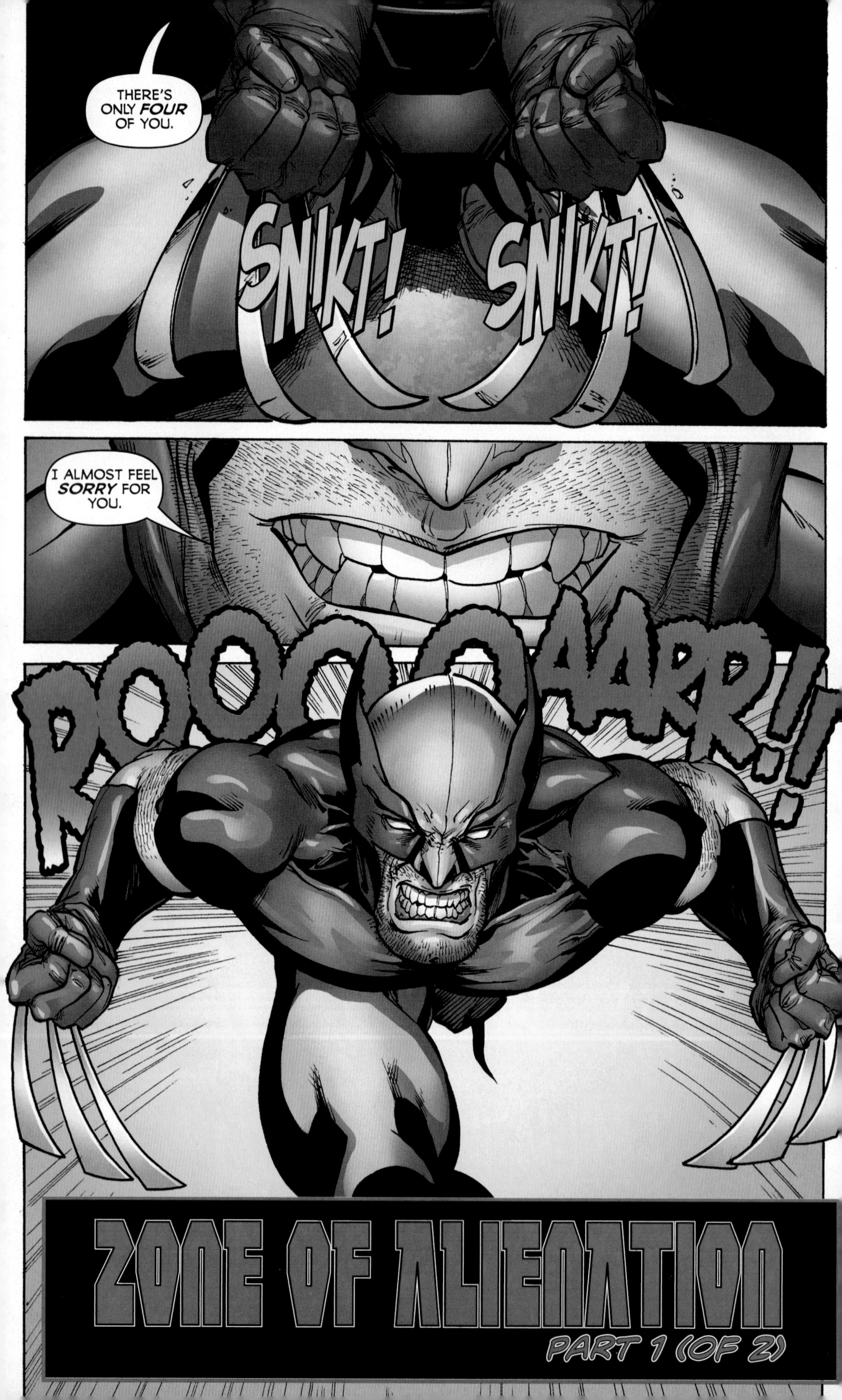
THERE'S ONLY FOUR OF YOU.
SNIKT! SNIKT!
I ALMOST FEEL SORRY FOR YOU.
ROOOOOAARR!!
ZONE OF ALIENATION
PART 1 (OF 2)

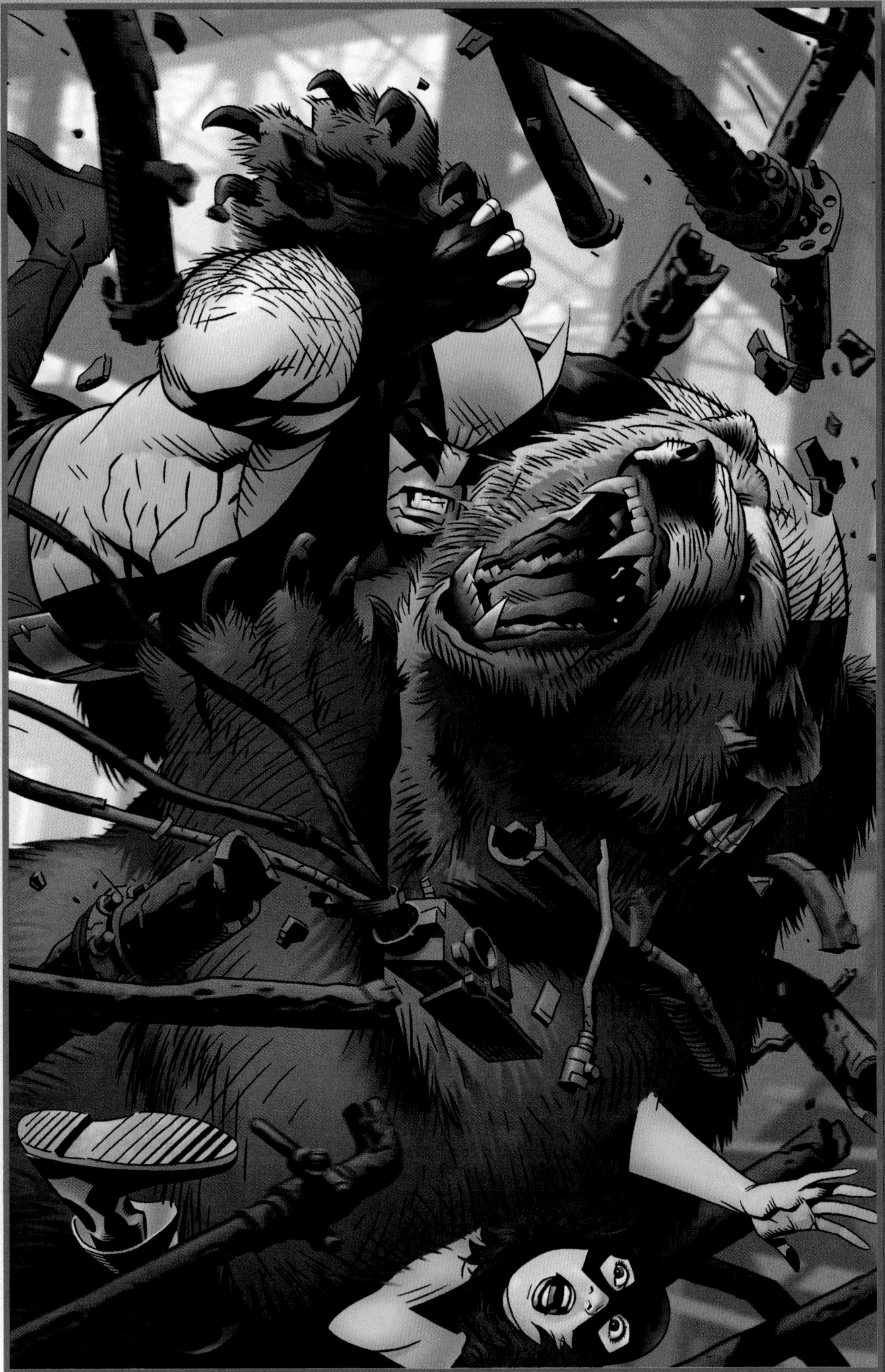

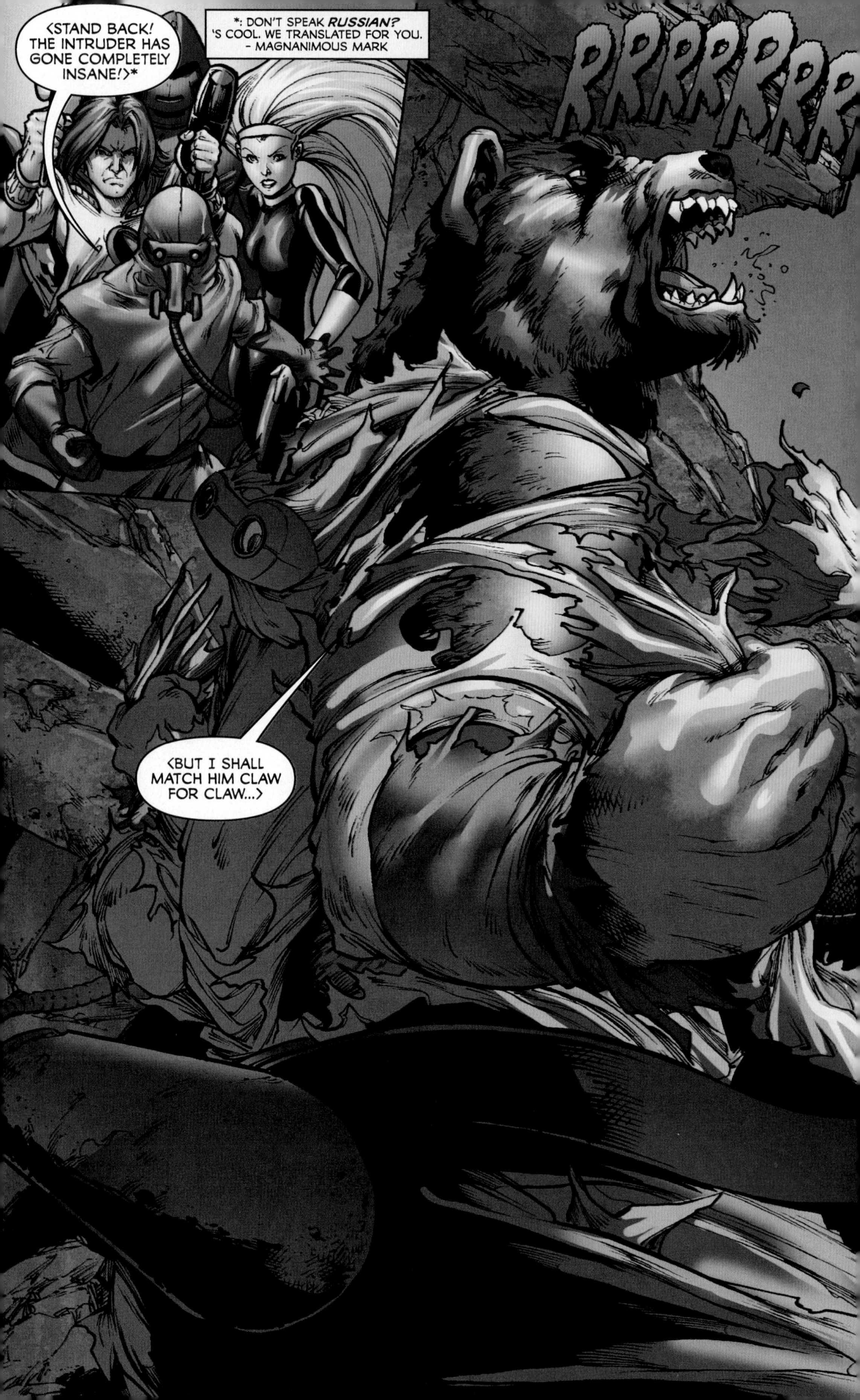
<STAND BACK! THE INTRUDER HAS GONE COMPLETELY INSANE!>*
*: DON'T SPEAK RUSSIAN? 'S COOL. WE TRANSLATED FOR YOU. - MAGNANIMOUS MARK
RRRRRRRR
<BUT I SHALL MATCH HIM CLAW FOR CLAW...>

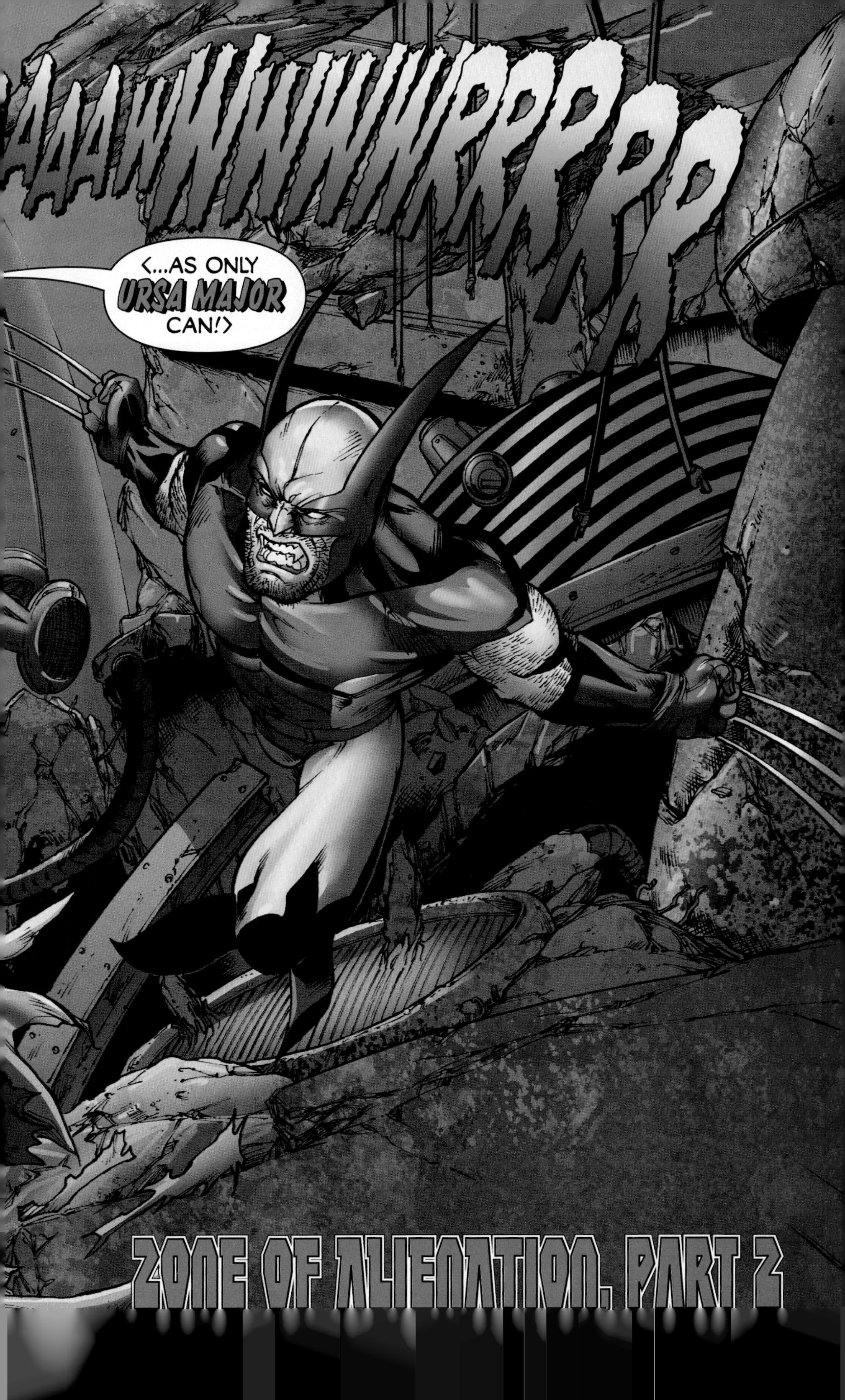
AAAAWWWWWWRRRRR
<...AS ONLY URSA MAJOR CAN!>
ZONE OF ALIENATION, PART 2

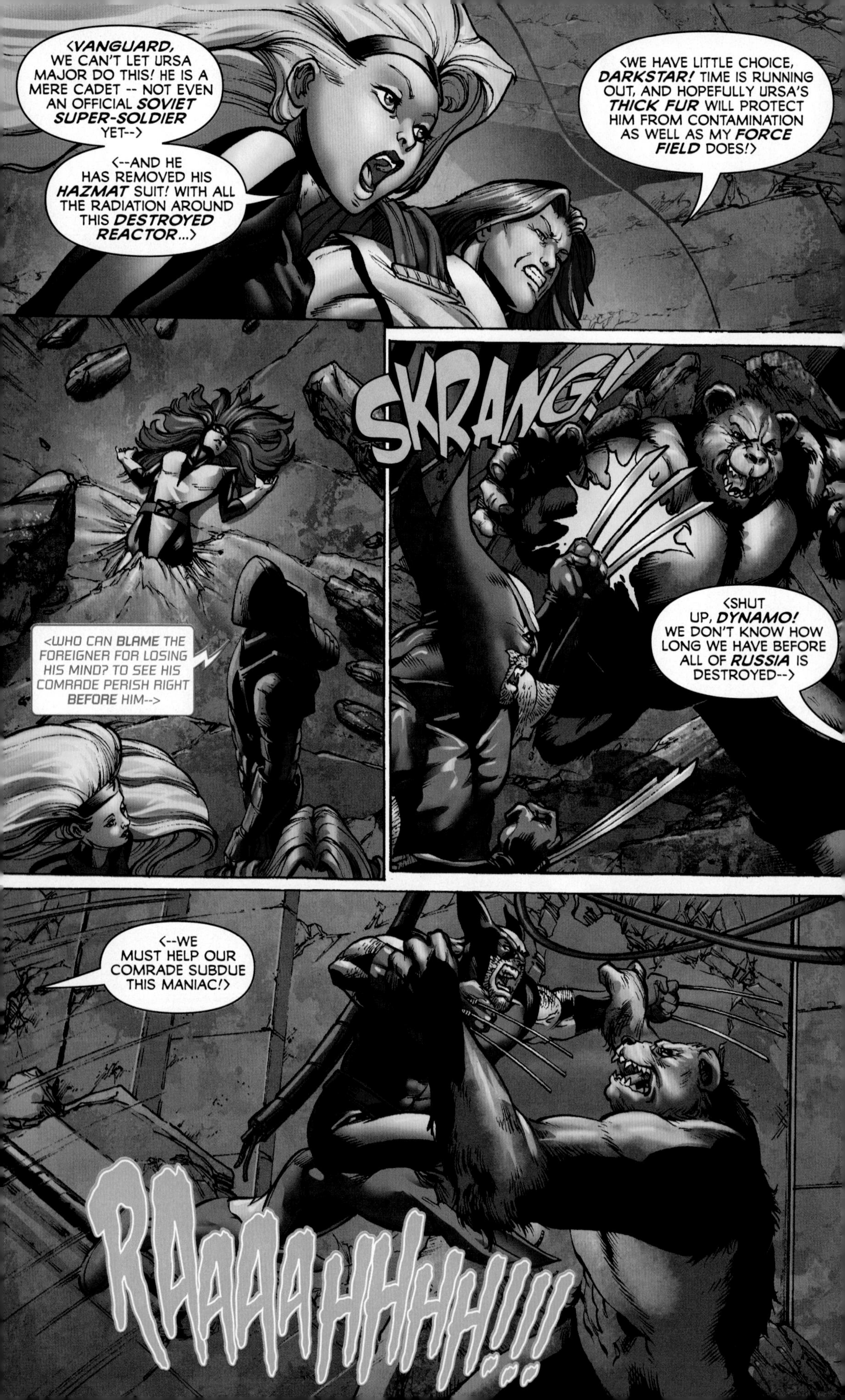
<VANGUARD, WE CAN'T LET URSA MAJOR DO THIS! HE IS A MERE CADET -- NOT EVEN AN OFFICIAL SOVIET SUPER-SOLDIER YET-->
<--AND HE HAS REMOVED HIS HAZMAT SUIT! WITH ALL THE RADIATION AROUND THIS DESTROYED REACTOR...>
<WE HAVE LITTLE CHOICE, DARKSTAR! TIME IS RUNNING OUT, AND HOPEFULLY URSA'S THICK FUR WILL PROTECT HIM FROM CONTAMINATION AS WELL AS MY FORCE FIELD DOES!>
SKRANG!
<WHO CAN BLAME THE FOREIGNER FOR LOSING HIS MIND? TO SEE HIS COMRADE PERISH RIGHT BEFORE HIM-->
<SHUT UP, DYNAMO! WE DON'T KNOW HOW LONG WE HAVE BEFORE ALL OF RUSSIA IS DESTROYED-->
<--WE MUST HELP OUR COMRADE SUBDUE THIS MANIAC!>
RAAAAHHHH!!!

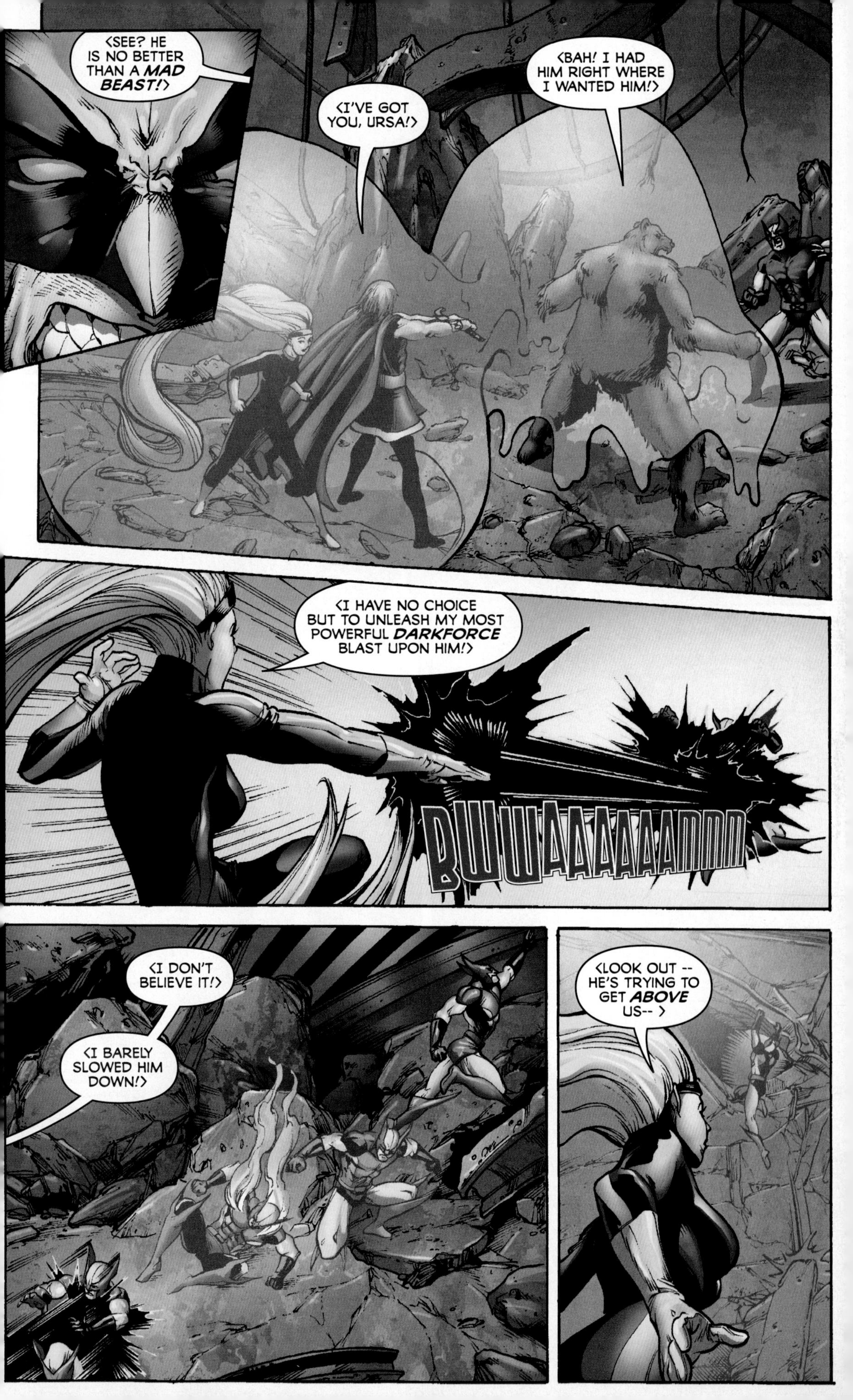
<SEE? HE IS NO BETTER THAN A *MAD BEAST!*>
<I'VE GOT YOU, URSA!>
<BAH! I HAD HIM RIGHT WHERE I WANTED HIM!>
<I HAVE NO CHOICE BUT TO UNLEASH MY MOST POWERFUL *DARKFORCE* BLAST UPON HIM!>
BWWAAAAAAAMMM
<I DON'T BELIEVE IT!>
<I BARELY SLOWED HIM DOWN!>
<LOOK OUT -- HE'S TRYING TO GET *ABOVE* US-- >

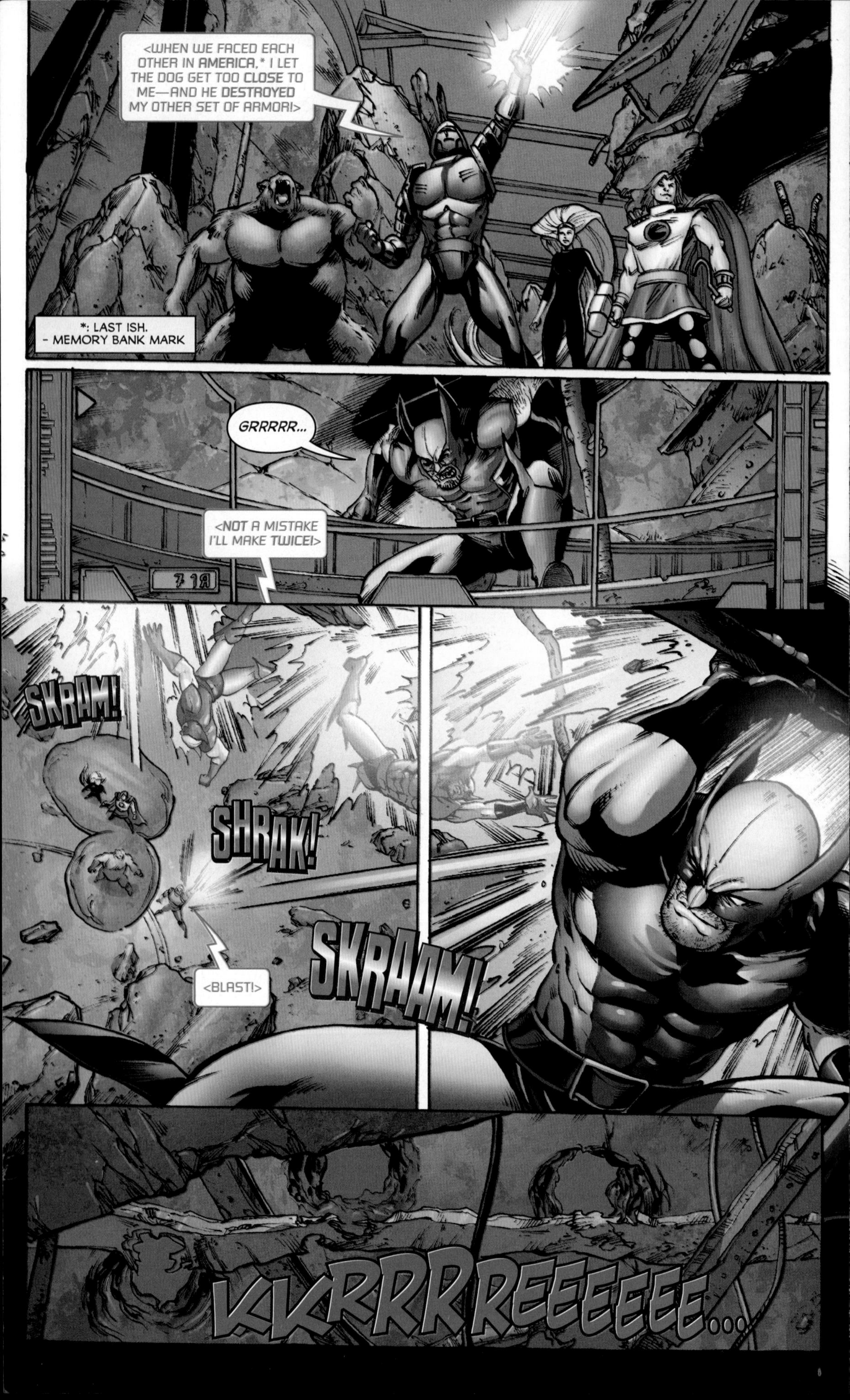
<WHEN WE FACED EACH OTHER IN AMERICA,* I LET THE DOG GET TOO CLOSE TO ME—AND HE DESTROYED MY OTHER SET OF ARMOR!>
*: LAST ISH. - MEMORY BANK MARK
GRRRRR...
<NOT A MISTAKE I'LL MAKE TWICE!>
SKRAM!
SHRAK!
<BLAST!>
SKRAAM!
KKRRRREEEEEEE...

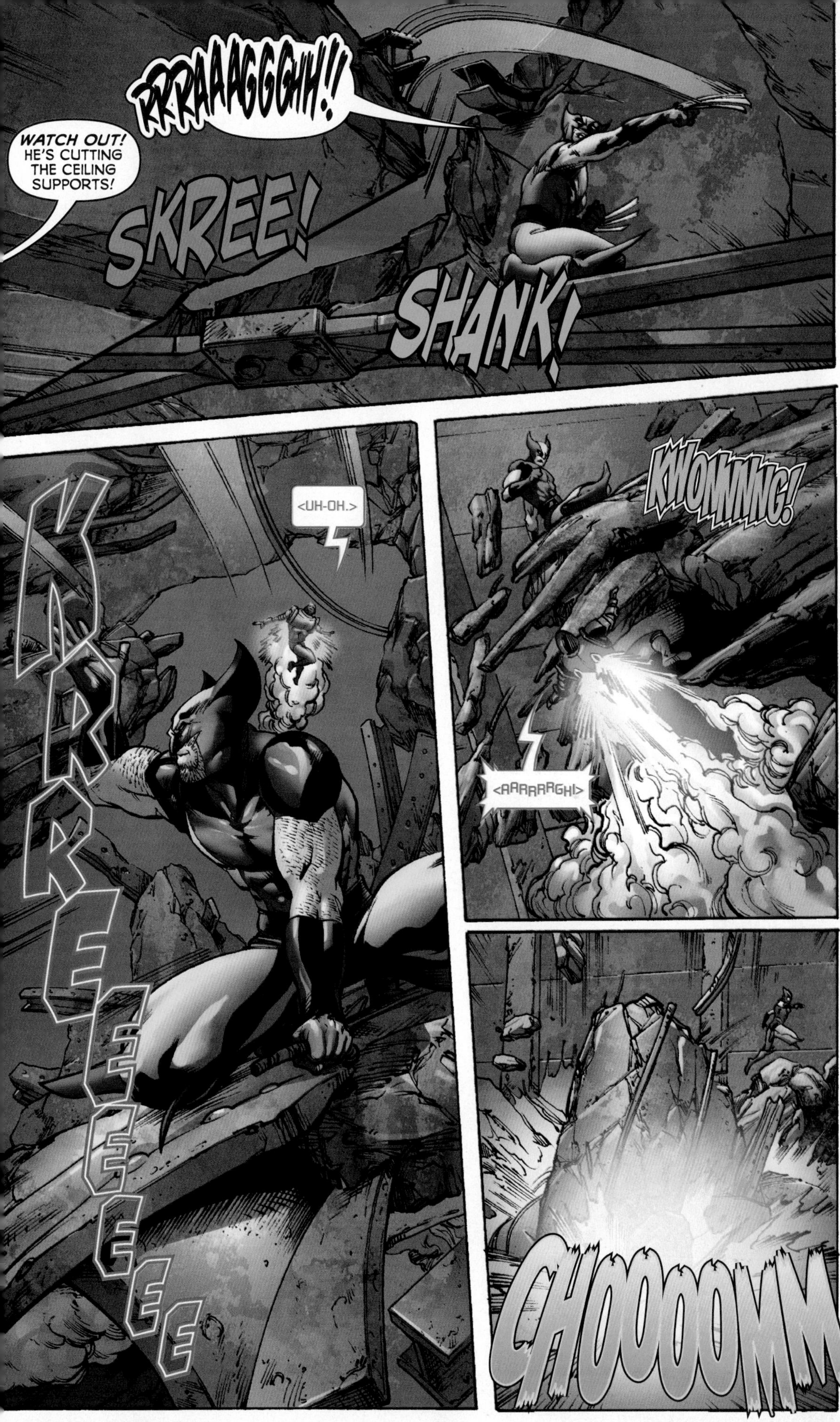
WATCH OUT! HE'S CUTTING THE CEILING SUPPORTS!
RRRAAAGGGHH!!
SKREE!
SHANK!
<UH-OH.>
KRREEEEEEEE
KWONNNNG!
<AAAAAAAGH!>
CHOOOOMM

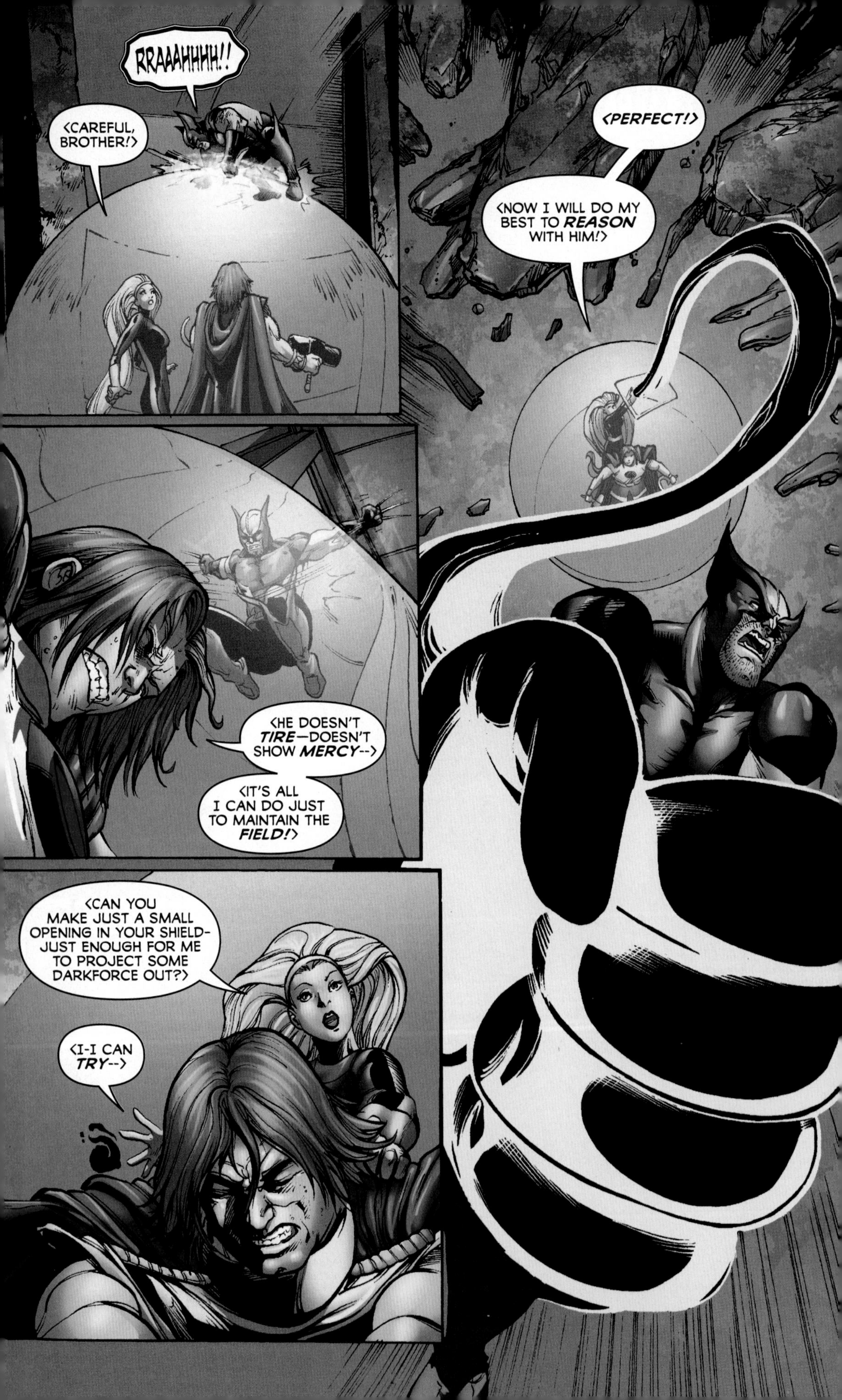
RRAAAHHHH!!
<CAREFUL, BROTHER!>
<PERFECT!>
<NOW I WILL DO MY BEST TO REASON WITH HIM!>
<HE DOESN'T TIRE—DOESN'T SHOW MERCY-->
<IT'S ALL I CAN DO JUST TO MAINTAIN THE FIELD!>
<CAN YOU MAKE JUST A SMALL OPENING IN YOUR SHIELD-JUST ENOUGH FOR ME TO PROJECT SOME DARKFORCE OUT?>
<I-I CAN TRY-->

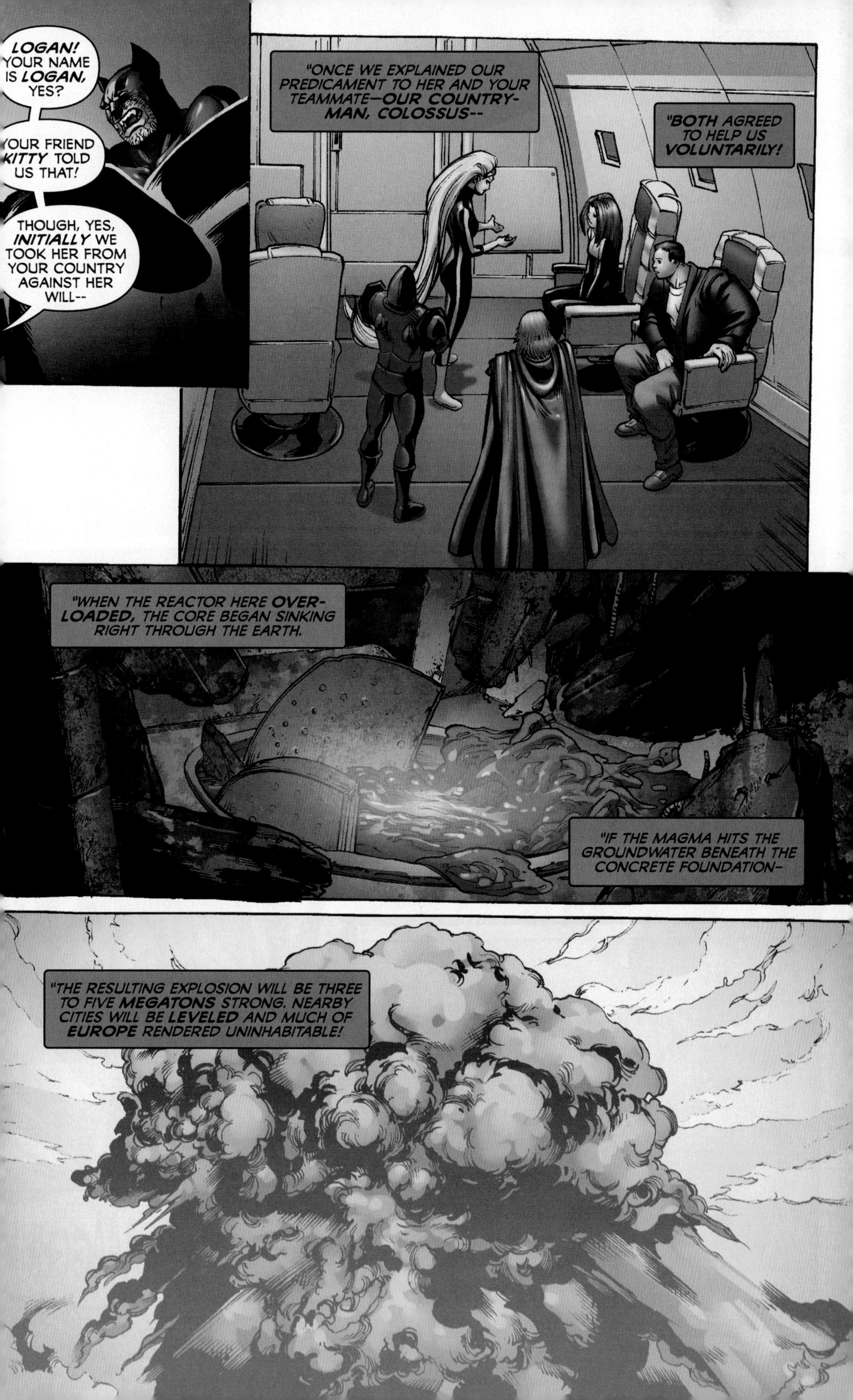
LOGAN! YOUR NAME IS LOGAN, YES?
YOUR FRIEND KITTY TOLD US THAT!
THOUGH, YES, INITIALLY WE TOOK HER FROM YOUR COUNTRY AGAINST HER WILL--
"ONCE WE EXPLAINED OUR PREDICAMENT TO HER AND YOUR TEAMMATE—OUR COUNTRYMAN, COLOSSUS--
"BOTH AGREED TO HELP US VOLUNTARILY!
"WHEN THE REACTOR HERE OVERLOADED, THE CORE BEGAN SINKING RIGHT THROUGH THE EARTH.
"IF THE MAGMA HITS THE GROUNDWATER BENEATH THE CONCRETE FOUNDATION-
"THE RESULTING EXPLOSION WILL BE THREE TO FIVE MEGATONS STRONG. NEARBY CITIES WILL BE LEVELED AND MUCH OF EUROPE RENDERED UNINHABITABLE!

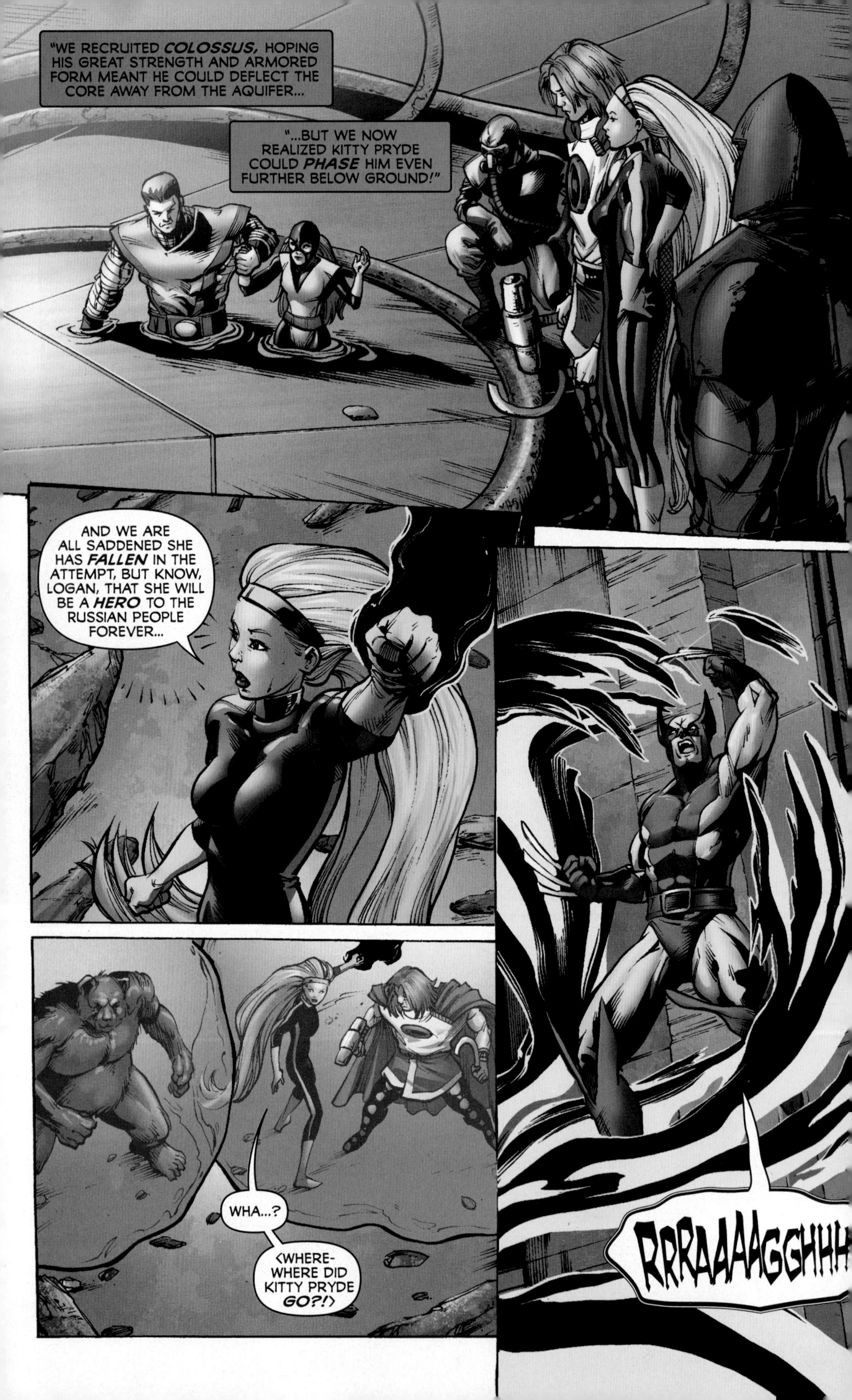
"WE RECRUITED COLOSSUS, HOPING HIS GREAT STRENGTH AND ARMORED FORM MEANT HE COULD DEFLECT THE CORE AWAY FROM THE AQUIFER...
"...BUT WE NOW REALIZED KITTY PRYDE COULD PHASE HIM EVEN FURTHER BELOW GROUND!"
AND WE ARE ALL SADDENED SHE HAS FALLEN IN THE ATTEMPT, BUT KNOW, LOGAN, THAT SHE WILL BE A HERO TO THE RUSSIAN PEOPLE FOREVER...
WHA...?
<WHERE-WHERE DID KITTY PRYDE GO?!>
RRRAAAAGGHHH

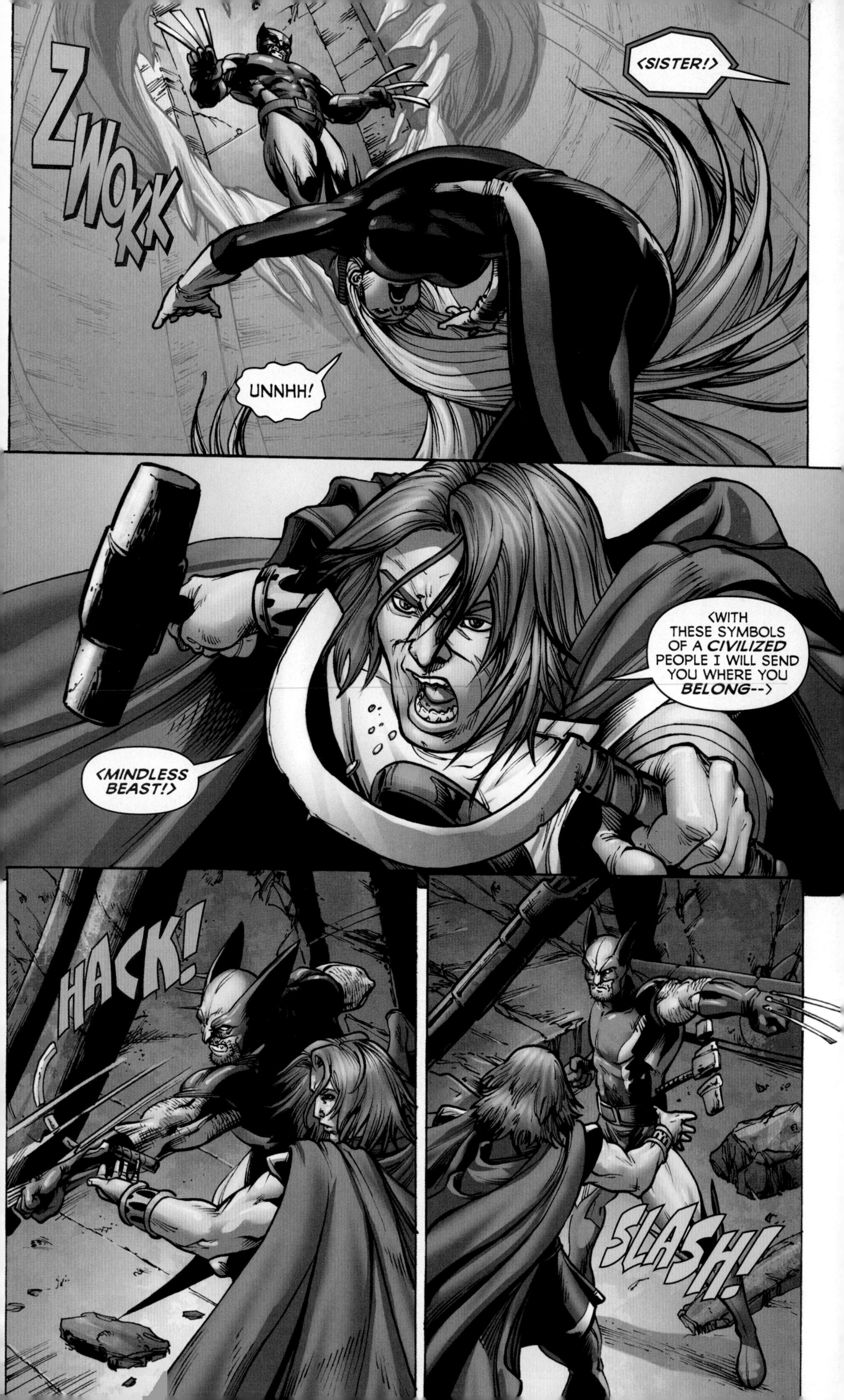
ZWOKK
<SISTER!>
UNNHH!
<WITH THESE SYMBOLS OF A *CIVILIZED* PEOPLE I WILL SEND YOU WHERE YOU *BELONG*-->
<MINDLESS BEAST!>
HACK!
SLASH!

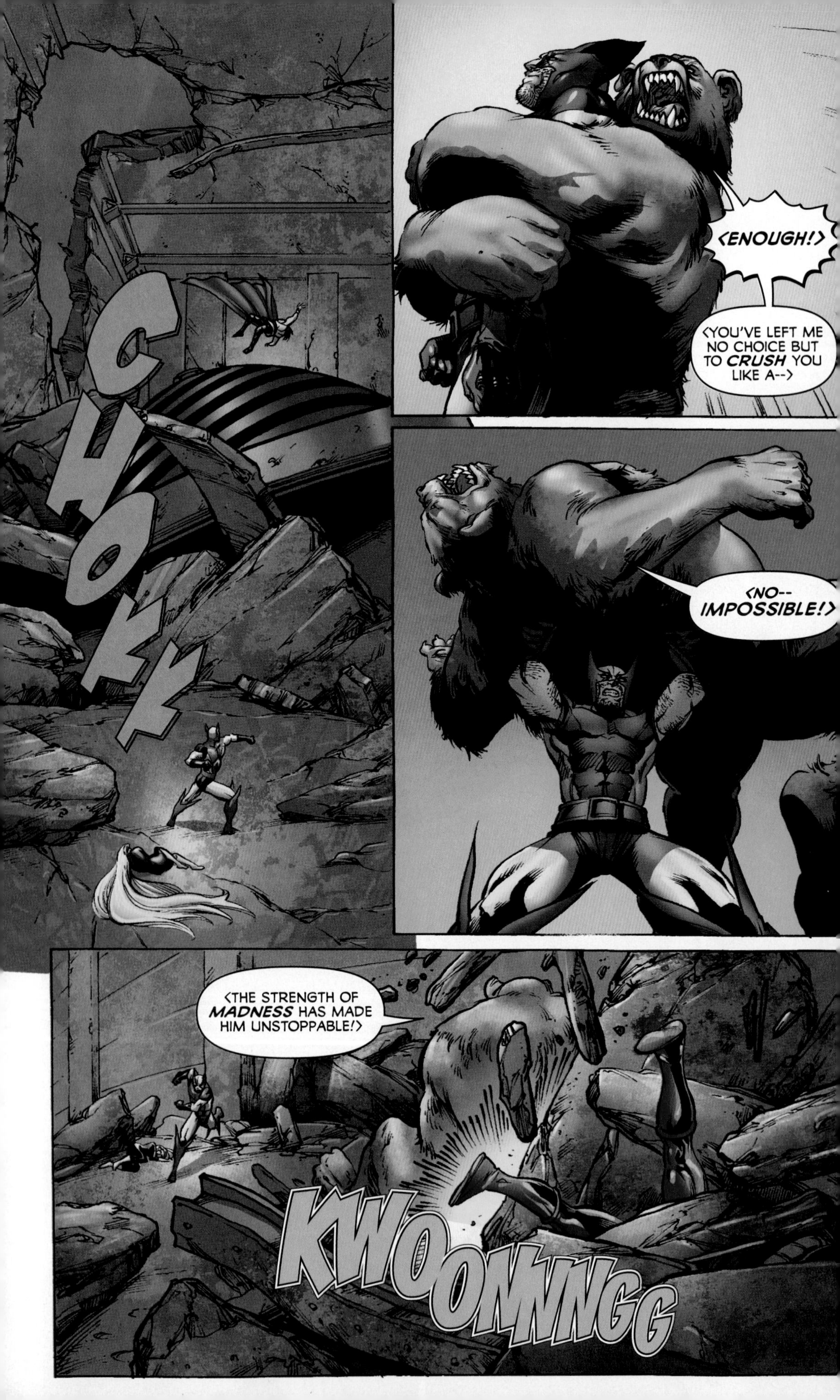
CHOKK
<ENOUGH!>
<YOU'VE LEFT ME NO CHOICE BUT TO CRUSH YOU LIKE A-->
<NO-- IMPOSSIBLE!>
<THE STRENGTH OF MADNESS HAS MADE HIM UNSTOPPABLE!>
KWOOONNNGG

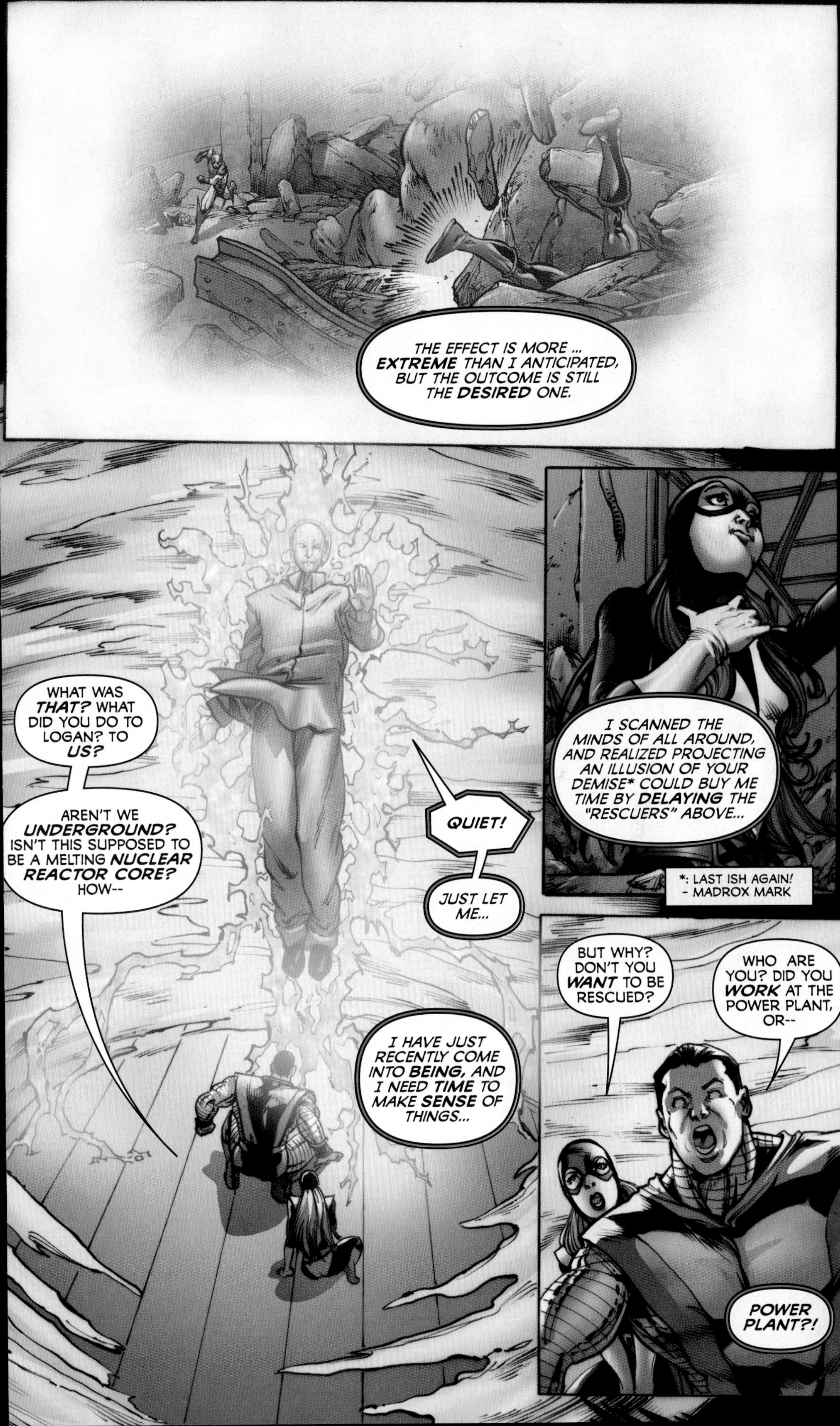
THE EFFECT IS MORE ... EXTREME THAN I ANTICIPATED, BUT THE OUTCOME IS STILL THE DESIRED ONE.
WHAT WAS THAT? WHAT DID YOU DO TO LOGAN? TO US?
AREN'T WE UNDERGROUND? ISN'T THIS SUPPOSED TO BE A MELTING NUCLEAR REACTOR CORE? HOW--
QUIET!
JUST LET ME...
I SCANNED THE MINDS OF ALL AROUND, AND REALIZED PROJECTING AN ILLUSION OF YOUR DEMISE* COULD BUY ME TIME BY DELAYING THE "RESCUERS" ABOVE...
*: LAST ISH AGAIN! - MADROX MARK
I HAVE JUST RECENTLY COME INTO BEING, AND I NEED TIME TO MAKE SENSE OF THINGS...
BUT WHY? DON'T YOU WANT TO BE RESCUED?
WHO ARE YOU? DID YOU WORK AT THE POWER PLANT, OR--
POWER PLANT?!

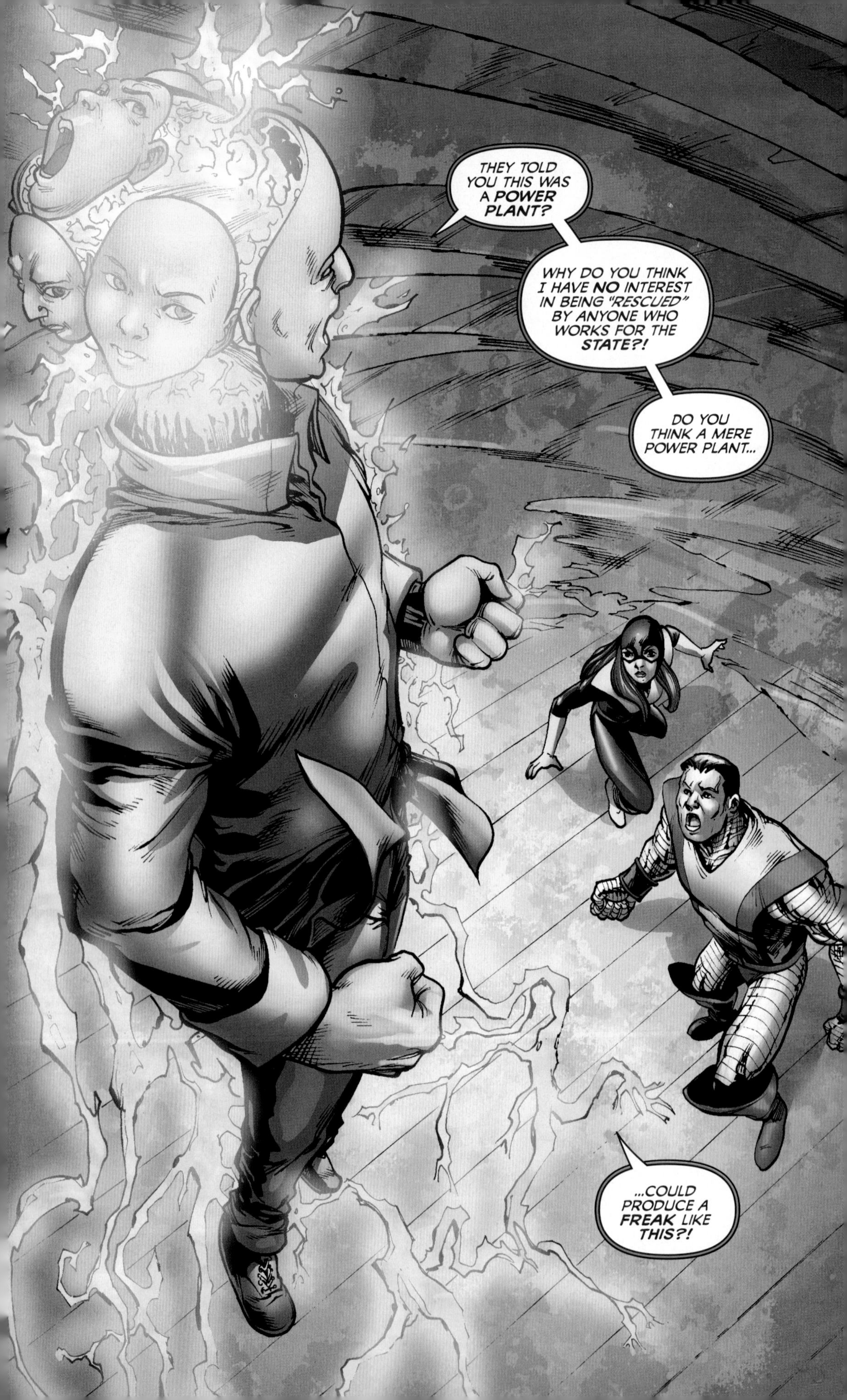
THEY TOLD YOU THIS WAS A **POWER PLANT?**
WHY DO YOU THINK I HAVE **NO** INTEREST IN BEING "RESCUED" BY ANYONE WHO WORKS FOR THE **STATE?!**
DO YOU THINK A MERE POWER PLANT...
...COULD PRODUCE A **FREAK** LIKE **THIS?!**

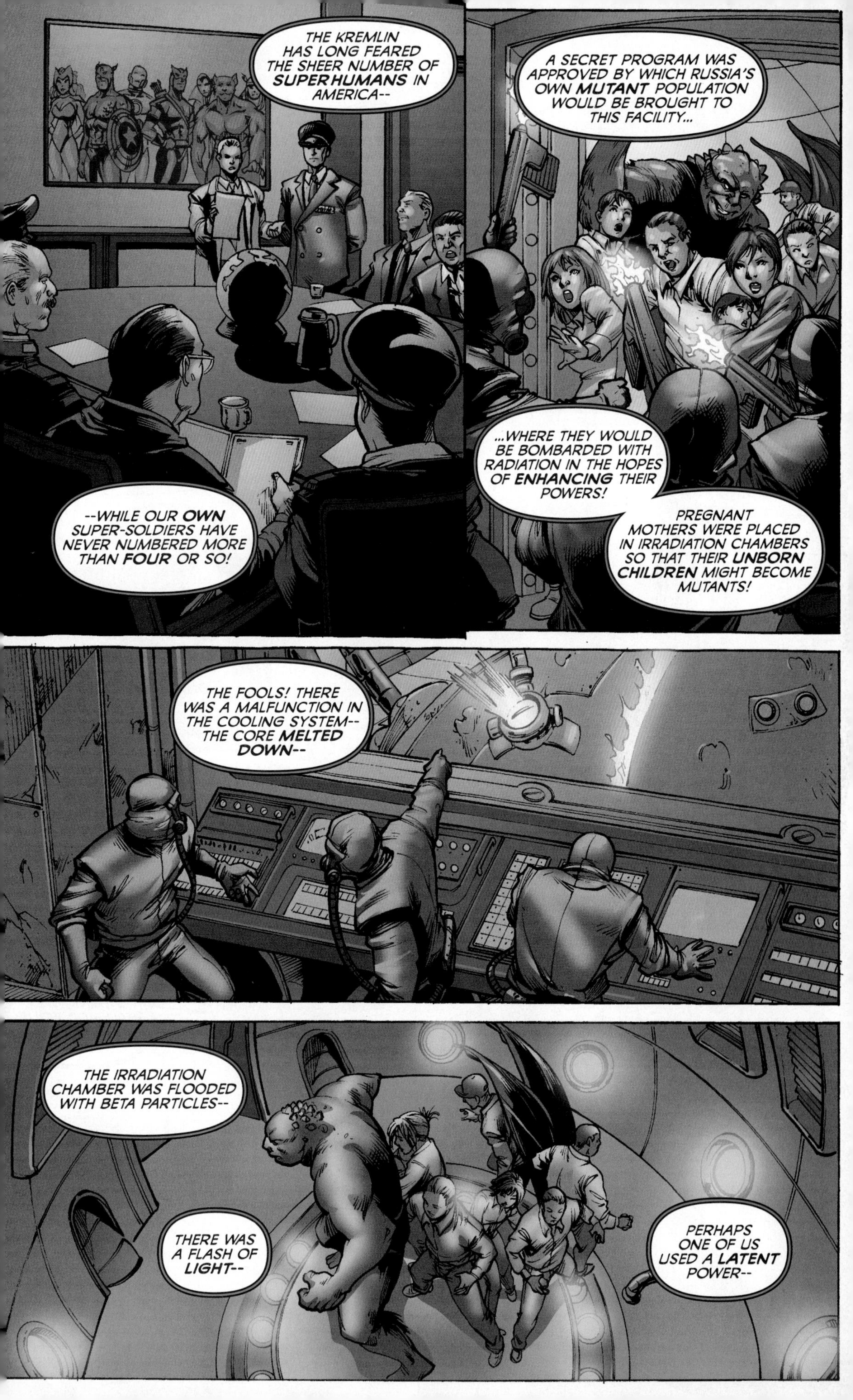
THE KREMLIN HAS LONG FEARED THE SHEER NUMBER OF SUPERHUMANS IN AMERICA--
--WHILE OUR OWN SUPER-SOLDIERS HAVE NEVER NUMBERED MORE THAN FOUR OR SO!
A SECRET PROGRAM WAS APPROVED BY WHICH RUSSIA'S OWN MUTANT POPULATION WOULD BE BROUGHT TO THIS FACILITY...
...WHERE THEY WOULD BE BOMBARDED WITH RADIATION IN THE HOPES OF ENHANCING THEIR POWERS!
PREGNANT MOTHERS WERE PLACED IN IRRADIATION CHAMBERS SO THAT THEIR UNBORN CHILDREN MIGHT BECOME MUTANTS!
THE FOOLS! THERE WAS A MALFUNCTION IN THE COOLING SYSTEM-- THE CORE MELTED DOWN--
THE IRRADIATION CHAMBER WAS FLOODED WITH BETA PARTICLES--
THERE WAS A FLASH OF LIGHT--
PERHAPS ONE OF US USED A LATENT POWER--

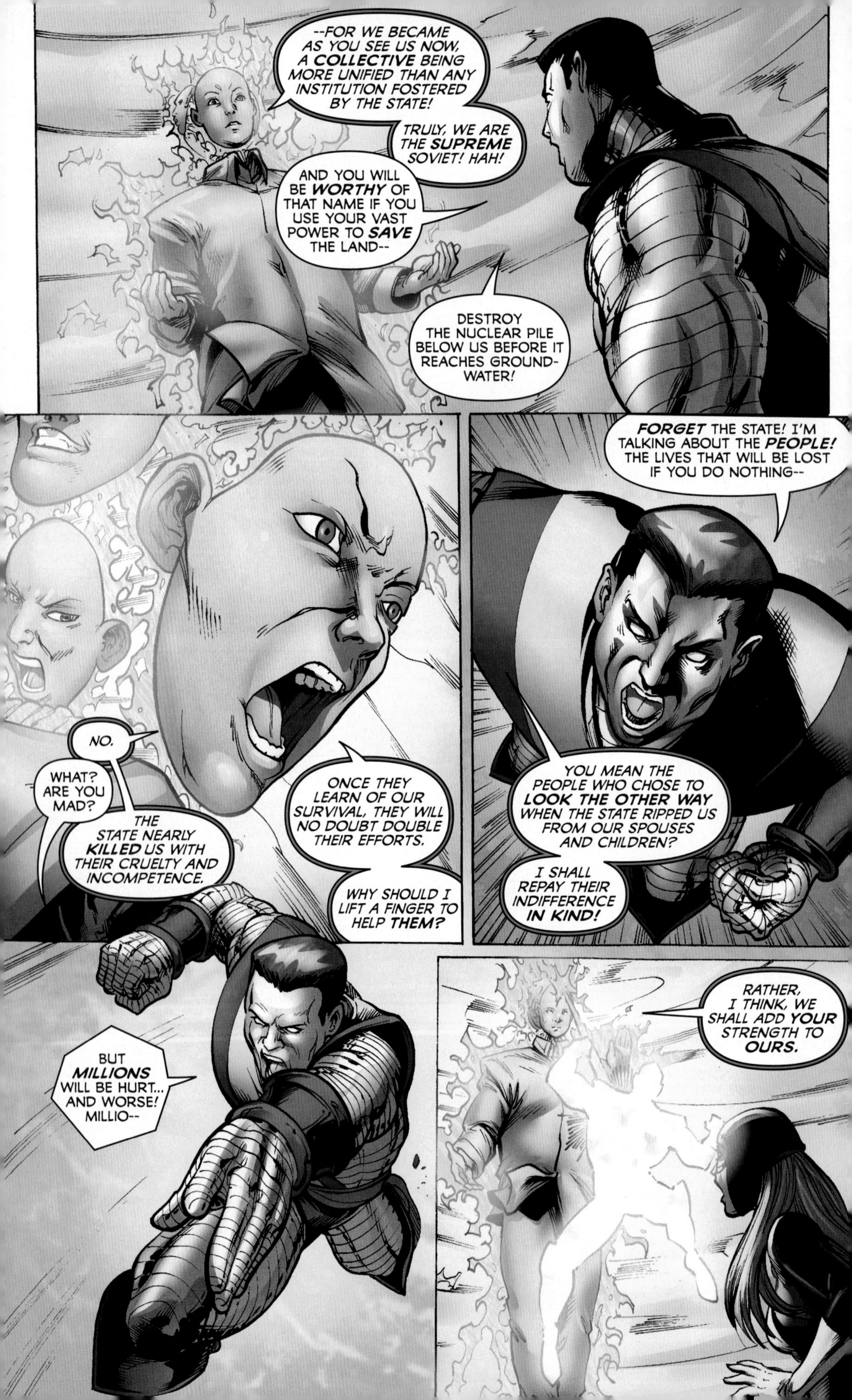

--FOR WE BECAME AS YOU SEE US NOW, A **COLLECTIVE** BEING MORE UNIFIED THAN ANY INSTITUTION FOSTERED BY THE STATE!
*TRULY, WE ARE THE **SUPREME** SOVIET! HAH!*
AND YOU WILL BE ***WORTHY*** OF THAT NAME IF YOU USE YOUR VAST POWER TO ***SAVE*** THE LAND--
DESTROY THE NUCLEAR PILE BELOW US BEFORE IT REACHES GROUND-WATER!
NO.
WHAT? ARE YOU MAD?
*THE STATE NEARLY **KILLED** US WITH THEIR CRUELTY AND INCOMPETENCE.*
ONCE THEY LEARN OF OUR SURVIVAL, THEY WILL NO DOUBT DOUBLE THEIR EFFORTS.
*WHY SHOULD I LIFT A FINGER TO HELP **THEM?***
FORGET THE STATE! I'M TALKING ABOUT THE ***PEOPLE!*** THE LIVES THAT WILL BE LOST IF YOU DO NOTHING--
*YOU MEAN THE PEOPLE WHO CHOSE TO **LOOK THE OTHER WAY** WHEN THE STATE RIPPED US FROM OUR SPOUSES AND CHILDREN?*
*I SHALL REPAY THEIR INDIFFERENCE **IN KIND!***
BUT ***MILLIONS*** WILL BE HURT... AND WORSE! MILLIO--
*RATHER, I THINK, WE SHALL ADD **YOUR** STRENGTH TO **OURS.***

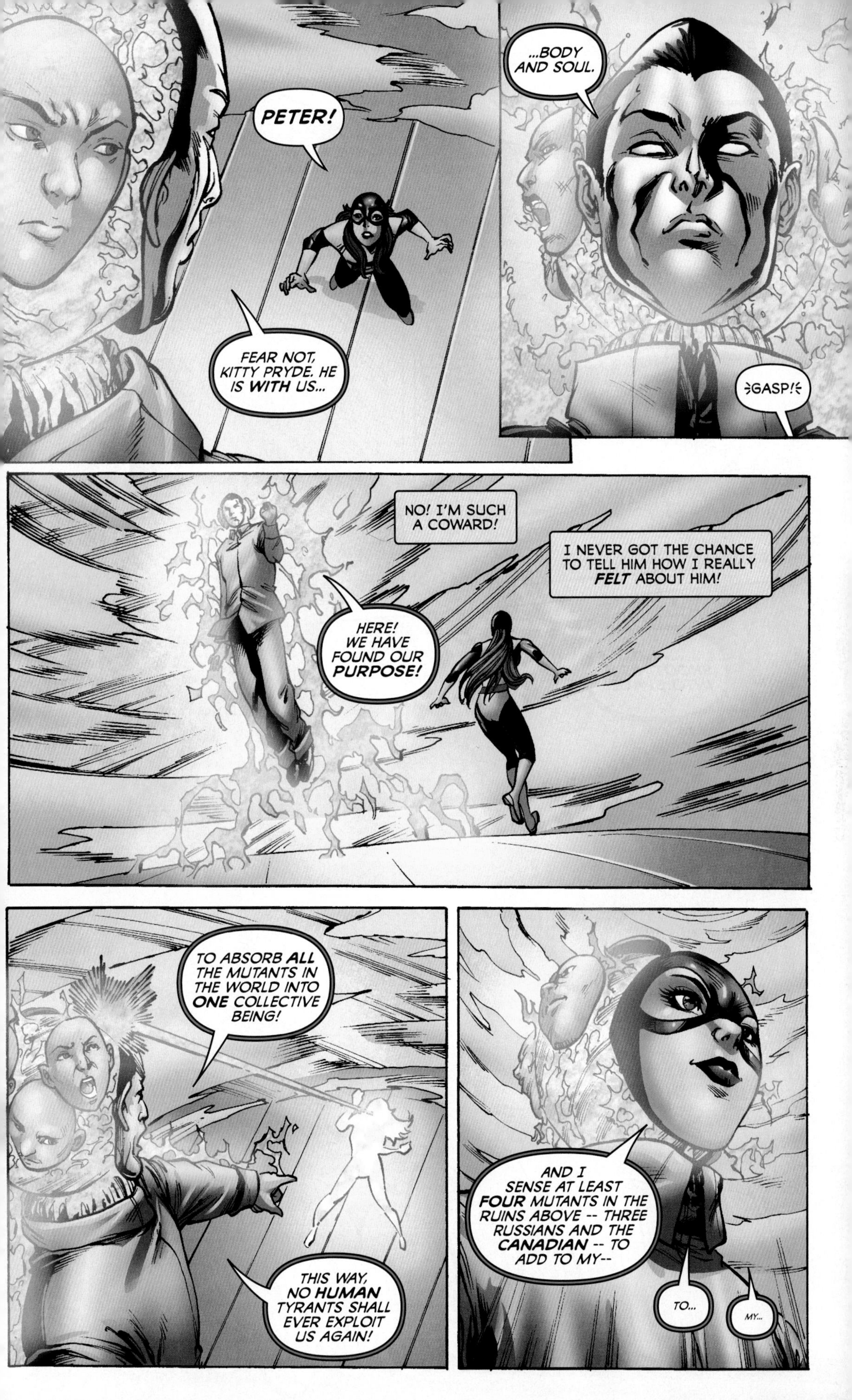
PETER!
FEAR NOT, KITTY PRYDE. HE IS WITH US...
...BODY AND SOUL.
GASP!
NO! I'M SUCH A COWARD!
I NEVER GOT THE CHANCE TO TELL HIM HOW I REALLY FELT ABOUT HIM!
HERE! WE HAVE FOUND OUR PURPOSE!
TO ABSORB ALL THE MUTANTS IN THE WORLD INTO ONE COLLECTIVE BEING!
THIS WAY, NO HUMAN TYRANTS SHALL EVER EXPLOIT US AGAIN!
AND I SENSE AT LEAST FOUR MUTANTS IN THE RUINS ABOVE -- THREE RUSSIANS AND THE CANADIAN -- TO ADD TO MY--
TO...
MY...

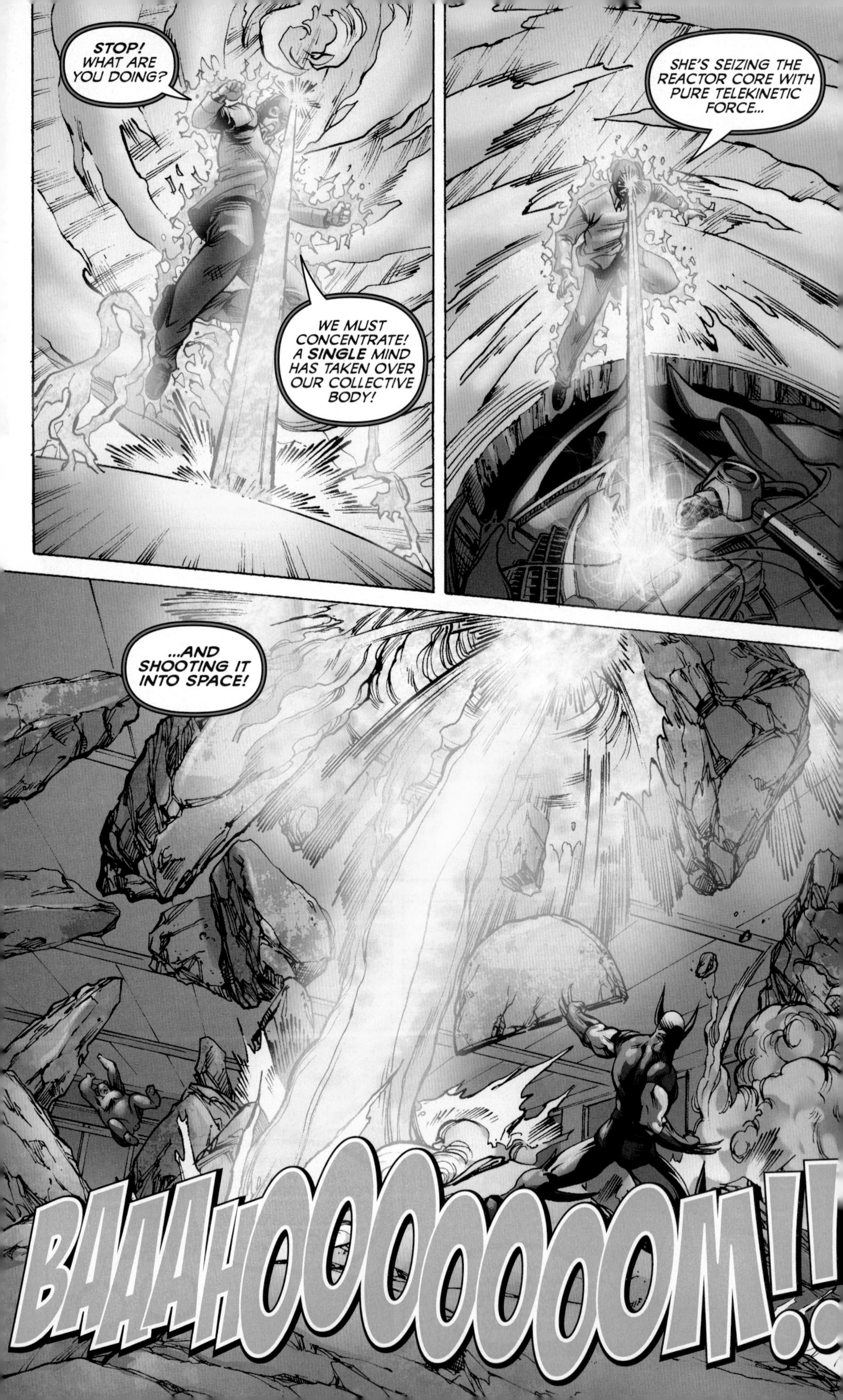
STOP! WHAT ARE YOU DOING?
WE MUST CONCENTRATE! A SINGLE MIND HAS TAKEN OVER OUR COLLECTIVE BODY!
SHE'S SEIZING THE REACTOR CORE WITH PURE TELEKINETIC FORCE...
...AND SHOOTING IT INTO SPACE!
BAAAHOOOOOOOM!!

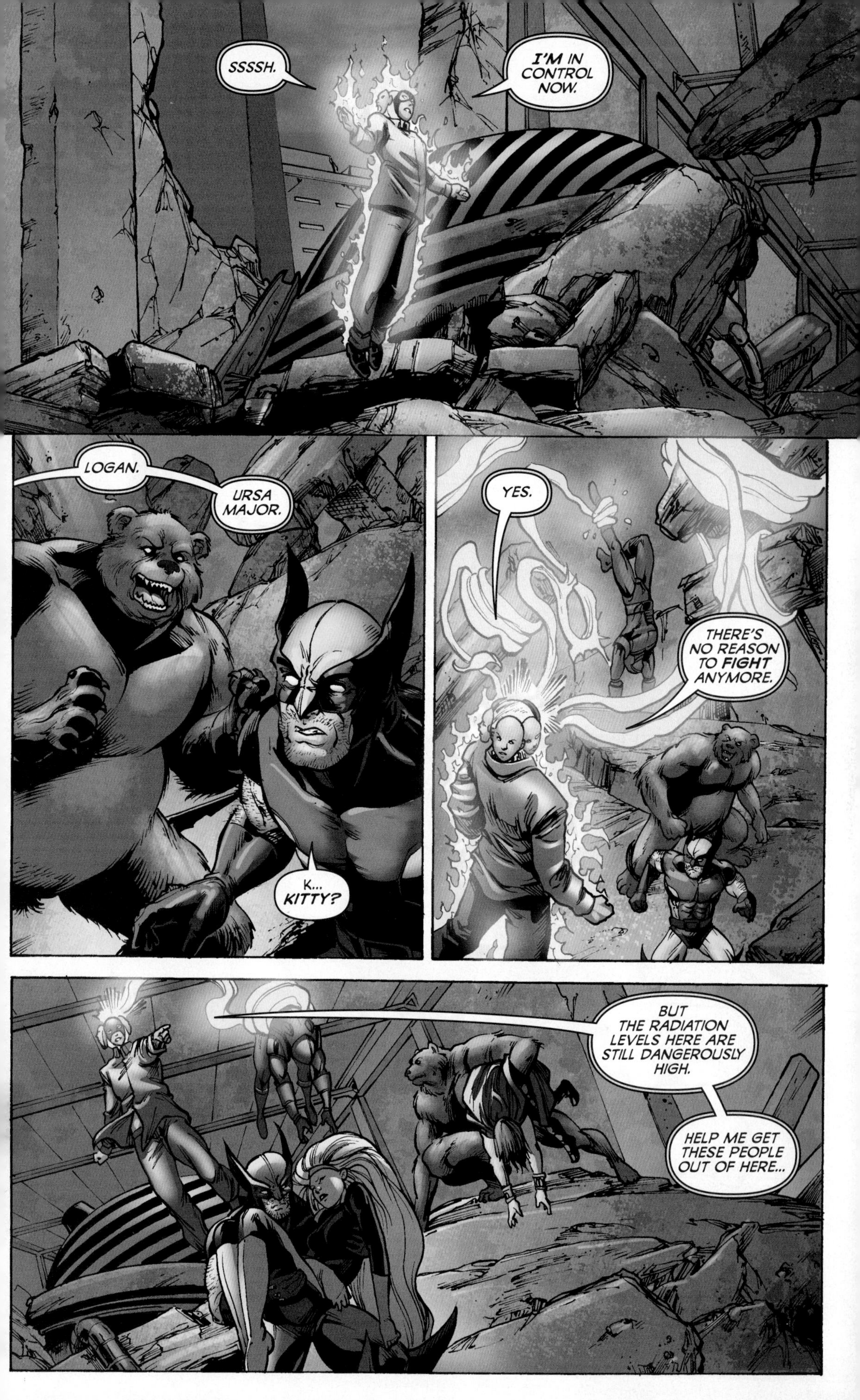
SSSSH.
I'M IN CONTROL NOW.
LOGAN.
URSA MAJOR.
K... KITTY?
YES.
THERE'S NO REASON TO FIGHT ANYMORE.
BUT THE RADIATION LEVELS HERE ARE STILL DANGEROUSLY HIGH.
HELP ME GET THESE PEOPLE OUT OF HERE...

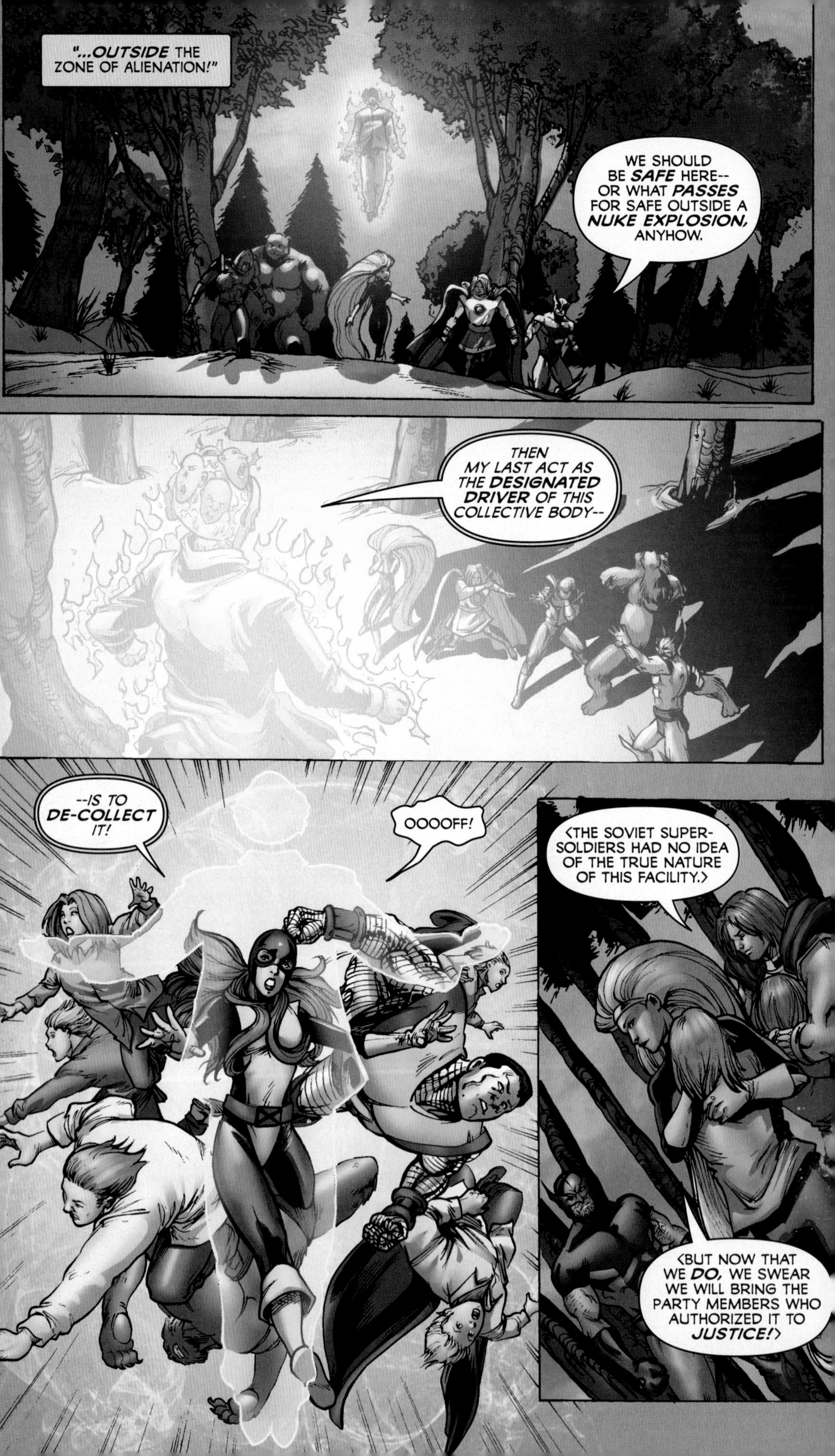
"...OUTSIDE THE ZONE OF ALIENATION!"
WE SHOULD BE SAFE HERE-- OR WHAT PASSES FOR SAFE OUTSIDE A NUKE EXPLOSION, ANYHOW.
THEN MY LAST ACT AS THE DESIGNATED DRIVER OF THIS COLLECTIVE BODY--
--IS TO DE-COLLECT IT!
OOOOFF!
<THE SOVIET SUPER-SOLDIERS HAD NO IDEA OF THE TRUE NATURE OF THIS FACILITY.>
<BUT NOW THAT WE DO, WE SWEAR WE WILL BRING THE PARTY MEMBERS WHO AUTHORIZED IT TO JUSTICE!>

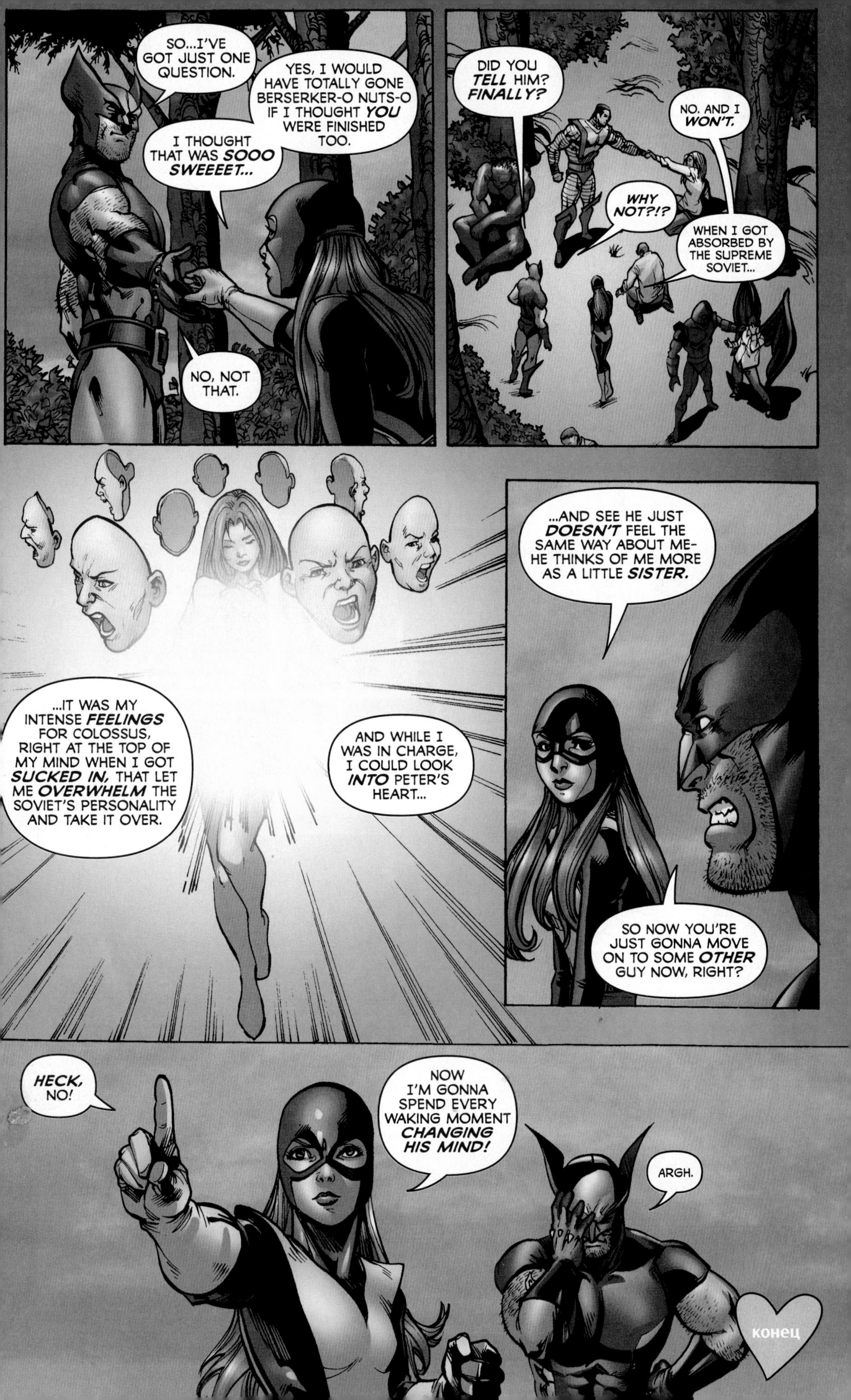

SO...I'VE GOT JUST ONE QUESTION.
I THOUGHT THAT WAS SOOO SWEEEET...
YES, I WOULD HAVE TOTALLY GONE BERSERKER-O NUTS-O IF I THOUGHT YOU WERE FINISHED TOO.
NO, NOT THAT.
DID YOU TELL HIM? FINALLY?
NO. AND I WON'T.
WHY NOT?!?
WHEN I GOT ABSORBED BY THE SUPREME SOVIET...
...IT WAS MY INTENSE FEELINGS FOR COLOSSUS, RIGHT AT THE TOP OF MY MIND WHEN I GOT SUCKED IN, THAT LET ME OVERWHELM THE SOVIET'S PERSONALITY AND TAKE IT OVER.
AND WHILE I WAS IN CHARGE, I COULD LOOK INTO PETER'S HEART...
...AND SEE HE JUST DOESN'T FEEL THE SAME WAY ABOUT ME- HE THINKS OF ME MORE AS A LITTLE SISTER.
SO NOW YOU'RE JUST GONNA MOVE ON TO SOME OTHER GUY NOW, RIGHT?
HECK, NO!
NOW I'M GONNA SPEND EVERY WAKING MOMENT CHANGING HIS MIND!
ARGH.
конец

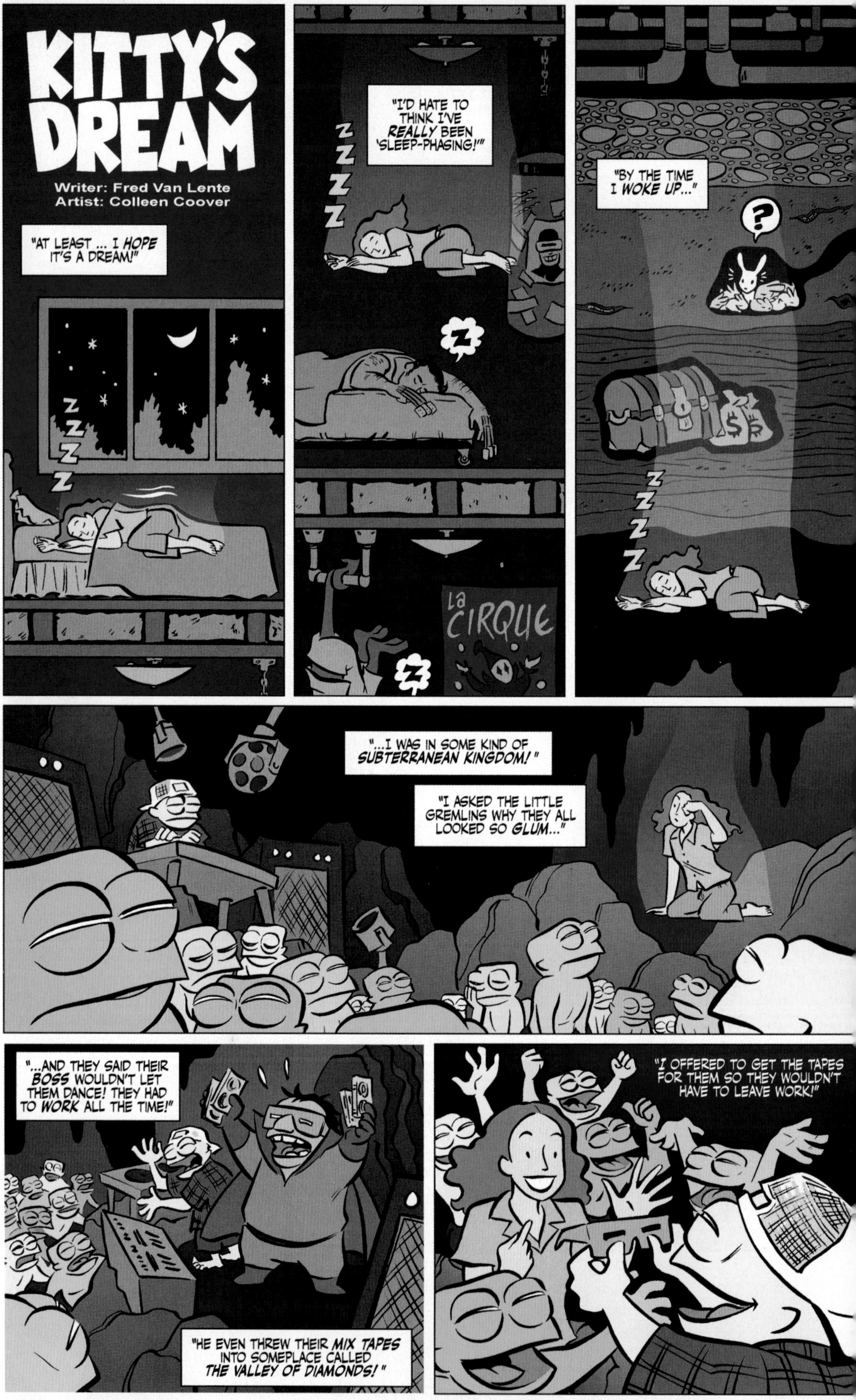
KITTY'S DREAM
Writer: Fred Van Lente
Artist: Colleen Coover
"AT LEAST ... I HOPE IT'S A DREAM!"
Z Z Z Z
"I'D HATE TO THINK I'VE REALLY BEEN 'SLEEP-PHASING!'"
Z Z Z Z
Z
LA CIRQUE
Z
"BY THE TIME I WOKE UP..."
?
Z Z Z Z
"...I WAS IN SOME KIND OF SUBTERRANEAN KINGDOM!"
"I ASKED THE LITTLE GREMLINS WHY THEY ALL LOOKED SO GLUM..."
"...AND THEY SAID THEIR BOSS WOULDN'T LET THEM DANCE! THEY HAD TO WORK ALL THE TIME!"
"HE EVEN THREW THEIR MIX TAPES INTO SOMEPLACE CALLED THE VALLEY OF DIAMONDS!"
"I OFFERED TO GET THE TAPES FOR THEM SO THEY WOULDN'T HAVE TO LEAVE WORK!"

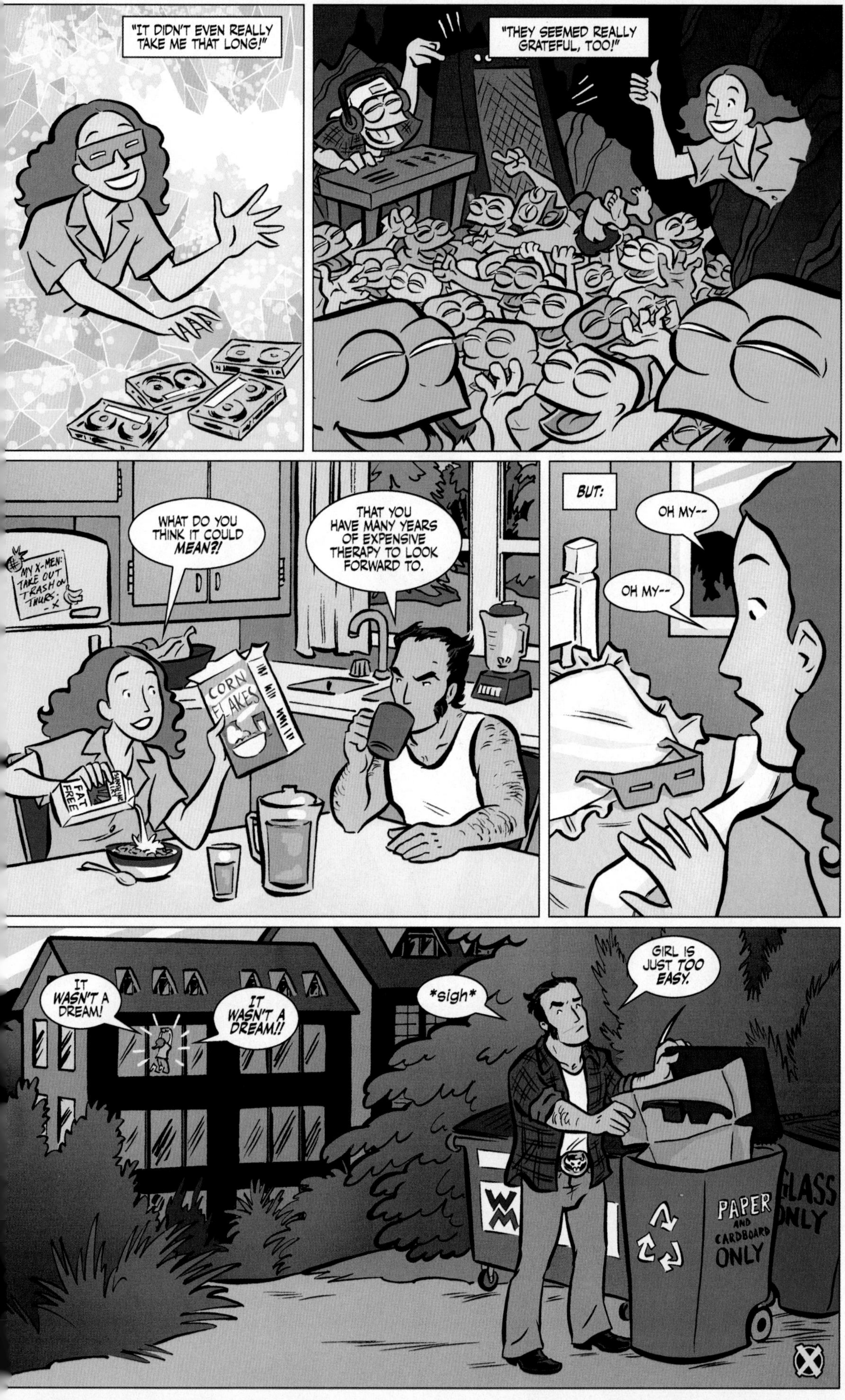
"IT DIDN'T EVEN REALLY TAKE ME THAT LONG!"
"THEY SEEMED REALLY GRATEFUL, TOO!"
MY X-MEN: TAKE OUT TRASH ON THURS. -X
WHAT DO YOU THINK IT COULD MEAN?!
THAT YOU HAVE MANY YEARS OF EXPENSIVE THERAPY TO LOOK FORWARD TO.
CORN FLAKES
FAT FREE
BUT:
OH MY--
OH MY--
IT WASN'T A DREAM!
IT WASN'T A DREAM!!
sigh
GIRL IS JUST TOO EASY.
PAPER AND CARDBOARD ONLY
GLASS ONLY

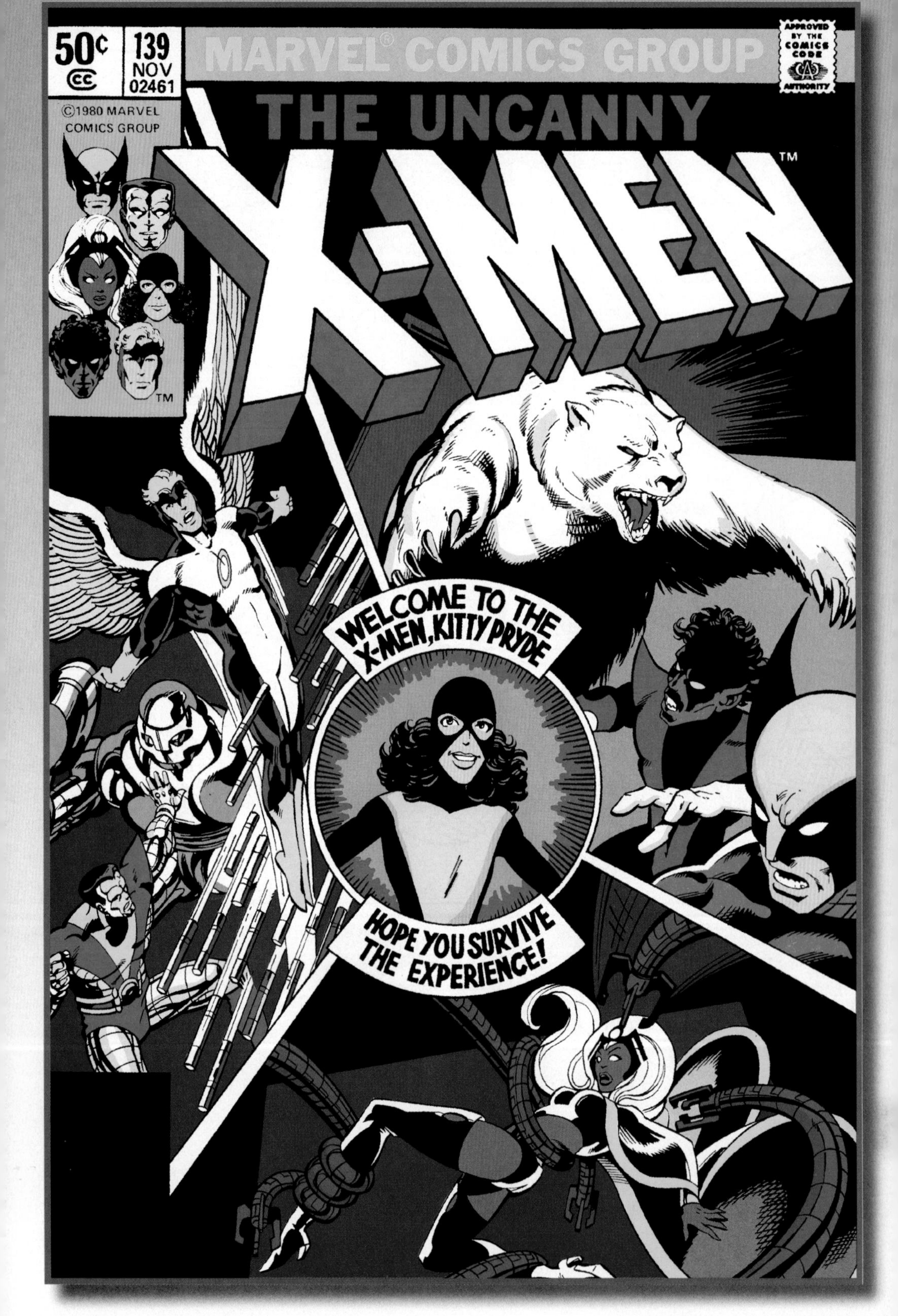
50¢
CC
139
NOV
02461
MARVEL® COMICS GROUP
APPROVED BY THE COMICS CODE AUTHORITY
©1980 MARVEL COMICS GROUP
THE UNCANNY
X-MEN™
TM
WELCOME TO THE X-MEN, KITTY PRYDE
HOPE YOU SURVIVE THE EXPERIENCE!

Cyclops. Storm. Nightcrawler. Wolverine. Colossus. Children of the atom, students of Charles Xavier, MUTANTS — feared and hated by the world they have sworn to protect. These are the STRANGEST heroes of all!

Stan Lee PRESENTS: THE UNCANNY X-MEN!™

CHRIS CLAREMONT WRITER | JOHN BYRNE PLOT-PENCILS | TERRY AUSTIN INKER | TOM ORZECHOWSKI, letterer GLYNIS WEIN, colorist | LOUISE JONES EDITOR | JIM SHOOTER Ed. in CHIEF

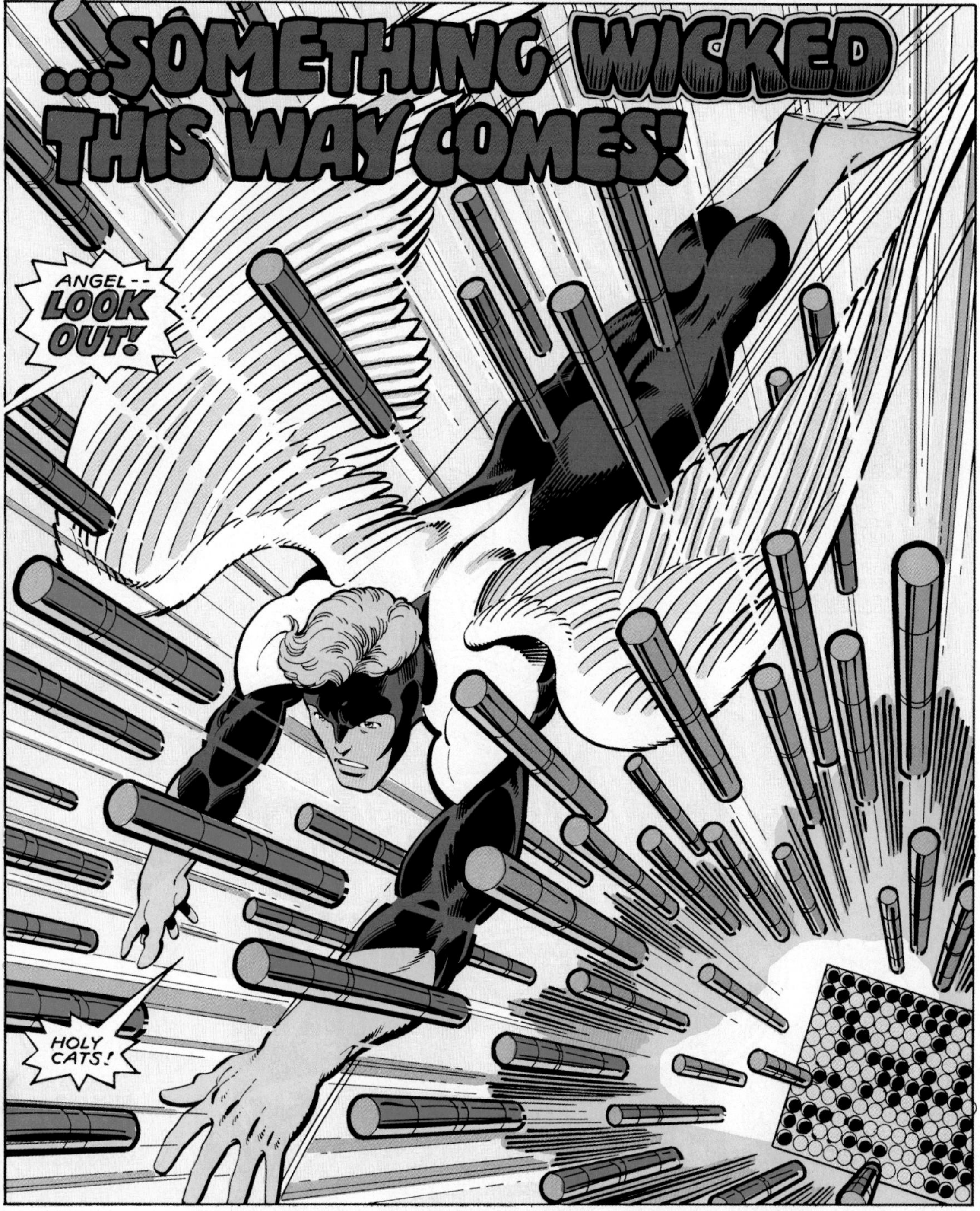
...SOMETHING WICKED THIS WAY COMES!
ANGEL-- LOOK OUT!
HOLY CATS!

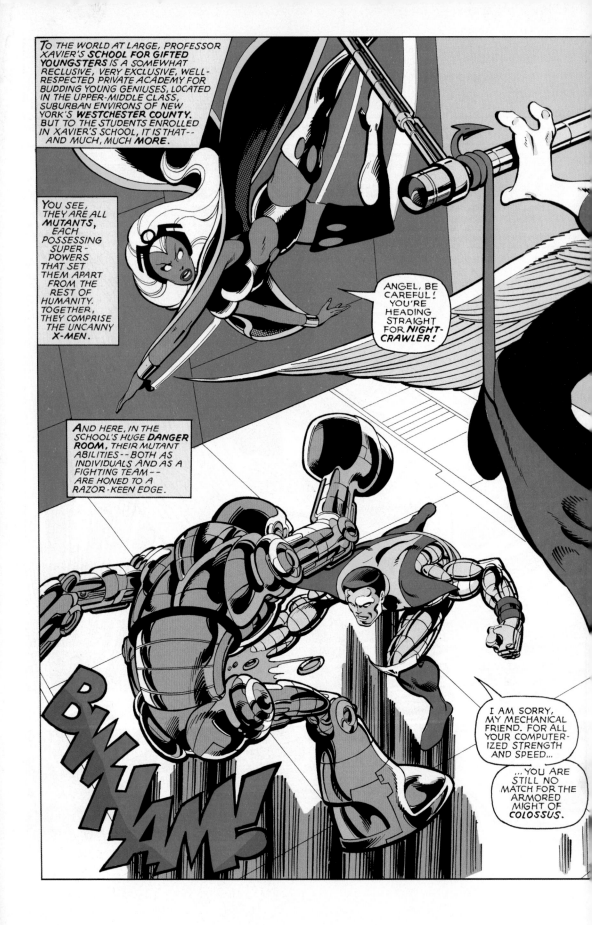

TO THE WORLD AT LARGE, PROFESSOR XAVIER'S **SCHOOL FOR GIFTED YOUNGSTERS** IS A SOMEWHAT RECLUSIVE, VERY EXCLUSIVE, WELL-RESPECTED PRIVATE ACADEMY FOR BUDDING YOUNG GENIUSES, LOCATED IN THE UPPER-MIDDLE CLASS, SUBURBAN ENVIRONS OF NEW YORK'S **WESTCHESTER COUNTY.** BUT TO THE STUDENTS ENROLLED IN XAVIER'S SCHOOL, IT IS THAT-- AND MUCH, MUCH **MORE.**

YOU SEE, THEY ARE ALL **MUTANTS,** EACH POSSESSING SUPER-POWERS THAT SET THEM APART FROM THE REST OF HUMANITY. TOGETHER, THEY COMPRISE THE UNCANNY **X-MEN.**

ANGEL, BE CAREFUL! YOU'RE HEADING STRAIGHT FOR **NIGHT-CRAWLER!**

AND HERE, IN THE SCHOOL'S HUGE **DANGER ROOM,** THEIR MUTANT ABILITIES--BOTH AS INDIVIDUALS AND AS A FIGHTING TEAM-- ARE HONED TO A RAZOR-KEEN EDGE.

BWHAMM!

I AM SORRY, MY MECHANICAL FRIEND. FOR ALL YOUR COMPUTER-IZED STRENGTH AND SPEED...

...YOU ARE STILL NO MATCH FOR THE ARMORED MIGHT OF **COLOSSUS.**

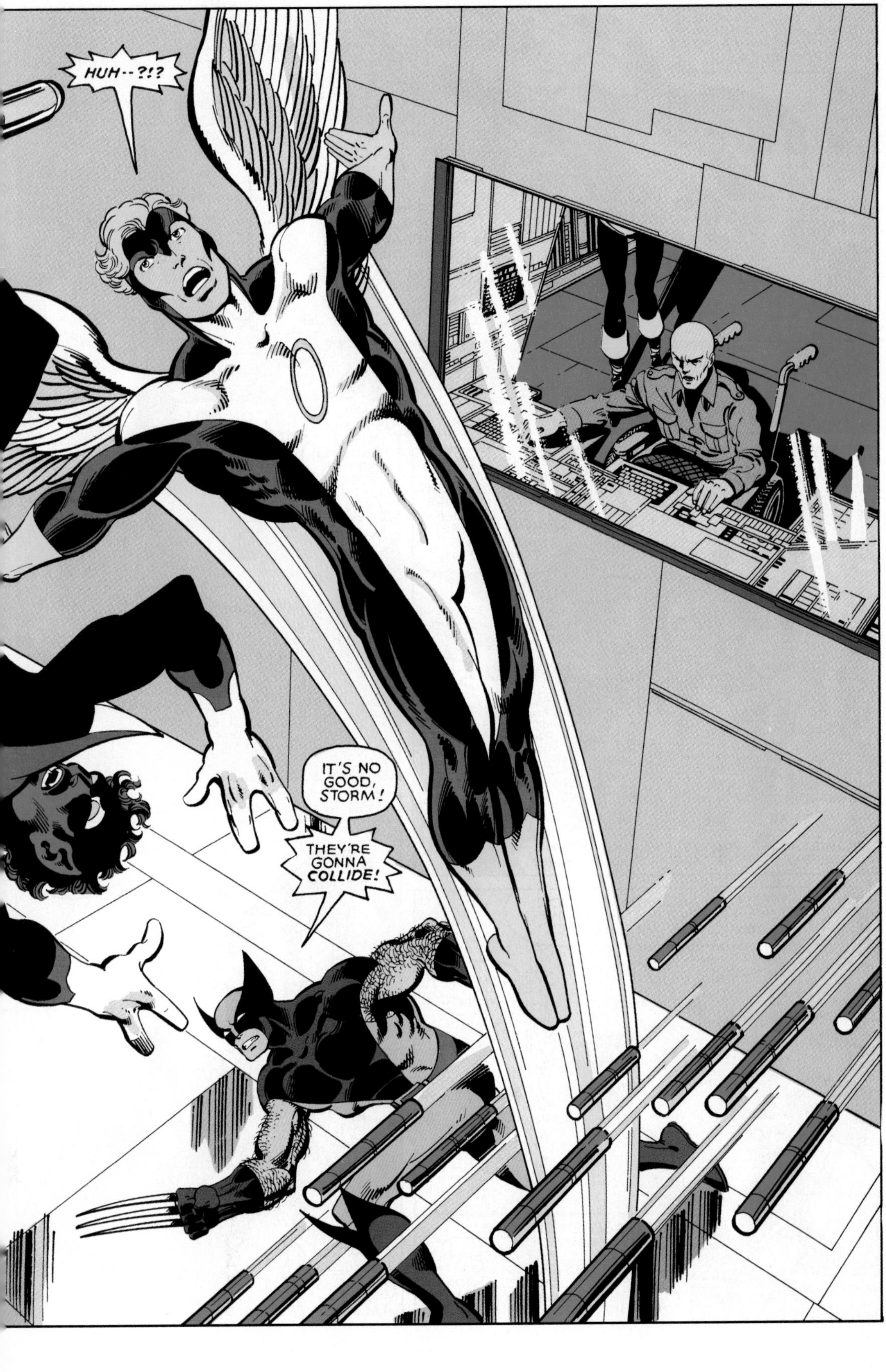
HUH--?!?
IT'S NO GOOD, STORM!
THEY'RE GONNA COLLIDE!

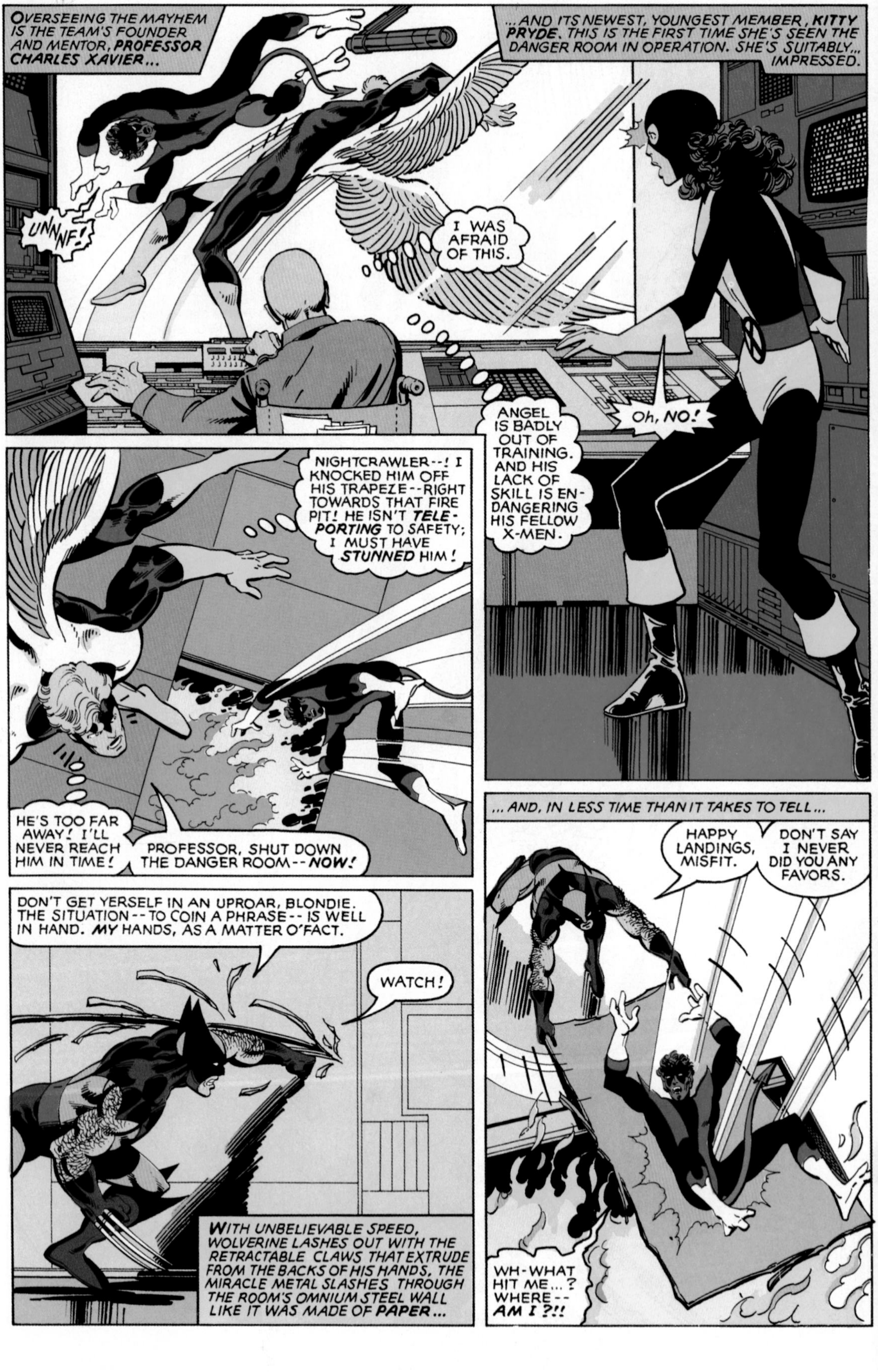
OVERSEEING THE MAYHEM IS THE TEAM'S FOUNDER AND MENTOR, PROFESSOR CHARLES XAVIER...
...AND ITS NEWEST, YOUNGEST MEMBER, KITTY PRYDE. THIS IS THE FIRST TIME SHE'S SEEN THE DANGER ROOM IN OPERATION. SHE'S SUITABLY... IMPRESSED.
UNNNF!
I WAS AFRAID OF THIS.
ANGEL IS BADLY OUT OF TRAINING. AND HIS LACK OF SKILL IS ENDANGERING HIS FELLOW X-MEN.
Oh, NO!
NIGHTCRAWLER--! I KNOCKED HIM OFF HIS TRAPEZE--RIGHT TOWARDS THAT FIRE PIT! HE ISN'T TELEPORTING TO SAFETY; I MUST HAVE STUNNED HIM!
HE'S TOO FAR AWAY! I'LL NEVER REACH HIM IN TIME!
PROFESSOR, SHUT DOWN THE DANGER ROOM--NOW!
DON'T GET YERSELF IN AN UPROAR, BLONDIE. THE SITUATION--TO COIN A PHRASE--IS WELL IN HAND. MY HANDS, AS A MATTER O'FACT.
WATCH!
WITH UNBELIEVABLE SPEED, WOLVERINE LASHES OUT WITH THE RETRACTABLE CLAWS THAT EXTRUDE FROM THE BACKS OF HIS HANDS. THE MIRACLE METAL SLASHES THROUGH THE ROOM'S OMNIUM STEEL WALL LIKE IT WAS MADE OF PAPER...
...AND, IN LESS TIME THAN IT TAKES TO TELL...
HAPPY LANDINGS, MISFIT.
DON'T SAY I NEVER DID YOU ANY FAVORS.
WH-WHAT HIT ME...? WHERE--AM I?!!

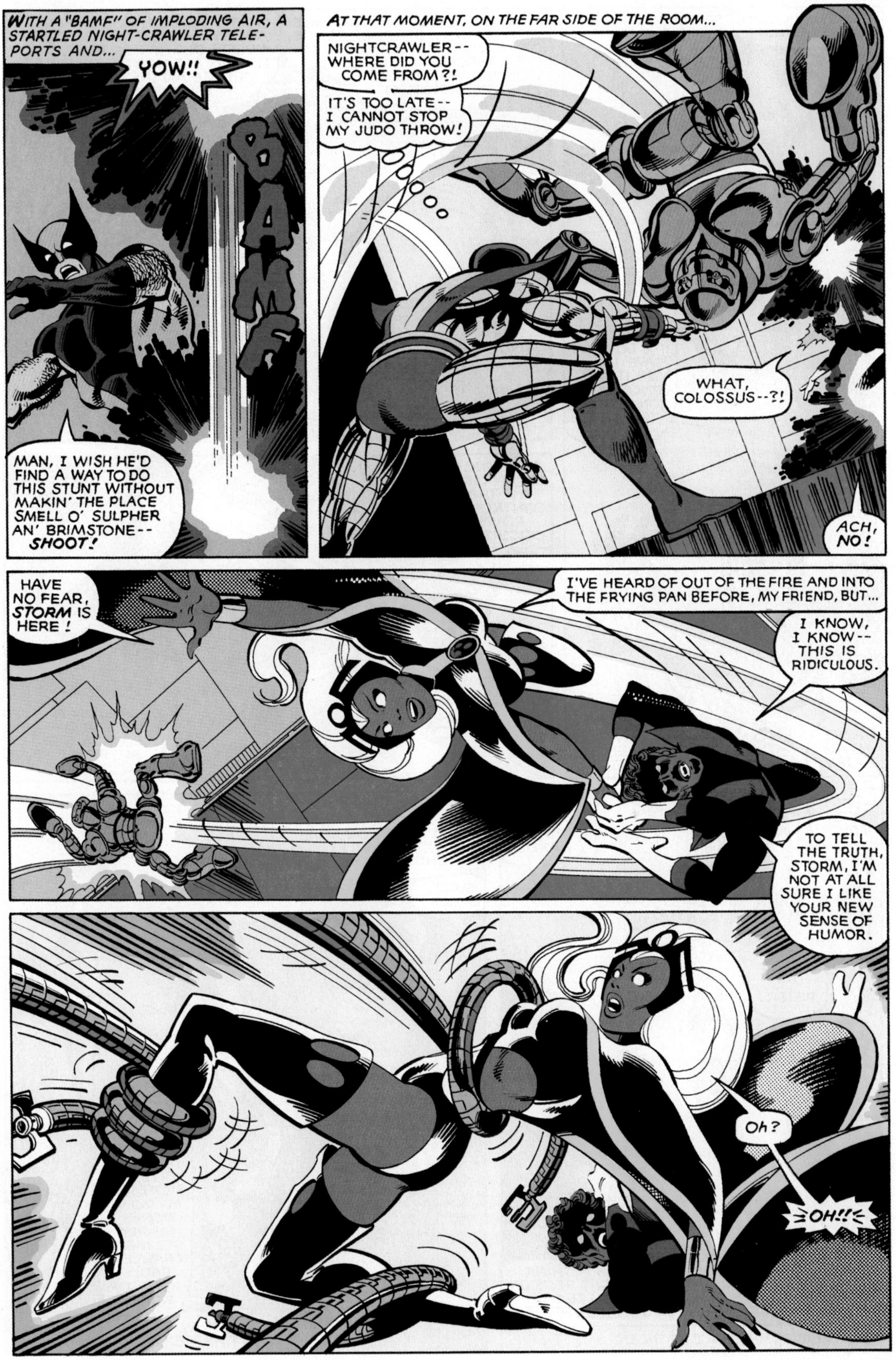
WITH A "BAMF" OF IMPLODING AIR, A STARTLED NIGHT-CRAWLER TELE-PORTS AND...
YOW!!
BAMF
MAN, I WISH HE'D FIND A WAY TO DO THIS STUNT WITHOUT MAKIN' THE PLACE SMELL O' SULPHER AN' BRIMSTONE-- SHOOT!
AT THAT MOMENT, ON THE FAR SIDE OF THE ROOM...
NIGHTCRAWLER-- WHERE DID YOU COME FROM?!
IT'S TOO LATE-- I CANNOT STOP MY JUDO THROW!
WHAT, COLOSSUS--?!
ACH, NO!
HAVE NO FEAR, STORM IS HERE!
I'VE HEARD OF OUT OF THE FIRE AND INTO THE FRYING PAN BEFORE, MY FRIEND, BUT...
I KNOW, I KNOW-- THIS IS RIDICULOUS.
TO TELL THE TRUTH, STORM, I'M NOT AT ALL SURE I LIKE YOUR NEW SENSE OF HUMOR.
Oh?
OH!!

COLOSSUS, CATCH NIGHTCRAWLER!

SORRY TO DROP YOU LIKE THIS, KURT...

...BUT I'LL HAVE A BETTER CHANCE OF DEALING WITH THESE TENTACLES IF I DON'T HAVE TO SPLIT MY CONCENTRATION BETWEEN THEM AND YOU.

I HAVE HIM, STORM.

I WILL EVEN BE GENTLE.

Hmm -- I'M NOT THE ONLY ONE DEVELOPING A STRANGE SENSE OF HUMOR. AFTER ALL WE'VE BEEN THROUGH LATELY, I WONDER IF I SHOULD EVEN BE SURPRISED.

THAT'S SOMETHING TO THINK ABOUT -- *AFTER* I'VE GOTTEN MYSELF OUT OF THIS TRAP. I'LL USE MY *ELEMENTAL* POWERS TO CREATE AN INSTANT MINI-THUNDERSHOWER.

THERE WE ARE.

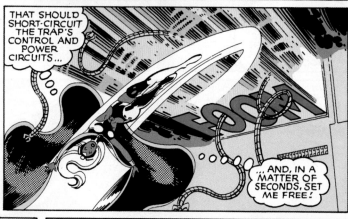

THAT SHOULD SHORT-CIRCUIT THE TRAP'S CONTROL AND POWER CIRCUITS...

...AND, IN A MATTER OF SECONDS, SET ME *FREE!*

WELL DONE, ORORO!

I GOTTA ADMIT, DARLIN'...

THANK YOU, PETER.

...I'M BEGINNING TA THINK CHARLEY MADE THE RIGHT DECISION WHEN HE NAMED YOU *TEAM LEADER* AFTER CYCLOPS LEFT. *

*ON A LEAVE OF ABSENCE, AT THE END OF LAST ISSUE.

WOLVERINE, CALL ME 'PROFESSOR,' 'PROFESSOR X', 'PROFESSOR XAVIER', OR EVEN, IF YOU MUST, 'CHARLES'. BUT NOT 'CHARLEY'. IS THAT UNDERSTOOD?

SURE, CHUCK.

Uh, GUYS, IS IT *SAFE* TO COME IN NOW?

I KNOW WHAT YOU'RE GOING TO SAY, PROFESSOR. MY DUMB MOVES NEARLY GOT NIGHT-CRAWLER BADLY HURT--OR WORSE.

I'M SORRY. IT WON'T HAPPEN AGAIN.

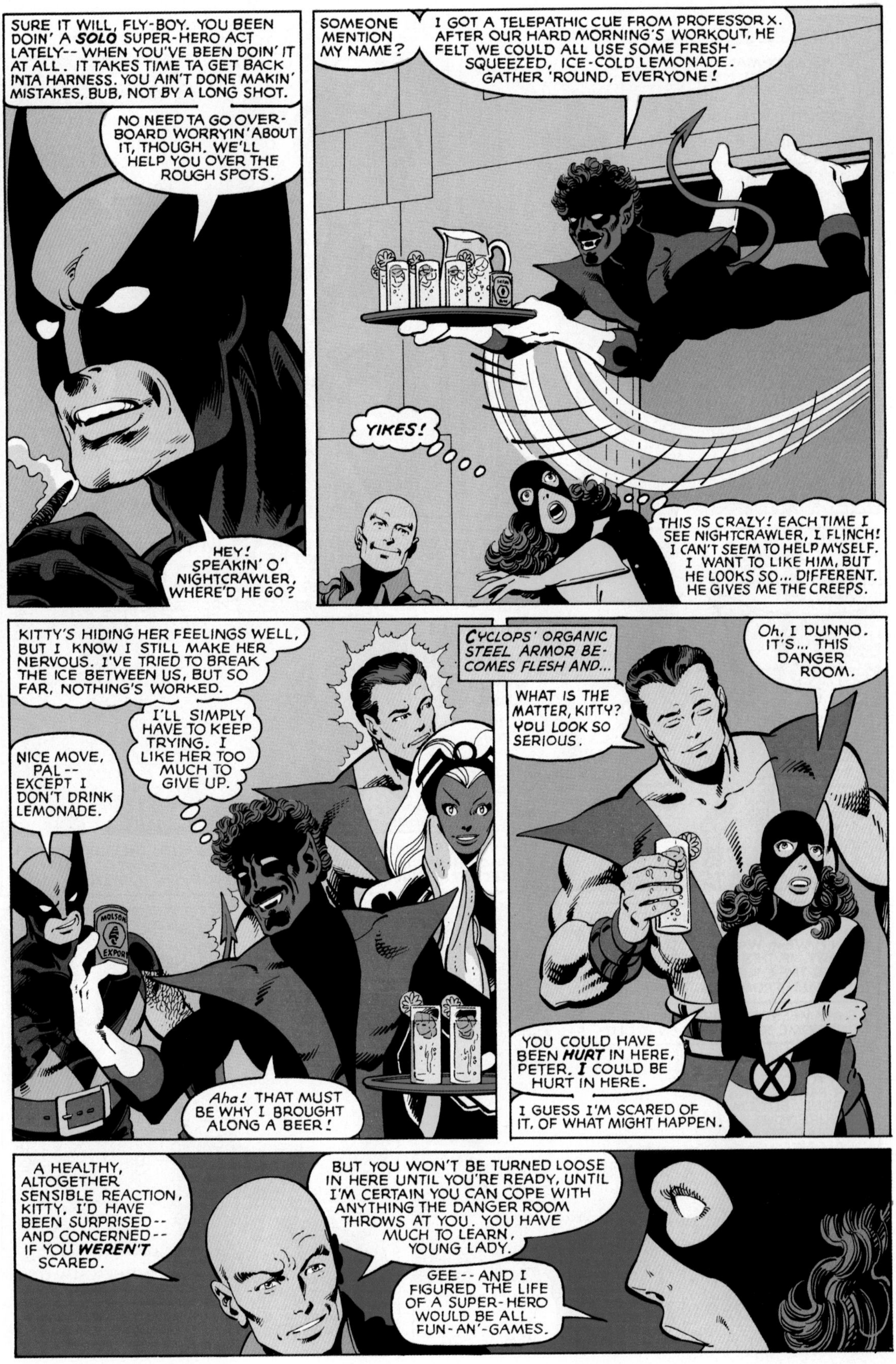

SURE IT WILL, FLY-BOY. YOU BEEN DOIN' A SOLO SUPER-HERO ACT LATELY-- WHEN YOU'VE BEEN DOIN' IT AT ALL. IT TAKES TIME TA GET BACK INTA HARNESS. YOU AIN'T DONE MAKIN' MISTAKES, BUB, NOT BY A LONG SHOT.
NO NEED TA GO OVER-BOARD WORRYIN' ABOUT IT, THOUGH. WE'LL HELP YOU OVER THE ROUGH SPOTS.
HEY! SPEAKIN' O' NIGHTCRAWLER, WHERE'D HE GO?
SOMEONE MENTION MY NAME?
I GOT A TELEPATHIC CUE FROM PROFESSOR X. AFTER OUR HARD MORNING'S WORKOUT, HE FELT WE COULD ALL USE SOME FRESH-SQUEEZED, ICE-COLD LEMONADE. GATHER 'ROUND, EVERYONE!
YIKES!
THIS IS CRAZY! EACH TIME I SEE NIGHTCRAWLER, I FLINCH! I CAN'T SEEM TO HELP MYSELF. I WANT TO LIKE HIM, BUT HE LOOKS SO... DIFFERENT. HE GIVES ME THE CREEPS.
KITTY'S HIDING HER FEELINGS WELL, BUT I KNOW I STILL MAKE HER NERVOUS. I'VE TRIED TO BREAK THE ICE BETWEEN US, BUT SO FAR, NOTHING'S WORKED.
I'LL SIMPLY HAVE TO KEEP TRYING. I LIKE HER TOO MUCH TO GIVE UP.
NICE MOVE, PAL-- EXCEPT I DON'T DRINK LEMONADE.
MOLSON EXPORT
Aha! THAT MUST BE WHY I BROUGHT ALONG A BEER!
CYCLOPS' ORGANIC STEEL ARMOR BECOMES FLESH AND...
WHAT IS THE MATTER, KITTY? YOU LOOK SO SERIOUS.
Oh, I DUNNO. IT'S... THIS DANGER ROOM.
YOU COULD HAVE BEEN HURT IN HERE, PETER. I COULD BE HURT IN HERE.
I GUESS I'M SCARED OF IT, OF WHAT MIGHT HAPPEN.
A HEALTHY, ALTOGETHER SENSIBLE REACTION, KITTY. I'D HAVE BEEN SURPRISED-- AND CONCERNED-- IF YOU WEREN'T SCARED.
BUT YOU WON'T BE TURNED LOOSE IN HERE UNTIL YOU'RE READY, UNTIL I'M CERTAIN YOU CAN COPE WITH ANYTHING THE DANGER ROOM THROWS AT YOU. YOU HAVE MUCH TO LEARN, YOUNG LADY.
GEE-- AND I FIGURED THE LIFE OF A SUPER-HERO WOULD BE ALL FUN-AN'-GAMES.

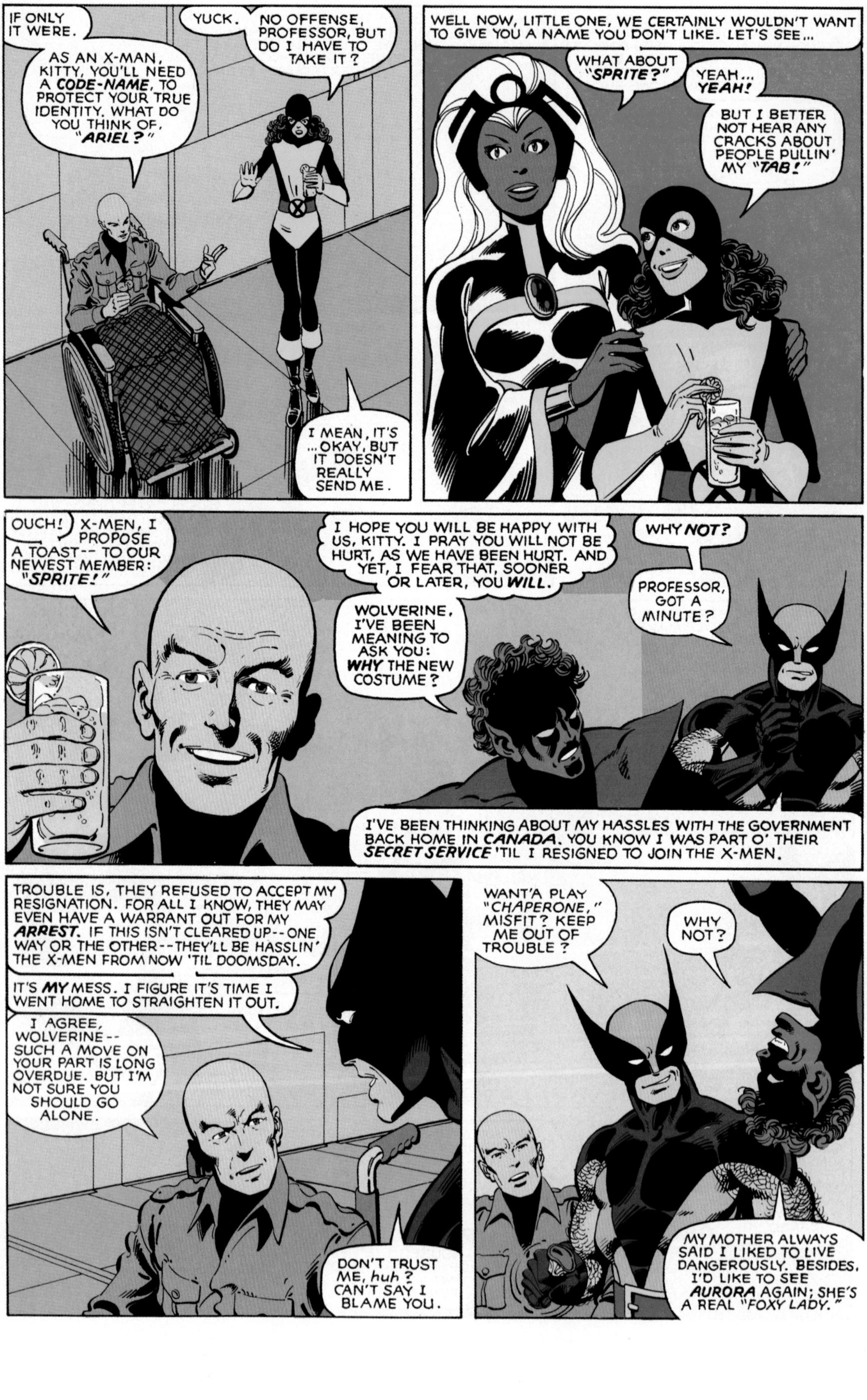

IF ONLY IT WERE.
AS AN X-MAN, KITTY, YOU'LL NEED A CODE-NAME, TO PROTECT YOUR TRUE IDENTITY. WHAT DO YOU THINK OF, "ARIEL?"
YUCK.
NO OFFENSE, PROFESSOR, BUT DO I HAVE TO TAKE IT?
I MEAN, IT'S ...OKAY, BUT IT DOESN'T REALLY SEND ME.
WELL NOW, LITTLE ONE, WE CERTAINLY WOULDN'T WANT TO GIVE YOU A NAME YOU DON'T LIKE. LET'S SEE...
WHAT ABOUT "SPRITE?"
YEAH... YEAH!
BUT I BETTER NOT HEAR ANY CRACKS ABOUT PEOPLE PULLIN' MY "TAB!"
OUCH!
X-MEN, I PROPOSE A TOAST-- TO OUR NEWEST MEMBER: "SPRITE!"
I HOPE YOU WILL BE HAPPY WITH US, KITTY. I PRAY YOU WILL NOT BE HURT, AS WE HAVE BEEN HURT. AND YET, I FEAR THAT, SOONER OR LATER, YOU WILL.
WOLVERINE, I'VE BEEN MEANING TO ASK YOU: WHY THE NEW COSTUME?
WHY NOT?
PROFESSOR, GOT A MINUTE?
I'VE BEEN THINKING ABOUT MY HASSLES WITH THE GOVERNMENT BACK HOME IN CANADA. YOU KNOW I WAS PART O' THEIR SECRET SERVICE 'TIL I RESIGNED TO JOIN THE X-MEN.
TROUBLE IS, THEY REFUSED TO ACCEPT MY RESIGNATION. FOR ALL I KNOW, THEY MAY EVEN HAVE A WARRANT OUT FOR MY ARREST. IF THIS ISN'T CLEARED UP--ONE WAY OR THE OTHER--THEY'LL BE HASSLIN' THE X-MEN FROM NOW 'TIL DOOMSDAY.
IT'S MY MESS. I FIGURE IT'S TIME I WENT HOME TO STRAIGHTEN IT OUT.
I AGREE, WOLVERINE-- SUCH A MOVE ON YOUR PART IS LONG OVERDUE. BUT I'M NOT SURE YOU SHOULD GO ALONE.
DON'T TRUST ME, huh? CAN'T SAY I BLAME YOU.
WANT'A PLAY "CHAPERONE," MISFIT? KEEP ME OUT OF TROUBLE?
WHY NOT?
MY MOTHER ALWAYS SAID I LIKED TO LIVE DANGEROUSLY. BESIDES, I'D LIKE TO SEE AURORA AGAIN; SHE'S A REAL "FOXY LADY."

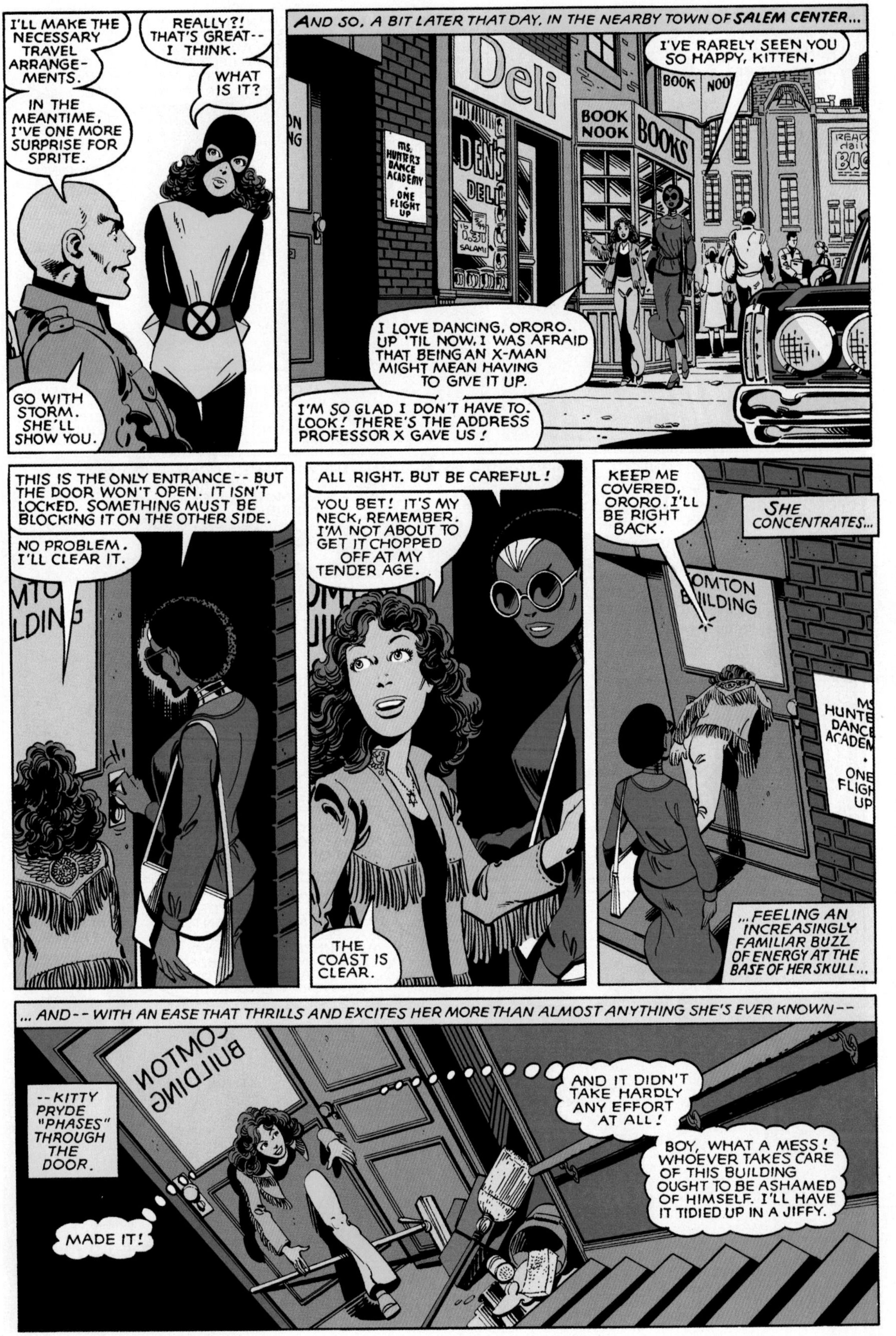
I'LL MAKE THE NECESSARY TRAVEL ARRANGE-MENTS.
IN THE MEANTIME, I'VE ONE MORE SURPRISE FOR SPRITE.
REALLY?! THAT'S GREAT-- I THINK.
WHAT IS IT?
GO WITH STORM. SHE'LL SHOW YOU.
AND SO, A BIT LATER THAT DAY, IN THE NEARBY TOWN OF SALEM CENTER...
I'VE RARELY SEEN YOU SO HAPPY, KITTEN.
I LOVE DANCING, ORORO. UP 'TIL NOW, I WAS AFRAID THAT BEING AN X-MAN MIGHT MEAN HAVING TO GIVE IT UP.
I'M SO GLAD I DON'T HAVE TO. LOOK! THERE'S THE ADDRESS PROFESSOR X GAVE US!
Deli
BOOK NOOK
BOOKS
MS. HUNTER'S DANCE ACADEMY • ONE FLIGHT UP
THIS IS THE ONLY ENTRANCE-- BUT THE DOOR WON'T OPEN. IT ISN'T LOCKED. SOMETHING MUST BE BLOCKING IT ON THE OTHER SIDE.
NO PROBLEM. I'LL CLEAR IT.
ALL RIGHT. BUT BE CAREFUL!
YOU BET! IT'S MY NECK, REMEMBER. I'M NOT ABOUT TO GET IT CHOPPED OFF AT MY TENDER AGE.
THE COAST IS CLEAR.
KEEP ME COVERED, ORORO. I'LL BE RIGHT BACK.
SHE CONCENTRATES...
...FEELING AN INCREASINGLY FAMILIAR BUZZ OF ENERGY AT THE BASE OF HER SKULL...
... AND-- WITH AN EASE THAT THRILLS AND EXCITES HER MORE THAN ALMOST ANYTHING SHE'S EVER KNOWN--
--KITTY PRYDE "PHASES" THROUGH THE DOOR.
MADE IT!
AND IT DIDN'T TAKE HARDLY ANY EFFORT AT ALL!
BOY, WHAT A MESS! WHOEVER TAKES CARE OF THIS BUILDING OUGHT TO BE ASHAMED OF HIMSELF. I'LL HAVE IT TIDIED UP IN A JIFFY.

HI, THERE! MISS ME?

TERRIBLY.

Awww-- I BET YOU SAY THAT TO ALL THE X-MEN.

... I'M A CERTIFIED *GENIUS*, Y'KNOW. MY PEERS ARE IN THE NINTH GRADE, AN' I'M TAKING COLLEGE-LEVEL COURSES. ACADEMICALLY, WE DON'T FIT.

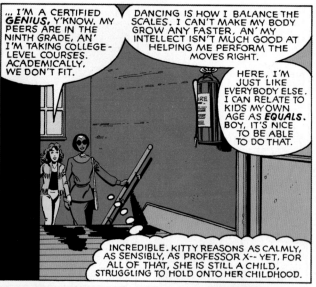

DANCING IS HOW I BALANCE THE SCALES. I CAN'T MAKE MY BODY GROW ANY FASTER, AN' MY INTELLECT ISN'T MUCH GOOD AT HELPING ME PERFORM THE MOVES RIGHT.

HERE, I'M JUST LIKE EVERYBODY ELSE. I CAN RELATE TO KIDS MY OWN AGE AS *EQUALS*. BOY, IT'S NICE TO BE ABLE TO DO THAT.

INCREDIBLE. KITTY REASONS AS CALMLY, AS SENSIBLY, AS PROFESSOR X-- YET, FOR ALL OF THAT, SHE IS STILL A CHILD, STRUGGLING TO HOLD ONTO HER CHILDHOOD.

I, TOO, FACED SUCH A CONFLICT, IN CAIRO, AFTER MY PARENTS WERE KILLED. I HAD TO GROW UP VERY QUICKLY-- PERHAPS *TOO* QUICKLY. NOW, I REMEMBER ORORO THE GODDESS, AND ORORO THE GIRL-THIEF-- BUT NOT ORORO THE CHILD.

I WILL DO WHATEVER I CAN TO HELP KITTY WIN *HER* BATTLE, TO LIVE AS *NORMAL* A LIFE AS POSSIBLE.

MS. HUNTER DANCE ACADEMY

WELL, KITTEN, WE'VE ARRIVED.

I DON'T BELIEVE THIS. I'M SO... *NERVOUS!*

AFTERNOON, FOLKS! YOU'RE RIGHT ON TIME!

I'M *STEVIE HUNTER*. WELCOME TO MY STUDIO.

AND YOU MUST BE MS. MONROE AND MS. PRYDE, FROM PROFESSOR XAVIER'S SCHOOL, RIGHT?

I AM... ORORO.

I'M KITTY, KITTY PRYDE. I'M... I'M YOUR NEW STUDENT. I'M REAL PLEASED TO MEET YOU, MS. HUNTER. I SAW YOU DANCE IN CHICAGO, BEFORE YOUR ACCIDENT. YOU WERE WONDERFUL.

THANK YOU. AND THE NAME'S *STEVIE*.

SOME ICED TEA, ANYONE?

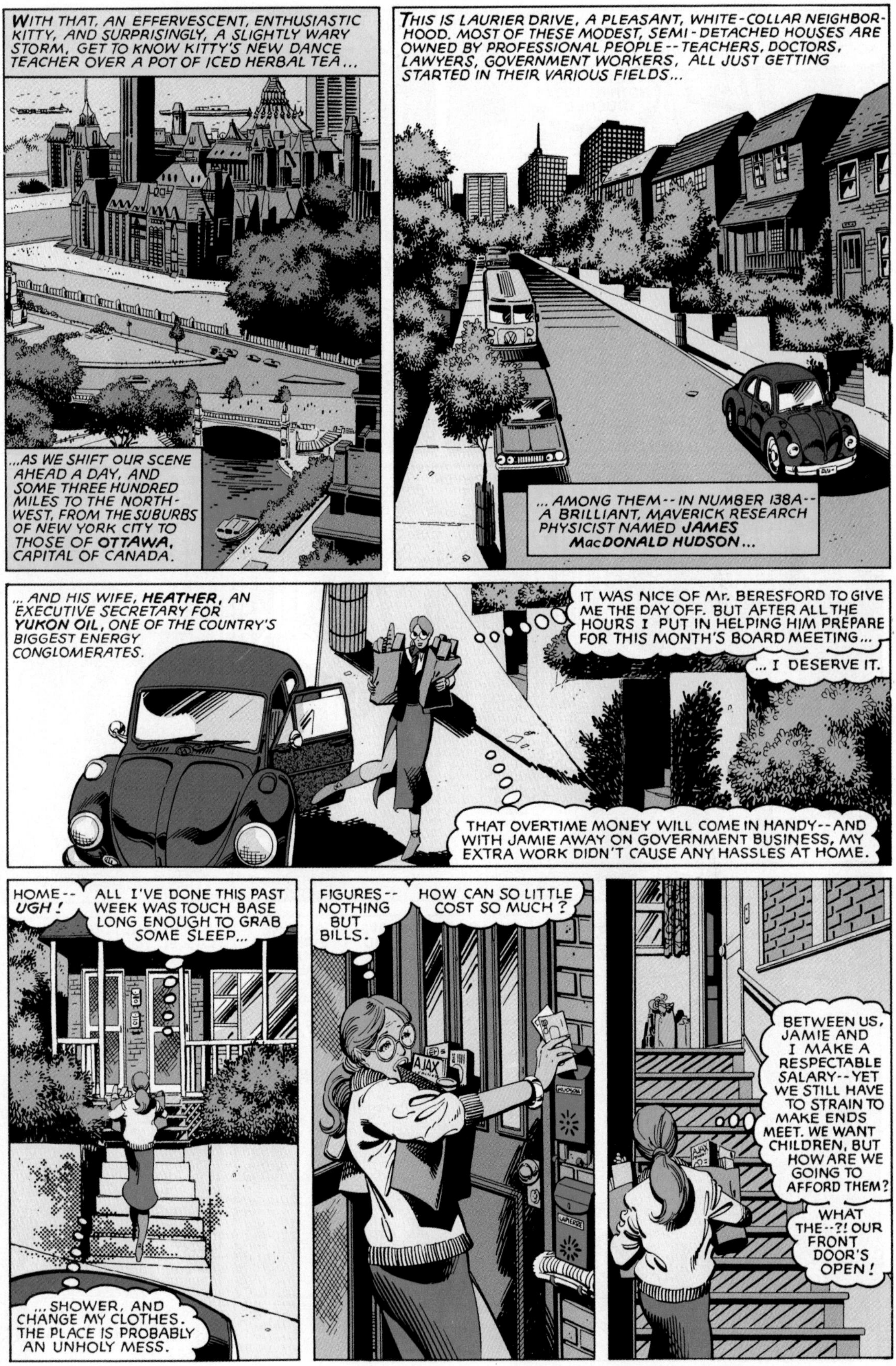
WITH THAT, AN EFFERVESCENT, ENTHUSIASTIC KITTY, AND SURPRISINGLY, A SLIGHTLY WARY STORM, GET TO KNOW KITTY'S NEW DANCE TEACHER OVER A POT OF ICED HERBAL TEA...
...AS WE SHIFT OUR SCENE AHEAD A DAY, AND SOME THREE HUNDRED MILES TO THE NORTH-WEST, FROM THE SUBURBS OF NEW YORK CITY TO THOSE OF OTTAWA, CAPITAL OF CANADA.
THIS IS LAURIER DRIVE, A PLEASANT, WHITE-COLLAR NEIGHBORHOOD. MOST OF THESE MODEST, SEMI-DETACHED HOUSES ARE OWNED BY PROFESSIONAL PEOPLE--TEACHERS, DOCTORS, LAWYERS, GOVERNMENT WORKERS, ALL JUST GETTING STARTED IN THEIR VARIOUS FIELDS...
...AMONG THEM--IN NUMBER 138A--A BRILLIANT, MAVERICK RESEARCH PHYSICIST NAMED JAMES MacDONALD HUDSON...
...AND HIS WIFE, HEATHER, AN EXECUTIVE SECRETARY FOR YUKON OIL, ONE OF THE COUNTRY'S BIGGEST ENERGY CONGLOMERATES.
IT WAS NICE OF Mr. BERESFORD TO GIVE ME THE DAY OFF. BUT AFTER ALL THE HOURS I PUT IN HELPING HIM PREPARE FOR THIS MONTH'S BOARD MEETING...
...I DESERVE IT.
THAT OVERTIME MONEY WILL COME IN HANDY--AND WITH JAMIE AWAY ON GOVERNMENT BUSINESS, MY EXTRA WORK DIDN'T CAUSE ANY HASSLES AT HOME.
HOME--UGH!
ALL I'VE DONE THIS PAST WEEK WAS TOUCH BASE LONG ENOUGH TO GRAB SOME SLEEP...
...SHOWER, AND CHANGE MY CLOTHES. THE PLACE IS PROBABLY AN UNHOLY MESS.
FIGURES--NOTHING BUT BILLS.
HOW CAN SO LITTLE COST SO MUCH?
AJAX
BETWEEN US, JAMIE AND I MAKE A RESPECTABLE SALARY--YET WE STILL HAVE TO STRAIN TO MAKE ENDS MEET. WE WANT CHILDREN, BUT HOW ARE WE GOING TO AFFORD THEM?
WHAT THE--?! OUR FRONT DOOR'S OPEN!

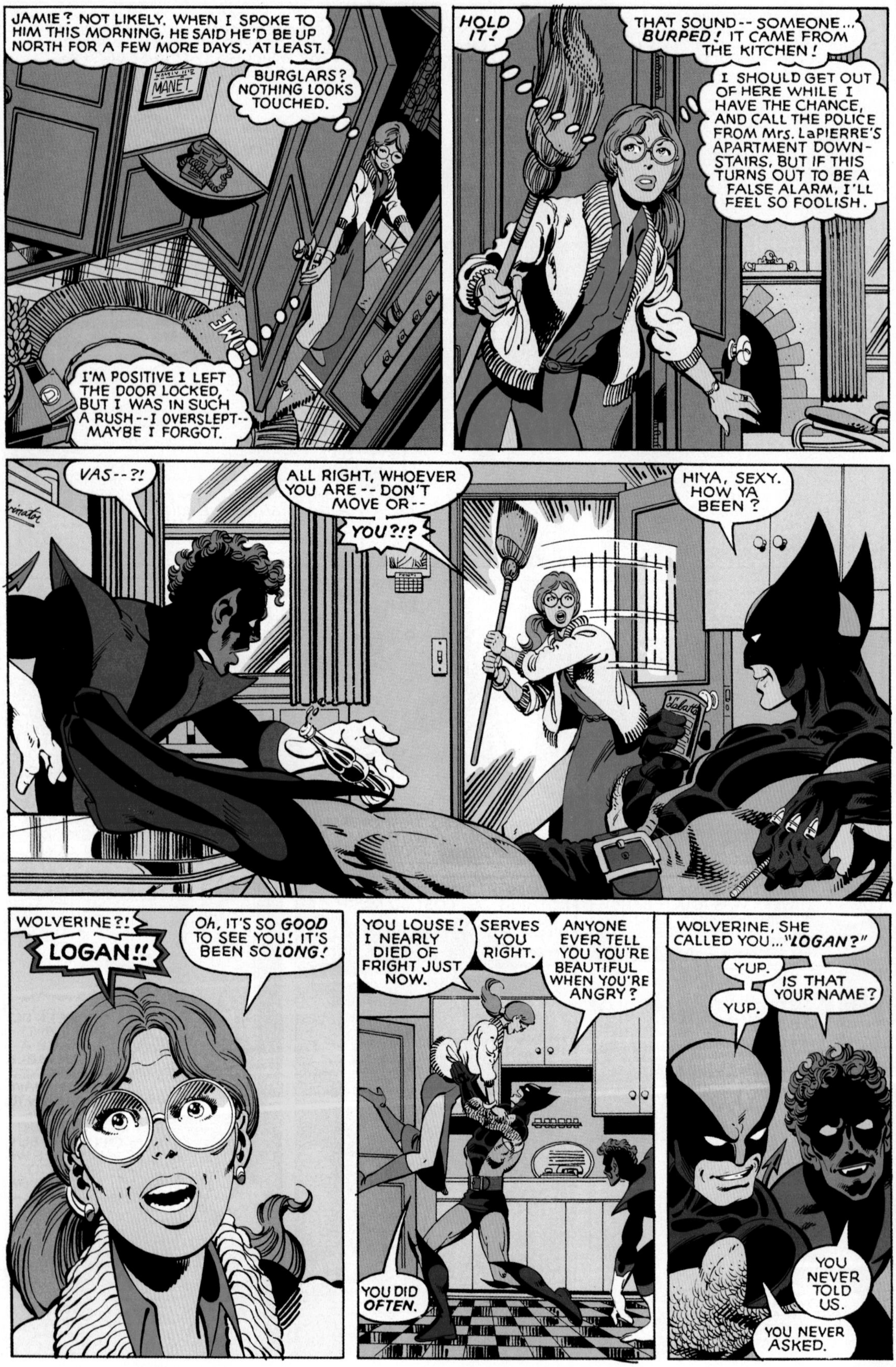

JAMIE? NOT LIKELY. WHEN I SPOKE TO HIM THIS MORNING, HE SAID HE'D BE UP NORTH FOR A FEW MORE DAYS, AT LEAST.
BURGLARS? NOTHING LOOKS TOUCHED.
MANET
I'M POSITIVE I LEFT THE DOOR LOCKED, BUT I WAS IN SUCH A RUSH--I OVERSLEPT--MAYBE I FORGOT.
HOLD IT!
THAT SOUND--SOMEONE... BURPED! IT CAME FROM THE KITCHEN!
I SHOULD GET OUT OF HERE WHILE I HAVE THE CHANCE, AND CALL THE POLICE FROM Mrs. LaPIERRE'S APARTMENT DOWNSTAIRS, BUT IF THIS TURNS OUT TO BE A FALSE ALARM, I'LL FEEL SO FOOLISH.
VAS--?!
ALL RIGHT, WHOEVER YOU ARE--DON'T MOVE OR--
YOU?!?
HIYA, SEXY. HOW YA BEEN?
WOLVERINE?!
LOGAN!!
Oh, IT'S SO GOOD TO SEE YOU! IT'S BEEN SO LONG!
YOU LOUSE! I NEARLY DIED OF FRIGHT JUST NOW.
SERVES YOU RIGHT.
ANYONE EVER TELL YOU YOU'RE BEAUTIFUL WHEN YOU'RE ANGRY?
YOU DID OFTEN.
WOLVERINE, SHE CALLED YOU..."LOGAN?"
YUP.
IS THAT YOUR NAME?
YUP.
YOU NEVER TOLD US.
YOU NEVER ASKED.

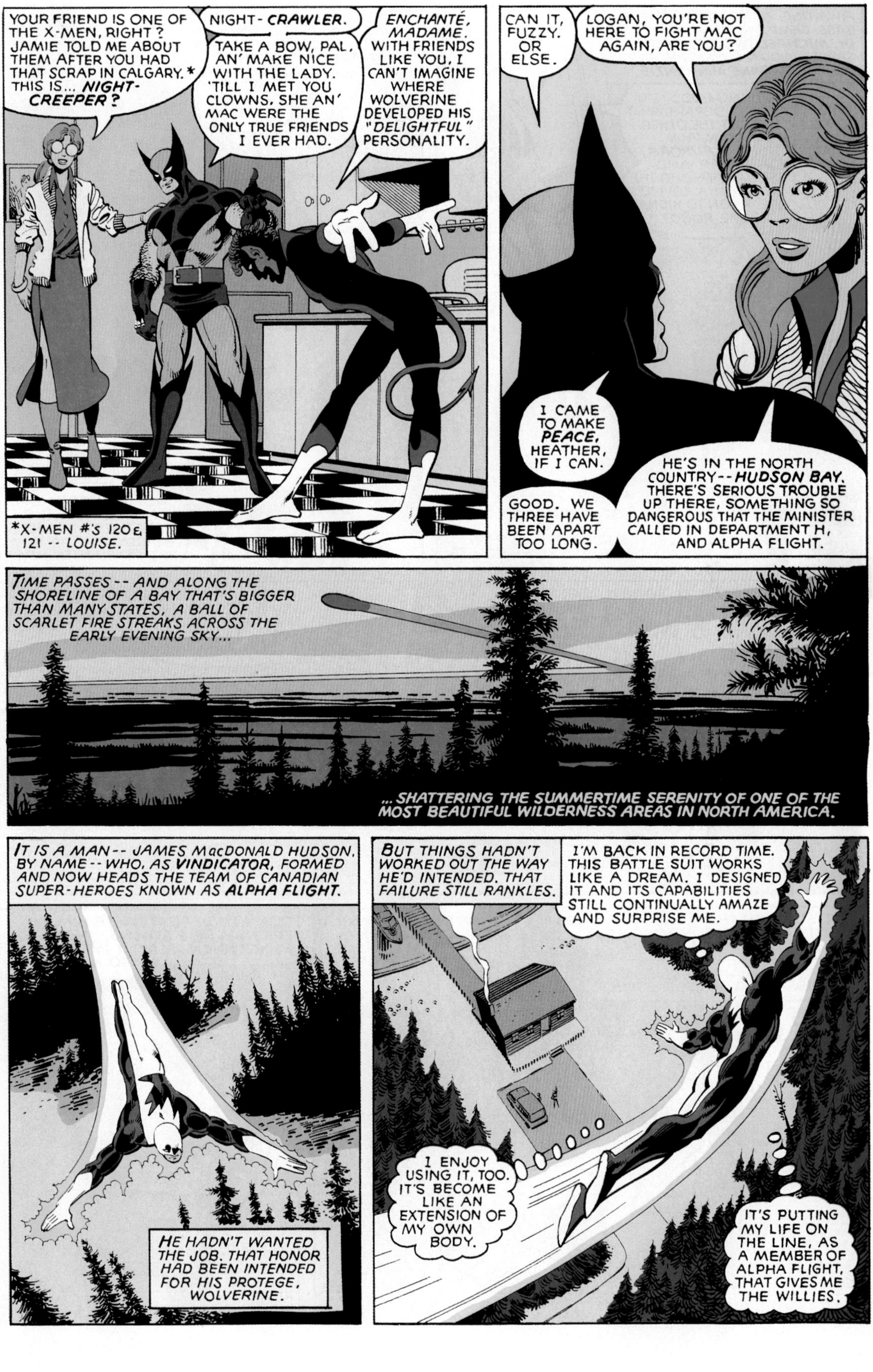

YOUR FRIEND IS ONE OF THE X-MEN, RIGHT? JAMIE TOLD ME ABOUT THEM AFTER YOU HAD THAT SCRAP IN CALGARY.* THIS IS... NIGHT-CREEPER?
NIGHT-CRAWLER.
TAKE A BOW, PAL, AN' MAKE NICE WITH THE LADY. 'TILL I MET YOU CLOWNS, SHE AN' MAC WERE THE ONLY TRUE FRIENDS I EVER HAD.
ENCHANTÉ, MADAME. WITH FRIENDS LIKE YOU, I CAN'T IMAGINE WHERE WOLVERINE DEVELOPED HIS "DELIGHTFUL" PERSONALITY.
*X-MEN #'S 120 & 121 -- LOUISE.
CAN IT, FUZZY. OR ELSE.
LOGAN, YOU'RE NOT HERE TO FIGHT MAC AGAIN, ARE YOU?
I CAME TO MAKE PEACE, HEATHER, IF I CAN.
GOOD. WE THREE HAVE BEEN APART TOO LONG.
HE'S IN THE NORTH COUNTRY--HUDSON BAY. THERE'S SERIOUS TROUBLE UP THERE, SOMETHING SO DANGEROUS THAT THE MINISTER CALLED IN DEPARTMENT H, AND ALPHA FLIGHT.
TIME PASSES-- AND ALONG THE SHORELINE OF A BAY THAT'S BIGGER THAN MANY STATES, A BALL OF SCARLET FIRE STREAKS ACROSS THE EARLY EVENING SKY...
...SHATTERING THE SUMMERTIME SERENITY OF ONE OF THE MOST BEAUTIFUL WILDERNESS AREAS IN NORTH AMERICA.
IT IS A MAN-- JAMES MacDONALD HUDSON, BY NAME-- WHO, AS VINDICATOR, FORMED AND NOW HEADS THE TEAM OF CANADIAN SUPER-HEROES KNOWN AS ALPHA FLIGHT.
HE HADN'T WANTED THE JOB. THAT HONOR HAD BEEN INTENDED FOR HIS PROTEGE, WOLVERINE.
BUT THINGS HADN'T WORKED OUT THE WAY HE'D INTENDED. THAT FAILURE STILL RANKLES.
I'M BACK IN RECORD TIME. THIS BATTLE SUIT WORKS LIKE A DREAM. I DESIGNED IT AND ITS CAPABILITIES STILL CONTINUALLY AMAZE AND SURPRISE ME.
I ENJOY USING IT, TOO. IT'S BECOME LIKE AN EXTENSION OF MY OWN BODY.
IT'S PUTTING MY LIFE ON THE LINE, AS A MEMBER OF ALPHA FLIGHT, THAT GIVES ME THE WILLIES.

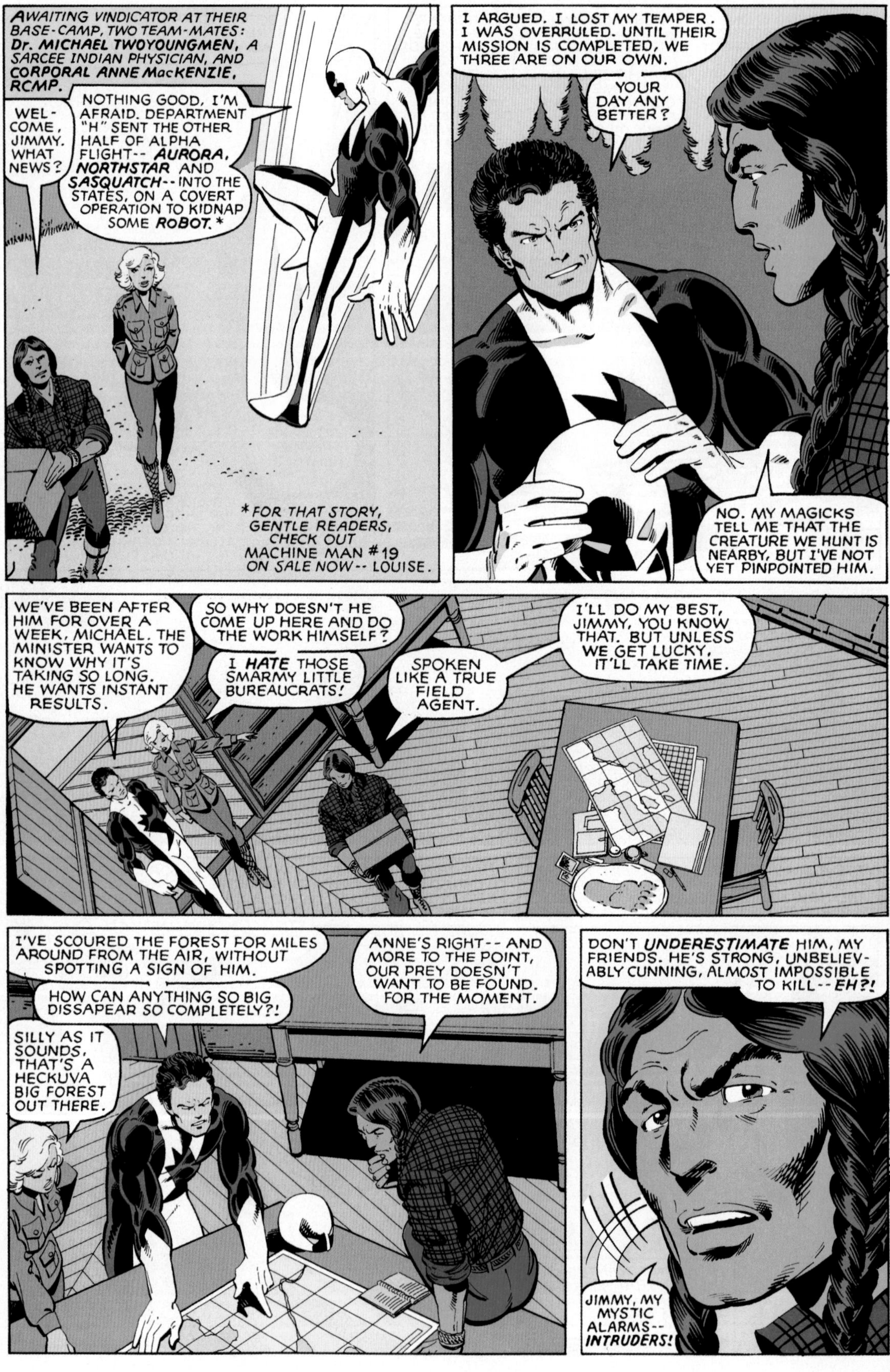
AWAITING VINDICATOR AT THEIR BASE-CAMP, TWO TEAM-MATES: Dr. MICHAEL TWOYOUNGMEN, A SARCEE INDIAN PHYSICIAN, AND CORPORAL ANNE MacKENZIE, RCMP.
WEL-COME, JIMMY. WHAT NEWS?
NOTHING GOOD, I'M AFRAID. DEPARTMENT "H" SENT THE OTHER HALF OF ALPHA FLIGHT-- AURORA, NORTHSTAR AND SASQUATCH-- INTO THE STATES, ON A COVERT OPERATION TO KIDNAP SOME ROBOT.*
*FOR THAT STORY, GENTLE READERS, CHECK OUT MACHINE MAN #19 ON SALE NOW -- LOUISE.
I ARGUED. I LOST MY TEMPER. I WAS OVERRULED. UNTIL THEIR MISSION IS COMPLETED, WE THREE ARE ON OUR OWN.
YOUR DAY ANY BETTER?
NO. MY MAGICKS TELL ME THAT THE CREATURE WE HUNT IS NEARBY, BUT I'VE NOT YET PINPOINTED HIM.
WE'VE BEEN AFTER HIM FOR OVER A WEEK, MICHAEL. THE MINISTER WANTS TO KNOW WHY IT'S TAKING SO LONG. HE WANTS INSTANT RESULTS.
SO WHY DOESN'T HE COME UP HERE AND DO THE WORK HIMSELF?
I HATE THOSE SMARMY LITTLE BUREAUCRATS!
SPOKEN LIKE A TRUE FIELD AGENT.
I'LL DO MY BEST, JIMMY, YOU KNOW THAT. BUT UNLESS WE GET LUCKY, IT'LL TAKE TIME.
I'VE SCOURED THE FOREST FOR MILES AROUND FROM THE AIR, WITHOUT SPOTTING A SIGN OF HIM.
HOW CAN ANYTHING SO BIG DISSAPEAR SO COMPLETELY?!
SILLY AS IT SOUNDS, THAT'S A HECKUVA BIG FOREST OUT THERE.
ANNE'S RIGHT-- AND MORE TO THE POINT, OUR PREY DOESN'T WANT TO BE FOUND. FOR THE MOMENT.
DON'T UNDERESTIMATE HIM, MY FRIENDS. HE'S STRONG, UNBELIEV-ABLY CUNNING, ALMOST IMPOSSIBLE TO KILL-- EH?!
JIMMY, MY MYSTIC ALARMS-- INTRUDERS!

THE THREE REACT IMMEDIATELY TO THE WARNING CRY. AS VINDICATOR DONS HIS HELMET, MICHAEL TWOYOUNG-MEN BRINGS A PAIR OF SACRED WRISTBANDS TOGETHER, MAGICALLY TRANSFORMING HIMSELF INTO THE SARCEE MEDICINE MAN KNOWN AS *SHAMAN*. AT THE SAME TIME, ANNE MacKENZIE'S FEATURES BLUR LIKE SMOKE; WHEN THEY SOLIDIFY ONCE MORE, THE YOUNG MOUNTIE IS GONE...

IN HER PLACE STANDS SNOW-BIRD, A SHAPE-CHANGER--A WOMAN OF HAUNTING, ELEMENTAL BEAUTY, YET ONE WHO IS NO LONGER QUITE... *HUMAN*.

SNOWBIRD-- *OUTSIDE!* FIND OUR VISITORS, BUT KEEP A LOW PROFILE. I WANT NO UNNECESSARY TROUBLE.

AFTER WHAT WE'VE SEEN HERE, JIM, I HOPE IT'S THE CREATURE WE'RE AFTER. I'D LIKE TO SEE HOW IMPRESSIVE HE IS AGAINST SOMEONE WHO CAN FIGHT BACK!

DON'T FRET, BOSS. I'LL BE CAREFUL. BE SEEING YOU, GUYS.

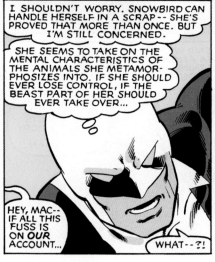

I SHOULDN'T WORRY. SNOWBIRD CAN HANDLE HERSELF IN A SCRAP -- SHE'S PROVED THAT MORE THAN ONCE. BUT I'M STILL CONCERNED.

SHE SEEMS TO TAKE ON THE MENTAL CHARACTERISTICS OF THE ANIMALS SHE METAMOR-PHOSIZES INTO. IF SHE SHOULD EVER LOSE CONTROL, IF THE BEAST PART OF HER SHOULD EVER TAKE OVER...

HEY, MAC-- IF ALL THIS FUSS IS ON *OUR* ACCOUNT...

WHAT--?!

...DON'T BOTHER.

WOLVERINE, I HOPE -- I *PRAY* -- YOU KNOW WHAT YOU'RE DOING.

BE COOL, PAL.

WOLVERINE! NIGHTCRAWLER!

WHAT ARE THE X-MEN DOING HERE ?!

I HAVEN'T THE FOGGIEST, SHAMAN. BUT IF IT'S TO SETTLE OLD SCORES, THEY'LL FIND US *READY* FOR THEM!

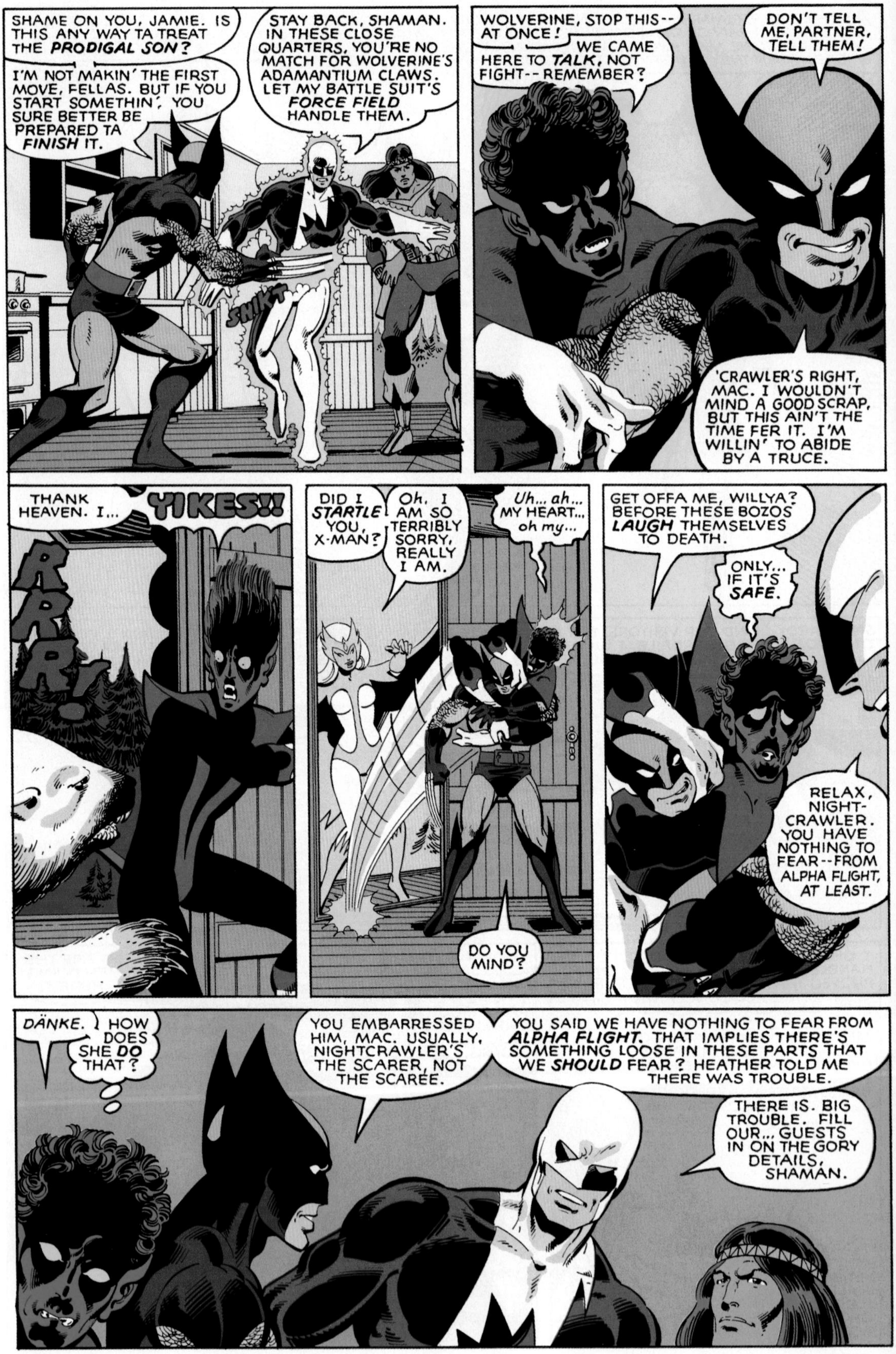
SHAME ON YOU, JAMIE. IS THIS ANY WAY TA TREAT THE PRODIGAL SON?
I'M NOT MAKIN' THE FIRST MOVE, FELLAS. BUT IF YOU START SOMETHIN', YOU SURE BETTER BE PREPARED TA FINISH IT.
STAY BACK, SHAMAN. IN THESE CLOSE QUARTERS, YOU'RE NO MATCH FOR WOLVERINE'S ADAMANTIUM CLAWS. LET MY BATTLE SUIT'S FORCE FIELD HANDLE THEM.
SNIKT
WOLVERINE, STOP THIS-- AT ONCE!
WE CAME HERE TO TALK, NOT FIGHT-- REMEMBER?
DON'T TELL ME, PARTNER, TELL THEM!
'CRAWLER'S RIGHT, MAC. I WOULDN'T MIND A GOOD SCRAP, BUT THIS AIN'T THE TIME FER IT. I'M WILLIN' TO ABIDE BY A TRUCE.
THANK HEAVEN. I...
YIKES!!
RRRR!
DID I STARTLE YOU, X-MAN?
Oh, I AM SO TERRIBLY SORRY, REALLY I AM.
Uh... ah... MY HEART... oh my...
DO YOU MIND?
GET OFFA ME, WILLYA? BEFORE THESE BOZOS LAUGH THEMSELVES TO DEATH.
ONLY... IF IT'S SAFE.
RELAX, NIGHT-CRAWLER. YOU HAVE NOTHING TO FEAR--FROM ALPHA FLIGHT, AT LEAST.
DÄNKE.
HOW DOES SHE DO THAT?
YOU EMBARRESSED HIM, MAC. USUALLY, NIGHTCRAWLER'S THE SCARER, NOT THE SCAREE.
YOU SAID WE HAVE NOTHING TO FEAR FROM ALPHA FLIGHT. THAT IMPLIES THERE'S SOMETHING LOOSE IN THESE PARTS THAT WE SHOULD FEAR? HEATHER TOLD ME THERE WAS TROUBLE.
THERE IS. BIG TROUBLE. FILL OUR... GUESTS IN ON THE GORY DETAILS, SHAMAN.

WOLVERINE, YOUR SENSE OF TIMING IS AS EXTRAORDINARY AS YOUR TEMPER. AT THE MOMENT, THOUGH, YOU'RE THE LEAST OF OUR CONCERNS.

WE'RE LOOKING FOR THE FAMILY OF A MOUNTIE NAMED *JOE PARNALL.* THEY WERE CAMPING ALONG BIG MOOSE CREEK, NEAR HUDSON BAY -- PARNALL, HIS WIFE, THEIR SIX-YEAR OLD SON AND INFANT DAUGHTER.

THEY WERE IN REMOTE, ROUGH COUNTRY-- BUT BOTH PARNALL AND HIS WIFE KNEW THE WOODS. THEY WERE WELL-SUPPLIED, ARMED, AND THEY HAD A PORTABLE, TWO-WAY, SHORTWAVE RADIO.

"THEY WERE CAREFUL PEOPLE. PARNALL CHECKED IN WITH UGALI STATION EVERY DAY."

"AT FIRST, EVERYTHING WAS NORMAL. THEY WERE HAVING A WONDERFUL TIME.

"THEN...

AARR

MOM? DAD?! SOMEONE'S SCREAMING--WHAT'S HAPPENING? *DAD?!*

RRIP

YOW!!

"TOMMY PARNALL RAN FOR HIS LIFE. HE DIDN'T STOP UNTIL A BUSH-PILOT FOUND HIM TWO DAYS LATER, WANDERING ALONG THE SHORE, HALF-DEAD FROM EXPOSURE.

"THE BOY'S STILL IN SHOCK, ALMOST CATATONIC. WHEN WE FOUND THE PARNALL CAMPSITE, AND WHAT WAS... LEFT OF HIS FATHER, WE UNDERSTOOD WHY."

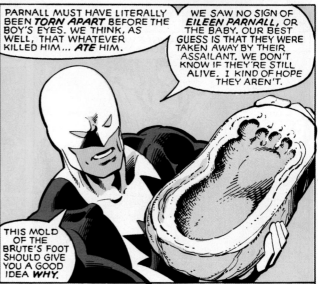

PARNALL MUST HAVE LITERALLY BEEN *TORN APART* BEFORE THE BOY'S EYES. WE THINK, AS WELL, THAT WHATEVER KILLED HIM... *ATE* HIM.

WE SAW NO SIGN OF *EILEEN PARNALL,* OR THE BABY. OUR BEST GUESS IS THAT THEY WERE TAKEN AWAY BY THEIR ASSAILANT. WE DON'T KNOW IF THEY'RE STILL ALIVE. I KIND OF HOPE THEY AREN'T.

THIS MOLD OF THE BRUTE'S FOOT SHOULD GIVE YOU A GOOD IDEA *WHY.*

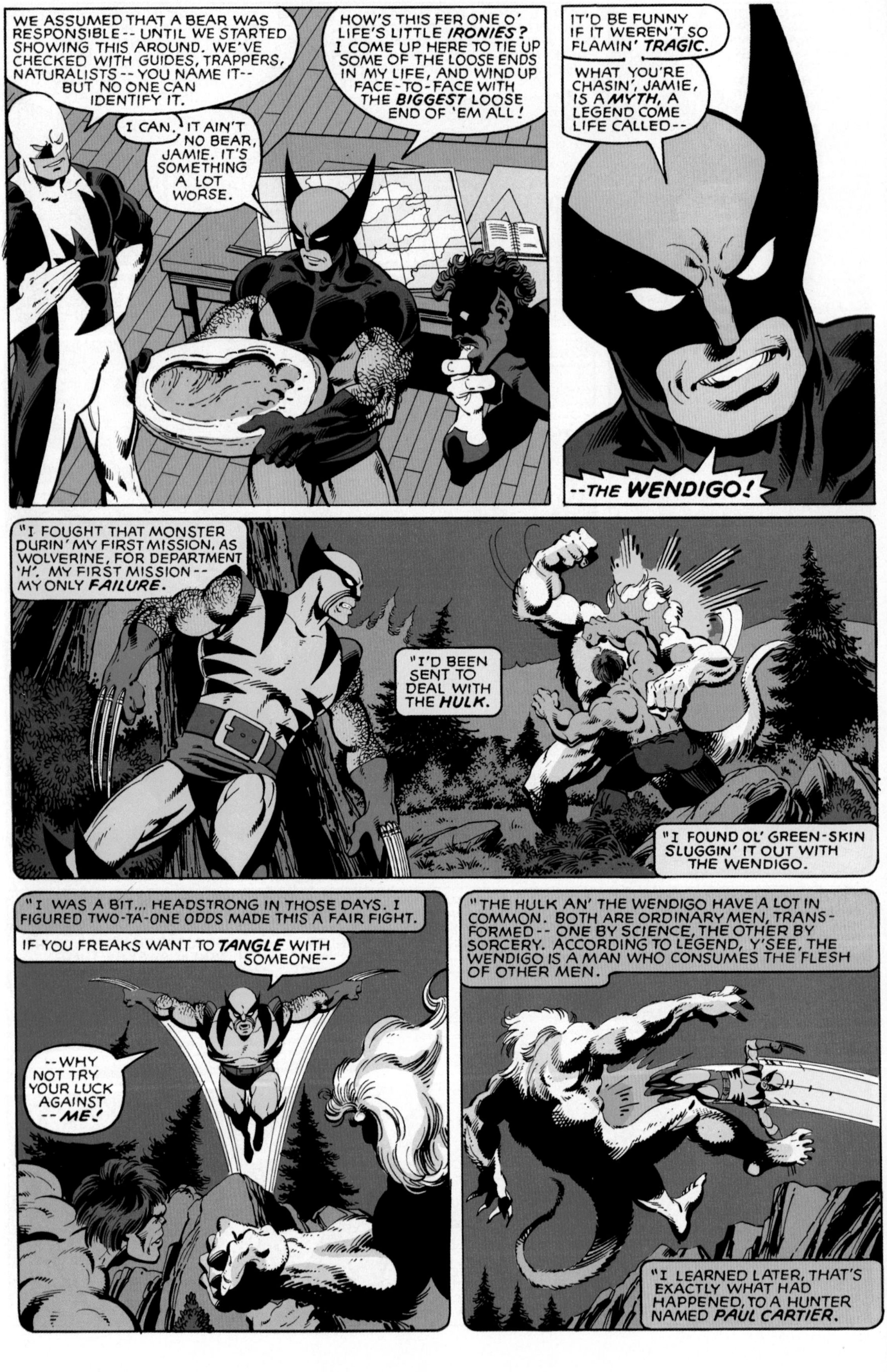
WE ASSUMED THAT A BEAR WAS RESPONSIBLE -- UNTIL WE STARTED SHOWING THIS AROUND. WE'VE CHECKED WITH GUIDES, TRAPPERS, NATURALISTS -- YOU NAME IT -- BUT NO ONE CAN IDENTIFY IT.
I CAN.
IT AIN'T NO BEAR, JAMIE. IT'S SOMETHING A LOT WORSE.
HOW'S THIS FER ONE O' LIFE'S LITTLE IRONIES? I COME UP HERE TO TIE UP SOME OF THE LOOSE ENDS IN MY LIFE, AND WIND UP FACE-TO-FACE WITH THE BIGGEST LOOSE END OF 'EM ALL!
IT'D BE FUNNY IF IT WEREN'T SO FLAMIN' TRAGIC.
WHAT YOU'RE CHASIN', JAMIE, IS A MYTH, A LEGEND COME LIFE CALLED--
--THE WENDIGO!
"I FOUGHT THAT MONSTER DURIN' MY FIRST MISSION, AS WOLVERINE, FOR DEPARTMENT 'H'. MY FIRST MISSION -- MY ONLY FAILURE.
"I'D BEEN SENT TO DEAL WITH THE HULK.
"I FOUND OL' GREEN-SKIN SLUGGIN' IT OUT WITH THE WENDIGO.
"I WAS A BIT... HEADSTRONG IN THOSE DAYS. I FIGURED TWO-TA-ONE ODDS MADE THIS A FAIR FIGHT.
IF YOU FREAKS WANT TO TANGLE WITH SOMEONE--
--WHY NOT TRY YOUR LUCK AGAINST --ME!
"THE HULK AN' THE WENDIGO HAVE A LOT IN COMMON. BOTH ARE ORDINARY MEN, TRANSFORMED -- ONE BY SCIENCE, THE OTHER BY SORCERY. ACCORDING TO LEGEND, Y'SEE, THE WENDIGO IS A MAN WHO CONSUMES THE FLESH OF OTHER MEN.
"I LEARNED LATER, THAT'S EXACTLY WHAT HAD HAPPENED, TO A HUNTER NAMED PAUL CARTIER.

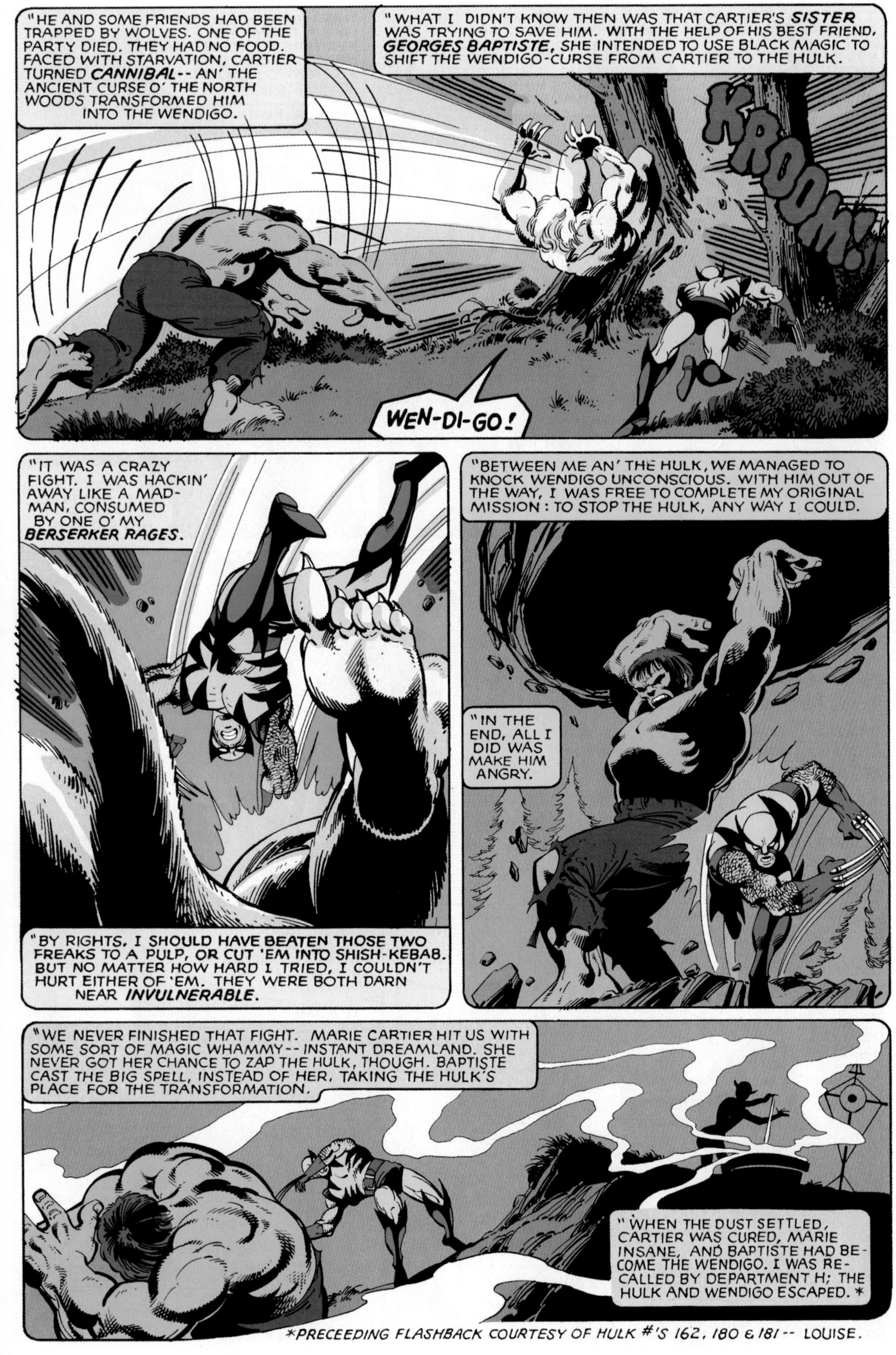
"HE AND SOME FRIENDS HAD BEEN TRAPPED BY WOLVES. ONE OF THE PARTY DIED. THEY HAD NO FOOD. FACED WITH STARVATION, CARTIER TURNED CANNIBAL-- AN' THE ANCIENT CURSE O' THE NORTH WOODS TRANSFORMED HIM INTO THE WENDIGO.
"WHAT I DIDN'T KNOW THEN WAS THAT CARTIER'S SISTER WAS TRYING TO SAVE HIM. WITH THE HELP OF HIS BEST FRIEND, GEORGES BAPTISTE, SHE INTENDED TO USE BLACK MAGIC TO SHIFT THE WENDIGO-CURSE FROM CARTIER TO THE HULK.
KROOM!
WEN-DI-GO!
"IT WAS A CRAZY FIGHT. I WAS HACKIN' AWAY LIKE A MAD-MAN, CONSUMED BY ONE O' MY BERSERKER RAGES.
"BY RIGHTS, I SHOULD HAVE BEATEN THOSE TWO FREAKS TO A PULP, OR CUT 'EM INTO SHISH-KEBAB. BUT NO MATTER HOW HARD I TRIED, I COULDN'T HURT EITHER OF 'EM. THEY WERE BOTH DARN NEAR INVULNERABLE.
"BETWEEN ME AN' THE HULK, WE MANAGED TO KNOCK WENDIGO UNCONSCIOUS. WITH HIM OUT OF THE WAY, I WAS FREE TO COMPLETE MY ORIGINAL MISSION: TO STOP THE HULK, ANY WAY I COULD.
"IN THE END, ALL I DID WAS MAKE HIM ANGRY.
"WE NEVER FINISHED THAT FIGHT. MARIE CARTIER HIT US WITH SOME SORT OF MAGIC WHAMMY-- INSTANT DREAMLAND. SHE NEVER GOT HER CHANCE TO ZAP THE HULK, THOUGH. BAPTISTE CAST THE BIG SPELL, INSTEAD OF HER, TAKING THE HULK'S PLACE FOR THE TRANSFORMATION.
"WHEN THE DUST SETTLED, CARTIER WAS CURED, MARIE INSANE, AND BAPTISTE HAD BECOME THE WENDIGO. I WAS RECALLED BY DEPARTMENT H; THE HULK AND WENDIGO ESCAPED.*

*PRECEEDING FLASHBACK COURTESY OF HULK #'S 162, 180 & 181 -- LOUISE.

I WAS OUT OF CANADA A LOT AFTER THAT-- DOIN' MY "JAMES BOND" NUMBER-- I NEVER GOT ANOTHER CHANCE TO GO AFTER EITHER HULK OR WENDIGO.

THERE'S JUST ME AN' THE MISFIT HERE, MAC, BUT IF YOU WANT OUR HELP AGAINST WENDIGO, IT'S YOURS FOR THE ASKING. TRUTH T' TELL, IT'S YOURS WHETHER YOU WANT IT OR NOT.

SINCE YOU PUT IT THAT WAY, LOGAN, HOW CAN I REFUSE?

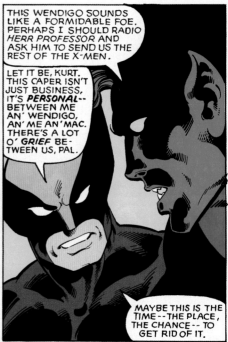

THIS WENDIGO SOUNDS LIKE A FORMIDABLE FOE. PERHAPS I SHOULD RADIO HERR PROFESSOR AND ASK HIM TO SEND US THE REST OF THE X-MEN.

LET IT BE, KURT. THIS CAPER ISN'T JUST BUSINESS, IT'S PERSONAL-- BETWEEN ME AN' WENDIGO, AN' ME AN' MAC. THERE'S A LOT O' GRIEF BETWEEN US, PAL.

MAYBE THIS IS THE TIME-- THE PLACE, THE CHANCE-- TO GET RID OF IT.

MEANWHILE, WE NEED OUR GEAR.

I'LL GET IT.

BAMF

OH!

NIGHTCRAWLER-- VANISHED!

HOW DOES HE DO THAT?

Y'KNOW, IF I REMEMBER RIGHT, WENDIGO'S PREFERENCE IS SUPPOSED TO BE FOR FRESH-KILLED MEAT. IF THAT HOLDS TRUE, EILEEN PARNALL AN' HER BABY MIGHT STILL BE ALIVE.

I MIGHT BE ABLE TO TRACK THEIR SCENT.

WE'VE TRIED. JUST ABOUT EVERYTHING ELSE.

FACE IT, JAMIE, IF ANYONE ON EARTH HAS A PRAYER O' FINDIN' 'EM, AN' BRINGIN' 'EM BACK WHOLE--

-- IT'S ME.

I'M REALLY LOOKIN' FORWARD TO IT.

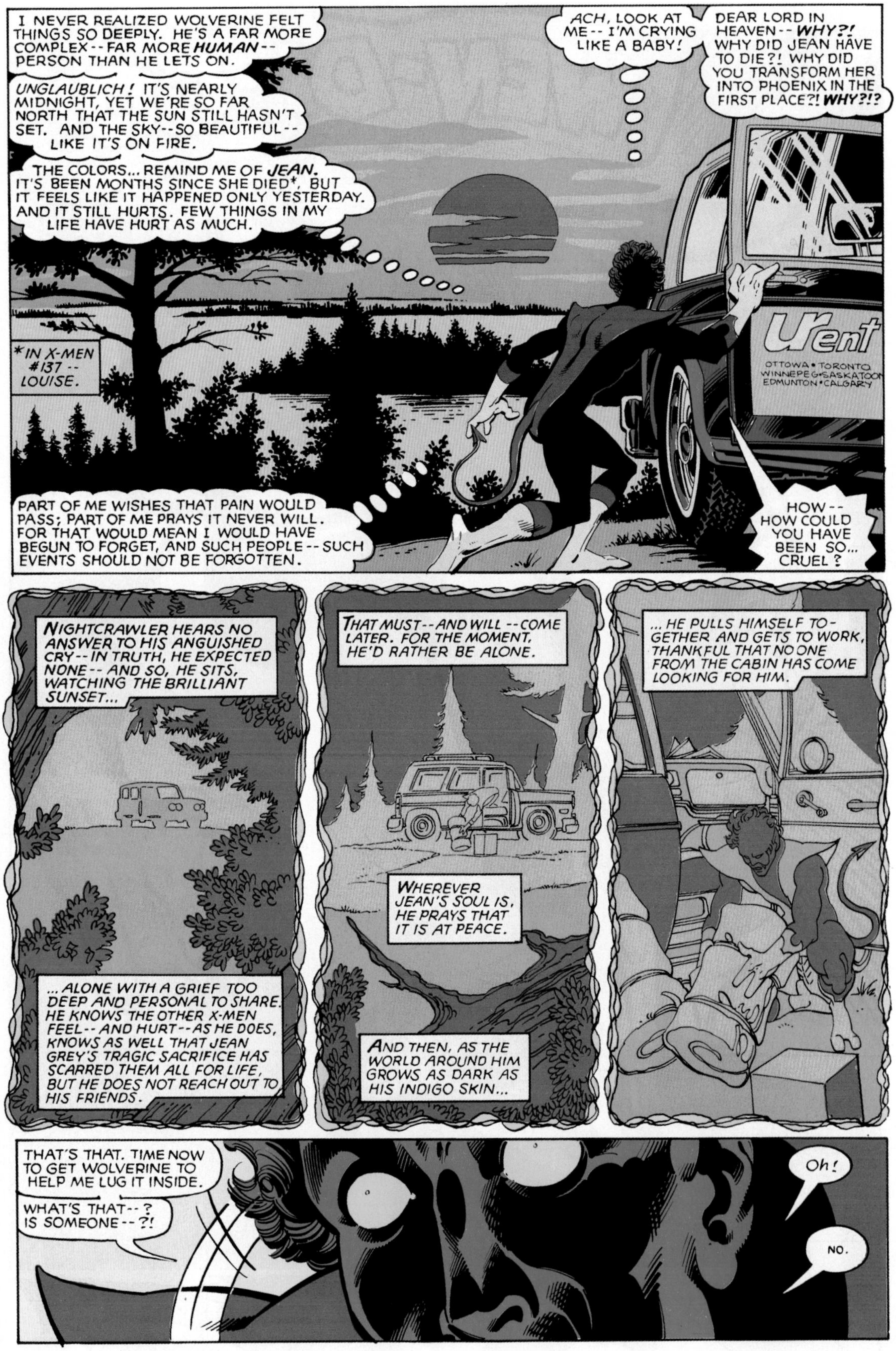

I NEVER REALIZED WOLVERINE FELT THINGS SO DEEPLY. HE'S A FAR MORE COMPLEX -- FAR MORE HUMAN -- PERSON THAN HE LETS ON.
UNGLAUBLICH! IT'S NEARLY MIDNIGHT, YET WE'RE SO FAR NORTH THAT THE SUN STILL HASN'T SET. AND THE SKY -- SO BEAUTIFUL -- LIKE IT'S ON FIRE.
THE COLORS... REMIND ME OF JEAN. IT'S BEEN MONTHS SINCE SHE DIED*, BUT IT FEELS LIKE IT HAPPENED ONLY YESTERDAY. AND IT STILL HURTS. FEW THINGS IN MY LIFE HAVE HURT AS MUCH.
ACH, LOOK AT ME -- I'M CRYING LIKE A BABY!
DEAR LORD IN HEAVEN -- WHY?! WHY DID JEAN HAVE TO DIE?! WHY DID YOU TRANSFORM HER INTO PHOENIX IN THE FIRST PLACE?! WHY?!?
*IN X-MEN #137 -- LOUISE.
URent
OTTOWA • TORONTO
WINNEPEG • SASKATOON
EDMUNTON • CALGARY
PART OF ME WISHES THAT PAIN WOULD PASS; PART OF ME PRAYS IT NEVER WILL. FOR THAT WOULD MEAN I WOULD HAVE BEGUN TO FORGET, AND SUCH PEOPLE -- SUCH EVENTS SHOULD NOT BE FORGOTTEN.
HOW -- HOW COULD YOU HAVE BEEN SO... CRUEL?
NIGHTCRAWLER HEARS NO ANSWER TO HIS ANGUISHED CRY -- IN TRUTH, HE EXPECTED NONE -- AND SO, HE SITS, WATCHING THE BRILLIANT SUNSET...
... ALONE WITH A GRIEF TOO DEEP AND PERSONAL TO SHARE. HE KNOWS THE OTHER X-MEN FEEL -- AND HURT -- AS HE DOES, KNOWS AS WELL THAT JEAN GREY'S TRAGIC SACRIFICE HAS SCARRED THEM ALL FOR LIFE, BUT HE DOES NOT REACH OUT TO HIS FRIENDS.
THAT MUST -- AND WILL -- COME LATER. FOR THE MOMENT, HE'D RATHER BE ALONE.
WHEREVER JEAN'S SOUL IS, HE PRAYS THAT IT IS AT PEACE.
AND THEN, AS THE WORLD AROUND HIM GROWS AS DARK AS HIS INDIGO SKIN...
... HE PULLS HIMSELF TOGETHER AND GETS TO WORK, THANKFUL THAT NO ONE FROM THE CABIN HAS COME LOOKING FOR HIM.
THAT'S THAT. TIME NOW TO GET WOLVERINE TO HELP ME LUG IT INSIDE.
WHAT'S THAT -- ? IS SOMEONE -- ?!
Oh!
NO.

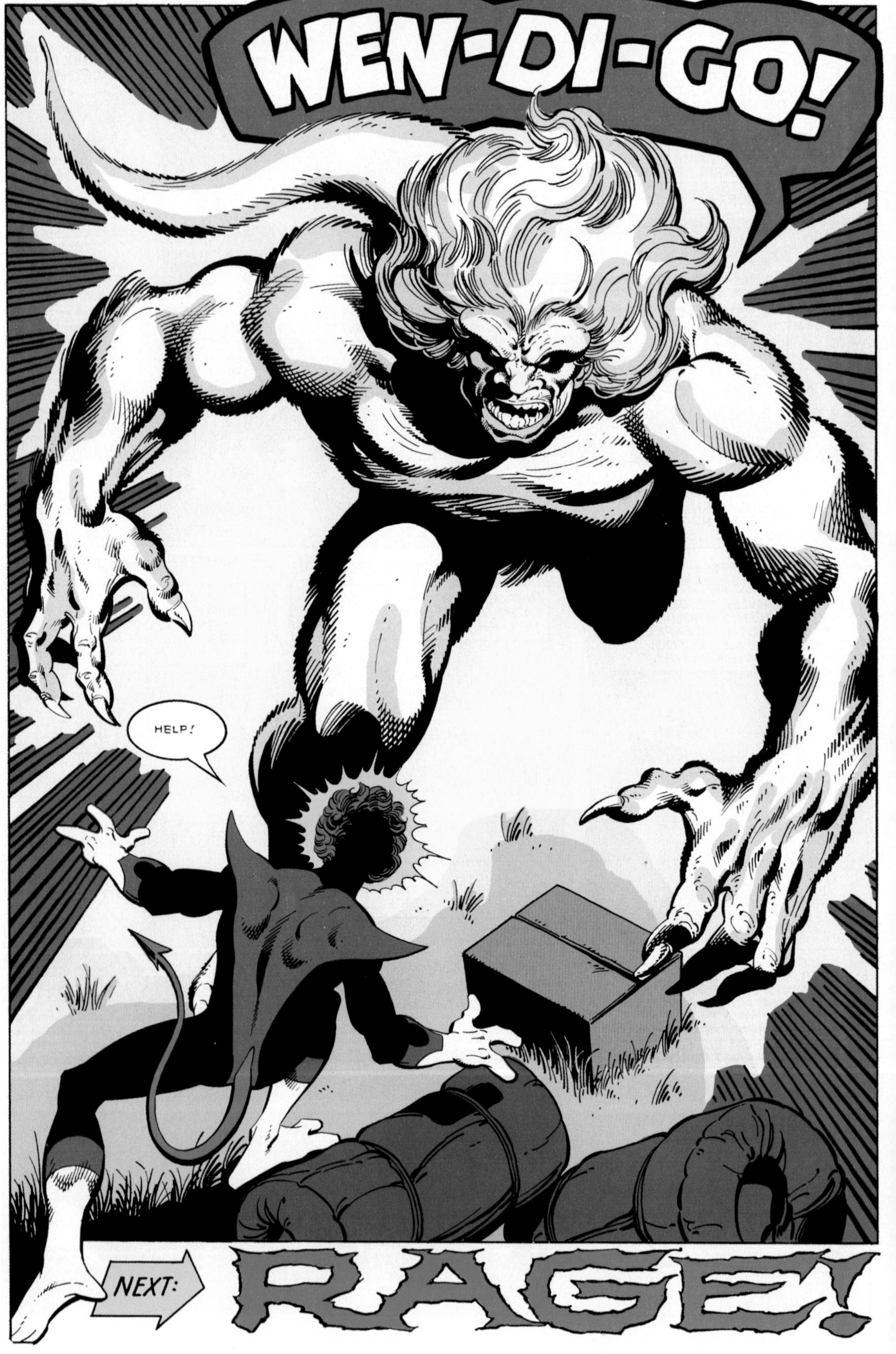
WEN-DI-GO!
HELP!
NEXT:
RAGE!

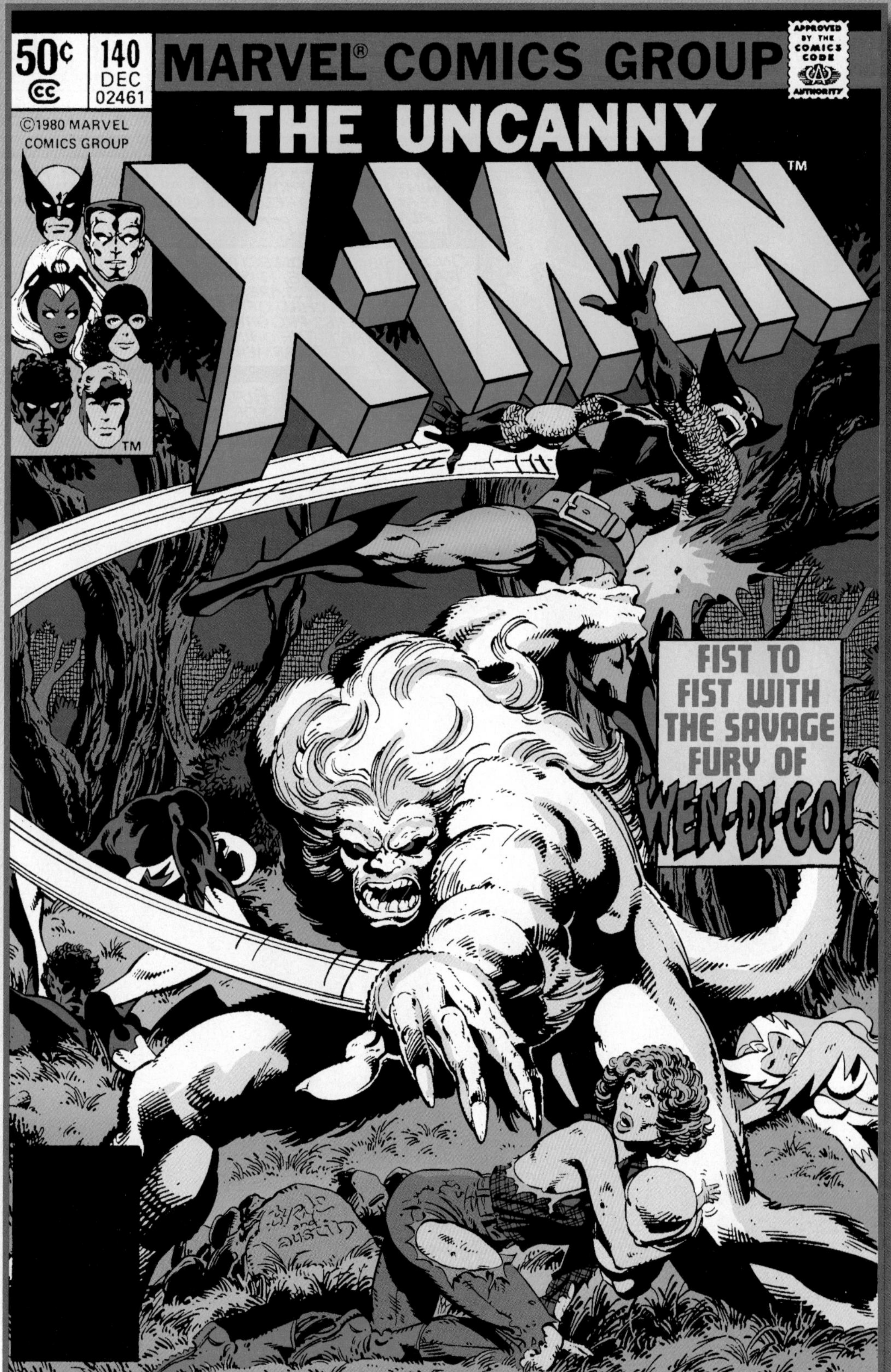
50¢
140
DEC
02461
MARVEL® COMICS GROUP
APPROVED BY THE COMICS CODE AUTHORITY
©1980 MARVEL COMICS GROUP
THE UNCANNY
X-MEN™
FIST TO FIST WITH THE SAVAGE FURY OF
WEN-DI-GO!

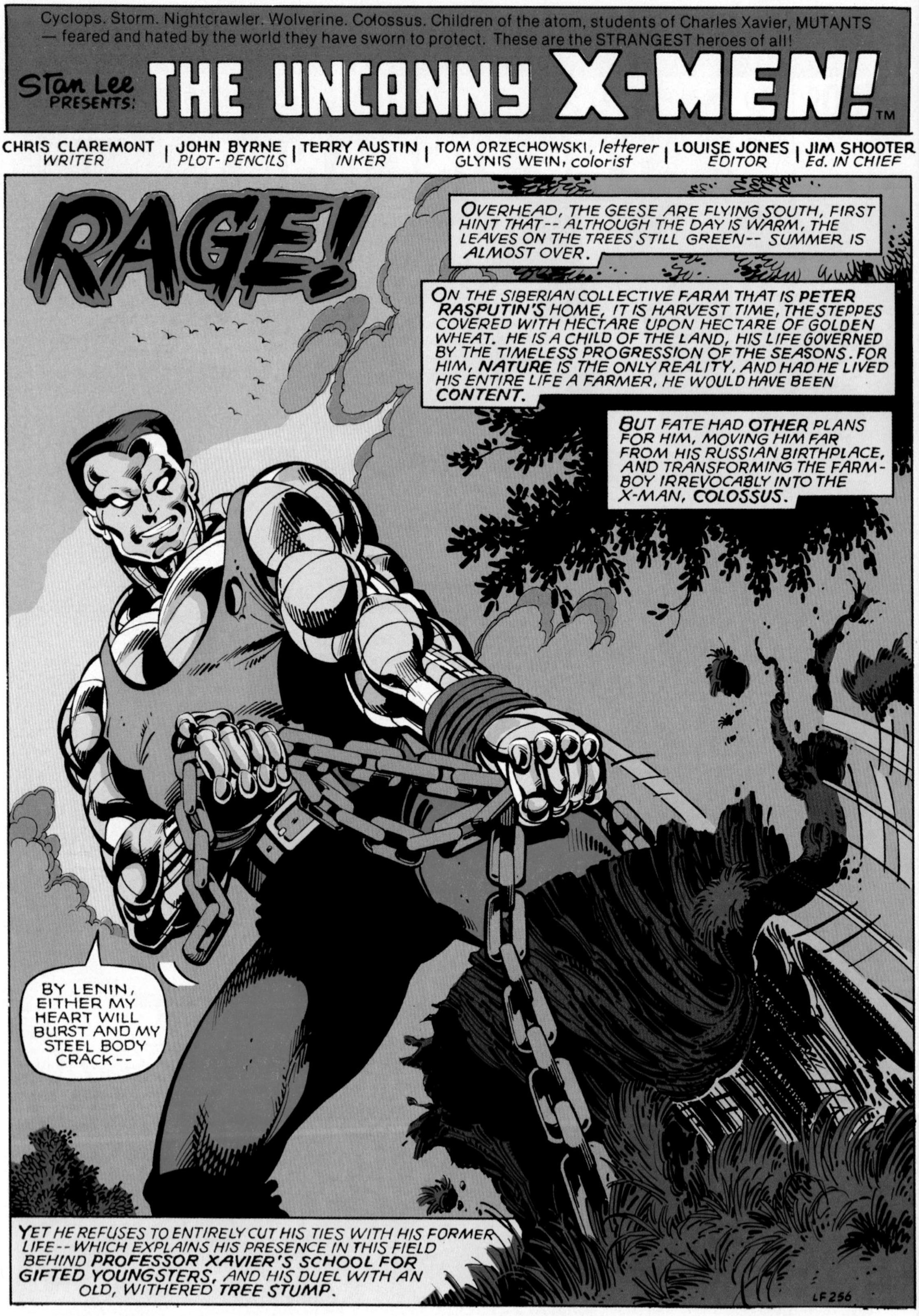
Cyclops. Storm. Nightcrawler. Wolverine. Colossus. Children of the atom, students of Charles Xavier, MUTANTS — feared and hated by the world they have sworn to protect. These are the STRANGEST heroes of all!
Stan Lee PRESENTS: THE UNCANNY X-MEN!
CHRIS CLAREMONT WRITER | JOHN BYRNE PLOT-PENCILS | TERRY AUSTIN INKER | TOM ORZECHOWSKI, letterer GLYNIS WEIN, colorist | LOUISE JONES EDITOR | JIM SHOOTER Ed. IN CHIEF
RAGE!
OVERHEAD, THE GEESE ARE FLYING SOUTH, FIRST HINT THAT-- ALTHOUGH THE DAY IS WARM, THE LEAVES ON THE TREES STILL GREEN-- SUMMER IS ALMOST OVER.
ON THE SIBERIAN COLLECTIVE FARM THAT IS PETER RASPUTIN'S HOME, IT IS HARVEST TIME, THE STEPPES COVERED WITH HECTARE UPON HECTARE OF GOLDEN WHEAT. HE IS A CHILD OF THE LAND, HIS LIFE GOVERNED BY THE TIMELESS PROGRESSION OF THE SEASONS. FOR HIM, NATURE IS THE ONLY REALITY, AND HAD HE LIVED HIS ENTIRE LIFE A FARMER, HE WOULD HAVE BEEN CONTENT.
BUT FATE HAD OTHER PLANS FOR HIM, MOVING HIM FAR FROM HIS RUSSIAN BIRTHPLACE, AND TRANSFORMING THE FARM-BOY IRREVOCABLY INTO THE X-MAN, COLOSSUS.
BY LENIN, EITHER MY HEART WILL BURST AND MY STEEL BODY CRACK--
YET HE REFUSES TO ENTIRELY CUT HIS TIES WITH HIS FORMER LIFE-- WHICH EXPLAINS HIS PRESENCE IN THIS FIELD BEHIND PROFESSOR XAVIER'S SCHOOL FOR GIFTED YOUNGSTERS, AND HIS DUEL WITH AN OLD, WITHERED TREE STUMP.
LF256

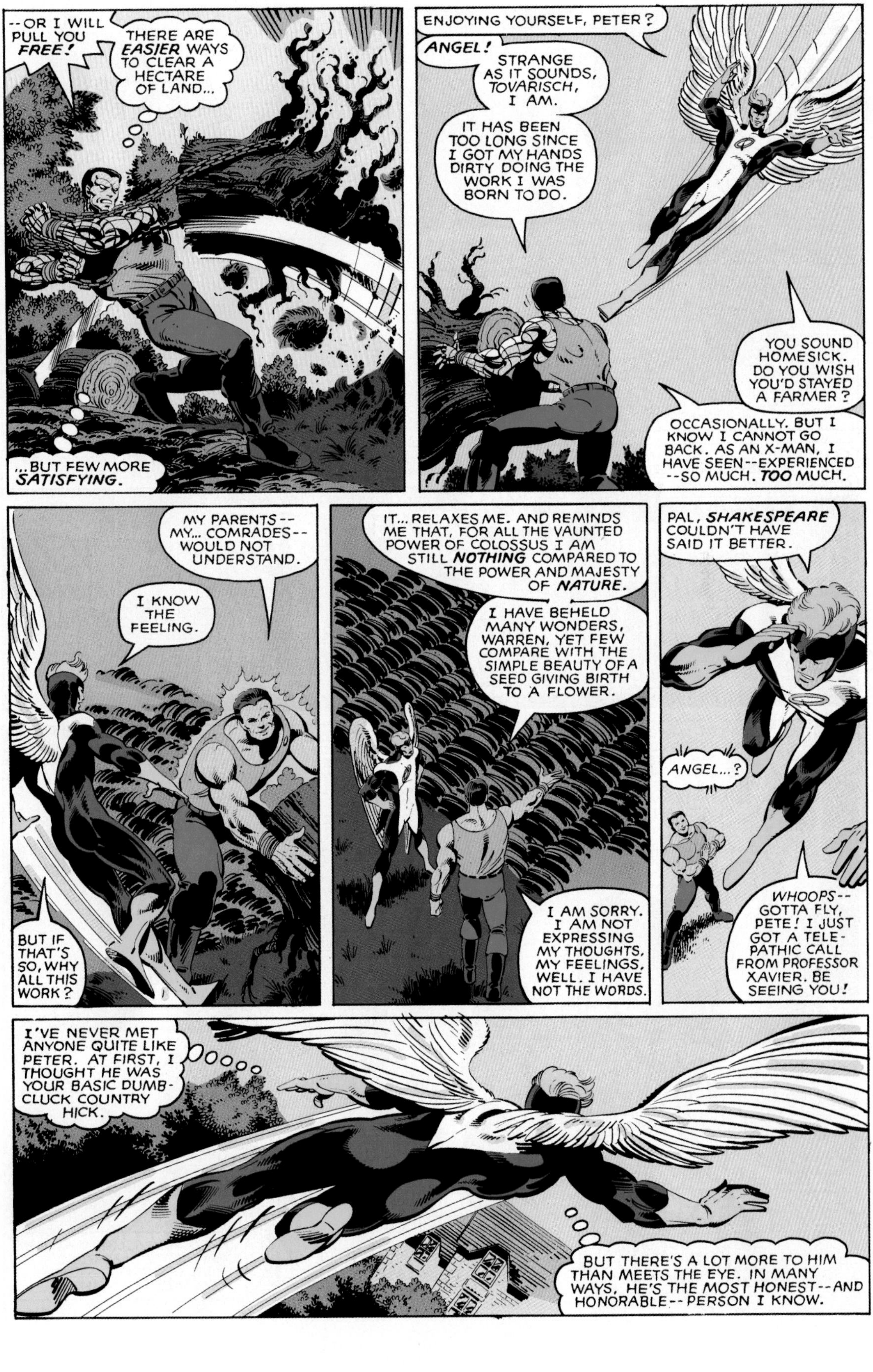
--OR I WILL PULL YOU FREE!
THERE ARE EASIER WAYS TO CLEAR A HECTARE OF LAND...
...BUT FEW MORE SATISFYING.
ENJOYING YOURSELF, PETER?
ANGEL!
STRANGE AS IT SOUNDS, TOVARISCH, I AM.
IT HAS BEEN TOO LONG SINCE I GOT MY HANDS DIRTY DOING THE WORK I WAS BORN TO DO.
YOU SOUND HOMESICK. DO YOU WISH YOU'D STAYED A FARMER?
OCCASIONALLY. BUT I KNOW I CANNOT GO BACK. AS AN X-MAN, I HAVE SEEN--EXPERIENCED --SO MUCH. TOO MUCH.
MY PARENTS-- MY... COMRADES-- WOULD NOT UNDERSTAND.
I KNOW THE FEELING.
BUT IF THAT'S SO, WHY ALL THIS WORK?
IT... RELAXES ME. AND REMINDS ME THAT, FOR ALL THE VAUNTED POWER OF COLOSSUS I AM STILL NOTHING COMPARED TO THE POWER AND MAJESTY OF NATURE.
I HAVE BEHELD MANY WONDERS, WARREN, YET FEW COMPARE WITH THE SIMPLE BEAUTY OF A SEED GIVING BIRTH TO A FLOWER.
I AM SORRY. I AM NOT EXPRESSING MY THOUGHTS, MY FEELINGS, WELL. I HAVE NOT THE WORDS.
PAL, SHAKESPEARE COULDN'T HAVE SAID IT BETTER.
ANGEL...?
WHOOPS-- GOTTA FLY, PETE! I JUST GOT A TELE-PATHIC CALL FROM PROFESSOR XAVIER. BE SEEING YOU!
I'VE NEVER MET ANYONE QUITE LIKE PETER. AT FIRST, I THOUGHT HE WAS YOUR BASIC DUMB-CLUCK COUNTRY HICK.
BUT THERE'S A LOT MORE TO HIM THAN MEETS THE EYE. IN MANY WAYS, HE'S THE MOST HONEST--AND HONORABLE--PERSON I KNOW.

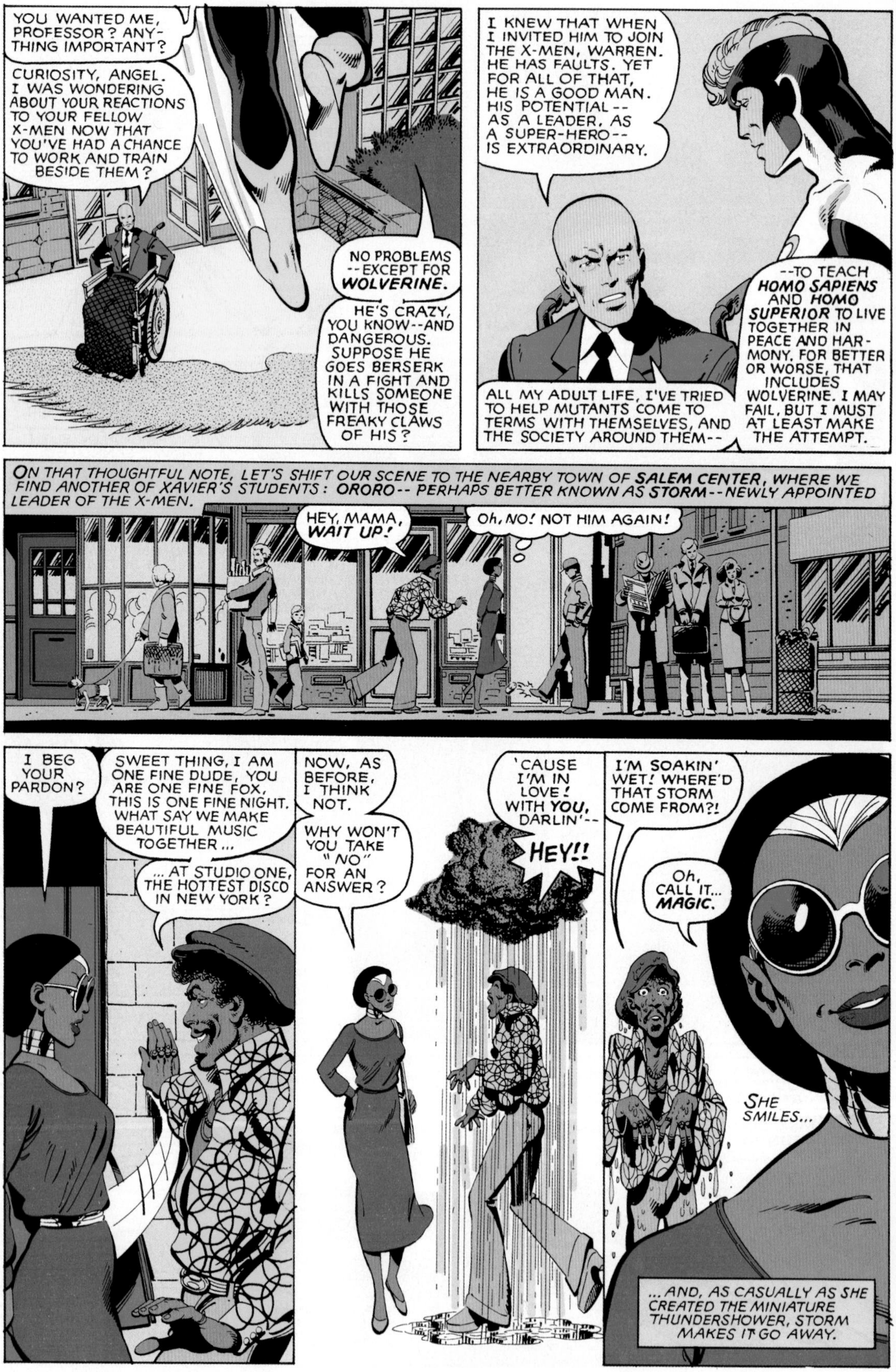

YOU WANTED ME, PROFESSOR? ANYTHING IMPORTANT?
CURIOSITY, ANGEL. I WAS WONDERING ABOUT YOUR REACTIONS TO YOUR FELLOW X-MEN NOW THAT YOU'VE HAD A CHANCE TO WORK AND TRAIN BESIDE THEM?
NO PROBLEMS --EXCEPT FOR **WOLVERINE.**
HE'S CRAZY, YOU KNOW--AND DANGEROUS. SUPPOSE HE GOES BERSERK IN A FIGHT AND KILLS SOMEONE WITH THOSE FREAKY CLAWS OF HIS?
I KNEW THAT WHEN I INVITED HIM TO JOIN THE X-MEN, WARREN. HE HAS FAULTS. YET FOR ALL OF THAT, HE IS A GOOD MAN. HIS POTENTIAL -- AS A LEADER, AS A SUPER-HERO-- IS EXTRAORDINARY.
ALL MY ADULT LIFE, I'VE TRIED TO HELP MUTANTS COME TO TERMS WITH THEMSELVES, AND THE SOCIETY AROUND THEM--
--TO TEACH **HOMO SAPIENS** AND **HOMO SUPERIOR** TO LIVE TOGETHER IN PEACE AND HARMONY. FOR BETTER OR WORSE, THAT INCLUDES WOLVERINE. I MAY FAIL, BUT I MUST AT LEAST MAKE THE ATTEMPT.
*ON THAT THOUGHTFUL NOTE, LET'S SHIFT OUR SCENE TO THE NEARBY TOWN OF **SALEM CENTER**, WHERE WE FIND ANOTHER OF XAVIER'S STUDENTS: **ORORO**-- PERHAPS BETTER KNOWN AS **STORM**--NEWLY APPOINTED LEADER OF THE X-MEN.*
HEY, MAMA, **WAIT UP!**
Oh, NO! NOT HIM AGAIN!
I BEG YOUR PARDON?
SWEET THING, I AM ONE FINE DUDE, YOU ARE ONE FINE FOX. THIS IS ONE FINE NIGHT. WHAT SAY WE MAKE BEAUTIFUL MUSIC TOGETHER...
...AT STUDIO ONE, THE HOTTEST DISCO IN NEW YORK?
NOW, AS BEFORE, I THINK NOT.
WHY WON'T YOU TAKE "NO" FOR AN ANSWER?
'CAUSE I'M IN LOVE! WITH **YOU**, DARLIN'--
HEY!!
I'M SOAKIN' WET! WHERE'D THAT STORM COME FROM?!
Oh, CALL IT... **MAGIC.**
SHE SMILES...
...AND, AS CASUALLY AS SHE CREATED THE MINIATURE THUNDERSHOWER, STORM MAKES IT GO AWAY.

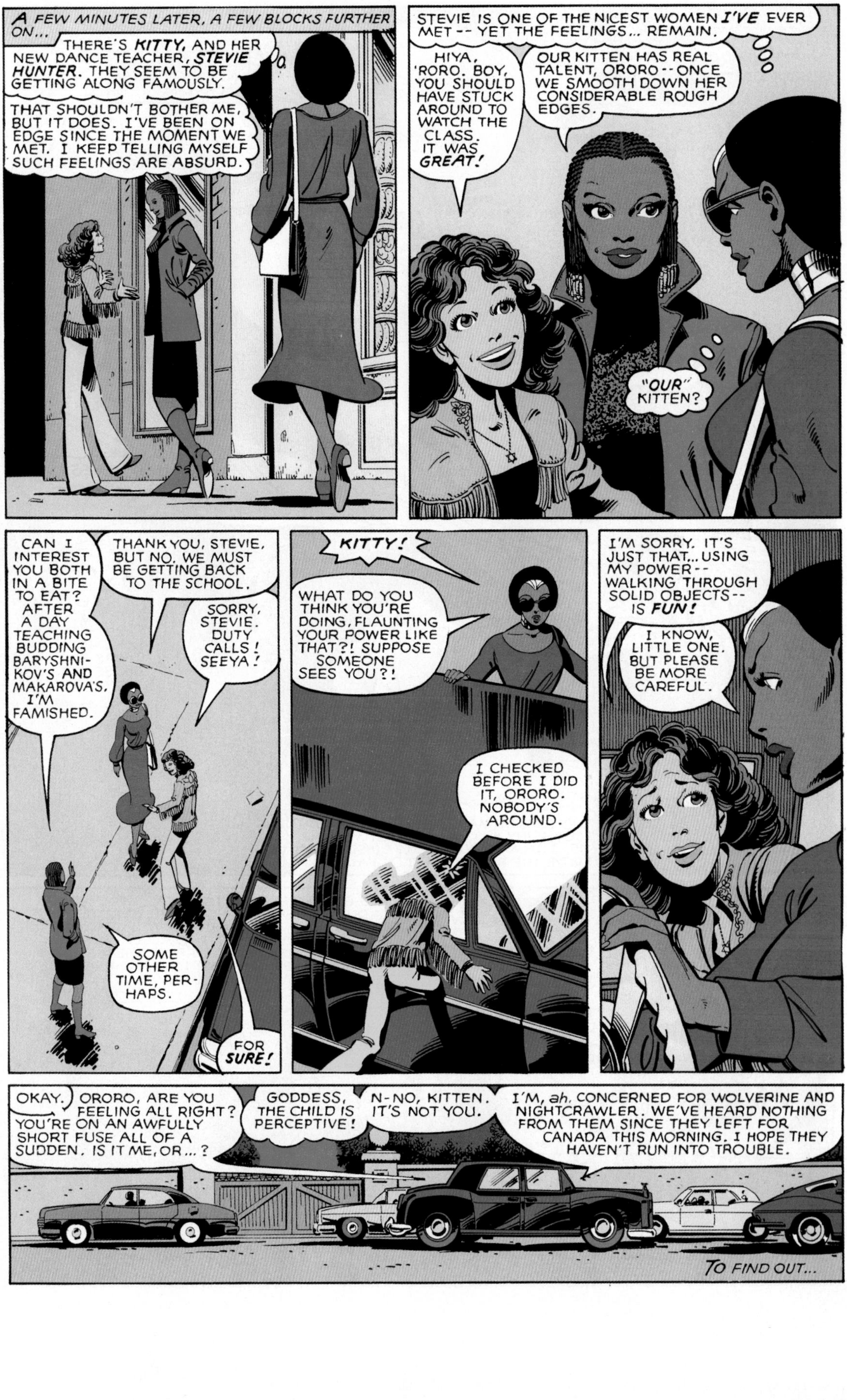
A FEW MINUTES LATER, A FEW BLOCKS FURTHER ON...
THERE'S KITTY, AND HER NEW DANCE TEACHER, STEVIE HUNTER. THEY SEEM TO BE GETTING ALONG FAMOUSLY.
THAT SHOULDN'T BOTHER ME, BUT IT DOES. I'VE BEEN ON EDGE SINCE THE MOMENT WE MET. I KEEP TELLING MYSELF SUCH FEELINGS ARE ABSURD.
STEVIE IS ONE OF THE NICEST WOMEN I'VE EVER MET -- YET THE FEELINGS... REMAIN.
HIYA, 'RORO. BOY, YOU SHOULD HAVE STUCK AROUND TO WATCH THE CLASS. IT WAS GREAT!
OUR KITTEN HAS REAL TALENT, ORORO -- ONCE WE SMOOTH DOWN HER CONSIDERABLE ROUGH EDGES.
"OUR" KITTEN?
CAN I INTEREST YOU BOTH IN A BITE TO EAT? AFTER A DAY TEACHING BUDDING BARYSHNIKOV'S AND MAKAROVA'S, I'M FAMISHED.
THANK YOU, STEVIE, BUT NO. WE MUST BE GETTING BACK TO THE SCHOOL.
SORRY, STEVIE. DUTY CALLS! SEEYA!
SOME OTHER TIME, PERHAPS.
FOR SURE!
KITTY!
WHAT DO YOU THINK YOU'RE DOING, FLAUNTING YOUR POWER LIKE THAT?! SUPPOSE SOMEONE SEES YOU?!
I CHECKED BEFORE I DID IT, ORORO. NOBODY'S AROUND.
I'M SORRY. IT'S JUST THAT... USING MY POWER -- WALKING THROUGH SOLID OBJECTS -- IS FUN!
I KNOW, LITTLE ONE. BUT PLEASE BE MORE CAREFUL.
OKAY.
ORORO, ARE YOU FEELING ALL RIGHT? YOU'RE ON AN AWFULLY SHORT FUSE ALL OF A SUDDEN. IS IT ME, OR...?
GODDESS, THE CHILD IS PERCEPTIVE!
N-NO, KITTEN. IT'S NOT YOU.
I'M, ah, CONCERNED FOR WOLVERINE AND NIGHTCRAWLER. WE'VE HEARD NOTHING FROM THEM SINCE THEY LEFT FOR CANADA THIS MORNING. I HOPE THEY HAVEN'T RUN INTO TROUBLE.
TO FIND OUT...

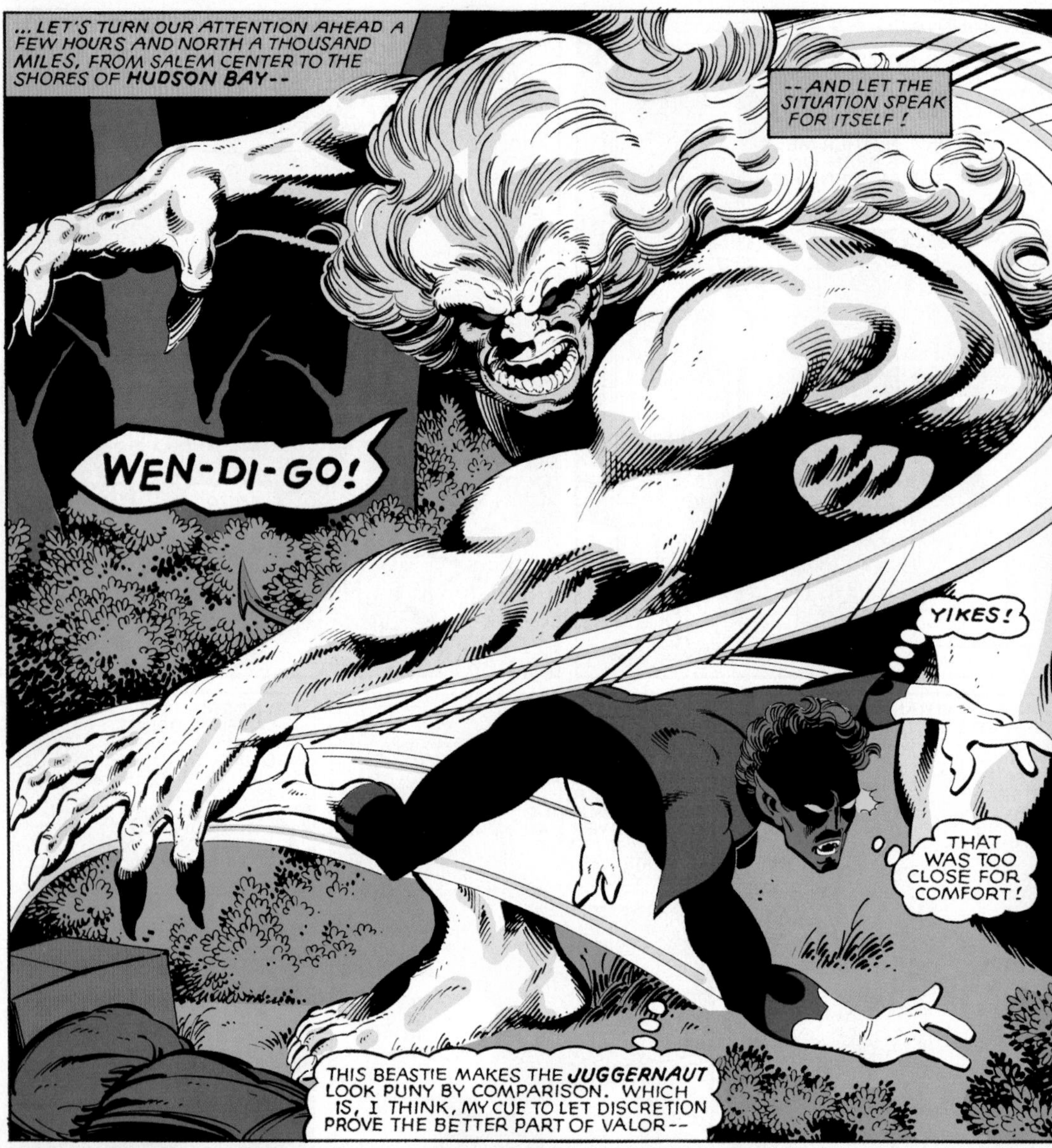
...LET'S TURN OUR ATTENTION AHEAD A FEW HOURS AND NORTH A THOUSAND MILES, FROM SALEM CENTER TO THE SHORES OF HUDSON BAY--
--AND LET THE SITUATION SPEAK FOR ITSELF!
WEN-DI-GO!
YIKES!
THAT WAS TOO CLOSE FOR COMFORT!
THIS BEASTIE MAKES THE JUGGERNAUT LOOK PUNY BY COMPARISON. WHICH IS, I THINK, MY CUE TO LET DISCRETION PROVE THE BETTER PART OF VALOR--

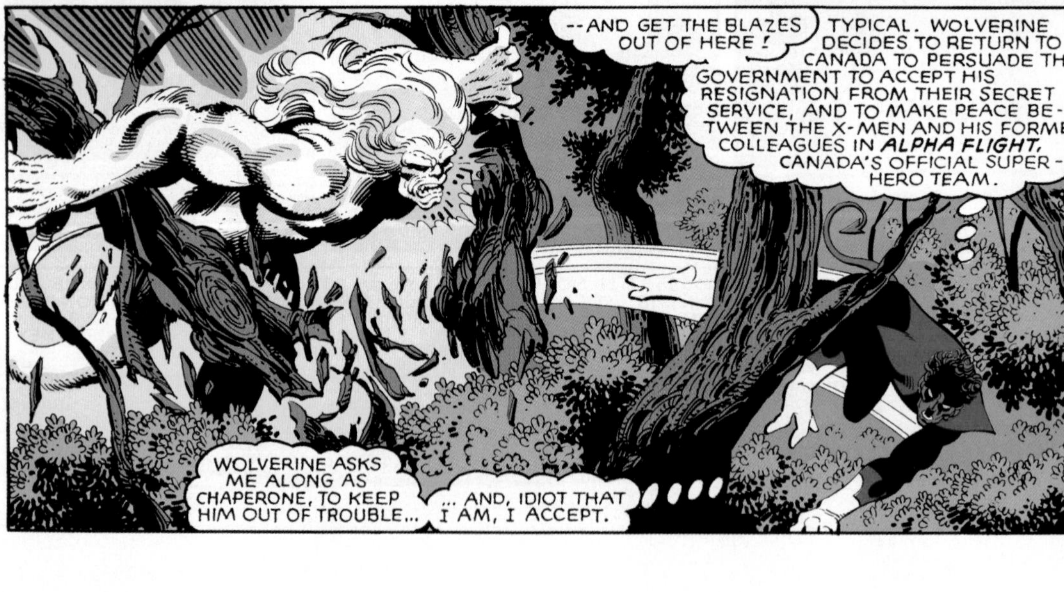
--AND GET THE BLAZES OUT OF HERE!
TYPICAL. WOLVERINE DECIDES TO RETURN TO CANADA TO PERSUADE THE GOVERNMENT TO ACCEPT HIS RESIGNATION FROM THEIR SECRET SERVICE, AND TO MAKE PEACE BETWEEN THE X-MEN AND HIS FORMER COLLEAGUES IN ALPHA FLIGHT, CANADA'S OFFICIAL SUPER-HERO TEAM.
WOLVERINE ASKS ME ALONG AS CHAPERONE, TO KEEP HIM OUT OF TROUBLE...
...AND, IDIOT THAT I AM, I ACCEPT.

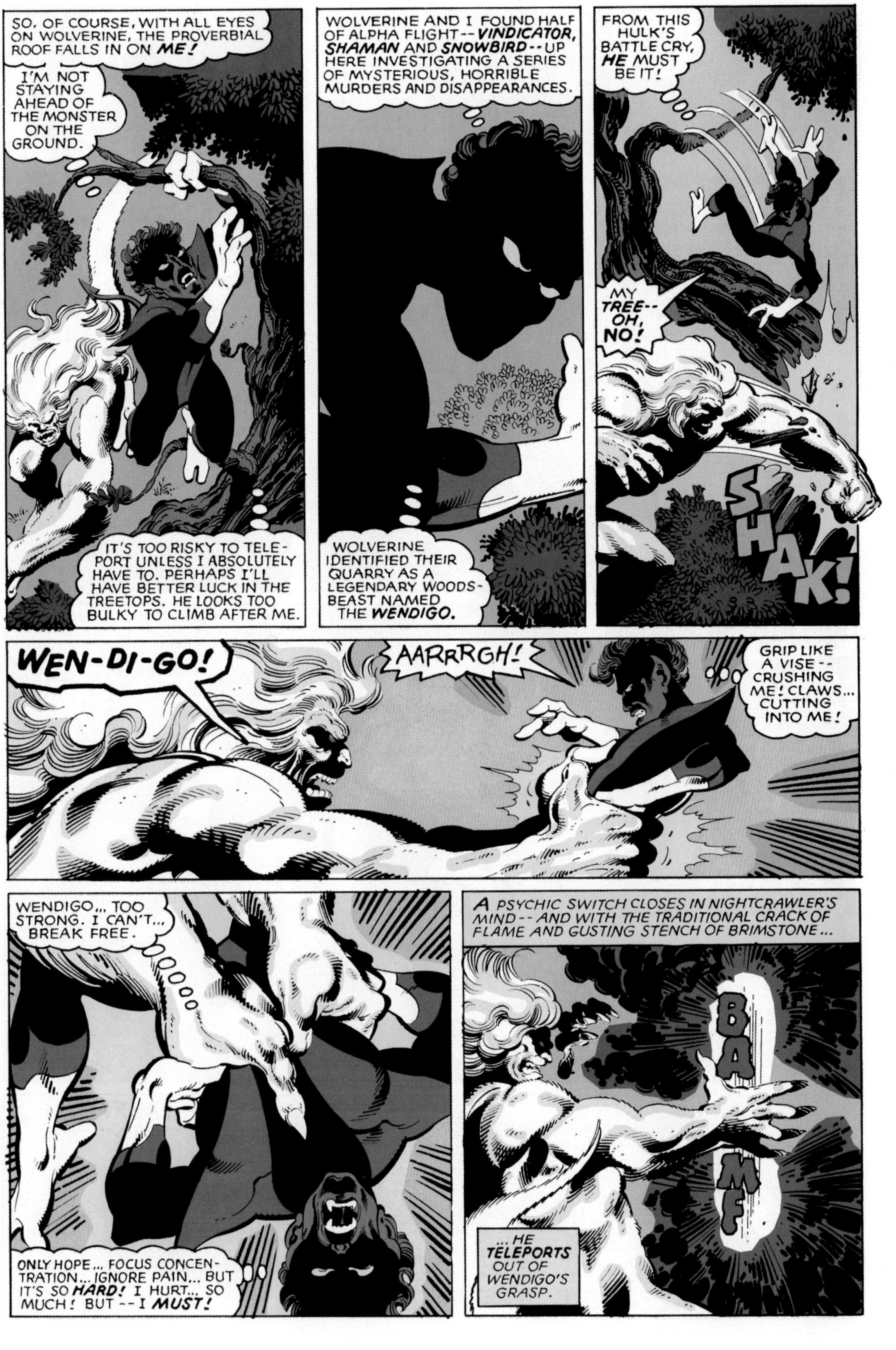

SO, OF COURSE, WITH ALL EYES ON WOLVERINE, THE PROVERBIAL ROOF FALLS IN ON ME!
I'M NOT STAYING AHEAD OF THE MONSTER ON THE GROUND.
IT'S TOO RISKY TO TELEPORT UNLESS I ABSOLUTELY HAVE TO. PERHAPS I'LL HAVE BETTER LUCK IN THE TREETOPS. HE LOOKS TOO BULKY TO CLIMB AFTER ME.
WOLVERINE AND I FOUND HALF OF ALPHA FLIGHT--VINDICATOR, SHAMAN AND SNOWBIRD--UP HERE INVESTIGATING A SERIES OF MYSTERIOUS, HORRIBLE MURDERS AND DISAPPEARANCES.
WOLVERINE IDENTIFIED THEIR QUARRY AS A LEGENDARY WOODS-BEAST NAMED THE WENDIGO.
FROM THIS HULK'S BATTLE CRY, HE MUST BE IT!
MY TREE-- OH, NO!
SHAK!
WEN-DI-GO!
AARRRGH!
GRIP LIKE A VISE--CRUSHING ME! CLAWS... CUTTING INTO ME!
WENDIGO... TOO STRONG. I CAN'T... BREAK FREE.
ONLY HOPE... FOCUS CONCENTRATION... IGNORE PAIN... BUT IT'S SO HARD! I HURT... SO MUCH! BUT--I MUST!
A PSYCHIC SWITCH CLOSES IN NIGHTCRAWLER'S MIND--AND WITH THE TRADITIONAL CRACK OF FLAME AND GUSTING STENCH OF BRIMSTONE...
BAMF
...HE TELEPORTS OUT OF WENDIGO'S GRASP.

THAT FEELS... SO MUCH BETTER!

I HAD TO TRY A *"BLIND"* 'PORT. I DON'T KNOW THE LAY OF THE LAND AROUND HERE. A WRONG MOVE -- EVEN A *SLIGHT* MIS-CALCULATION-- COULD HAVE HAD ME MATERIALIZING INSIDE A TREE.

AT BEST, I'D HAVE BEEN CRIPPLED OR MAIMED. AT WORST-- VERY MESSILY, AGONIZINGLY *KILLED.* LOVELY THOUGHT.

BAMF

AHA! THERE'S A CLEARING!

IT'S A FAR PIECE FROM WENDIGO, TOO. WITH LUCK, I'LL HAVE GIVEN HIM THE SLIP. I SHOULD BE ABLE TO GET BACK TO THE CABIN AND WARN THE OTHERS.

WEN-DI-GO!

ON THE OTHER HAND...

I CAN'T RUN AND IT'S TOO DARK-- TOO MANY TREES -- TO TRY ANOTHER 'PORT. I'LL HAVE TO *FIGHT.*

WENDIGO HAS THE EDGE -- AND WHAT AN EDGE -- IN TERMS OF RAW STRENGTH, AND HIS TRACKING SKILLS SEEM AS FORMIDABLE AS *WOLVERINE'S.*

IN *MY* FAVOR, I HAVE SPEED, AGILITY, MARTIAL ARTS TRAINING. I'LL HIT-AND-RUN, TRY TO KEEP HIM CONFUSED AND OFF-BALANCE...

OH BOY!

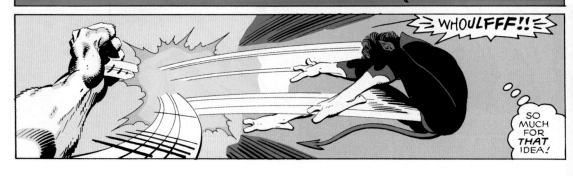

WHOULFFF!!

SO MUCH FOR *THAT* IDEA!

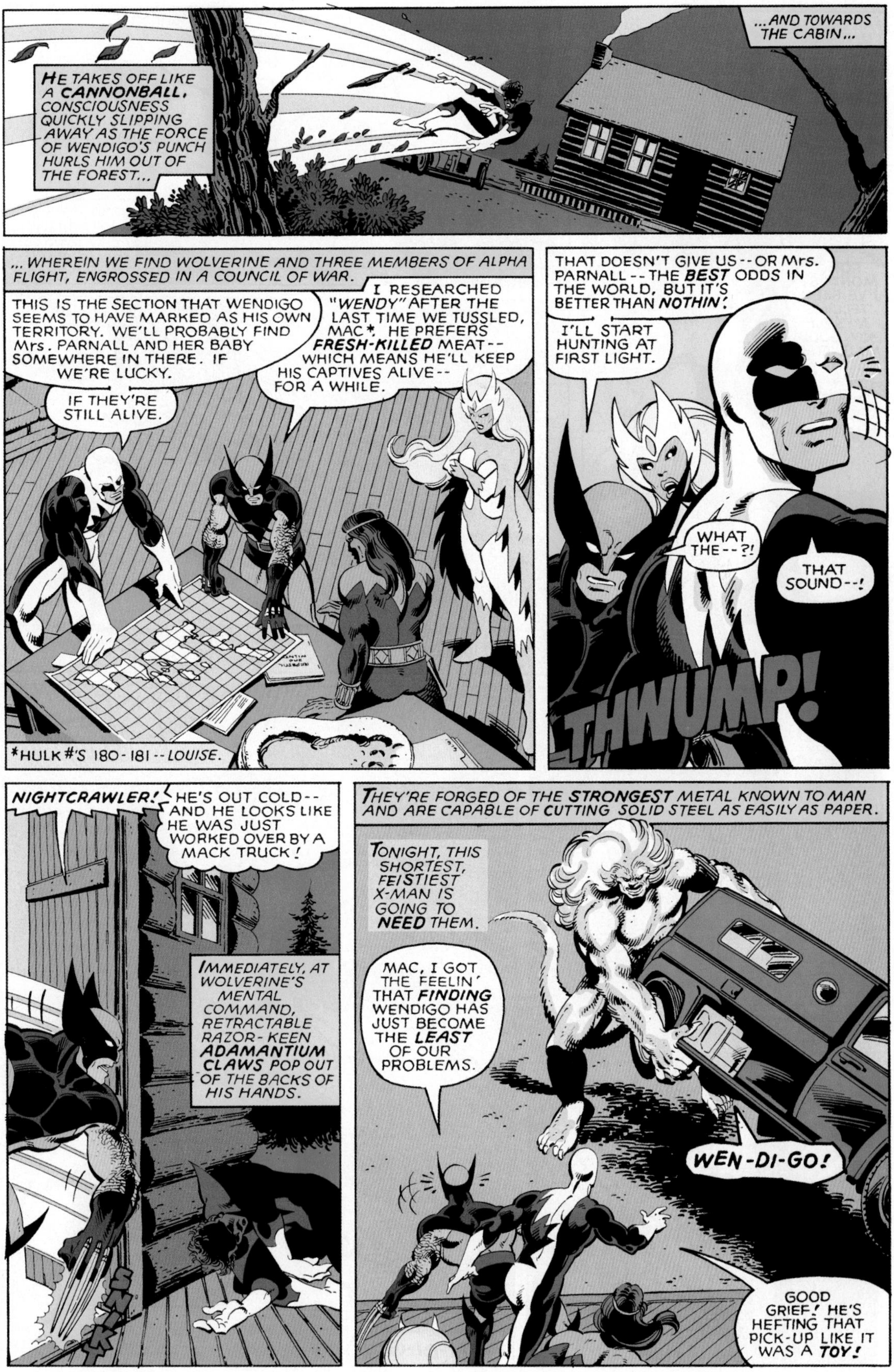

HE TAKES OFF LIKE A CANNONBALL, CONSCIOUSNESS QUICKLY SLIPPING AWAY AS THE FORCE OF WENDIGO'S PUNCH HURLS HIM OUT OF THE FOREST...
...AND TOWARDS THE CABIN...
...WHEREIN WE FIND WOLVERINE AND THREE MEMBERS OF ALPHA FLIGHT, ENGROSSED IN A COUNCIL OF WAR.
THIS IS THE SECTION THAT WENDIGO SEEMS TO HAVE MARKED AS HIS OWN TERRITORY. WE'LL PROBABLY FIND Mrs. PARNALL AND HER BABY SOMEWHERE IN THERE. IF WE'RE LUCKY.
IF THEY'RE STILL ALIVE.
I RESEARCHED "WENDY" AFTER THE LAST TIME WE TUSSLED, MAC*. HE PREFERS FRESH-KILLED MEAT-- WHICH MEANS HE'LL KEEP HIS CAPTIVES ALIVE-- FOR A WHILE.
*HULK #'S 180-181 --LOUISE.
THAT DOESN'T GIVE US--OR Mrs. PARNALL--THE BEST ODDS IN THE WORLD, BUT IT'S BETTER THAN NOTHIN'.
I'LL START HUNTING AT FIRST LIGHT.
WHAT THE--?!
THAT SOUND--!
THWUMP!
NIGHTCRAWLER!
HE'S OUT COLD-- AND HE LOOKS LIKE HE WAS JUST WORKED OVER BY A MACK TRUCK!
IMMEDIATELY, AT WOLVERINE'S MENTAL COMMAND, RETRACTABLE RAZOR-KEEN ADAMANTIUM CLAWS POP OUT OF THE BACKS OF HIS HANDS.
SNIKT
THEY'RE FORGED OF THE STRONGEST METAL KNOWN TO MAN AND ARE CAPABLE OF CUTTING SOLID STEEL AS EASILY AS PAPER.
TONIGHT, THIS SHORTEST, FEISTIEST X-MAN IS GOING TO NEED THEM.
MAC, I GOT THE FEELIN' THAT FINDING WENDIGO HAS JUST BECOME THE LEAST OF OUR PROBLEMS.
WEN-DI-GO!
GOOD GRIEF! HE'S HEFTING THAT PICK-UP LIKE IT WAS A TOY!

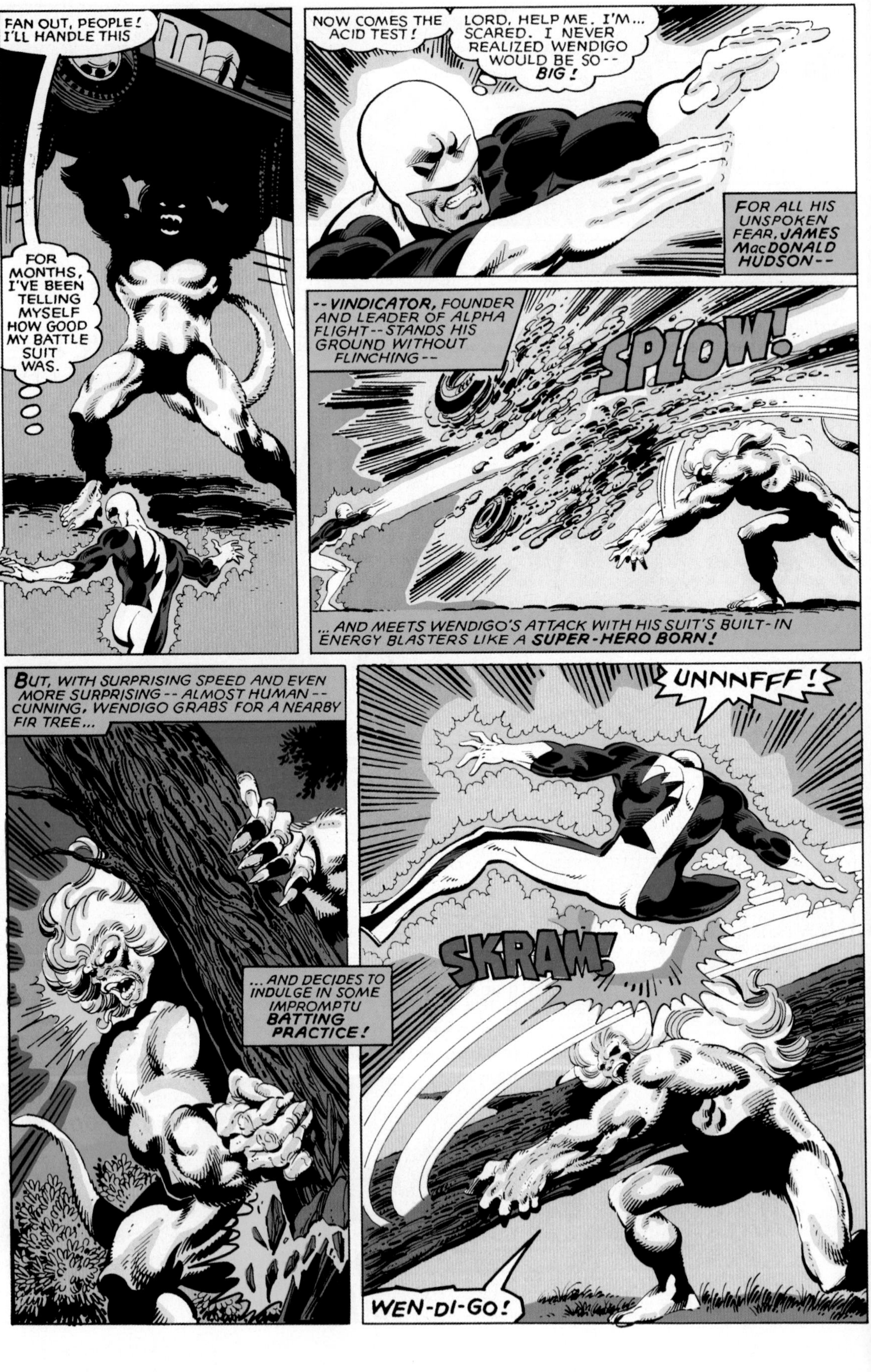
FAN OUT, PEOPLE! I'LL HANDLE THIS
FOR MONTHS, I'VE BEEN TELLING MYSELF HOW GOOD MY BATTLE SUIT WAS.
NOW COMES THE ACID TEST!
LORD, HELP ME. I'M... SCARED. I NEVER REALIZED WENDIGO WOULD BE SO-- BIG!
FOR ALL HIS UNSPOKEN FEAR, JAMES MacDONALD HUDSON--
--VINDICATOR, FOUNDER AND LEADER OF ALPHA FLIGHT--STANDS HIS GROUND WITHOUT FLINCHING--
SPLOW!
...AND MEETS WENDIGO'S ATTACK WITH HIS SUIT'S BUILT-IN ENERGY BLASTERS LIKE A SUPER-HERO BORN!
BUT, WITH SURPRISING SPEED AND EVEN MORE SURPRISING--ALMOST HUMAN--CUNNING, WENDIGO GRABS FOR A NEARBY FIR TREE...
...AND DECIDES TO INDULGE IN SOME IMPROMPTU BATTING PRACTICE!
UNNNFFF!
SKRAM!
WEN-DI-GO!

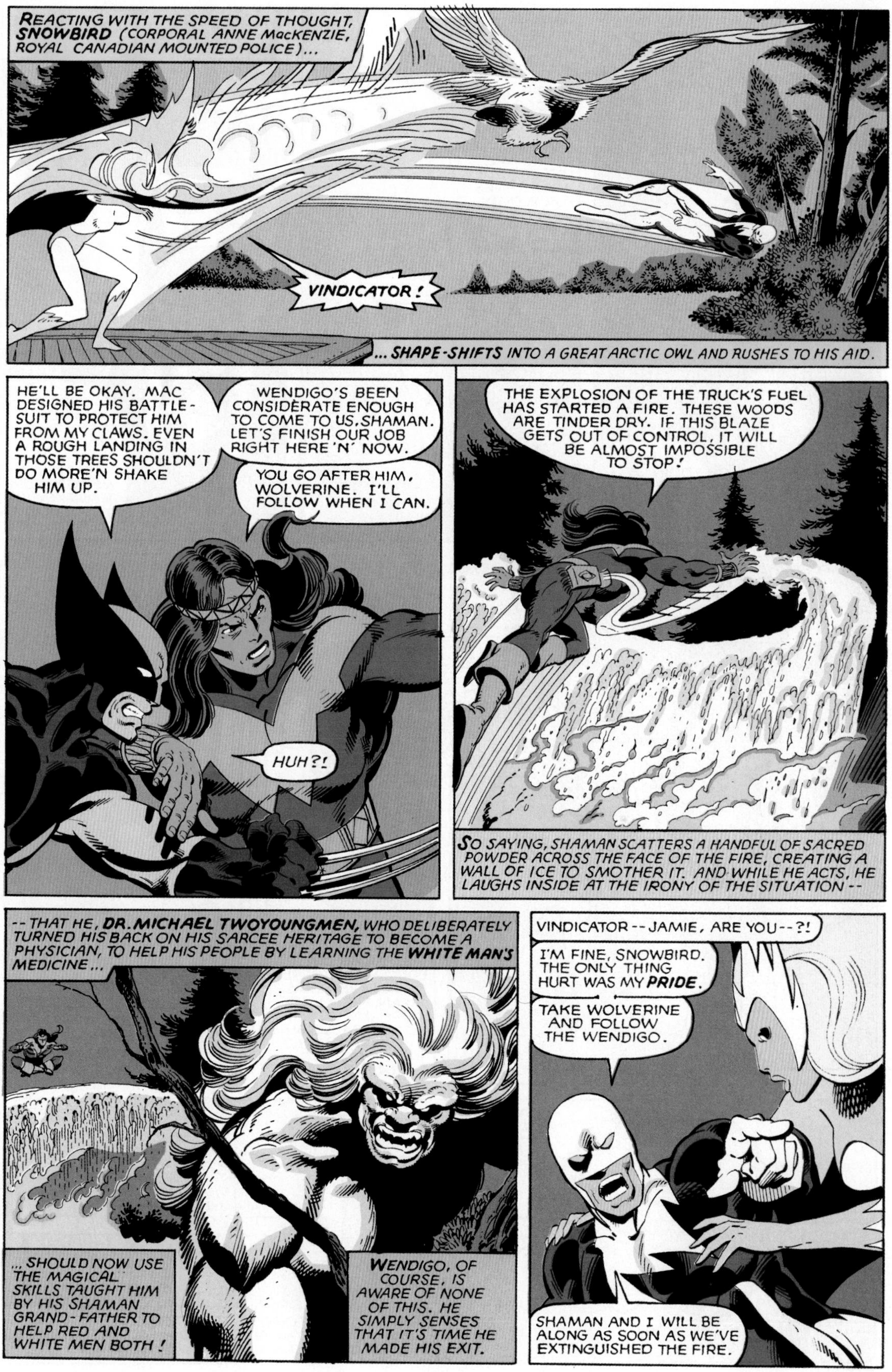
REACTING WITH THE SPEED OF THOUGHT, SNOWBIRD (CORPORAL ANNE MacKENZIE, ROYAL CANADIAN MOUNTED POLICE)...
VINDICATOR!
...SHAPE-SHIFTS INTO A GREAT ARCTIC OWL AND RUSHES TO HIS AID.
HE'LL BE OKAY. MAC DESIGNED HIS BATTLE-SUIT TO PROTECT HIM FROM MY CLAWS. EVEN A ROUGH LANDING IN THOSE TREES SHOULDN'T DO MORE'N SHAKE HIM UP.
WENDIGO'S BEEN CONSIDERATE ENOUGH TO COME TO US, SHAMAN. LET'S FINISH OUR JOB RIGHT HERE 'N' NOW.
YOU GO AFTER HIM, WOLVERINE. I'LL FOLLOW WHEN I CAN.
HUH?!
THE EXPLOSION OF THE TRUCK'S FUEL HAS STARTED A FIRE. THESE WOODS ARE TINDER DRY. IF THIS BLAZE GETS OUT OF CONTROL, IT WILL BE ALMOST IMPOSSIBLE TO STOP!
SO SAYING, SHAMAN SCATTERS A HANDFUL OF SACRED POWDER ACROSS THE FACE OF THE FIRE, CREATING A WALL OF ICE TO SMOTHER IT. AND WHILE HE ACTS, HE LAUGHS INSIDE AT THE IRONY OF THE SITUATION --
-- THAT HE, DR. MICHAEL TWOYOUNGMEN, WHO DELIBERATELY TURNED HIS BACK ON HIS SARCEE HERITAGE TO BECOME A PHYSICIAN, TO HELP HIS PEOPLE BY LEARNING THE WHITE MAN'S MEDICINE...
...SHOULD NOW USE THE MAGICAL SKILLS TAUGHT HIM BY HIS SHAMAN GRAND-FATHER TO HELP RED AND WHITE MEN BOTH!
WENDIGO, OF COURSE, IS AWARE OF NONE OF THIS. HE SIMPLY SENSES THAT IT'S TIME HE MADE HIS EXIT.
VINDICATOR -- JAMIE, ARE YOU --?!
I'M FINE, SNOWBIRD. THE ONLY THING HURT WAS MY PRIDE.
TAKE WOLVERINE AND FOLLOW THE WENDIGO.
SHAMAN AND I WILL BE ALONG AS SOON AS WE'VE EXTINGUISHED THE FIRE.

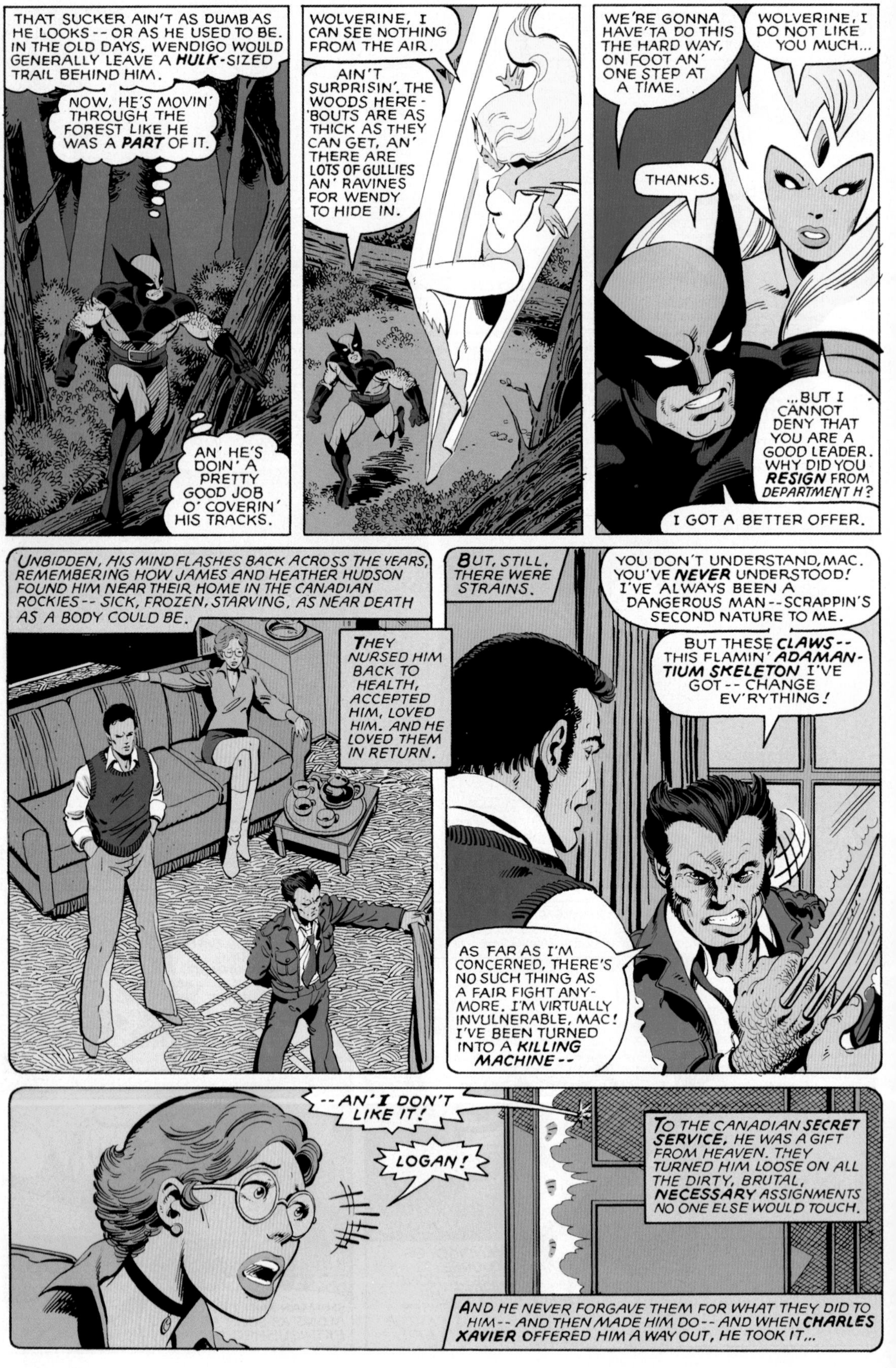
THAT SUCKER AIN'T AS DUMB AS HE LOOKS -- OR AS HE USED TO BE. IN THE OLD DAYS, WENDIGO WOULD GENERALLY LEAVE A HULK-SIZED TRAIL BEHIND HIM.
NOW, HE'S MOVIN' THROUGH THE FOREST LIKE HE WAS A PART OF IT.
AN' HE'S DOIN' A PRETTY GOOD JOB O' COVERIN' HIS TRACKS.
WOLVERINE, I CAN SEE NOTHING FROM THE AIR.
AIN'T SURPRISIN'. THE WOODS HERE-'BOUTS ARE AS THICK AS THEY CAN GET, AN' THERE ARE LOTS OF GULLIES AN' RAVINES FOR WENDY TO HIDE IN.
WE'RE GONNA HAVE'TA DO THIS THE HARD WAY, ON FOOT AN' ONE STEP AT A TIME.
WOLVERINE, I DO NOT LIKE YOU MUCH...
THANKS.
...BUT I CANNOT DENY THAT YOU ARE A GOOD LEADER. WHY DID YOU RESIGN FROM DEPARTMENT H?
I GOT A BETTER OFFER.
UNBIDDEN, HIS MIND FLASHES BACK ACROSS THE YEARS, REMEMBERING HOW JAMES AND HEATHER HUDSON FOUND HIM NEAR THEIR HOME IN THE CANADIAN ROCKIES -- SICK, FROZEN, STARVING, AS NEAR DEATH AS A BODY COULD BE.
THEY NURSED HIM BACK TO HEALTH, ACCEPTED HIM, LOVED HIM. AND HE LOVED THEM IN RETURN.
BUT, STILL, THERE WERE STRAINS.
YOU DON'T UNDERSTAND, MAC. YOU'VE NEVER UNDERSTOOD! I'VE ALWAYS BEEN A DANGEROUS MAN -- SCRAPPIN'S SECOND NATURE TO ME.
BUT THESE CLAWS -- THIS FLAMIN' ADAMANTIUM SKELETON I'VE GOT -- CHANGE EV'RYTHING!
AS FAR AS I'M CONCERNED, THERE'S NO SUCH THING AS A FAIR FIGHT ANY-MORE. I'M VIRTUALLY INVULNERABLE, MAC! I'VE BEEN TURNED INTO A KILLING MACHINE --
-- AN' I DON'T LIKE IT!
LOGAN!
TO THE CANADIAN SECRET SERVICE, HE WAS A GIFT FROM HEAVEN. THEY TURNED HIM LOOSE ON ALL THE DIRTY, BRUTAL, NECESSARY ASSIGNMENTS NO ONE ELSE WOULD TOUCH.
AND HE NEVER FORGAVE THEM FOR WHAT THEY DID TO HIM -- AND THEN MADE HIM DO -- AND WHEN CHARLES XAVIER OFFERED HIM A WAY OUT, HE TOOK IT...

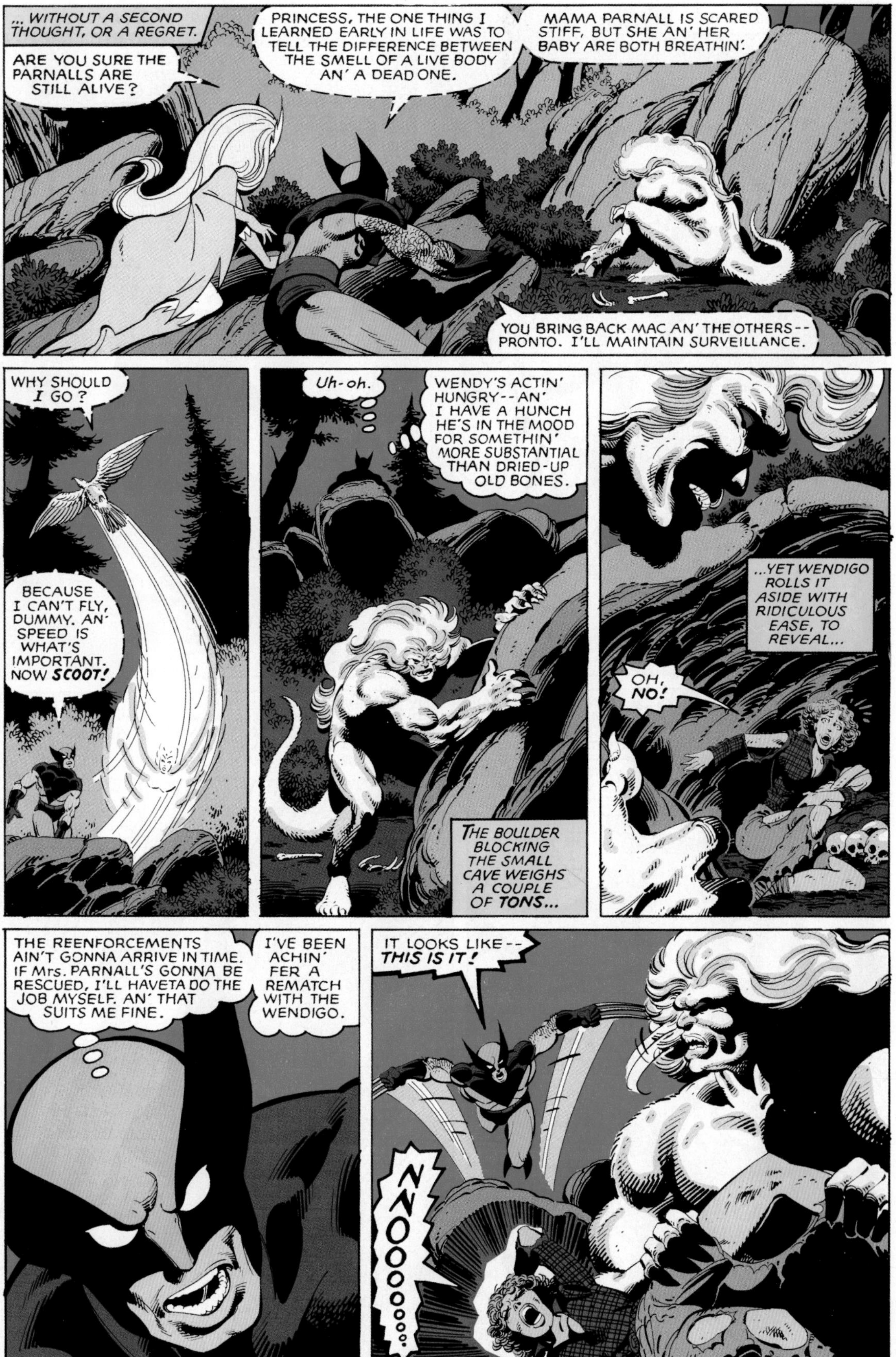

... WITHOUT A SECOND THOUGHT, OR A REGRET.
ARE YOU SURE THE PARNALLS ARE STILL ALIVE?
PRINCESS, THE ONE THING I LEARNED EARLY IN LIFE WAS TO TELL THE DIFFERENCE BETWEEN THE SMELL OF A LIVE BODY AN' A DEAD ONE.
MAMA PARNALL IS SCARED STIFF, BUT SHE AN' HER BABY ARE BOTH BREATHIN'.
YOU BRING BACK MAC AN' THE OTHERS -- PRONTO. I'LL MAINTAIN SURVEILLANCE.
WHY SHOULD I GO?
BECAUSE I CAN'T FLY, DUMMY. AN' SPEED IS WHAT'S IMPORTANT. NOW SCOOT!
Uh-oh.
WENDY'S ACTIN' HUNGRY -- AN' I HAVE A HUNCH HE'S IN THE MOOD FOR SOMETHIN' MORE SUBSTANTIAL THAN DRIED-UP OLD BONES.
THE BOULDER BLOCKING THE SMALL CAVE WEIGHS A COUPLE OF TONS...
...YET WENDIGO ROLLS IT ASIDE WITH RIDICULOUS EASE, TO REVEAL...
OH, NO!
THE REENFORCEMENTS AIN'T GONNA ARRIVE IN TIME. IF Mrs. PARNALL'S GONNA BE RESCUED, I'LL HAVETA DO THE JOB MYSELF. AN' THAT SUITS ME FINE.
I'VE BEEN ACHIN' FER A REMATCH WITH THE WENDIGO.
IT LOOKS LIKE -- THIS IS IT!
NNOOOOOoo.

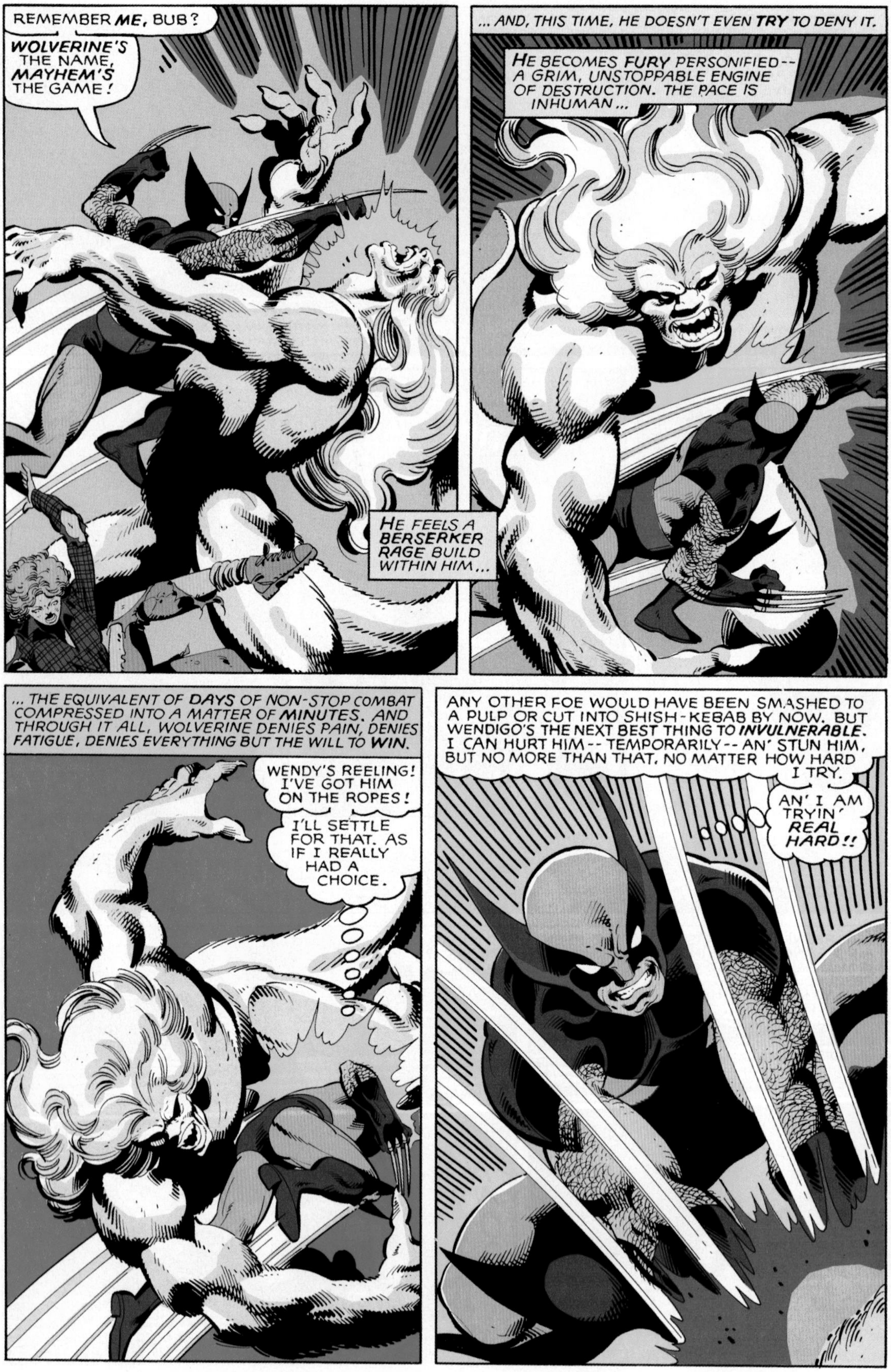
REMEMBER ME, BUB?
WOLVERINE'S THE NAME, MAYHEM'S THE GAME!
HE FEELS A BERSERKER RAGE BUILD WITHIN HIM...
... AND, THIS TIME, HE DOESN'T EVEN TRY TO DENY IT.
HE BECOMES FURY PERSONIFIED -- A GRIM, UNSTOPPABLE ENGINE OF DESTRUCTION. THE PACE IS INHUMAN...
... THE EQUIVALENT OF DAYS OF NON-STOP COMBAT COMPRESSED INTO A MATTER OF MINUTES. AND THROUGH IT ALL, WOLVERINE DENIES PAIN, DENIES FATIGUE, DENIES EVERYTHING BUT THE WILL TO WIN.
WENDY'S REELING! I'VE GOT HIM ON THE ROPES!
I'LL SETTLE FOR THAT. AS IF I REALLY HAD A CHOICE.
ANY OTHER FOE WOULD HAVE BEEN SMASHED TO A PULP OR CUT INTO SHISH-KEBAB BY NOW. BUT WENDIGO'S THE NEXT BEST THING TO INVULNERABLE. I CAN HURT HIM -- TEMPORARILY -- AN' STUN HIM, BUT NO MORE THAN THAT, NO MATTER HOW HARD I TRY.
AN' I AM TRYIN' REAL HARD!!

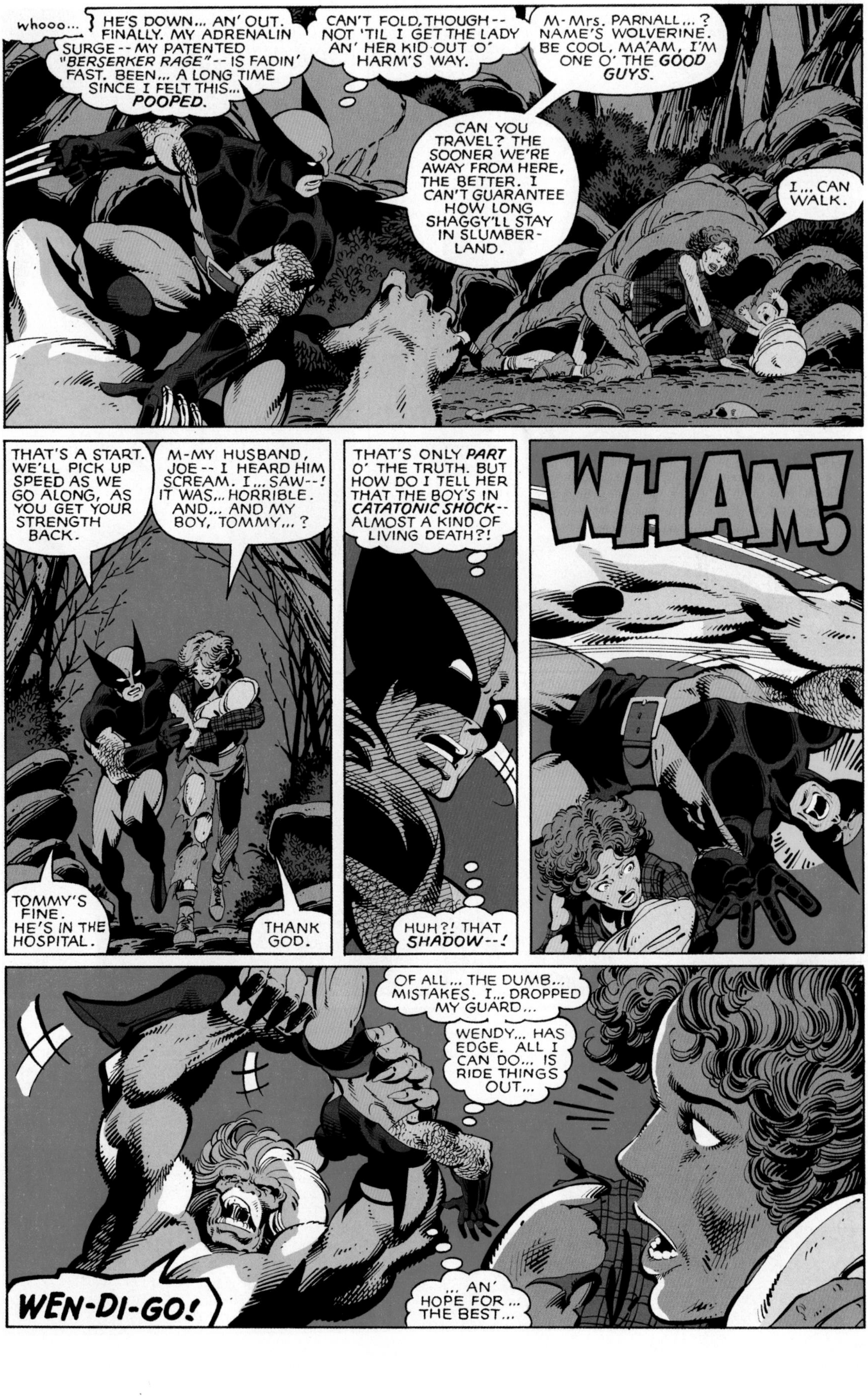
whooo...
HE'S DOWN... AN' OUT. FINALLY. MY ADRENALIN SURGE -- MY PATENTED "BERSERKER RAGE" -- IS FADIN' FAST. BEEN... A LONG TIME SINCE I FELT THIS... POOPED.
CAN'T FOLD, THOUGH -- NOT 'TIL I GET THE LADY AN' HER KID OUT O' HARM'S WAY.
M-Mrs. PARNALL...? NAME'S WOLVERINE. BE COOL, MA'AM, I'M ONE O' THE GOOD GUYS.
CAN YOU TRAVEL? THE SOONER WE'RE AWAY FROM HERE, THE BETTER. I CAN'T GUARANTEE HOW LONG SHAGGY'LL STAY IN SLUMBER-LAND.
I... CAN WALK.
THAT'S A START. WE'LL PICK UP SPEED AS WE GO ALONG, AS YOU GET YOUR STRENGTH BACK.
M-MY HUSBAND, JOE -- I HEARD HIM SCREAM. I... SAW--! IT WAS... HORRIBLE. AND... AND MY BOY, TOMMY...?
TOMMY'S FINE. HE'S IN THE HOSPITAL.
THANK GOD.
THAT'S ONLY PART O' THE TRUTH. BUT HOW DO I TELL HER THAT THE BOY'S IN CATATONIC SHOCK -- ALMOST A KIND OF LIVING DEATH?!
HUH?! THAT SHADOW--!
WHAM!
OF ALL... THE DUMB... MISTAKES. I... DROPPED MY GUARD...
WENDY... HAS EDGE. ALL I CAN DO... IS RIDE THINGS OUT...
WEN-DI-GO!
... AN' HOPE FOR... THE BEST...

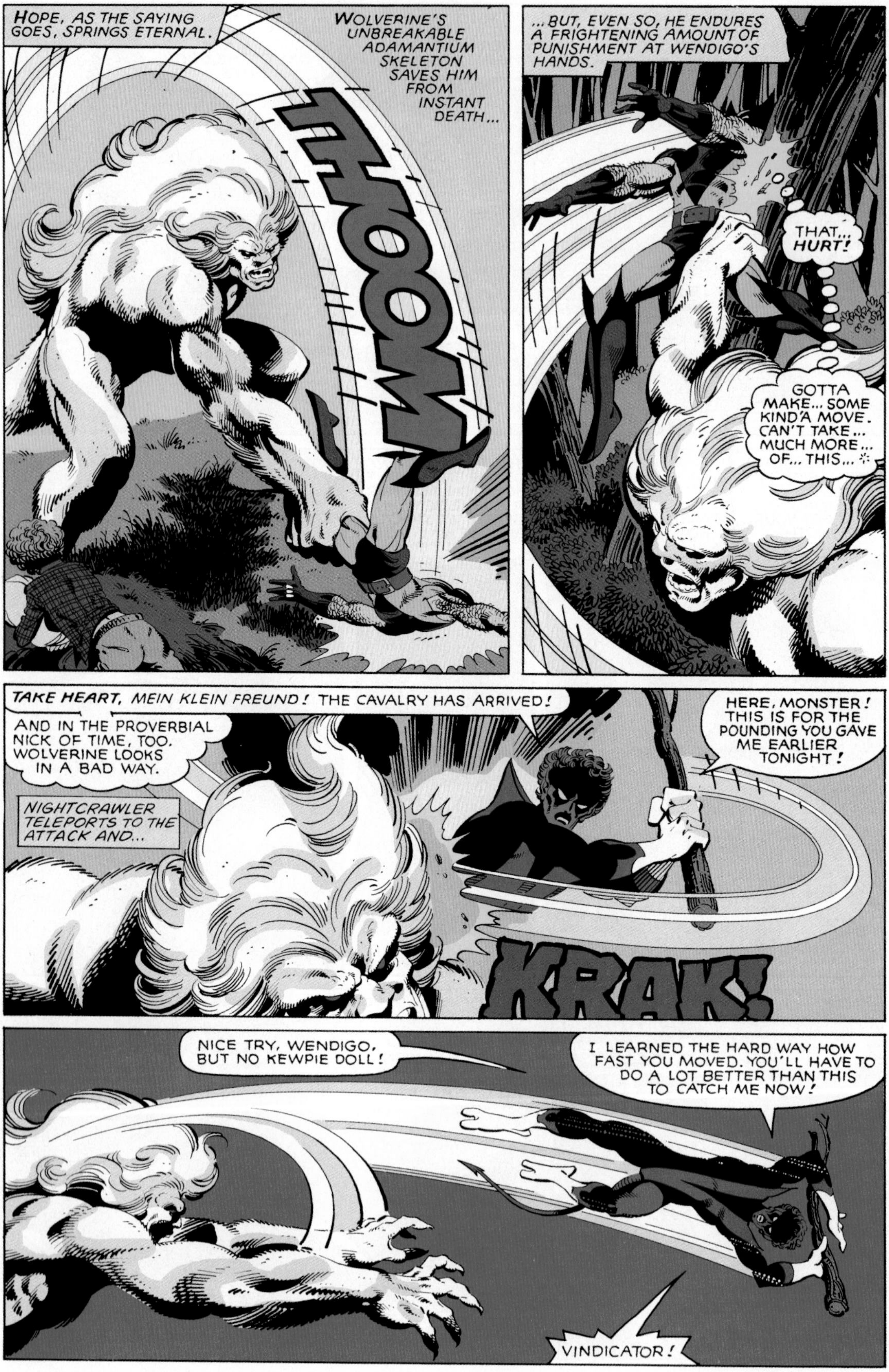
HOPE, AS THE SAYING GOES, SPRINGS ETERNAL.
WOLVERINE'S UNBREAKABLE ADAMANTIUM SKELETON SAVES HIM FROM INSTANT DEATH...
THOOM
...BUT, EVEN SO, HE ENDURES A FRIGHTENING AMOUNT OF PUNISHMENT AT WENDIGO'S HANDS.
THAT... HURT!
GOTTA MAKE... SOME KIND'A MOVE. CAN'T TAKE... MUCH MORE... OF... THIS...
TAKE HEART, MEIN KLEIN FREUND! THE CAVALRY HAS ARRIVED!
AND IN THE PROVERBIAL NICK OF TIME, TOO. WOLVERINE LOOKS IN A BAD WAY.
NIGHTCRAWLER TELEPORTS TO THE ATTACK AND...
HERE, MONSTER! THIS IS FOR THE POUNDING YOU GAVE ME EARLIER TONIGHT!
KRAK!
NICE TRY, WENDIGO, BUT NO KEWPIE DOLL!
I LEARNED THE HARD WAY HOW FAST YOU MOVED. YOU'LL HAVE TO DO A LOT BETTER THAN THIS TO CATCH ME NOW!
VINDICATOR!

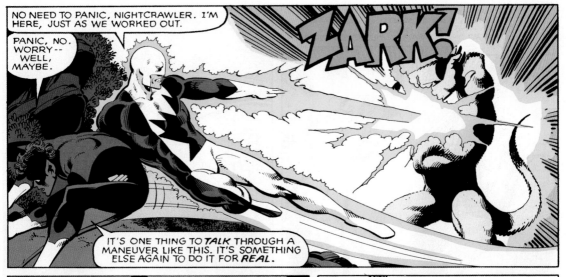

NO NEED TO PANIC, NIGHTCRAWLER. I'M HERE, JUST AS WE WORKED OUT.

PANIC, NO. WORRY-- WELL, MAYBE.

ZARK!

IT'S ONE THING TO *TALK* THROUGH A MANEUVER LIKE THIS. IT'S SOMETHING ELSE AGAIN TO DO IT FOR *REAL.*

I WAS AFRAID OF THIS. WE'RE STAGGERING WENDIGO, BUT NO MORE THAN THAT. THE ENCHANTMENT THAT CREATED HIM PROTECTS HIM FROM THE FULL FORCE OF OUR POWERS.

HE'S TOO STRONG. MY MAGICK CAN'T EVEN BIND HIM-- MUCH LESS *CURE* HIM-- WHILE HE'S CONSCIOUS.

PHYSICAL FORCE CAN OVERWHELM HIM. THE HULK AND WOLVERINE PROVED THAT.

WOLVERINE'S OUT COLD, SNOWBIRD. AND THE HULK ISN'T AVAILABLE.

TRUE

...BUT PERHAPS I CAN SHAPE-CHANGE INTO THE NEXT BEST THING.

THERE IS GREAT *DANGER* IN THIS. I ASSUME THE PERSONA OF WHATEVER CREATURE I BECOME. IF I AM CONSUMED BY *BLOOD-LUST,* I COULD BECOME AS TERRIBLE A THREAT TO MY FRIENDS AS WENDIGO HIMSELF. BUT I CAN SEE NO ALTERNATIVE. THE RISK MUST BE TAKEN.

OH, *HODIAK*-- SPIRIT OF THE NORTHERN LIGHTS-- GRANDFATHER--HELP ME! GIVE ME STRENGTH!

WITH THAT IMPASSIONED PRAYER, THE FORM OF THIS CHILD OF THE ICE AND SNOW BEGINS TO MELT AND FLOW LIKE MERCURY...

...TRANSFORMING A BEING WHO APPEARS HUMAN (BUT WHO, IN TRUTH, IS NOT)...

*...FROM AN EXOTICALLY BEAUTIFUL YOUNG WOMAN INTO A **WHITE WOLVERINE.***

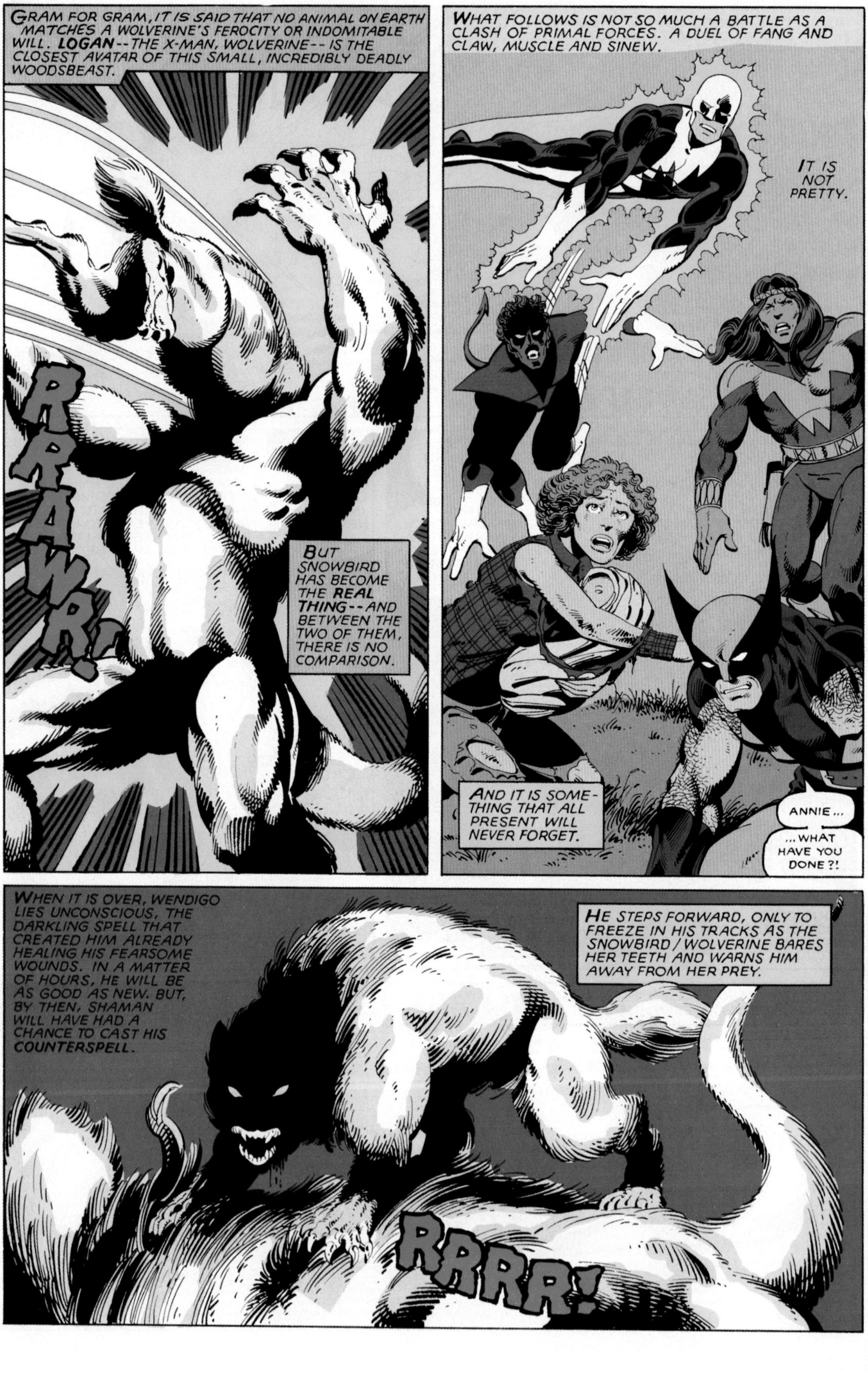
GRAM FOR GRAM, IT IS SAID THAT NO ANIMAL ON EARTH MATCHES A WOLVERINE'S FEROCITY OR INDOMITABLE WILL. LOGAN--THE X-MAN, WOLVERINE--IS THE CLOSEST AVATAR OF THIS SMALL, INCREDIBLY DEADLY WOODSBEAST.
RRAWR!
BUT SNOWBIRD HAS BECOME THE REAL THING--AND BETWEEN THE TWO OF THEM, THERE IS NO COMPARISON.
WHAT FOLLOWS IS NOT SO MUCH A BATTLE AS A CLASH OF PRIMAL FORCES. A DUEL OF FANG AND CLAW, MUSCLE AND SINEW.
IT IS NOT PRETTY.
AND IT IS SOMETHING THAT ALL PRESENT WILL NEVER FORGET.
ANNIE...
...WHAT HAVE YOU DONE?!
WHEN IT IS OVER, WENDIGO LIES UNCONSCIOUS, THE DARKLING SPELL THAT CREATED HIM ALREADY HEALING HIS FEARSOME WOUNDS. IN A MATTER OF HOURS, HE WILL BE AS GOOD AS NEW. BUT, BY THEN, SHAMAN WILL HAVE HAD A CHANCE TO CAST HIS COUNTERSPELL.
HE STEPS FORWARD, ONLY TO FREEZE IN HIS TRACKS AS THE SNOWBIRD/WOLVERINE BARES HER TEETH AND WARNS HIM AWAY FROM HER PREY.
RRRR!

SHE'S STILL A **WOLVERINE**! THE ANIMAL-PERSONA MUST HAVE TAKEN OVER!

MY **CHANGELING** SPELL WILL WORK AS WELL ON SNOWBIRD AS ON WENDIGO...

NO! SHE'LL FIGHT YOU, PHYSICALLY AND PSYCHICALLY. YOU COULD BE LEFT SO WASTED YOU WON'T BE ABLE TO HELP WENDIGO, AN' THEN ALL THIS PAIN AN' GRIEF WOULD HAVE BEEN FOR NOTHING.

LEAVE ANNIE TO ME.

GRRR!

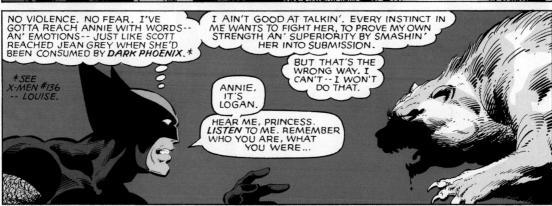

NO VIOLENCE. NO FEAR. I'VE GOTTA REACH ANNIE WITH WORDS-- AN' EMOTIONS-- JUST LIKE SCOTT REACHED JEAN GREY WHEN SHE'D BEEN CONSUMED BY **DARK PHOENIX**. *

*SEE X-MEN #136 -- LOUISE.

I AIN'T GOOD AT TALKIN'. EVERY INSTINCT IN ME WANTS TO FIGHT HER, TO PROVE MY OWN STRENGTH AN' SUPERIORITY BY SMASHIN' HER INTO SUBMISSION.

BUT THAT'S THE WRONG WAY. I CAN'T-- I WON'T DO THAT.

ANNIE, IT'S LOGAN.

HEAR ME, PRINCESS. **LISTEN** TO ME. REMEMBER WHO YOU ARE, WHAT YOU WERE...

*HE ISN'T AWARE OF HOW LONG HE TALKS, OR INDEED OF PRECISELY WHAT HE SAYS. IN A SENSE, HE BARES HIS **SOUL** TO HER, REACHING OUT WITH AS WILD AND FREE A PASSION AS HER OWN.*

RRAWR!

AND THEN, WITH A BLOOD-CURDLING SCREAM, THE SNOWBIRD/WOLVERINE RESPONDS.

LOGAN... OH, LOGAN...

...THANK YOU...

HUSH, DARLIN', HUSH. I KNOW HOW YOU FEEL. YOU'LL BE OKAY NOW, THOUGH. YOU'VE GONE THROUGH THE VALLEY, FACED THE WORST PARTS OF YOURSELF, AND **TRIUMPHED**. IT'LL NEVER BE AS ROUGH AGAIN.

THEY MOVE APART FROM THE OTHERS, THEIR WORDS AS PRIVATE AS THE EMOTIONS THEY STRUGGLE TO EXPRESS.

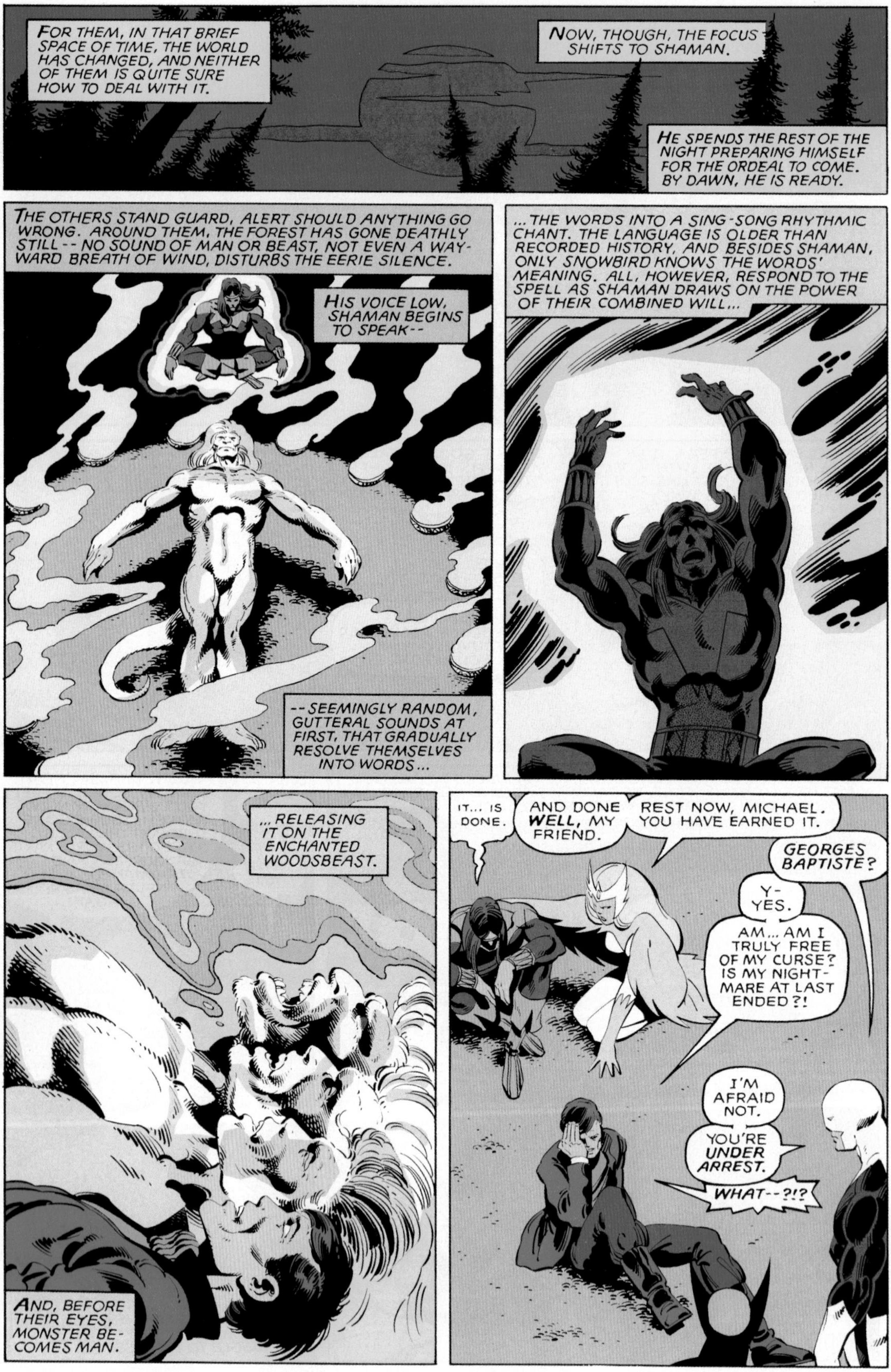
FOR THEM, IN THAT BRIEF SPACE OF TIME, THE WORLD HAS CHANGED, AND NEITHER OF THEM IS QUITE SURE HOW TO DEAL WITH IT.
NOW, THOUGH, THE FOCUS SHIFTS TO SHAMAN.
HE SPENDS THE REST OF THE NIGHT PREPARING HIMSELF FOR THE ORDEAL TO COME. BY DAWN, HE IS READY.
THE OTHERS STAND GUARD, ALERT SHOULD ANYTHING GO WRONG. AROUND THEM, THE FOREST HAS GONE DEATHLY STILL -- NO SOUND OF MAN OR BEAST, NOT EVEN A WAYWARD BREATH OF WIND, DISTURBS THE EERIE SILENCE.
HIS VOICE LOW, SHAMAN BEGINS TO SPEAK--
-- SEEMINGLY RANDOM, GUTTERAL SOUNDS AT FIRST, THAT GRADUALLY RESOLVE THEMSELVES INTO WORDS...
...THE WORDS INTO A SING-SONG RHYTHMIC CHANT. THE LANGUAGE IS OLDER THAN RECORDED HISTORY, AND BESIDES SHAMAN, ONLY SNOWBIRD KNOWS THE WORDS' MEANING. ALL, HOWEVER, RESPOND TO THE SPELL AS SHAMAN DRAWS ON THE POWER OF THEIR COMBINED WILL...
...RELEASING IT ON THE ENCHANTED WOODSBEAST.
AND, BEFORE THEIR EYES, MONSTER BECOMES MAN.
IT... IS DONE.
AND DONE WELL, MY FRIEND.
REST NOW, MICHAEL. YOU HAVE EARNED IT.
GEORGES BAPTISTE?
Y-YES.
AM... AM I TRULY FREE OF MY CURSE? IS MY NIGHTMARE AT LAST ENDED?!
I'M AFRAID NOT.
YOU'RE UNDER ARREST.
WHAT--?!?

LATER... I KNOW ARRESTING BAPTISTE SOUNDS CRUEL AND HEARTLESS, BUT I HAD NO CHOICE. HE BECAME WENDIGO OF HIS OWN FREE WILL. UNDER CANADIAN LAW, THAT RENDERS HIM CULPABLE FOR ANY CRIMES HE COMMITTED AS WENDIGO.

THE COURTS SHOULDN'T BE TOO HARD ON HIM, THOUGH. HIS ACTS WERE THOSE OF AN INSANE MAN, AND HIS MEMORIES OF WHAT HE DID ARE A FAR WORSE PUNISHMENT THAN A LIFETIME STRETCH IN PRISON.

THANKS FOR YOUR HELP, LOGAN. WE COULDN'T HAVE STOPPED HIM WITHOUT YOU. I'LL SPEAK TO THE MINISTER ABOUT YOUR RESIGNATION. THERE'LL BE NO MORE HASSLES, OF YOU OR THE X-MEN.

AND NOW THAT YOU'RE A FREE MAN, COME VISIT ME AND HEATHER MORE OFTEN. WE'RE YOUR FRIENDS, LOGAN. WE CARE ABOUT YOU. WE MISS YOU.

I KNOW, MAC. AND... I WILL.

WILL I SEE WOLVERINE AGAIN? WHO CAN SAY? DO I *WISH* TO?

YES.

LOOKING AT GEORGES BAPTISTE, *MEIN FREUND,* I CAN'T HELP THINKING, *"THERE BUT FOR THE GRACE OF GOD GOES YOU."*

HOW SO?

BAPTISTE, AS WENDIGO, KILLED. NOW HE MUST PAY THE PRICE. AND YOU, WOLVERINE? SHOULD YOU NOT PAY A PRICE AS WELL?

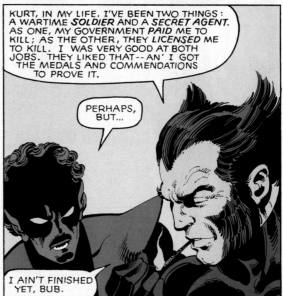

KURT, IN MY LIFE, I'VE BEEN TWO THINGS: A WARTIME *SOLDIER* AND A *SECRET AGENT.* AS ONE, MY GOVERNMENT *PAID* ME TO KILL; AS THE OTHER, THEY *LICENSED* ME TO KILL. I WAS VERY GOOD AT BOTH JOBS. THEY LIKED THAT-- AN' I GOT THE MEDALS AND COMMENDATIONS TO PROVE IT.

PERHAPS, BUT...

I AIN'T FINISHED YET, BUB.

A MAN COMES AT ME WITH HIS FISTS, I'LL MEET HIM WITH FISTS. BUT IF HE PULLS A GUN -- OR THREATENS PEOPLE I'M PROTECTIN'-- THEN I GOT NO SYMPATHY FOR HIM. HE MADE HIS CHOICE. HE'LL HAVE TO LIVE -- OR DIE -- WITH IT.

I NEVER USED MY CLAWS ON SOMEONE WHO HADN'T TRIED TO KILL ME FIRST. I CALL THAT *SELF-DEFENSE.*

I UNDERSTAND, LOGAN. WHAT YOU SAY IS REASONABLE, LOGICAL, JUSTIFIABLE.

BUT DOES THAT MAKE IT *RIGHT?*

WOLVERINE DOES NOT REPLY AND, FOR A LONG WHILE, THERE IS SILENCE BETWEEN THE TWO MEN...

... AND THE FEW TIMES HE DOES SPEAK, DURING THEIR LEISURELY MEANDER -- A VACATION BY ANY OTHER NAME -- HOME, HIS TONE IS THOUGHTFUL. NIGHTCRAWLER'S WORDS -- HIS FINAL QUESTION -- STRUCK DEEP.

NOW -- LIKE IT OR NOT, FOR BETTER OR WORSE -- WOLVERINE MUST DEAL WITH THEM.

MEANWHILE, IN THE PARLIAMENT BUILDING IN OTTAWA ...

YOU WANTED TO SEE ME, PRIME MINISTER?

YES, Dr. HUDSON. FIRSTLY, I'D LIKE TO CONGRATULATE ALPHA FLIGHT FOR YOUR HANDLING OF THIS "WENDIGO" BUSINESS. YOU DID WELL. I WISH I HAD A ... BETTER REWARD.

SIR?

THERE'S NO EASY WAY TO SAY THIS. I'M AFRAID DEPARTMENT H AND ALPHA FLIGHT ARE BEING DISBANDED.

TIMES ARE HARD. MONEY IS IN SHORT SUPPLY. THE HOUSE FELT THAT SUPER-HEROES WERE A LUXURY THE FEDERAL GOVERNMENT COULD NO LONGER AFFORD.

MANY MEMBERS -- LIKE THEIR CONSTITUENTS -- HAVE NEVER FELT ENTIRELY... COMFORTABLE WITH THE IDEA OF SUPER-BEINGS. THE CURRENT ANTI-MUTANT SENTIMENT IN THE UNITED STATES IS A GOOD EXAMPLE OF THAT.

REGRETTABLY, IGNORING YOUR EXISTENCE -- AS MANY ARE TRYING TO DO -- WILL NOT MAKE YOU DISAPPEAR.

THE GENIE IS OUT OF THE BOTTLE. PANDORA'S BOX IS OPEN. WE MUST LIVE WITH THIS REALITY AS BEST WE CAN. IF FOR NO OTHER REASON THAN THAT WE HAVE NO OTHER CHOICE.

I'M SORRY, JAMES. I WILL GIVE YOU AND ALPHA FLIGHT WHAT AID I CAN. YOU CAN KEEP YOUR SECURITY CLEARANCES AND YOUR STATUS AS R.C.M.P. AUXILIARIES. I WISH I COULD DO MORE.

I KNOW, SIR. DON'T WORRY, THOUGH. WE'LL MANAGE. SOMEHOW. WE'VE WORKED AND FOUGHT TOO HARD TO CHUCK EVERY-THING NOW.

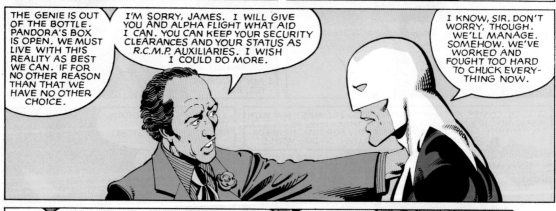

THAT'S THE SPIRIT.

VINDICATOR -- WHATEVER HAPPENS, I PRAY YOU'LL KEEP THE WELFARE OF CANADA AND HER PEOPLE FOREMOST IN YOUR THOUGHTS AND ACTIONS.

IN TIME, THEY WILL COME TO RESPECT -- AND HONOR -- YOU AND ALPHA FLIGHT, AS I DO.

I WILL, PRIME MINISTER. AND I HOPE YOU'RE RIGHT. GOOD-BYE.

AN ENDING OF SORTS, YET ALSO A BEGINNING -- OF A NEW, POSSIBLY BRIGHTER CHAP-TER IN THE LIFE OF ALPHA FLIGHT.

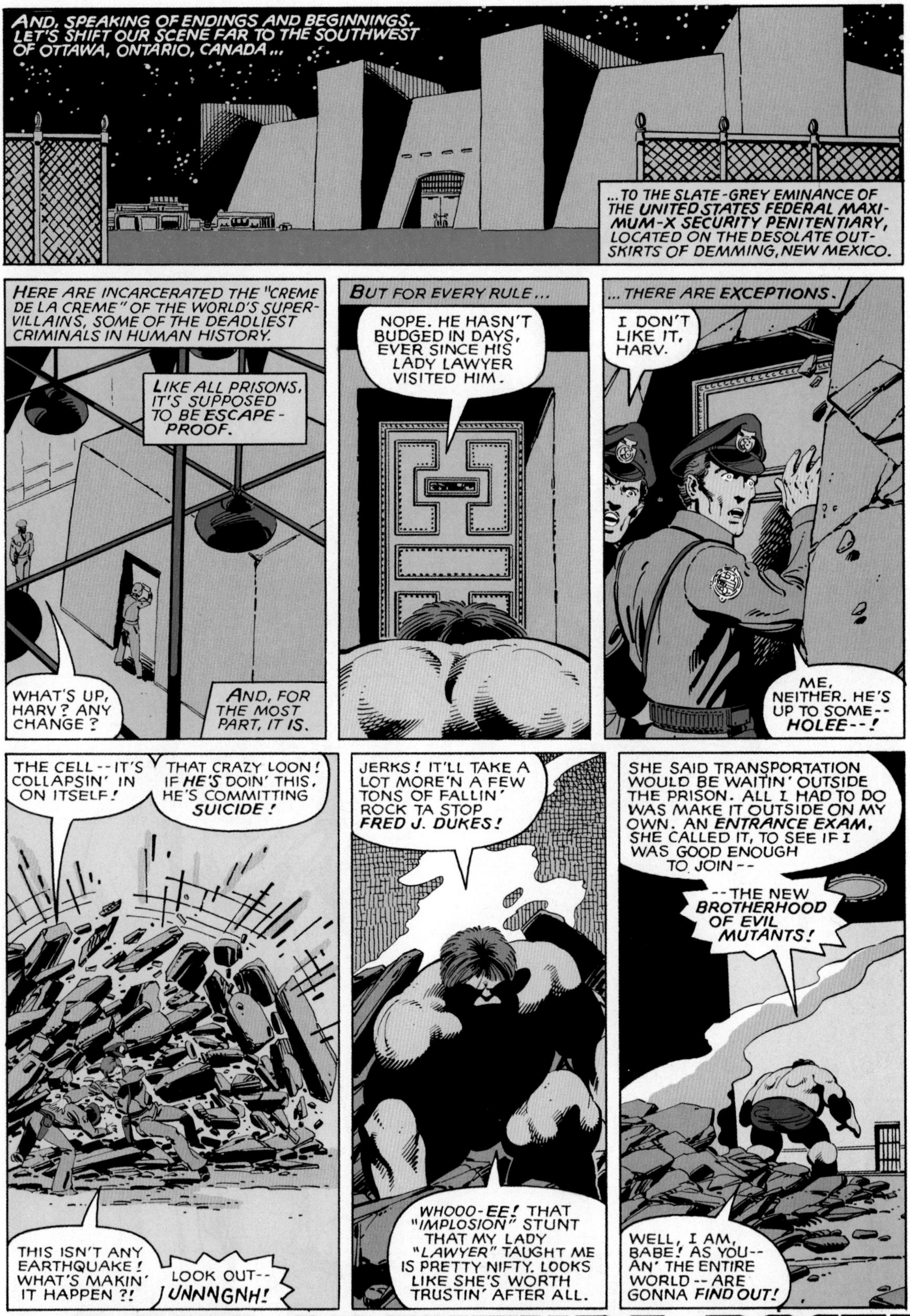

AND, SPEAKING OF ENDINGS AND BEGINNINGS, LET'S SHIFT OUR SCENE FAR TO THE SOUTHWEST OF OTTAWA, ONTARIO, CANADA...
...TO THE SLATE-GREY EMINANCE OF THE UNITED STATES FEDERAL MAXI-MUM-X SECURITY PENITENTIARY, LOCATED ON THE DESOLATE OUT-SKIRTS OF DEMMING, NEW MEXICO.
HERE ARE INCARCERATED THE "CREME DE LA CREME" OF THE WORLD'S SUPER-VILLAINS, SOME OF THE DEADLIEST CRIMINALS IN HUMAN HISTORY.
LIKE ALL PRISONS, IT'S SUPPOSED TO BE ESCAPE-PROOF.
WHAT'S UP, HARV? ANY CHANGE?
AND, FOR THE MOST PART, IT IS.
BUT FOR EVERY RULE...
NOPE. HE HASN'T BUDGED IN DAYS, EVER SINCE HIS LADY LAWYER VISITED HIM.
...THERE ARE EXCEPTIONS.
I DON'T LIKE IT, HARV.
ME, NEITHER. HE'S UP TO SOME-- HOLEE--!
THE CELL--IT'S COLLAPSIN' IN ON ITSELF!
THAT CRAZY LOON! IF HE'S DOIN' THIS, HE'S COMMITTING SUICIDE!
THIS ISN'T ANY EARTHQUAKE! WHAT'S MAKIN' IT HAPPEN ?!
LOOK OUT-- UNNNGNH!
JERKS! IT'LL TAKE A LOT MORE'N A FEW TONS OF FALLIN' ROCK TA STOP FRED J. DUKES!
WHOOO-EE! THAT "IMPLOSION" STUNT THAT MY LADY "LAWYER" TAUGHT ME IS PRETTY NIFTY. LOOKS LIKE SHE'S WORTH TRUSTIN' AFTER ALL.
SHE SAID TRANSPORTATION WOULD BE WAITIN' OUTSIDE THE PRISON. ALL I HAD TO DO WAS MAKE IT OUTSIDE ON MY OWN. AN ENTRANCE EXAM, SHE CALLED IT, TO SEE IF I WAS GOOD ENOUGH TO JOIN--
--THE NEW BROTHERHOOD OF EVIL MUTANTS!
WELL, I AM, BABE! AS YOU-- AN' THE ENTIRE WORLD--ARE GONNA FIND OUT!

NEXT DAYS OF FUTURE, PAST!

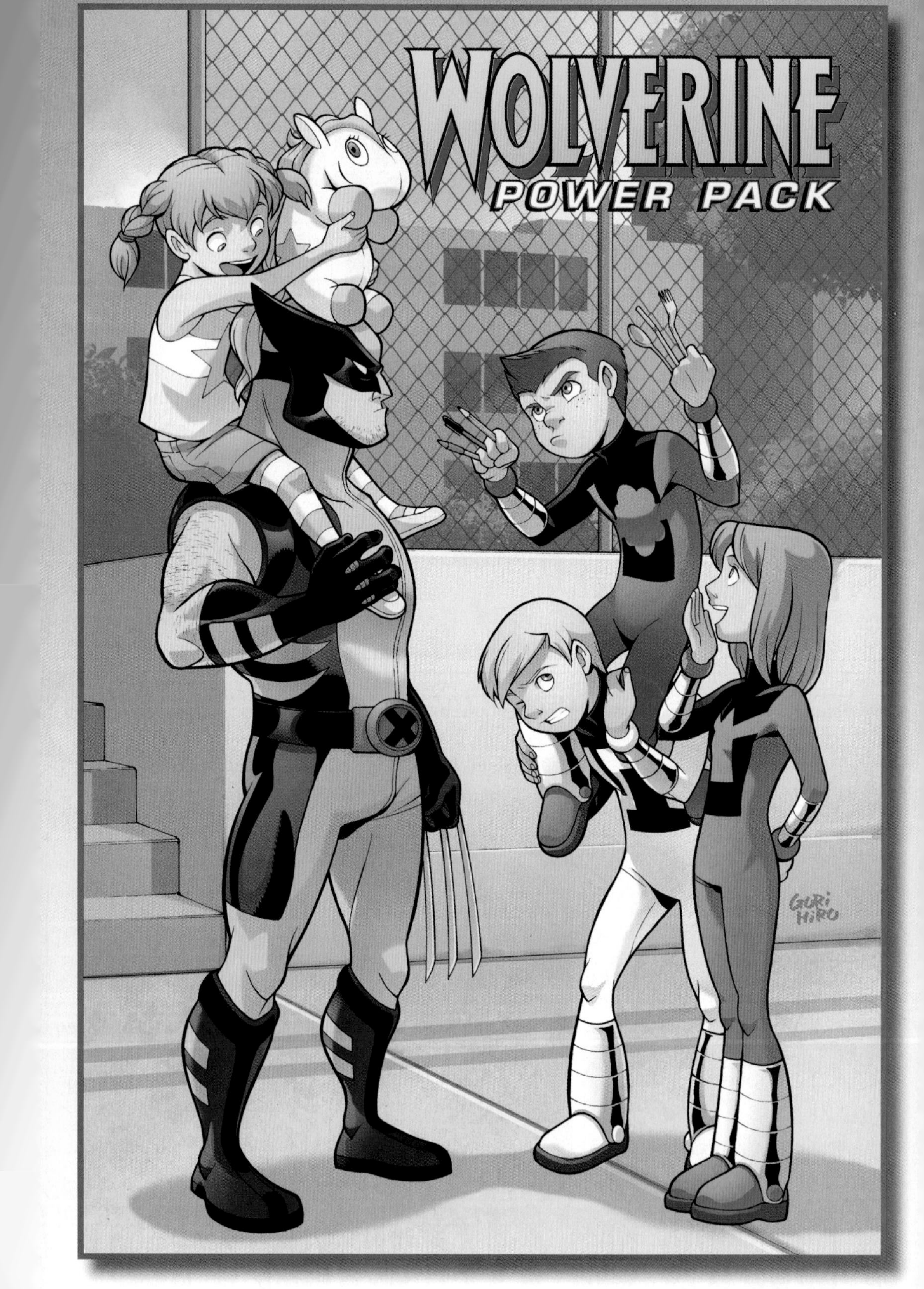
WOLVERINE
POWER PACK
GURIHIRU

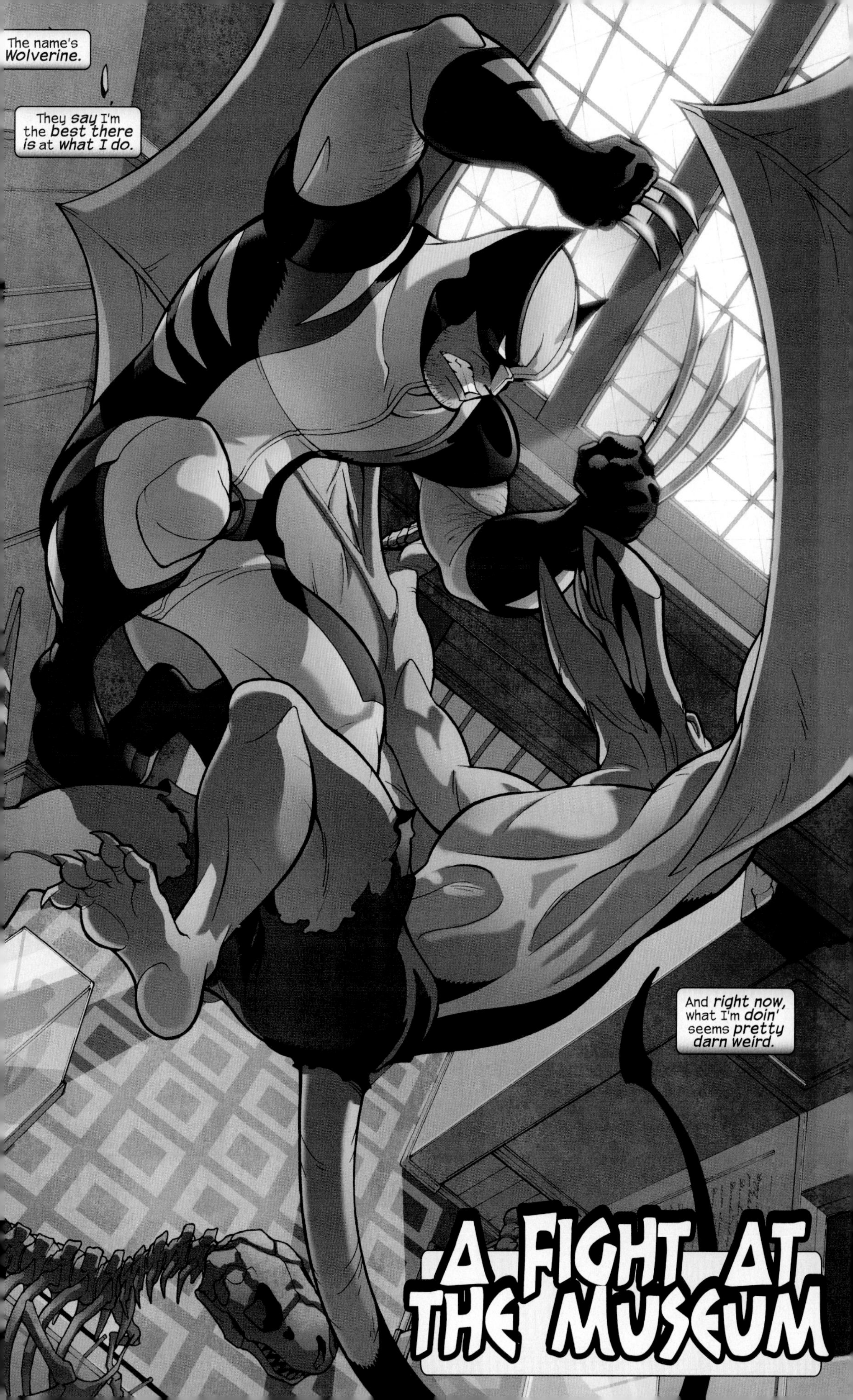
The name's Wolverine.
They say I'm the best there is at what I do.
And right now, what I'm doin' seems pretty darn weird.
A FIGHT AT THE MUSEUM

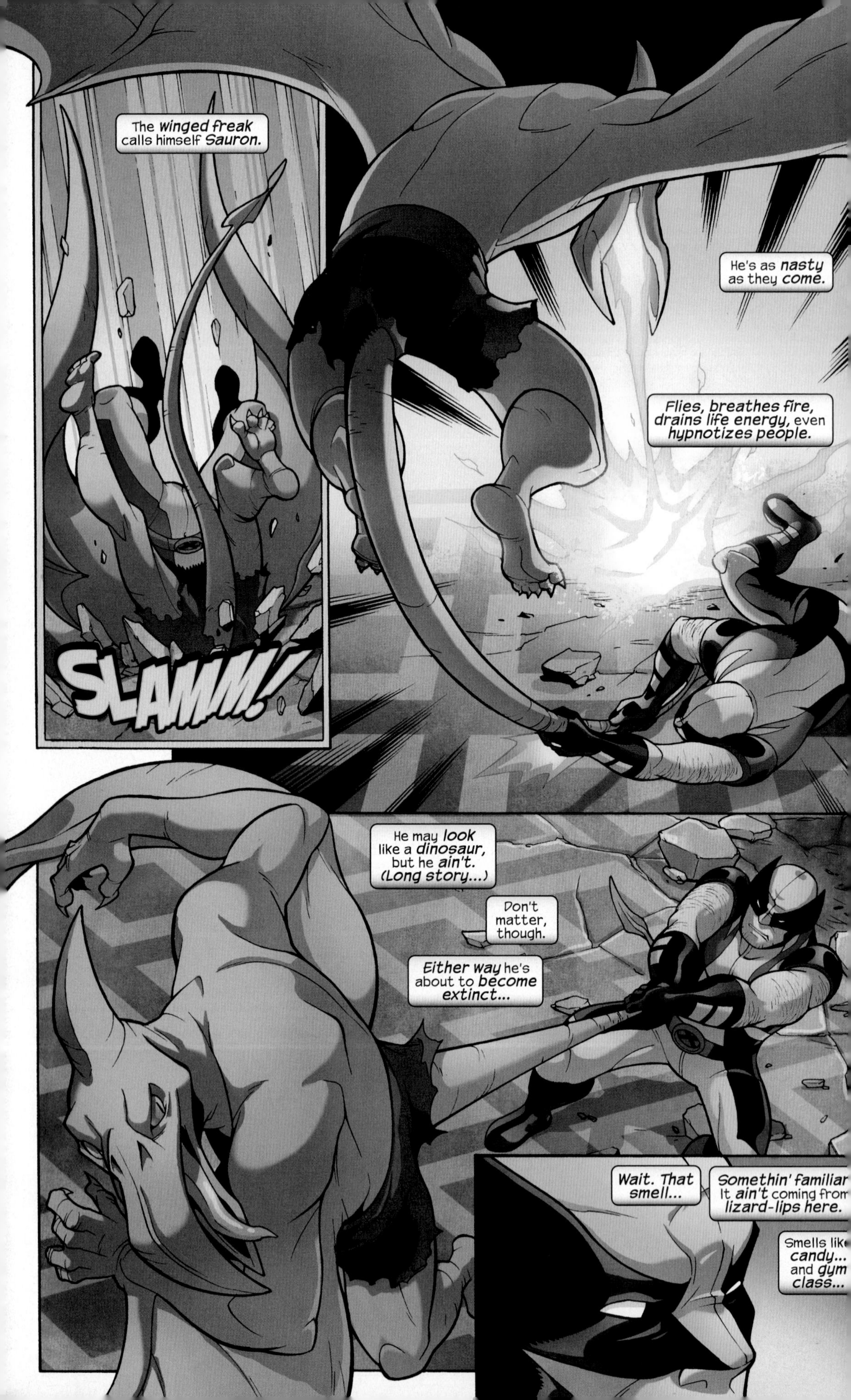
The winged freak calls himself Sauron.
SLAMM!
He's as nasty as they come.
Flies, breathes fire, drains life energy, even hypnotizes people.
He may look like a dinosaur, but he ain't. (Long story...)
Don't matter, though.
Either way he's about to become extinct...
Wait. That smell...
Somethin' familiar. It ain't coming from lizard-lips here.
Smells like candy... and gym class...

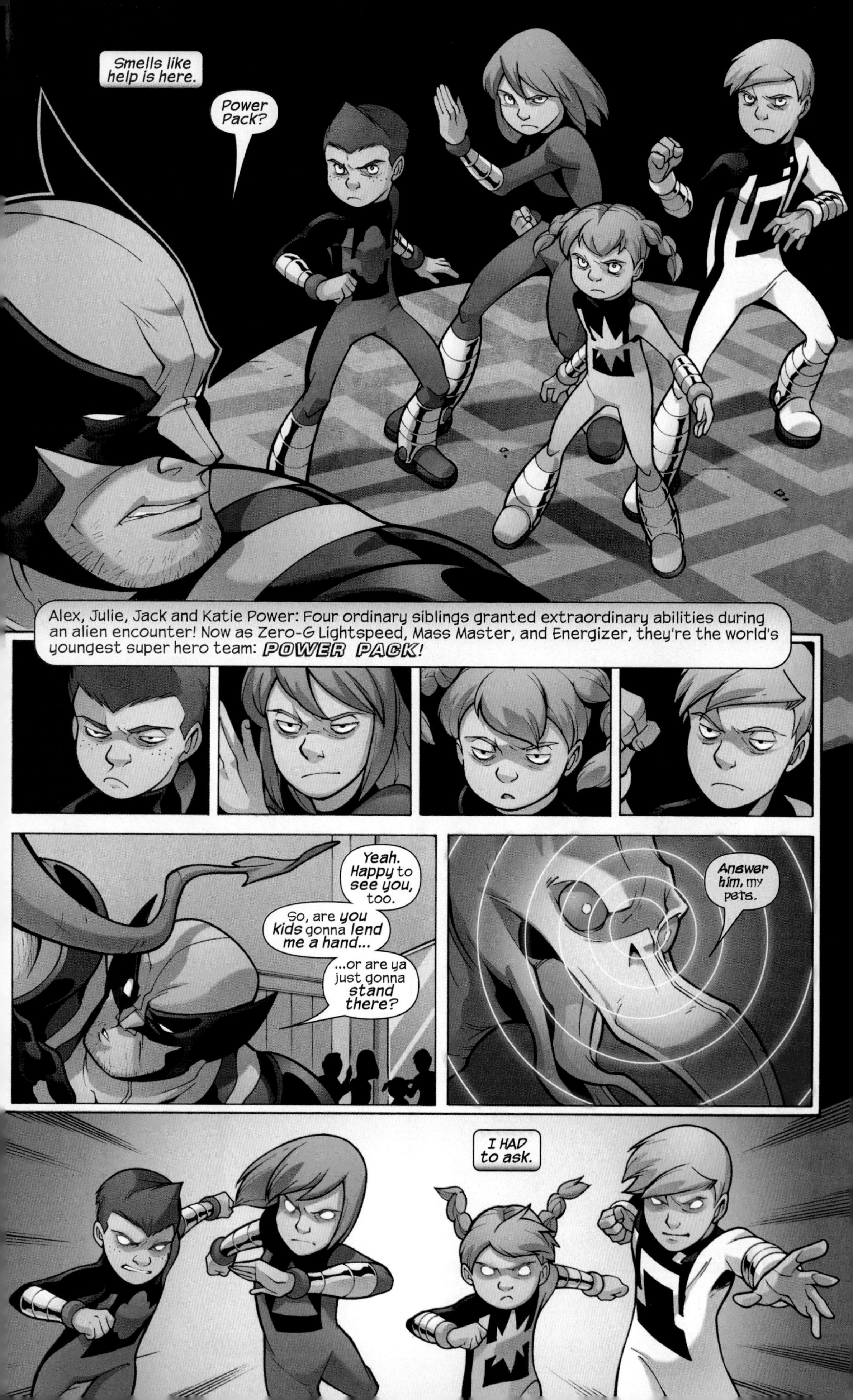
Smells like help is here.
Power Pack?
Alex, Julie, Jack and Katie Power: Four ordinary siblings granted extraordinary abilities during an alien encounter! Now as Zero-G Lightspeed, Mass Master, and Energizer, they're the world's youngest super hero team: POWER PACK!
Yeah. Happy to see you, too.
So, are you kids gonna lend me a hand...
...or are ya just gonna stand there?
Answer him, my pets.
I HAD to ask.

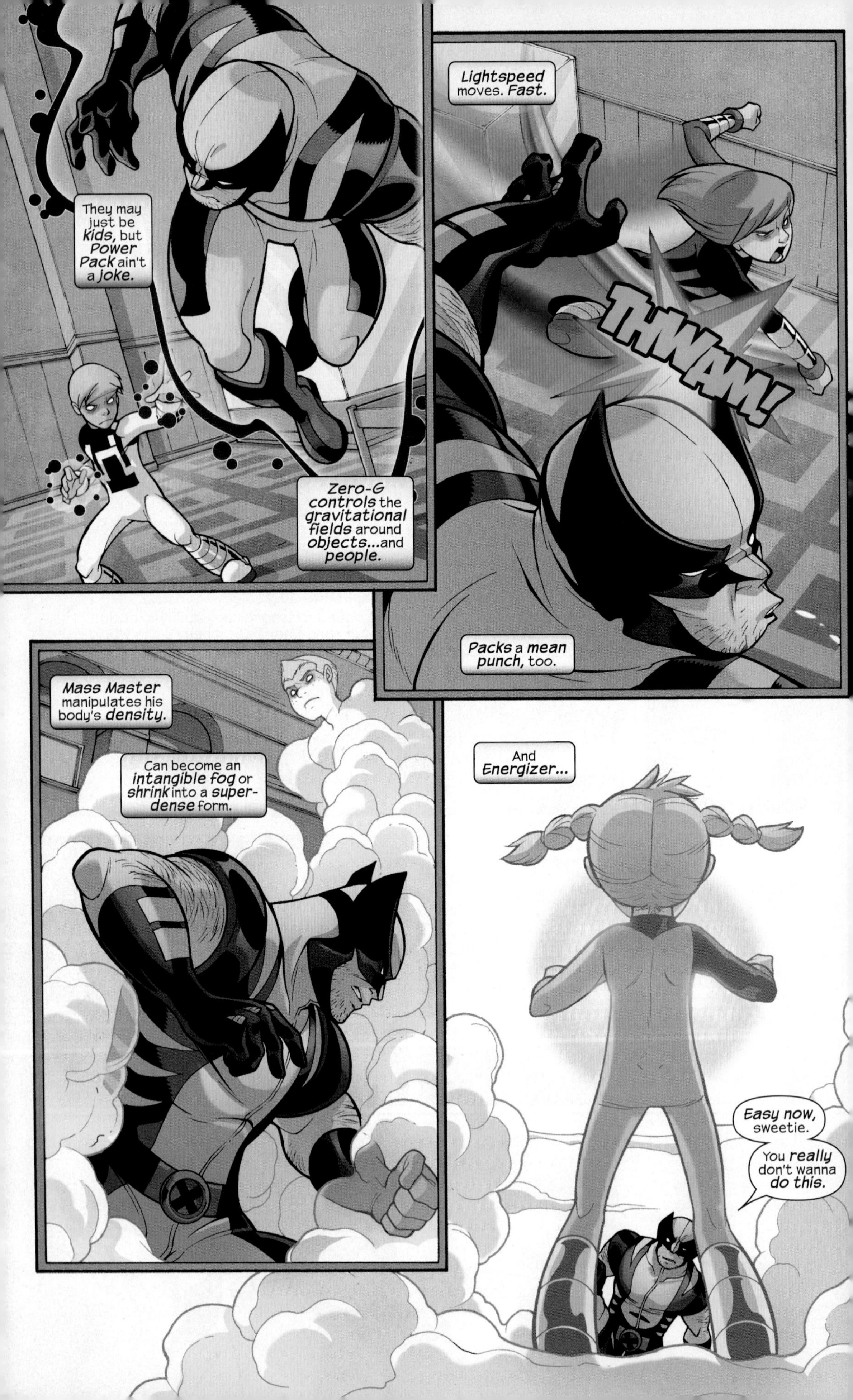

They may just be *kids*, but *Power Pack* ain't a *joke*.
Zero-G controls the *gravitational fields* around *objects*...and *people*.
Lightspeed moves. *Fast.*
THWAM!
Packs a *mean punch*, too.
Mass Master manipulates his body's *density*.
Can become an *intangible fog* or *shrink* into a *super-dense* form.
And *Energizer*...
Easy now, sweetie.
You *really* don't wanna *do this*.

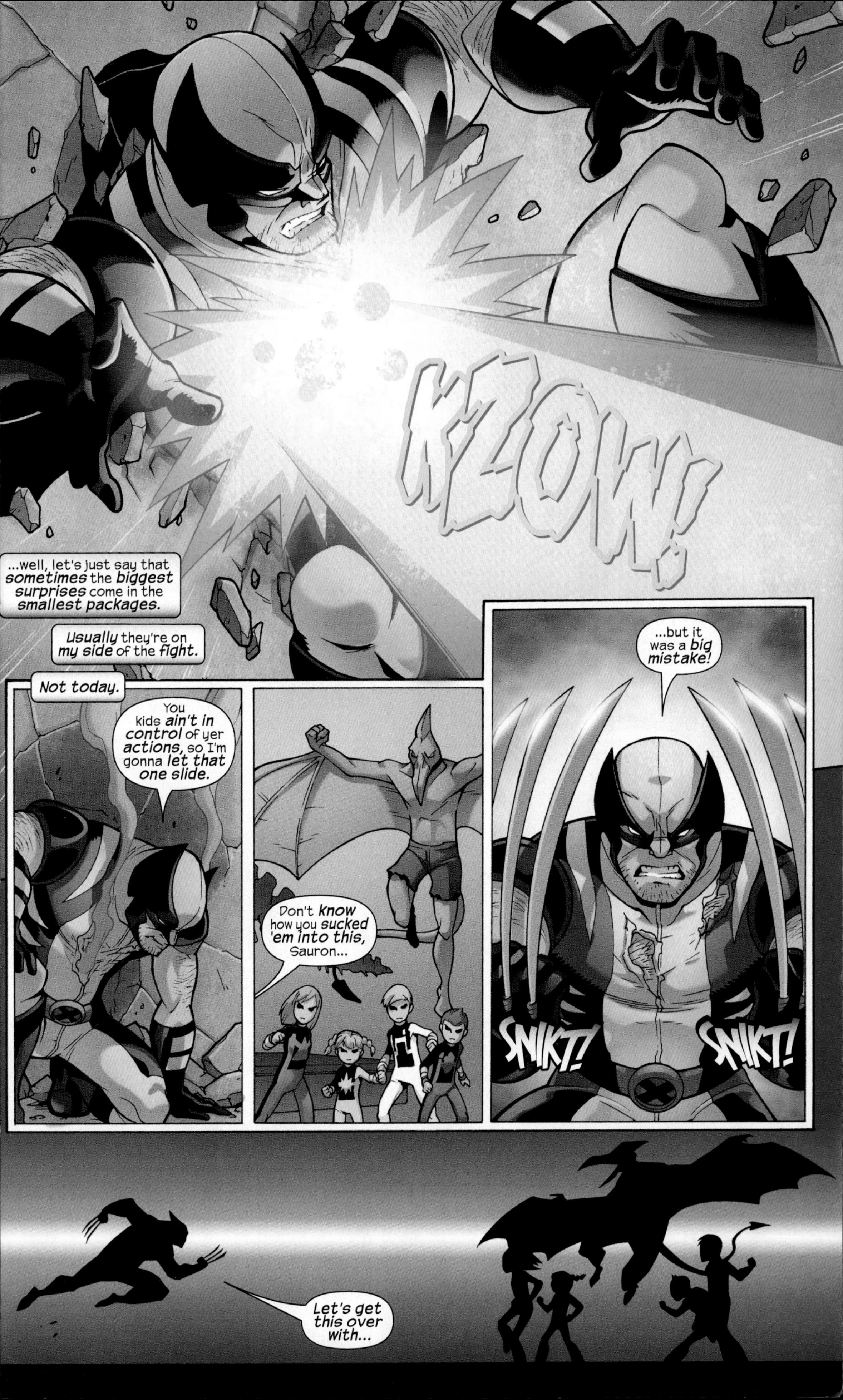
KZOW!
...well, let's just say that sometimes the biggest surprises come in the smallest packages.
Usually they're on my side of the fight.
Not today.
You kids ain't in control of yer actions, so I'm gonna let that one slide.
Don't know how you sucked 'em into this, Sauron...
...but it was a big mistake!
SNIKT!
SNIKT!
Let's get this over with...

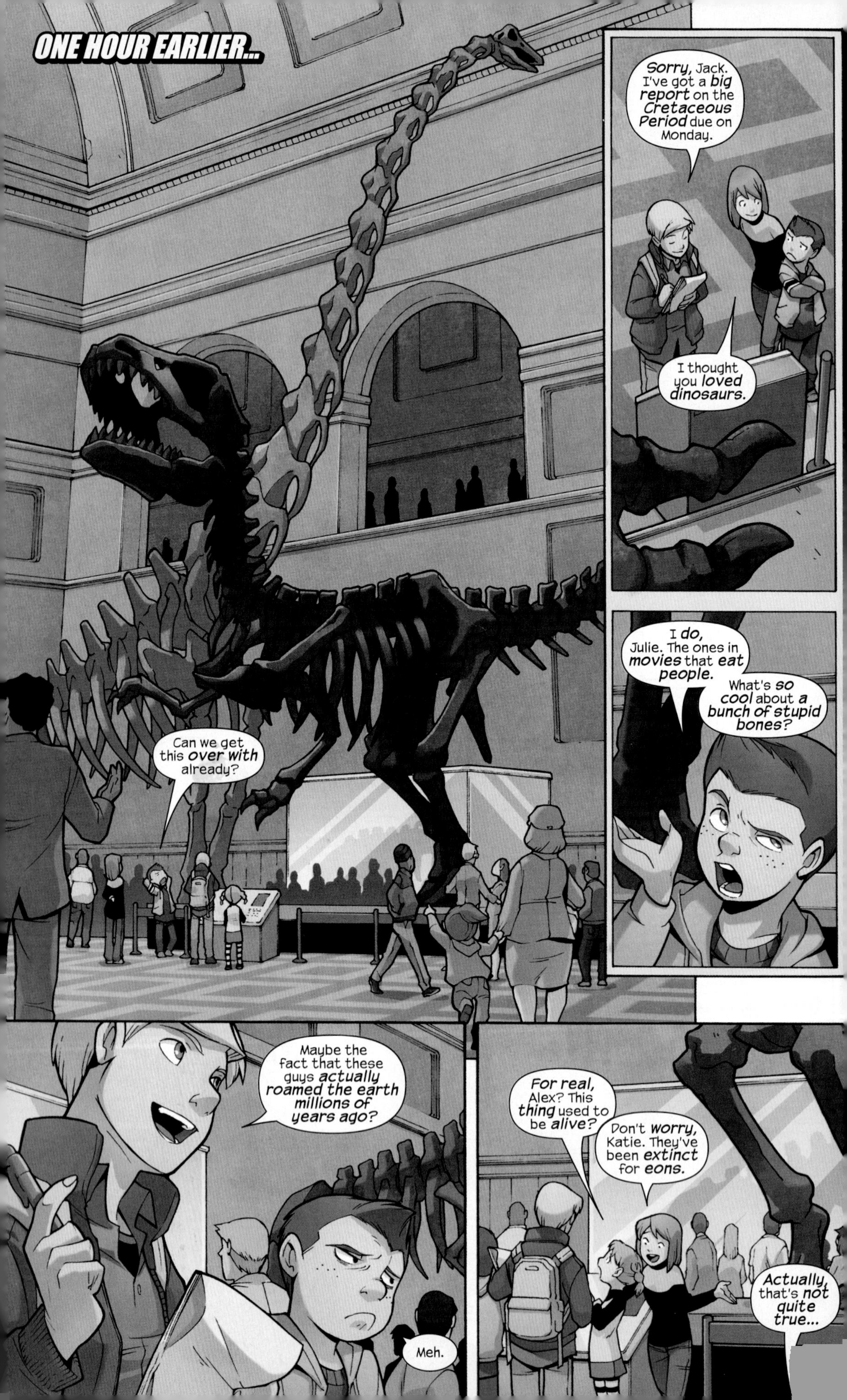
ONE HOUR EARLIER...
Sorry, Jack. I've got a big report on the Cretaceous Period due on Monday.
I thought you loved dinosaurs.
I do, Julie. The ones in movies that eat people.
What's so cool about a bunch of stupid bones?
Can we get this over with already?
Maybe the fact that these guys actually roamed the earth millions of years ago?
Meh.
For real, Alex? This thing used to be alive?
Don't worry, Katie. They've been extinct for eons.
Actually, that's not quite true...

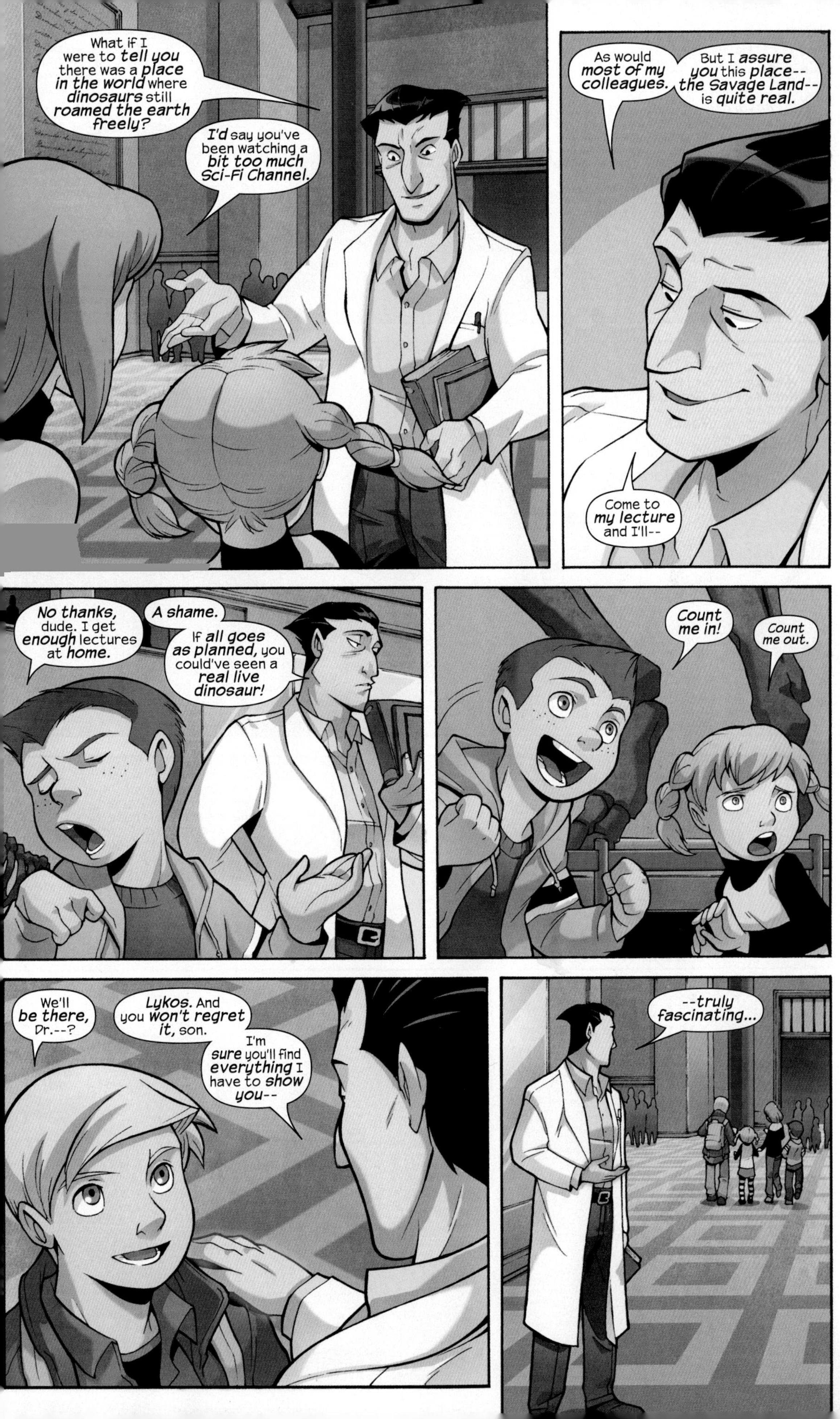
What if I were to tell you there was a place in the world where dinosaurs still roamed the earth freely?
I'd say you've been watching a bit too much Sci-Fi Channel.
As would most of my colleagues.
But I assure you this place-- the Savage Land-- is quite real.
Come to my lecture and I'll--
No thanks, dude. I get enough lectures at home.
A shame.
If all goes as planned, you could've seen a real live dinosaur!
Count me in!
Count me out.
We'll be there, Dr.--?
Lykos. And you won't regret it, son.
I'm sure you'll find everything I have to show you--
--truly fascinating...

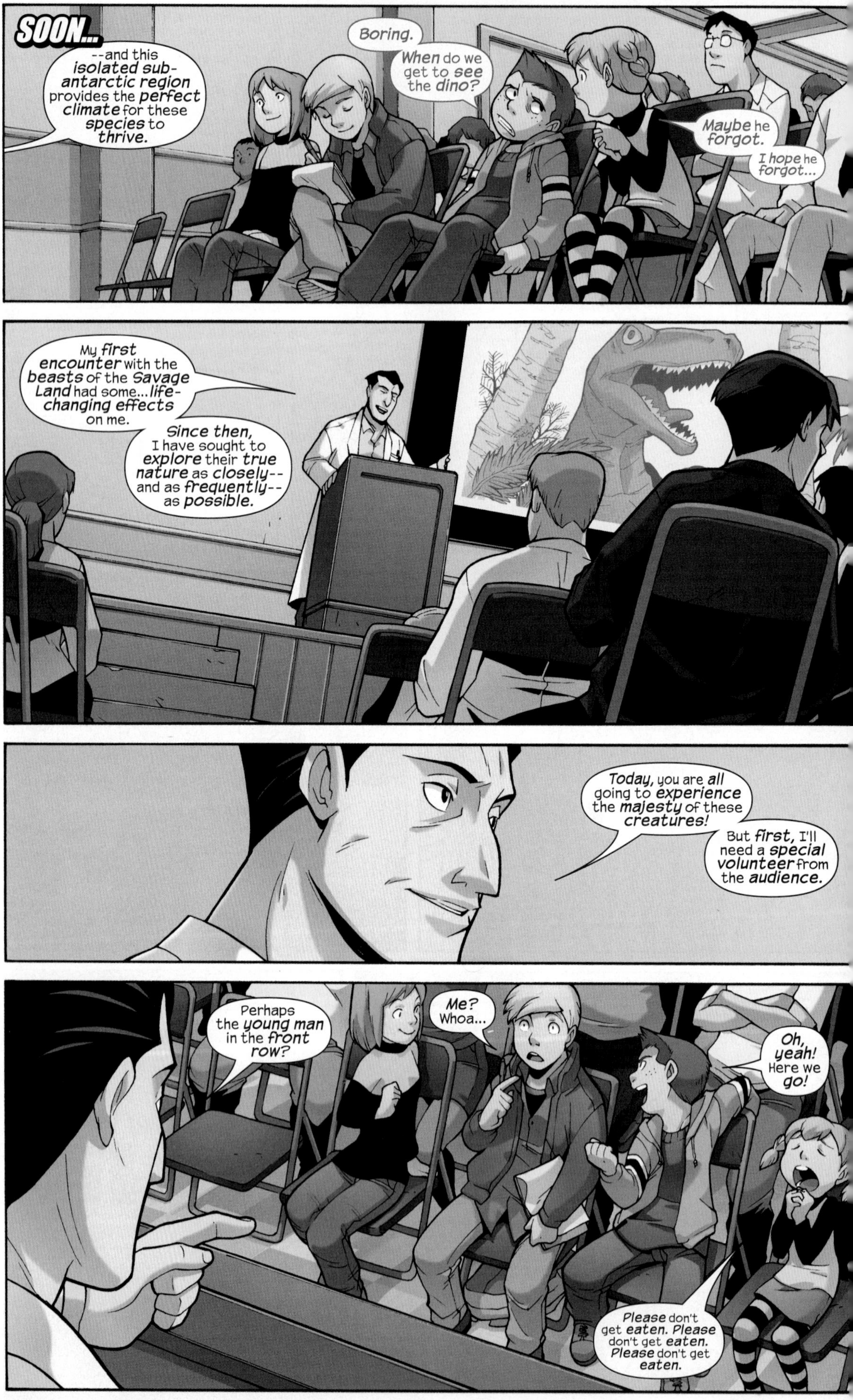
SOON...
--and this isolated sub-antarctic region provides the perfect climate for these species to thrive.
Boring.
When do we get to see the dino?
Maybe he forgot.
I hope he forgot...
My first encounter with the beasts of the Savage Land had some... life-changing effects on me.
Since then, I have sought to explore their true nature as closely-- and as frequently-- as possible.
Today, you are all going to experience the majesty of these creatures!
But first, I'll need a special volunteer from the audience.
Perhaps the young man in the front row?
Me? Whoa...
Oh, yeah! Here we go!
Please don't get eaten. Please don't get eaten. Please don't get eaten.

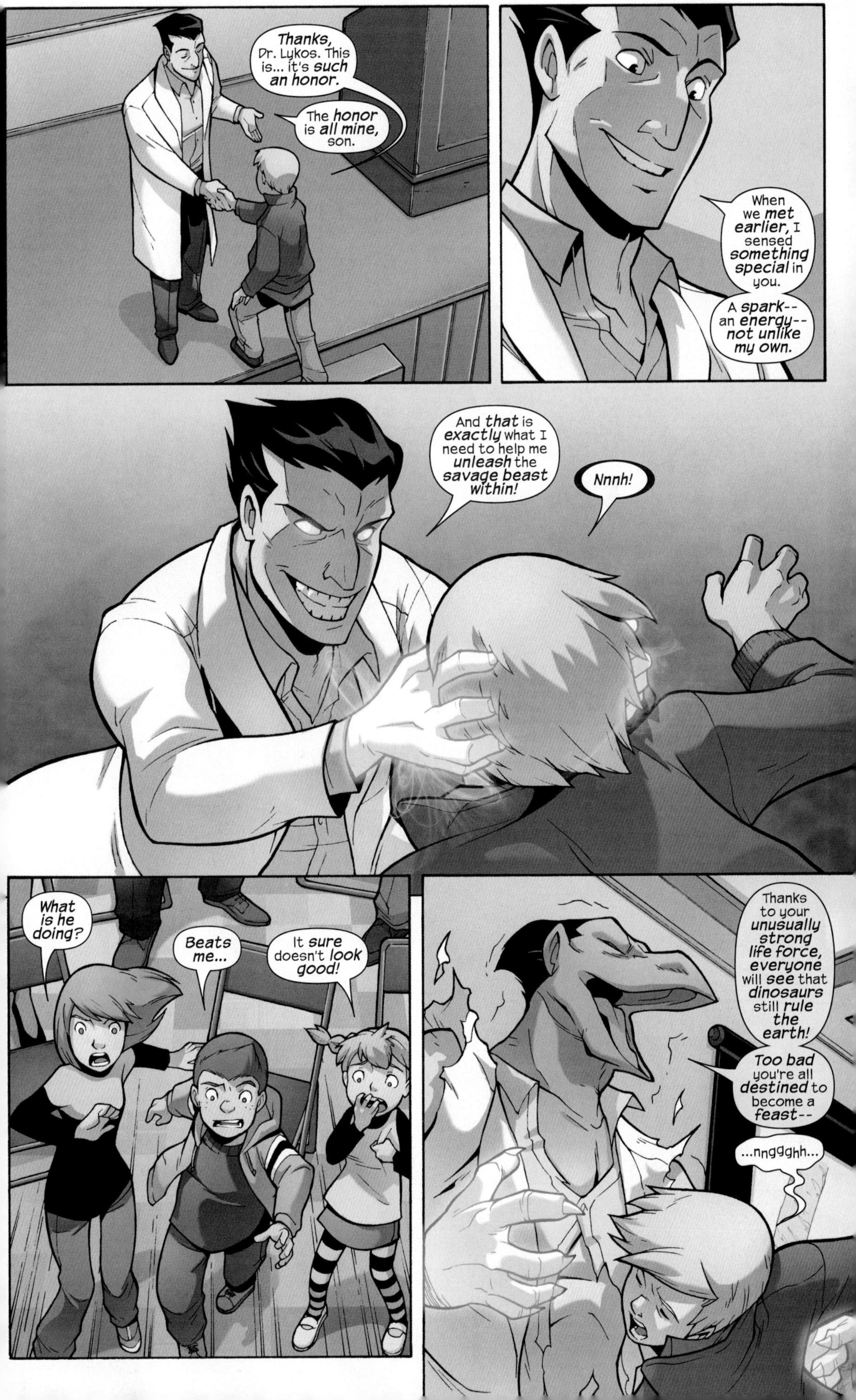
Thanks, Dr. Lykos. This is... it's such an honor.
The honor is all mine, son.
When we met earlier, I sensed something special in you.
A spark-- an energy-- not unlike my own.
And that is exactly what I need to help me unleash the savage beast within!
Nnnh!
What is he doing?
Beats me...
It sure doesn't look good!
Thanks to your unusually strong life force, everyone will see that dinosaurs still rule the earth!
Too bad you're all destined to become a feast--
...nngggh...

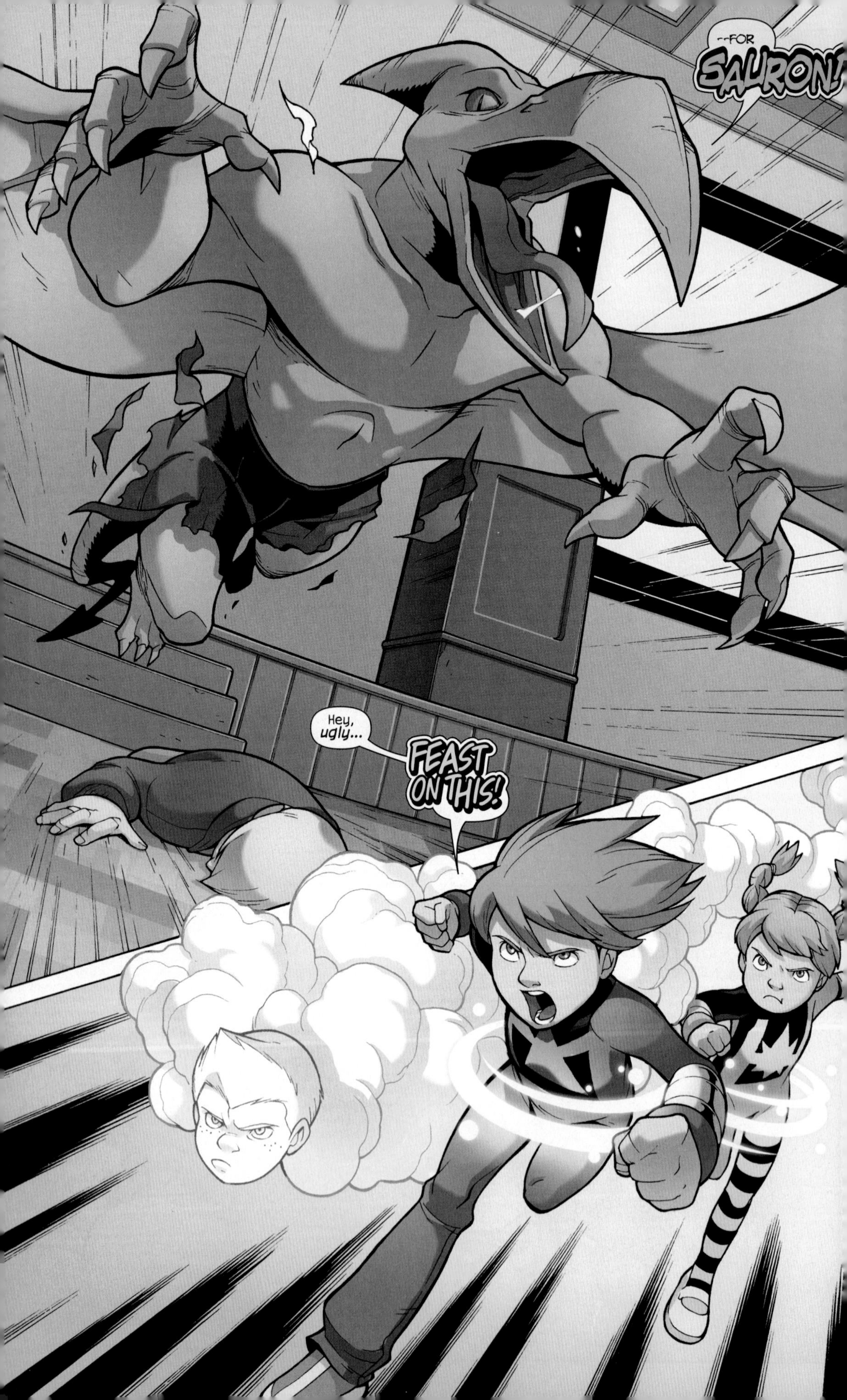
--FOR
SAURON!
Hey, ugly...
FEAST ON THIS!

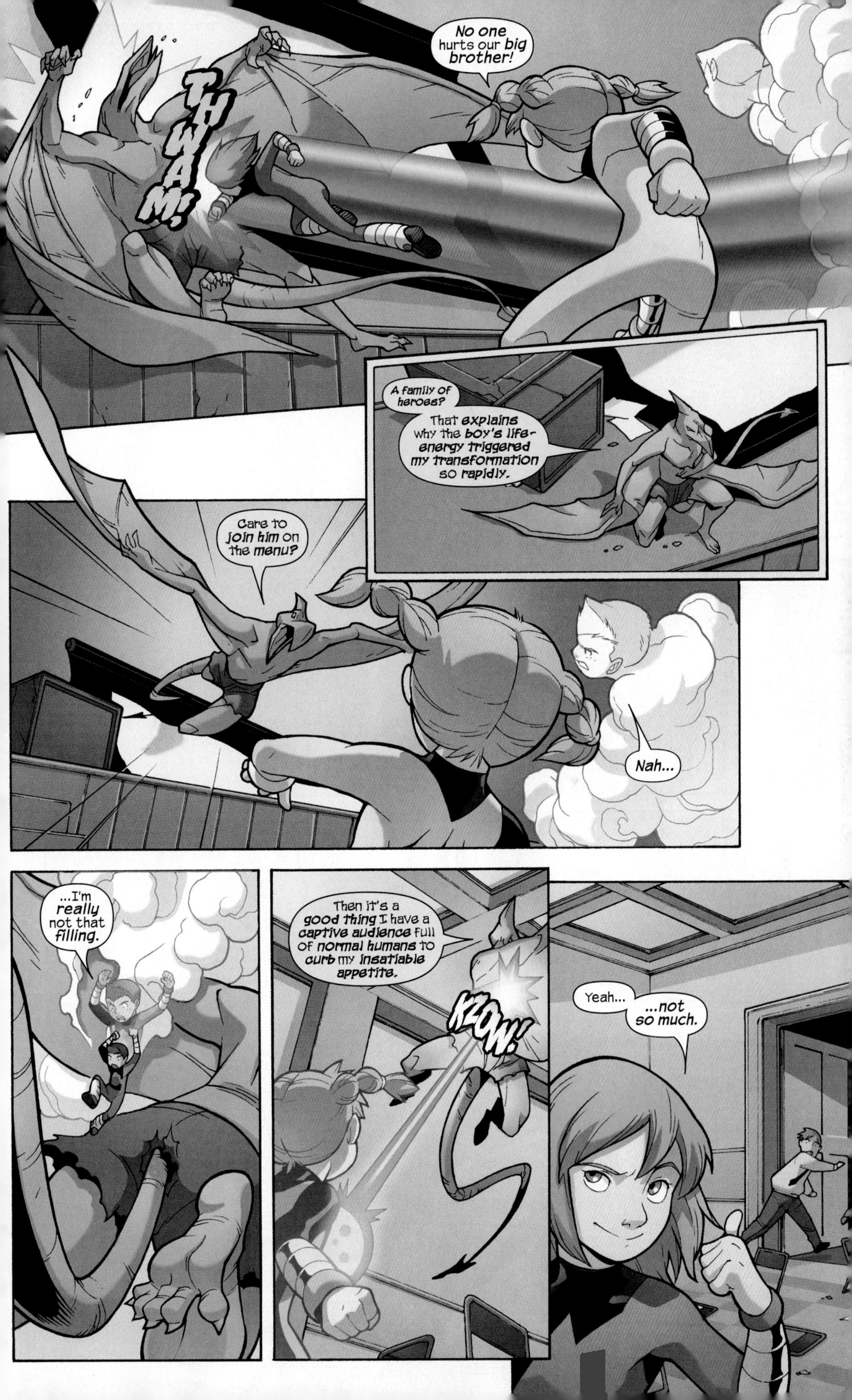
No one hurts our big brother!
THWAM!
A family of heroes?
That explains why the boy's life-energy triggered my transformation so rapidly.
Care to join him on the menu?
Nah...
...I'm really not that filling.
Then it's a good thing I have a captive audience full of normal humans to curb my insatiable appetite.
KZOW!
Yeah...
...not so much.

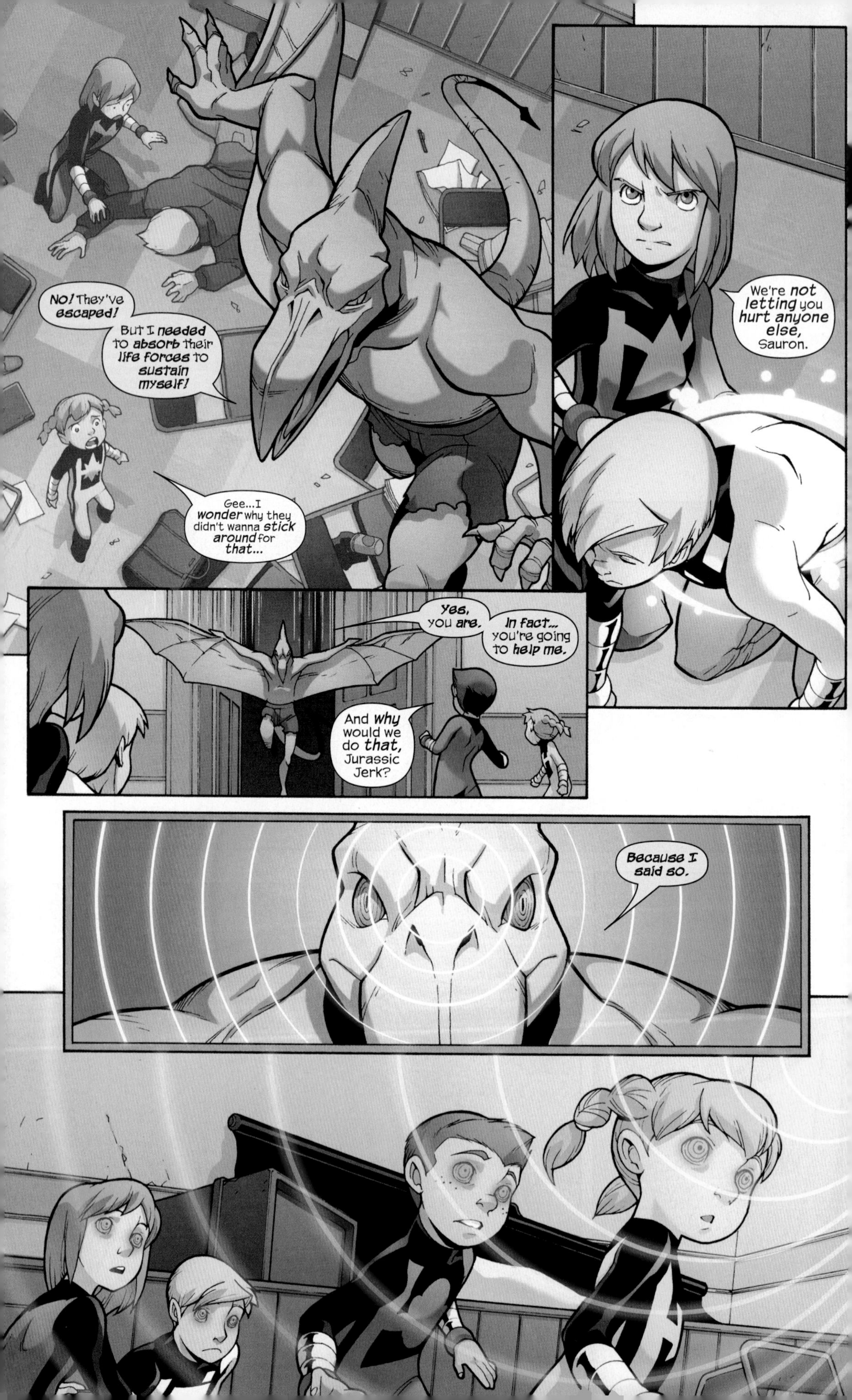
NO! They've escaped!
But I needed to absorb their life forces to sustain myself!
Gee...I wonder why they didn't wanna stick around for that...
We're not letting you hurt anyone else, Sauron.
Yes, you are.
In fact... you're going to help me.
And why would we do that, Jurassic Jerk?
Because I said so.

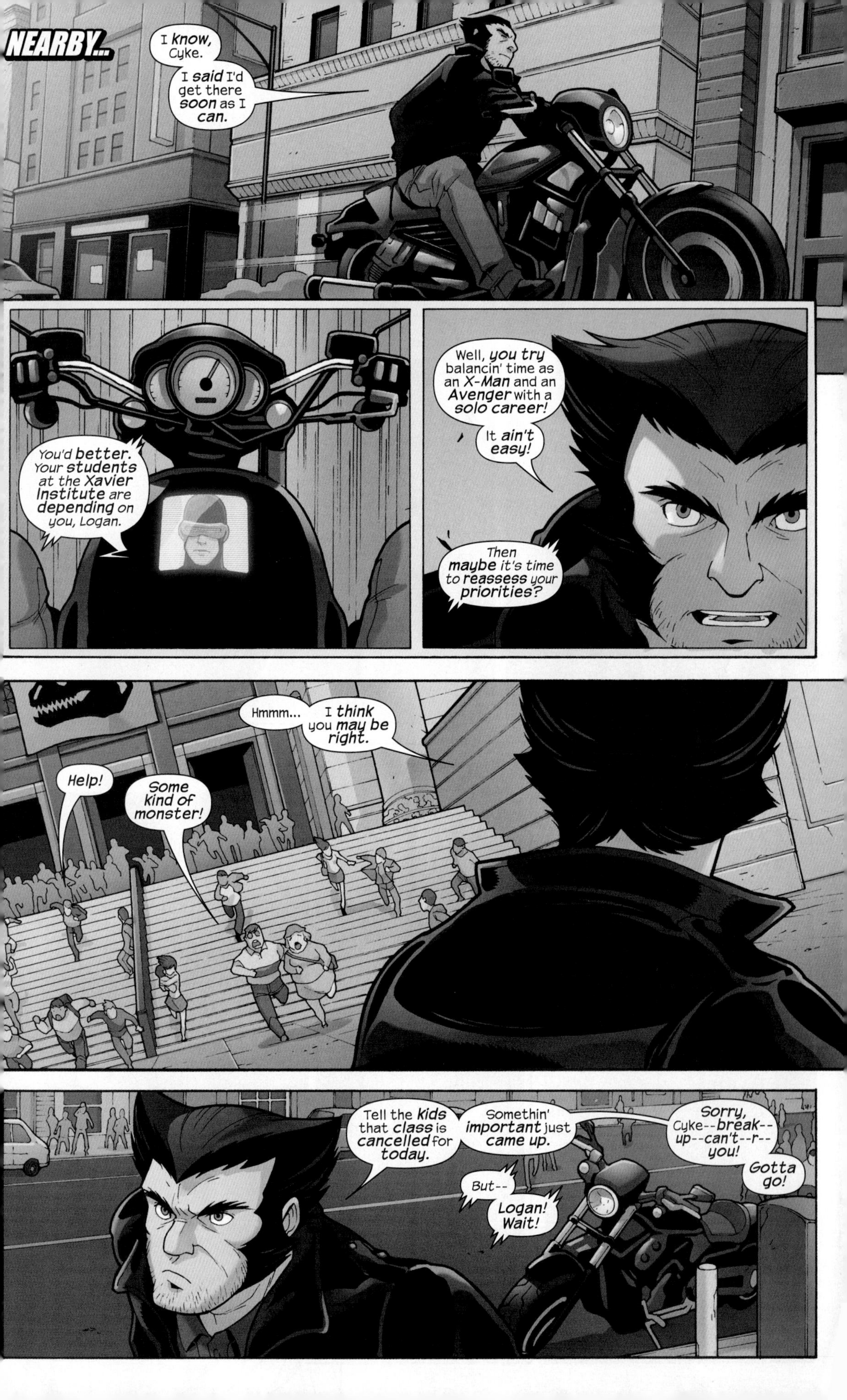
NEARBY...
I know, Cyke.
I said I'd get there soon as I can.
You'd better. Your students at the Xavier Institute are depending on you, Logan.
Well, you try balancin' time as an X-Man and an Avenger with a solo career!
It ain't easy!
Then maybe it's time to reassess your priorities?
Hmmm...
I think you may be right.
Help!
Some kind of monster!
Tell the kids that class is cancelled for today.
Somethin' important just came up.
Sorry, Cyke--break--up--can't--r--you!
Gotta go!
But--
Logan! Wait!

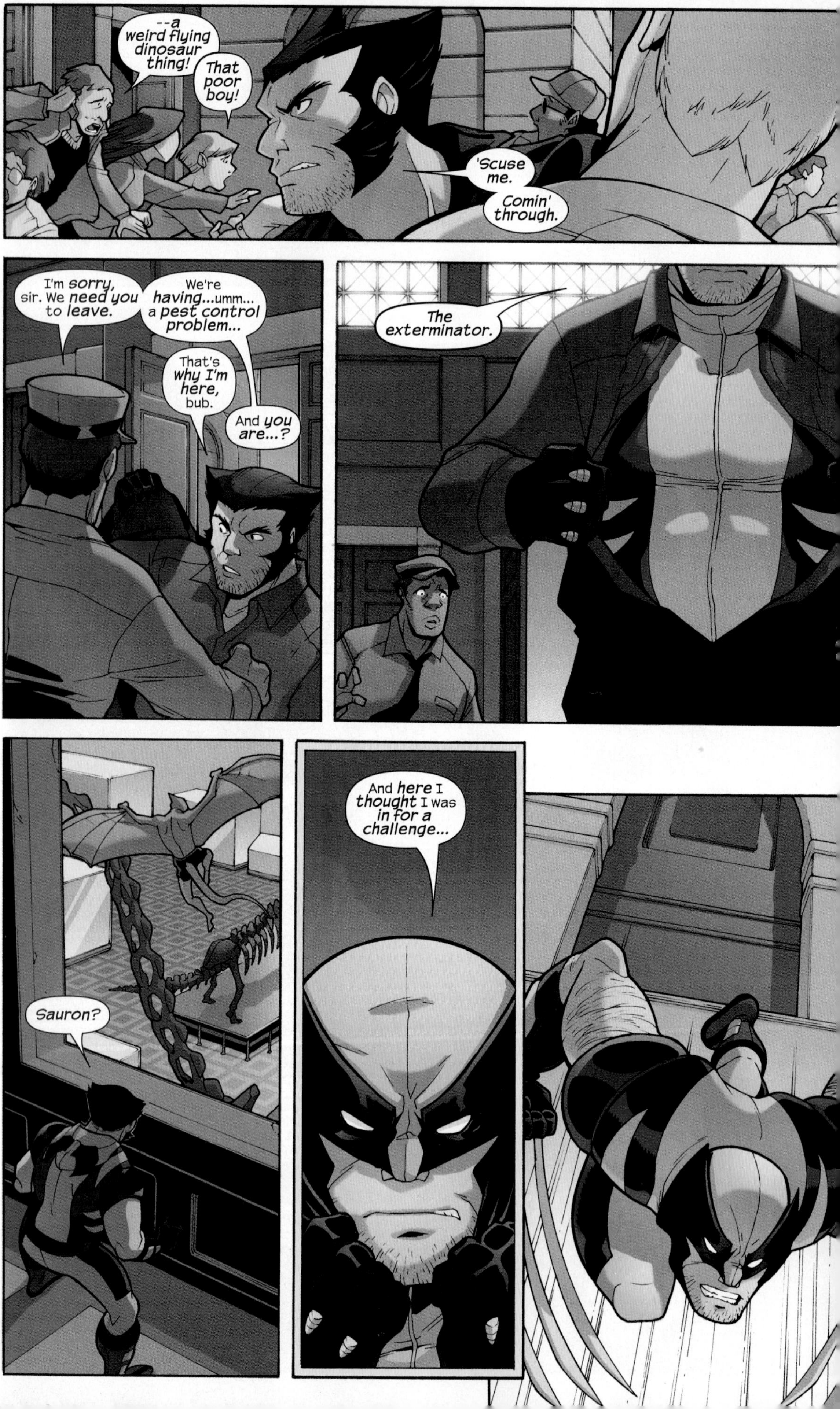
--a weird flying dinosaur thing!
That poor boy!
'Scuse me.
Comin' through.
I'm sorry, sir. We need you to leave.
We're having...umm... a pest control problem...
That's why I'm here, bub.
And you are...?
The exterminator.
Sauron?
And here I thought I was in for a challenge...

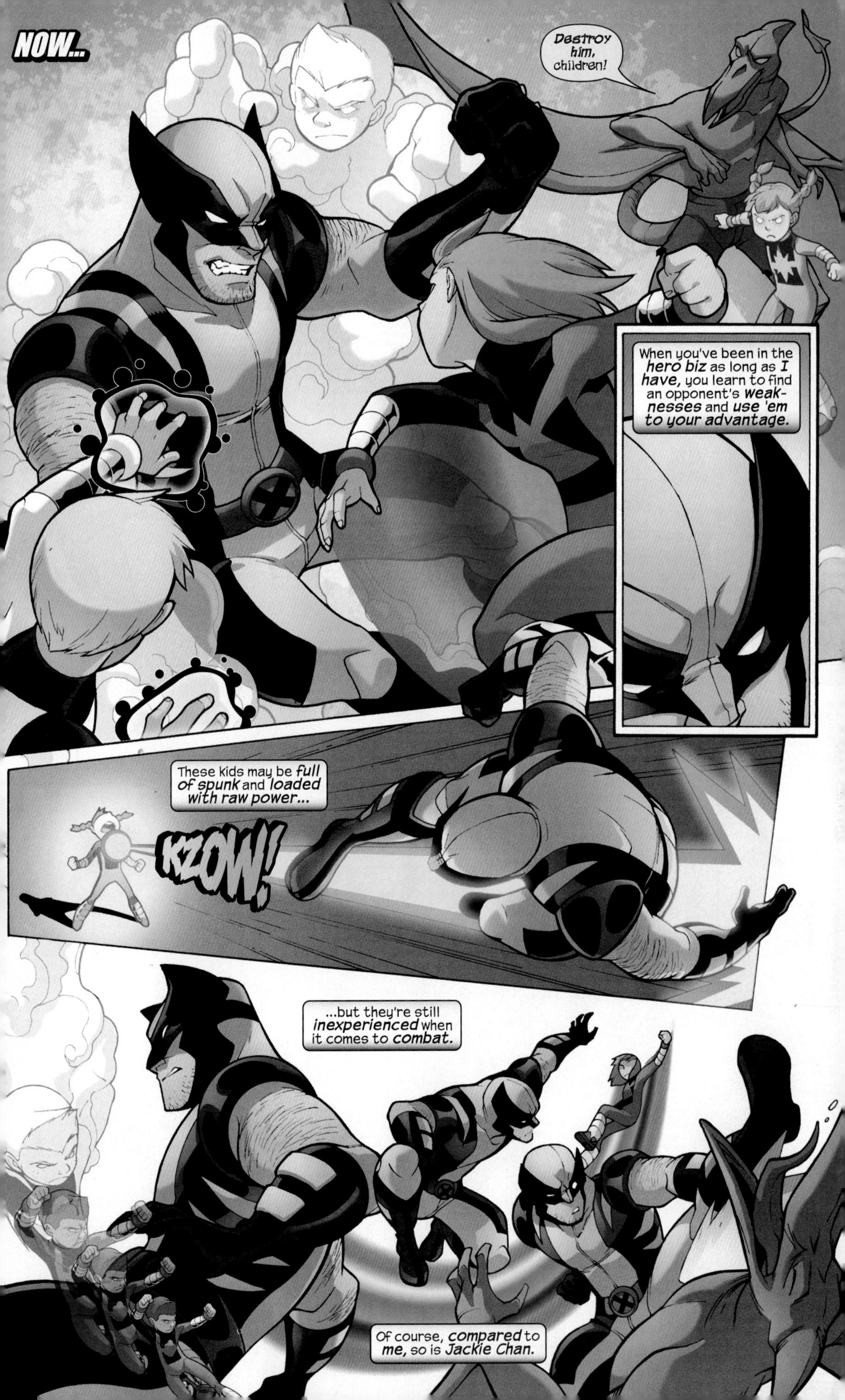
NOW...
Destroy him, children!
When you've been in the hero biz as long as I have, you learn to find an opponent's weak-nesses and use 'em to your advantage.
These kids may be full of spunk and loaded with raw power...
KZOW!
...but they're still inexperienced when it comes to combat.
Of course, compared to me, so is Jackie Chan.

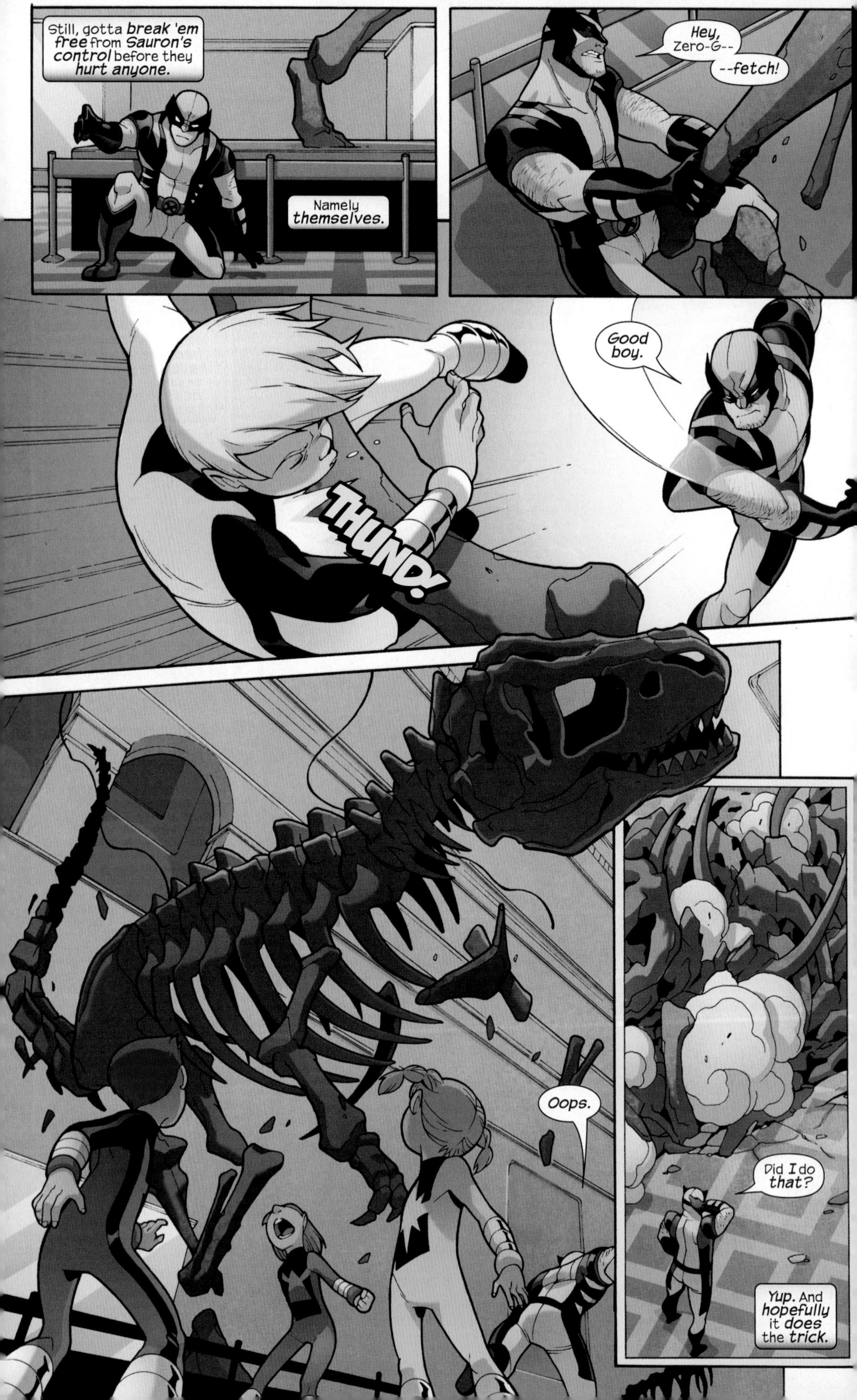
Still, gotta break 'em free from Sauron's control before they hurt anyone.
Namely themselves.
Hey, Zero-G--
--fetch!
Good boy.
THUND!
Oops.
Did I do that?
Yup. And hopefully it does the trick.

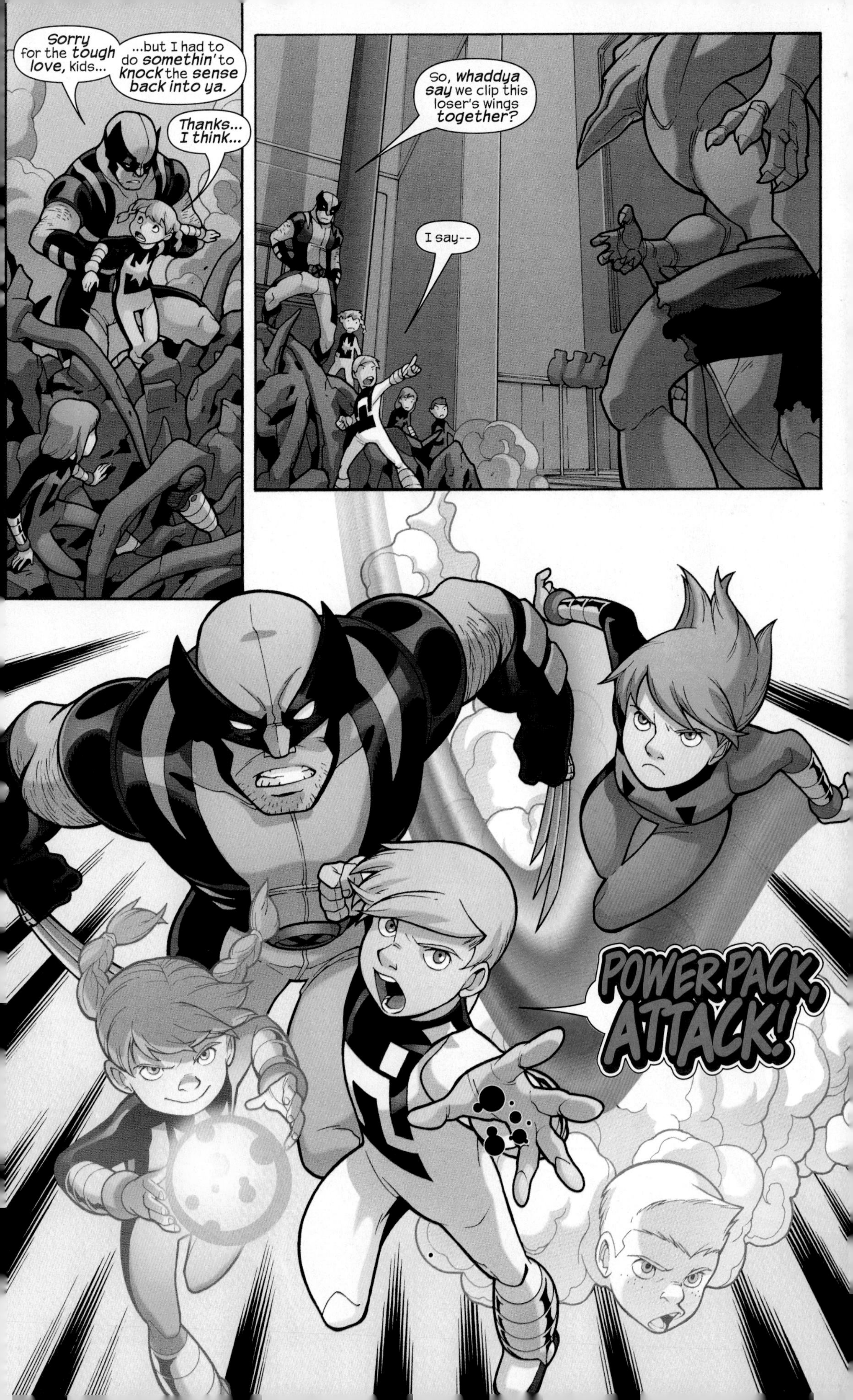
Sorry for the tough love, kids...
...but I had to do somethin' to knock the sense back into ya.
Thanks... I think...
So, whaddya say we clip this loser's wings together?
I say--
POWER PACK, ATTACK!

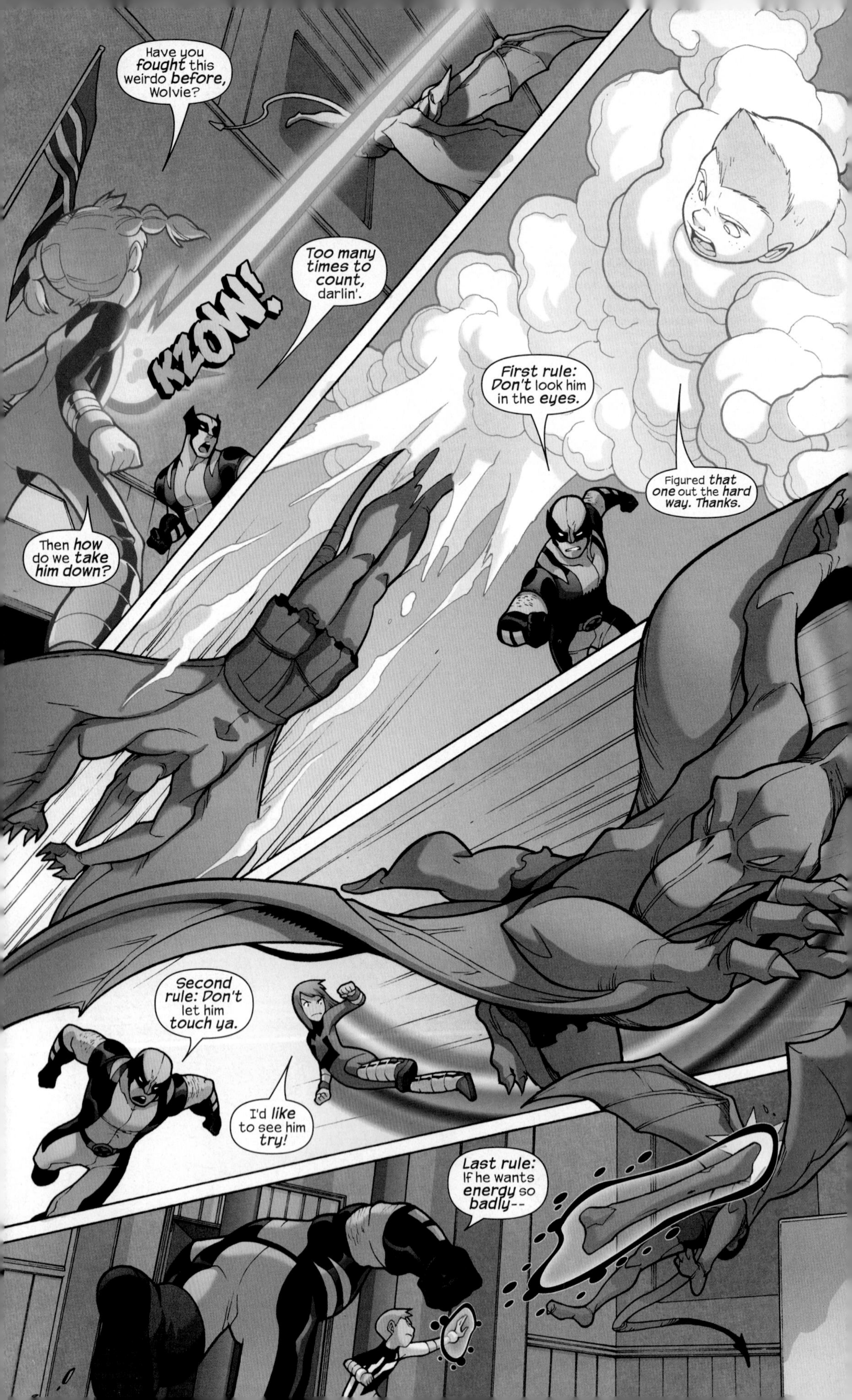
Have you fought this weirdo before, Wolvie?
KZOW!
Too many times to count, darlin'.
Then how do we take him down?
First rule: Don't look him in the eyes.
Figured that one out the hard way. Thanks.
Second rule: Don't let him touch ya.
I'd like to see him try!
Last rule: If he wants energy so badly--

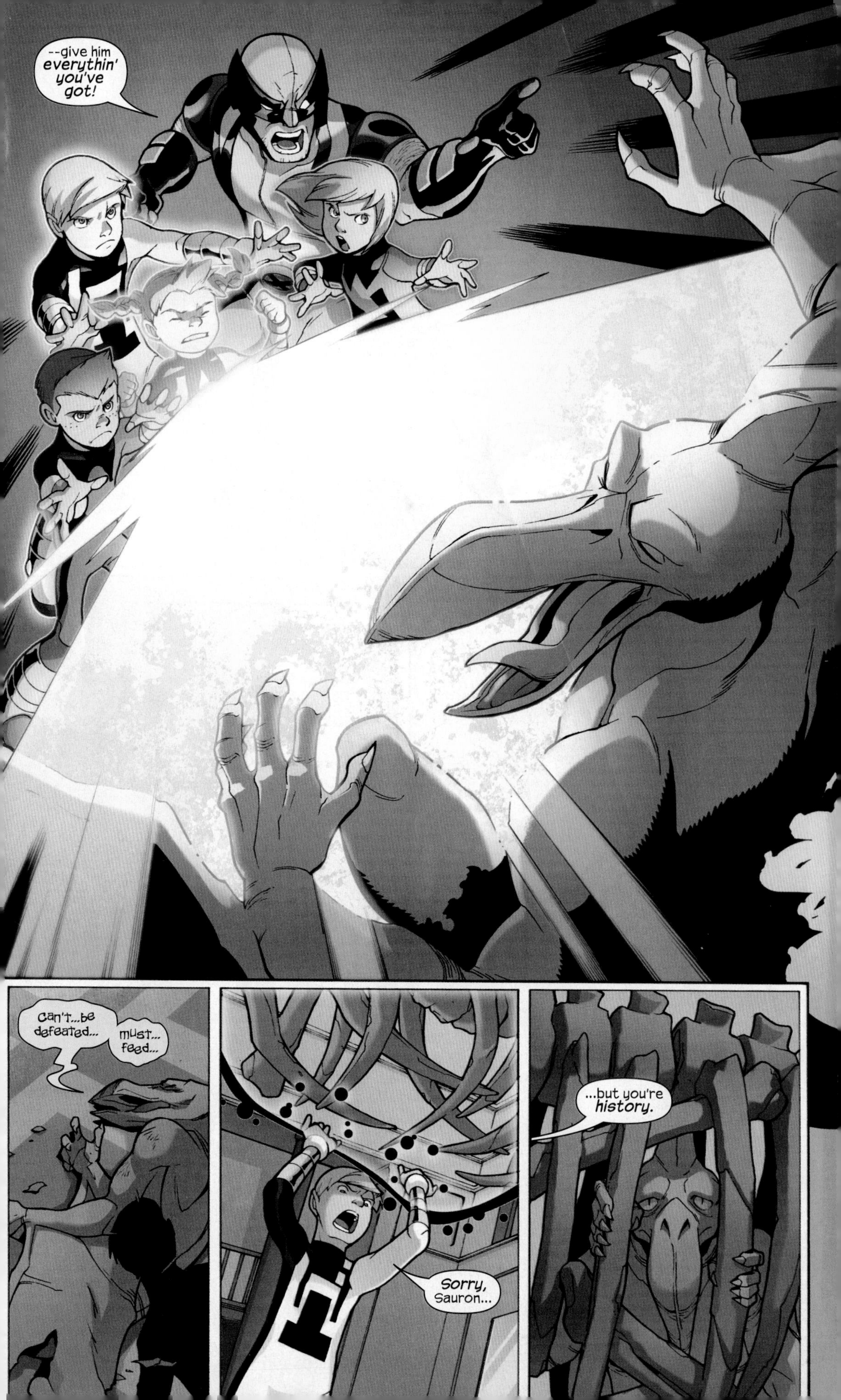
--give him everythin' you've got!
Can't...be defeated...
must... feed...
Sorry, Sauron...
...but you're history.

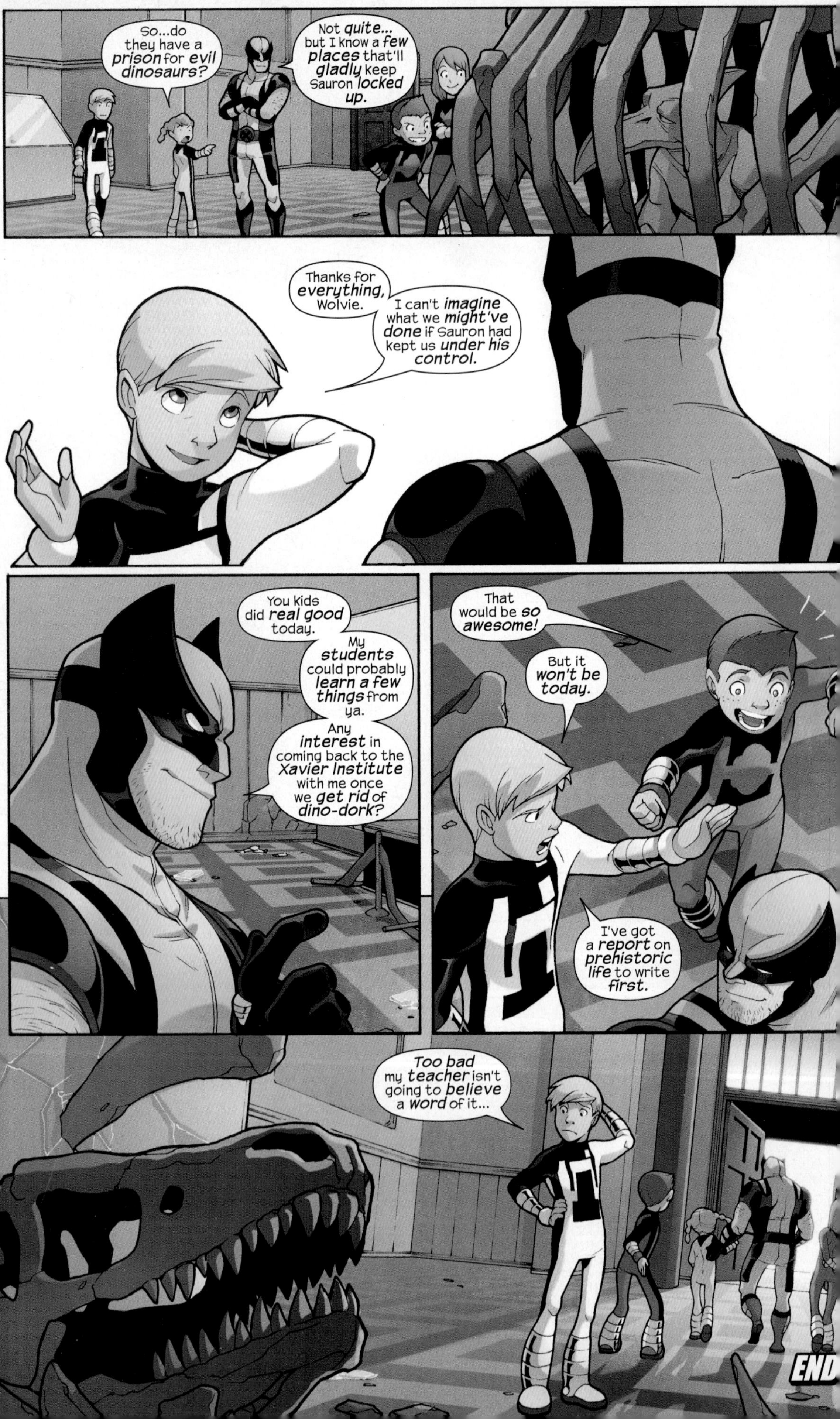

So...do they have a prison for evil dinosaurs?
Not quite... but I know a few places that'll gladly keep Sauron locked up.
Thanks for everything, Wolvie.
I can't imagine what we might've done if Sauron had kept us under his control.
You kids did real good today.
My students could probably learn a few things from ya.
Any interest in coming back to the Xavier Institute with me once we get rid of dino-dork?
That would be so awesome!
But it won't be today.
I've got a report on prehistoric life to write first.
Too bad my teacher isn't going to believe a word of it...
END